PHOTOSHOP
JUST THE SKINNY

Second Edition

Stephen Farnow

Justhe SKINNY™

PHOTOSHOP–JUST THE SKINNY
Second Edition
Stephen Farnow

Just the Skinny Publishing
P.O. Box 177
La Jolla, CA 92038
http://www.JustTheSkinny.com

Composed in Garamond Pro and Myriad Pro (Adobe Systems Incorporated).

ISBN 13: 978-0-9841845-0-7
ISBN 10: 0-9841845-0-3

9 8 7 6 5 4 3 2 1

Printed in China

DEDICATION

To my wife Janice, who provided the love, the inspiration, and the "gentle nudges."

TABLE of CONTENTS

PREFACE		**vii**
SECTION I	**BASIC CONCEPTS**	**1**
1	Pixels	2
2	The Workspace	6
3	Opening an Image	10
4	Panels	14
5	Image Size & Resolution	18
6	Selections–Part 1	22
7	Zoom & Hand Tools	26
8	Color	30
9	Histograms	34
10	File Formats	38
11	The Brush Tool	42
12	Selections–Part 2	46
	Section I CS4 Tips	50
SECTION II	**IMAGE ENHANCING**	**51**
13	Image Adjustments	52
14	Levels	56
15	Hue/Saturation	60
16	Cropping	64
17	Localized Enhancements	68
18	Fixing Defects	72
	Section II CS4 Tips	76
SECTION III	**INTRODUCTION TO LAYERS**	**77**
19	Layers	78
20	Layers Encore	82
21	Adjustment Layers	86
22	Adjustment Layers & Masking	90
23	Text	94
24	Layer Styles	98
	Section III CS4 Tips	102

SECTION IV	**MORE LAYER CONCEPTS**	**103**
25	Layer Masks	104
26	The Gradient Tool	108
27	Selections–Part 3	112
28	The Transform Command	116
29	Wanaka Sunrise Example	120
30	Opacity and Fill	124
31	Blending Modes	128
	Section IV CS4 Tips	132
SECTION V	**MORE IMAGE ENHANCING**	**133**
32	The Clone Tool	134
33	The Clone Tool–Part 2	138
34	Filters	142
35	The Sharpen Filter	146
36	The Blur Filter	150
	Section V CS4 Tips	154
SECTION VI	**DRAWING AND PAINTING**	**155**
37	Brush Encore & Pencil Tool	156
38	Vector Graphics	160
39	The Shape Tool	164
40	Paths & The Pen Tool	168
	Section VI CS4 Tips	172
SECTION VII	**FINISHING UP**	**173**
41	Saving Your Work	174
42	Save for Web & Devices	178
43	Printing	182
	Section VII CS4 Tips	186
SECTION VIII	**SOME EXAMPLES**	**187**
44	The Zebra	188
45	Wanaka Sunrise Reflection	190
46	Faux Matting	192
47	Cinque Terra	194
48	An Image Grouping	196
49	The Taj Mahal	198
50	Final Thoughts	202
INDEX		**203**

PREFACE

By my last count, there are a gazillion books out there on Photoshop. (I know because I have probably purchased half of them.) They are roughly divided into two categories, the reference books and the tutorial books. As a beginning Photoshop user, I found that I lacked the patience to read the reference books cover to cover. After all, I wanted to get going with Photoshop. And while the tutorial books were fun and instructive, I found that the click-here-click-there approach taught me techniques, but not the program. And the techniques didn't stick.

Photoshop is a lot of things. But one of the things it is not is intuitively obvious, especially for those of us that grew up with Microsoft applications. As I was learning the program, I wished I had a short book (a skinny one if you will) that gave me just the basics. Something that I could get through quickly, that would get me up and running, and that would teach me just enough that I could be dangerous.

And since I couldn't find that book, I've written it. I am not a 20-year Photoshop veteran. In fact, I've learned it recently enough that I remember the things that initially confused me and how I eventually demystifyed them. I remember which topics were the most important and the best order in which to absorb them. And I remember those topics that while neat, didn't really stick because they weren't really all that useful. All that's in this book. Just what you need–just the skinny.

WHICH VERSION OF PHOTOSHOP?

Because we're discussing "just the skinny," your version of Photoshop is not all that important. For this second edition, the screenshots were made in CS4, and some of them might have a slightly different look and feel if you are using a different version. But the concepts we'll be discussing are the foundations of the program so they are pretty universal to any moderately recent version. Aside from the menus perhaps looking a little different, you will be able to follow along just fine.

As I write this, Photoshop CS4 is the current version on the market. While we will be discussing the basics common to all recent versions, in some cases CS4 gives us easier ways to do things. So at the end of each section, I have an extra CS4 tips page that highlights some of these for you.

ORGANIZATION OF THE BOOK

In order to make this book easy to get through, I have organized each chapter with exactly four pages, bite size if you will. They do build on each other so it is best to read from beginning to end. But each short chapter presents a complete concept so you won't need to set aside hours to make any progress.

The little status bar in the upper right hand corner of each page (see it up there?) is a visual clue as to which page in the chapter, first through fourth, you are on.

One of the by-products of restricting chapter length to four pages is that I was forced to prioritize what I could include. One of the things you will find about Photoshop is that there are generally three or more ways to do any one operation. There are main menus, contextual menus, keyboard shortcuts, icons, etc. In almost all cases, I show only the simplest, most straightforward method. Maybe not the fastest, but the most straightforward. After all, we are trying to get up and running, not fill our brains with endless options. So prioritizing is a good thing.

For the most part, I avoid showing keyboard shortcuts. You will figure out which operations you use all the time and will undoubtedly learn those shortcuts. (I do show the really, really important ones.) With a few exceptions, though, they get in the way of the initial learning process.

- Section I goes through the basic concepts of Photoshop. We will learn how the program thinks and how to interact with it. In Section II, we will learn the basics of image enhancement–how to improve contrast, color, size and how to fix little defects.
- Sections III and IV get right down to it with a solid introduction to the power of layers, arguably the most important feature of Photoshop. Here is where we will learn how to put a cat's head on a dog! Section V gets back to image enhancing, but this time utilizing the power of layers.
- Section VI changes gears and talks about the drawing and painting features in Photoshop. Included is a short discussion of vector tools, including the Pen tool.
- Section VII helps us with the endgame of digital photography, saving and printing.
- And finally, Section VIII goes through some examples of personal travel photos and the simple enhancements made possible with Photoshop. (I know, this smells a little bit like tutorials.)

Many of the images I used in writing this book are available for download if you would like to follow along. Just go to www.justtheskinny.com/support.html for the link. Not all images are included in the file, but most that you would find useful are. The sample image icon, Ⓢ, next to an image in this book means it has been included in the file.

PC VERSUS MAC

I own 'em both and I use 'em both. And for our purposes, Photoshop works equally well on either platform. But my current workhorse laptop is a Mac, so with my apologies to Windows users, I have done all of the screen shots on the Mac version. When there are keystrokes described that differ between Mac and Windows, I list the Mac keystroke first followed by the Windows keystroke in parentheses. Cmd(Ctrl)-Click for example, corresponds to holding down the command key on the Mac while clicking and to holding down the control key on Windows while clicking.

I will also mention here that, when describing navigation through menus, I use a ">" between nested commands. So Image>Adjustments>Levels means to select the Image menu and scroll down to Adjustments and from the Adjustments menu that then appears, scroll down and select Levels.

THANKS...

First and foremost, I'd like to thank my wife Janice for her endless love, patience and inspiration. And for her many appearances in the images.

Secondly, I'd like to thank Amanda (my daughter) and Nate Reierson for providing many of the around-the-world images. They had quite the trip.

To my readers–Steve Edelson, Janice Farnow, Bruce Lightner, and Ray Vellinga–thanks for the careful reading, honest feedback, and great suggestions.

To Lauren Reiland, thanks for providing the Illustrator example in Section VI. I can't draw to save my life.

And finally, I would like to recognize the fine Creative Suite classes at San Diego Continuing Education and in particular, those of instructors Carolyn O'Barr and Paul Richard.

Stephen Farnow
La Jolla, CA
September 2009

SECTION I

BASIC CONCEPTS

In this first section, we will go through the basic concepts of digital imaging and learn our way around the Photoshop environment.

If you have not used Adobe software, you may find the user interface somewhat unnatural. This might be especially true if most of your software experience is on applications authored by a large company whose name starts with an M. In fact you may have even purchased this book because you have played with Photoshop and, well, it's not making any sense.

Have faith. The Adobe user interface is very well thought out and, with a little time, will come to feel quite comfortable for you. And many of Adobe's applications, especially within the Creative Suite, have a common look and feel. So once you have gotten used to Photoshop, you will find yourself comfortable with those applications as well.

After reading this section, you will be familiar with the basic Photoshop workspace and be well along the way to being able to navigate around within it. We will talk about the menus, the array of tools, and what are known as panels. We will also get to fool around with a few of the tools.

Photoshop works with (and can create) digital images. So this is where we will need to start. We will talk about what digital images are, how they are stored (file formats), and how color is incorporated.

1. PIXELS

Pixels, or picture elements, are the fundamental unit in digital photography, and for Photoshop. Our digital cameras are rated in terms of mega-pixels or millions of pixels. My 6 Mp camera, for example, has a sensor with approximately six million pixels, arranged in an array (or grid) of around 3,000 pixels (wide) by 2,000 pixels (tall).

A digital camera works by creating an optical image of the scene on its sensor, this grid of pixels. Each pixel measures, or senses, information about that little piece of our scene that falls on it, sensing color (by measuring red, green, and blue components) and brightness. This information, along with the pixel's location in the array, and some basic camera data, is then saved on our camera's memory card as an image file.

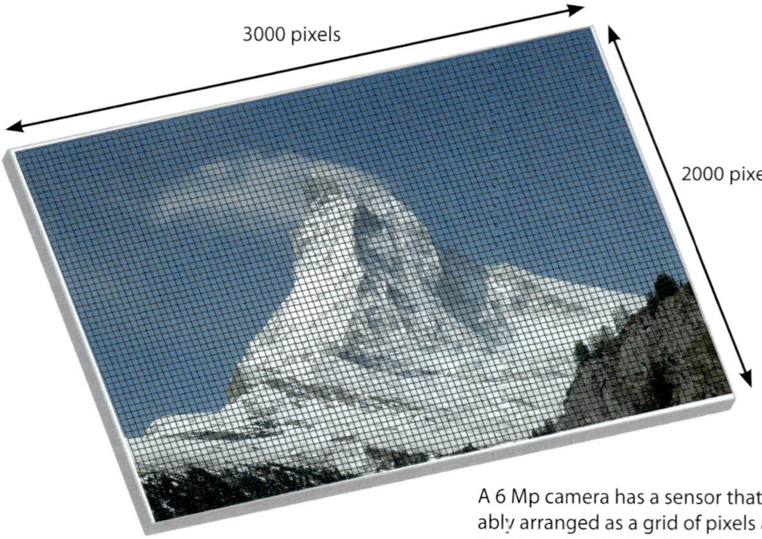

A 6 Mp camera has a sensor that is probably arranged as a grid of pixels around 3000 pixels wide by 2000 pixels tall. Each camera manufacturer will have different numbers depending on their design.

This turns out to be a lot of information to store. A 6 Mp raw (unprocessed) image takes around 8 MB or megabytes to store – a healthy bite out of our memory card. Fortunately, our camera can compress or simplify this data into what is known as a JPEG (a special format), reducing the memory needed to store an image from 6 MB to maybe 1.5 MB, depending on what image quality we may have chosen in our camera settings.

We will talk more about the various file formats, like JPEG, in Chapter 10. For now, it is really enough to know digital images are comprised of an array of bits of information and that these bits of information are called pixels.

When we save our image file on our computer and open it in Photoshop, the program decodes the pixel information that was saved by the camera and creates its own new file. This new file is also organized as a pixel array with dimensions the same as the camera sensor (3000 by 2000 in my 6 Mp example). But where the file on our memory card was 1.5 MB, Photoshop's file size will be closer to 17MB. The reasons for this are twofold. First of all, Photoshop's files are uncompressed. Secondly, Photoshop's file format allows it to store more information about each pixel than just color and intensity–this is part of how Photoshop does its magic.

We will talk more about this in Chapter 10 but I would be remiss if I didn't point out that compression, specifically JPEG compression, is what is known as lossy. When we compress our image, we lose some of its detail, and that detail is thrown away. And the loss is irreversible. The quality setting on our digital cameras is really setting the amount of compression that the camera uses on the image data when saving it. The best quality has the least compression (i.e. throws away the least detail). I always use the best quality when shooting in JPEG mode. (Memory cards are cheap and getting cheaper.) When Photoshop uncompresses a JPEG, it takes the image out of its compressed JPEG format. But it can't reconstruct the detail that was thrown away during the original compression. As I said, that's unfortunately lost.

File size is almost directly related to the number of pixels in our image. (There is a small amount of additional size needed to store overhead information that is independent of pixel count.) The file size of a 6 Mp image will be roughly double that of a 3 Mp image. A 10 Mp image will be approximately 67% larger than a 6 Mp image. And in each case, file size can vary tremendously depending on format type.

File Size in MB (Megabytes)
(Approximate)

Format	3MP	6MP	10MP
Raw	4	8	13
JPEG High	1.5	3	5
JPEG Low	0.5	1	1.5
Photoshop	8	17	29

Our **computer display** is made up of pixels as well, in this case, display pixels. (Our camera has sensor pixels.) The number of pixels varies depending on size and settings but a common display size is 1024 x 768 pixels. This is much smaller than our 6 Mp, 3000 x 2000 example. So what happens? The answer is that Photoshop adjusts for this and displays the image at a reduced size so that it fits. It is important to remember, though, that Photoshop still has every bit of data stored; it is just showing us a smaller version so that it will all fit on our screen. Photoshop displays current magnification in its lower left-hand corner.

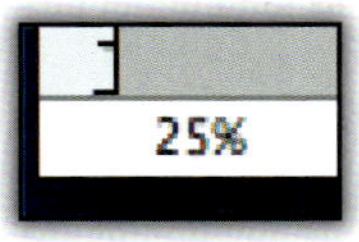

Current Magnification

Digital printing, such as with an ink jet printer, is very similar in nature. Print output has discrete elements as well, but instead of being called pixels, they are called dots. It will be a while before we get back to this (Chapter 43), but get back to it we will. For now, we just need to visualize that when we capture our image, we are saving it as little bits of information, called pixels. And when we view it on our computer display, we are looking at that same information, mapped to our display pixels. And when we print, we are printing the same information, now in the form of ink dots.

The sooner we start to think of images in terms of pixels, and not dimensions, the faster Photoshop will begin to make sense. Pixels are the basic building blocks of Photoshop. They are how images are displayed and they are how all of the image data is stored. They contain information on color divided up into red, green, and blue components (called RGB), on light intensity (with 256 discreet levels for each of the color components) and, in the case of Photoshop, transparency, visibility, locking, and a whole host of other attributes. The number of pixels in an image is most often the very first thing I look at in assessing whether that image is usable in a particular application. It's all about the pixels!

This whole pixel idea works because they are so small and tightly bunched that they look continuous to our eyes. On our monitor, the pixels measure 14 thousandths of an inch in size. Our eyes are attuned to better quality on a printed page, so the dots have to be smaller and closer together to look continuous. So printers create dots about 1.4 thousandths of an inch in size, an order of magnitude smaller. And if you think that is impressive, compare it to the image sensor itself, where the pixels have dimensions of less than a third of a thousandth of an inch.

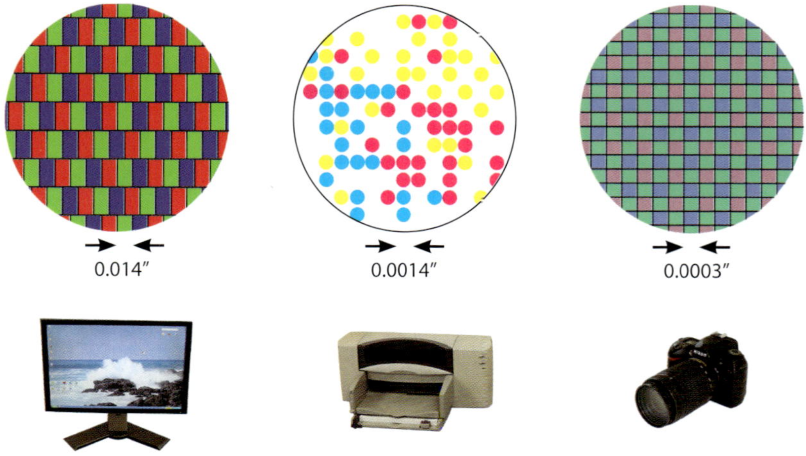

Here is an image printed at full resolution. It looks pretty pleasing to the eye and we really cannot make out that it is made up of discreet pixels. (This is the Matterhorn in Zermatt, Switzerland on a rare clear morning.)

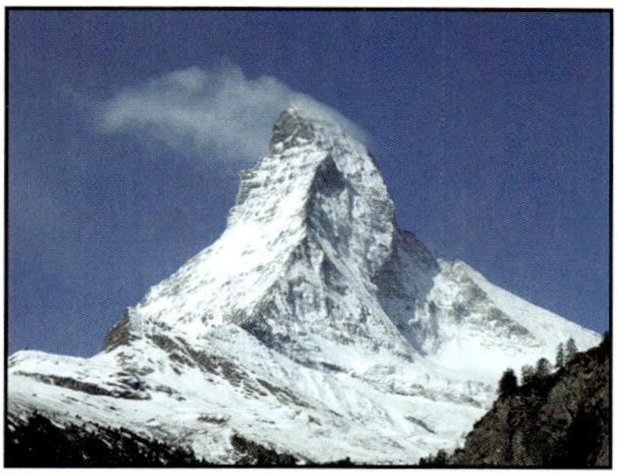

When we start to blow up the picture, however, our eyes begin to pick up the discrete nature of digital photos; the features no longer looks quite as crisp. Smooth curves start to look jagged and the image begins to look more blurry.

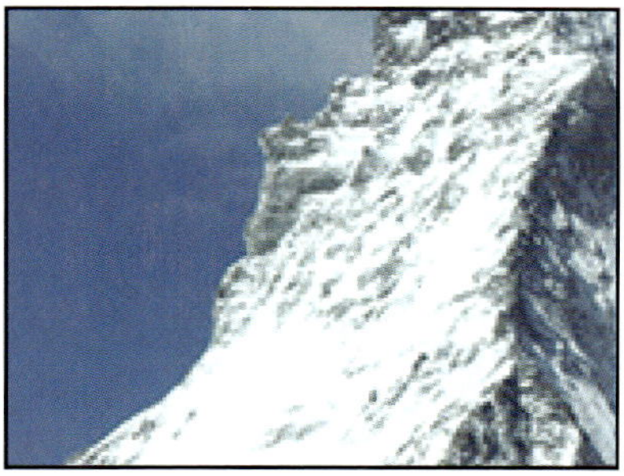

At excessive magnifications, we can easily see the discrete pixels, each of which appears to be like a little block. This effect is known as pixelization.

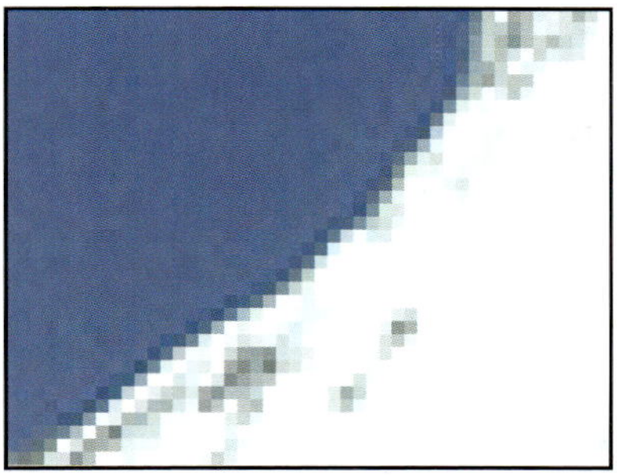

Of course this is why our thirst for more megapixels never seems to get quenched. The number of pixels we start out with puts an upper limit on how much we can enlarge our pictures without running into pixelization, or quality loss.

So pixels are pretty straightforward. Our camera takes images as an array of pixels. When we load it into our computer and open it with Photoshop, the image data is interpreted, massaged, and reconfigured into a Photoshop file, also organized as pixels. And then Photoshop displays the image for us to see on our computer screen using the screen's, you guessed it, pixels.

Keep the perspective of pixels in your head at all times. They are that fundamental.

2. THE WORKSPACE

Now that we know what we will be working with pixels, let's familiarize ourselves with where we will work with them, the **Photoshop workspace**. Launch Photoshop and do the following:

1. Click CLOSE on the welcoming screen if it appears. (Check the box in the lower left hand corner of the dialog box to bypass this screen in the future.)
2. From the menu bar at the top, choose File>New.
3. Name your document "trial" and make sure Preset is set to Default Photoshop Size. Click OK. We are opening a new document with Photoshop's default settings. More on these settings later.

The Basic Photoshop Workspace

Your screen probably looks a bit different than this one. I am working with a 16x9 widescreen format monitor–if you're using a 4x3 format monitor then your workspace won't be as wide. I am working on a Mac so if you're on a PC, there will be those interface differences. And last, I am working with Photoshop CS4 and if you're on a different version, the Photoshop workspace will also have some slight variations.

I have also dragged the border of the document window (the large central window) out a bit, creating a large gray border around the Photoshop canvas (the white rectangle). We will do that together in the next chapter.

The primary components of the Photoshop workspace are:

1. **Menu Bar** – This is a standard drop-down menu bar–we click on a heading to access its list of commands. Many of these commands are available as keyboard shortcuts (see the drop-down menu) or as clickable icons.

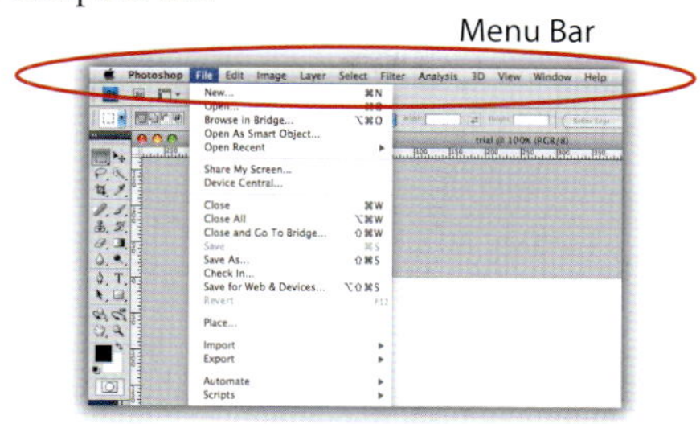

2. **Document Window** – This is where our working image resides. It has a title bar with the file name (in this case, "trial"), scroll bars, resizing handles, and a Status Bar.

3. **Status Bar** – This area at the bottom of the Document Window keeps us updated on document properties, like magnification, file size, etc.

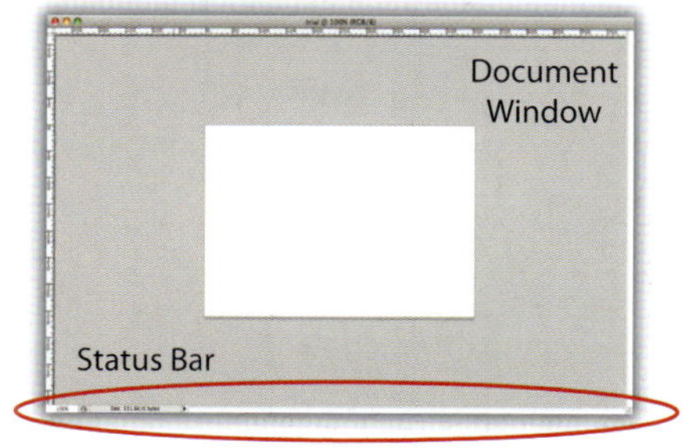

4. **Toolbox** – This area gives us instant access to all of the tools we will use (like the brush, eraser, and zoom tools) to edit our images. In a moment we will see how to switch between one and two column views.

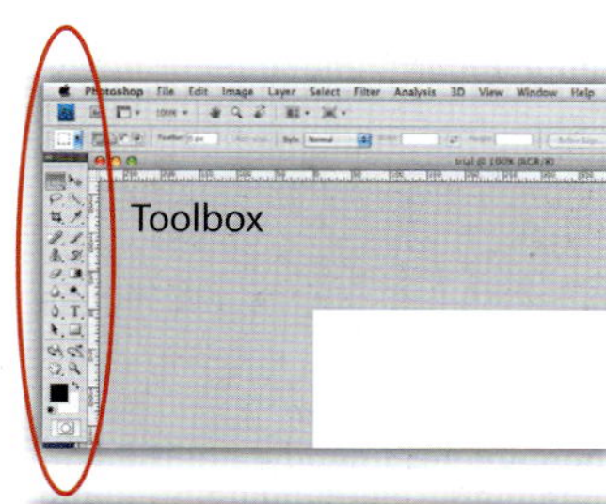

5. **Options Bar** – This area displays tool options for the currently selected tool (as shown by the icon to the left). These options vary, depending on which tool is selected.

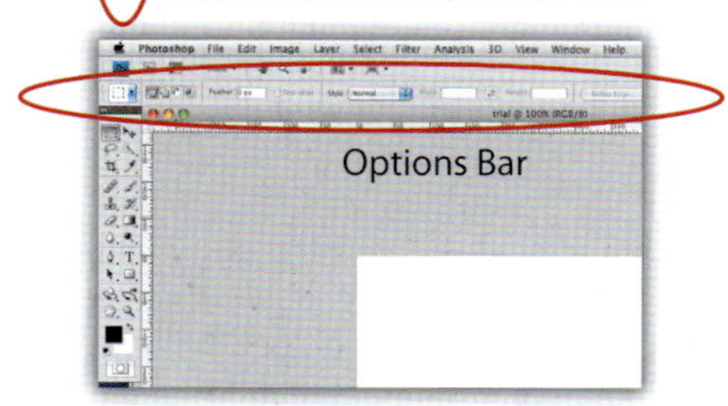

6. **Panel Dock** – The panels help us edit and keep track of our work. We click on a particular panel's tab to bring it forward and make its contents visible. (This is where CS4's interface has some dramatic changes.)

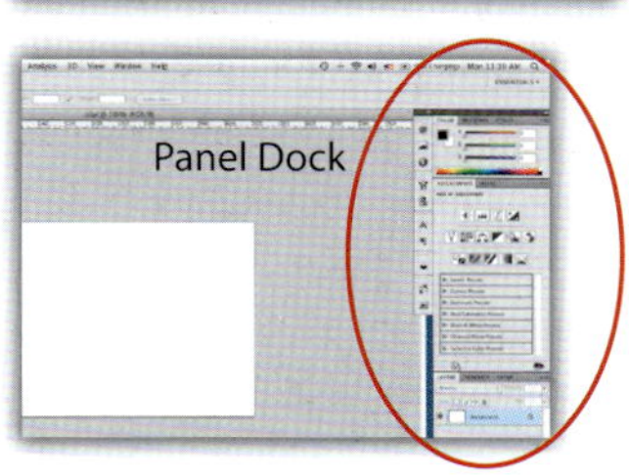

The toolbox shows over twenty tools available to us, but that's not all of them. Those tools with a little black triangle in the lower right hand corner of their box have even more, related tools hiding (nested) underneath. If we click and hold on the rectangle shape tool, for example, we see five other shapes that we can use. If we choose one, it replaces the rectangle in the toolbox.

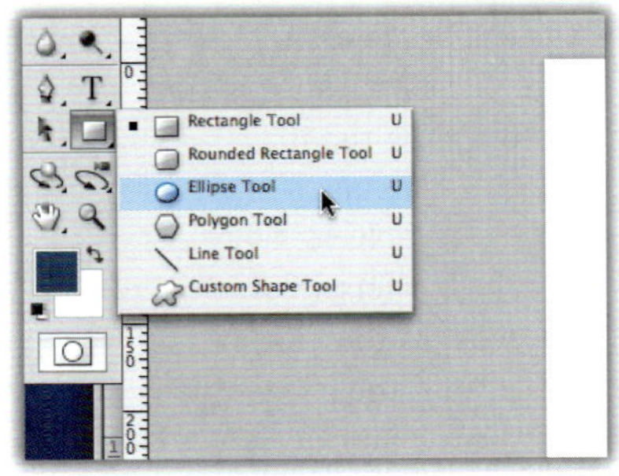

Here are all of the tools at our disposal in the toolbox. (If your screen shows a single column of tools as opposed to this double column, simply click in the top of the toolbox by the double triangles to toggle back and forth between one column and two.)

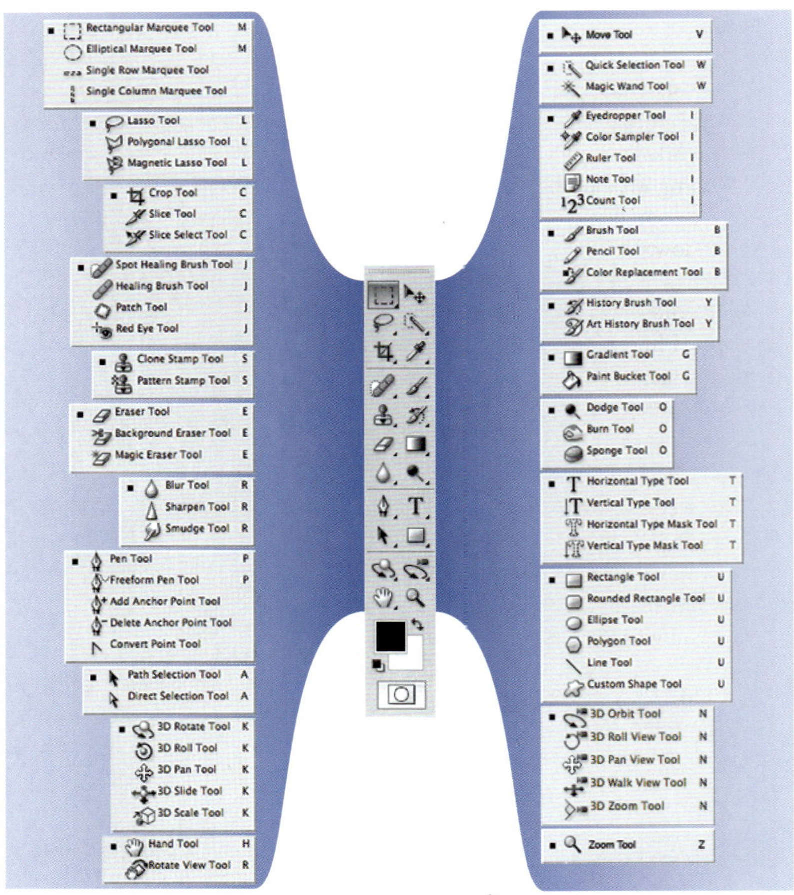

There are many more panels than meet the eye as well. Some of these hidden panels are available by clicking on its tab, if it's visible, bringing that particular panel to the top of its group. (The panels grouped together usually have some sort of relationship.) Many others are available by selecting Window in the menu bar and then choosing from the panels that are shown there. Most of the panels we will use often, however, are visible by default.

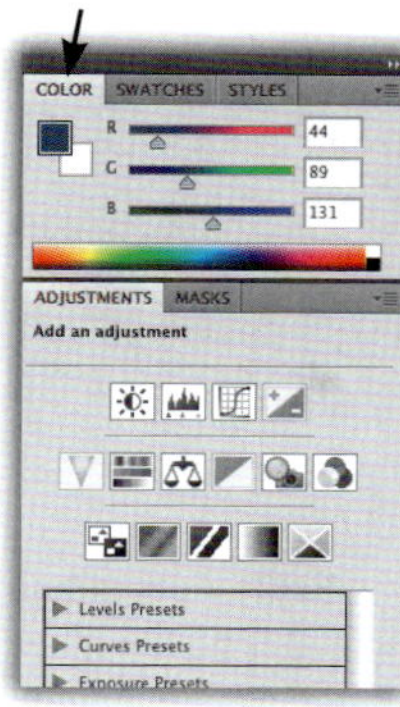

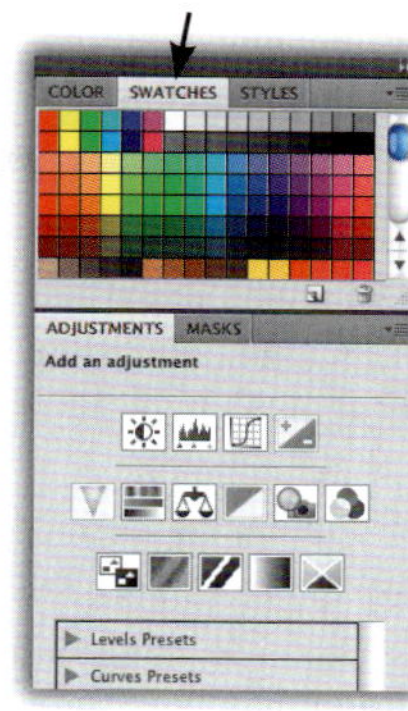

For right now, don't worry about what any of these things do. We are simply nosing around to see where things are located. We are seeing where all the pots and pans are stored before trying to bake something.

The document window, toolbox, and panels are all floating; they can be left docked where they are or, if we are the type that likes to personalize our workspace, they can be dragged around. And if we find a particular configuration of panels to our liking, we can save that workspace configuration by choosing Window>Workspace>Save Workspace and naming it. Let's say we have a configuration we like for web design and we call it "Web." At some later time, we can immediately return to that configuration by choosing Window>Workspace and then selecting "Web" from the menu.

I'm not one of those who does well personalizing his workspace. In fact, more often than not, I find that I inadvertently lose panels or get them undocked by mistake. So for me, the most useful command regarding workspaces is Window>Workspace>Default Workspace. This puts everything back the way it was. Phew!

One last point. In the menu bar, at the far right of the commands, is Help. Here is where we can access local (CS3 and earlier) or online (CS4) Photoshop help. Don't hesitate to use it. There is a table of contents tree as well as search capability. I generally use the search box and keywords to narrow what it finds. Each page you open also has related links in it so getting to the information you're seeking is usually pretty quick. The local version with CS3 and earlier is a bit easier to use but both work well.

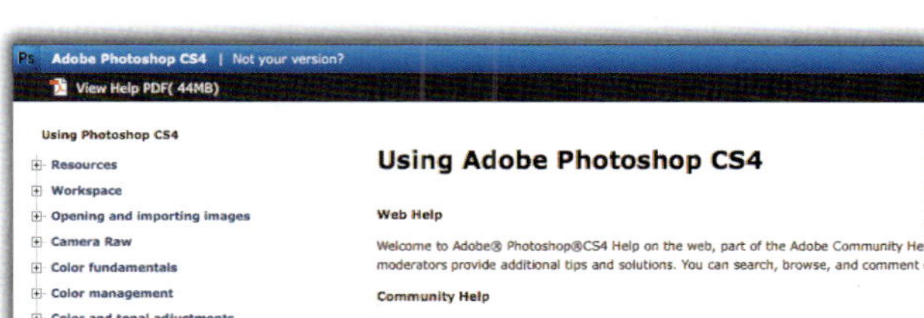

3. OPENING AN IMAGE

So let's open up an image in Photoshop. This is done as it is in most programs by going to the File command in the menu bar. When we do, we see that we actually have a few options:

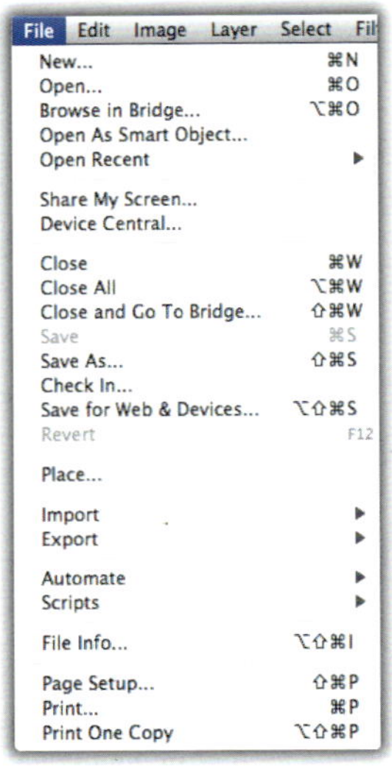

File>New brings up a new blank canvas, as we saw in Chapter 2.

File>Open brings up a standard Open dialog box that allows us to navigate to our desired file and then open it.

File>Browse brings up an Adobe program called Bridge (which came with Photoshop) that has a more graphical interface to help us navigate to our desired file. (We pay for the fancy interface, of course. Bridge is much slower than Open.) For now, just use File>Open.

File>Open Recent shows us a list of the most recent files we have worked on. This is very handy for opening work in progress.

Using File>Open, navigate to a photo that you have saved on you computer. If you have none, you can still follow along. But it would be best to get an image, either from your camera or even off the web. More than likely, you will be opening up a JPEG. But Photoshop is adept at opening almost any graphical file type, including PDF, PNG, AI, EPS, TIFF and so on.

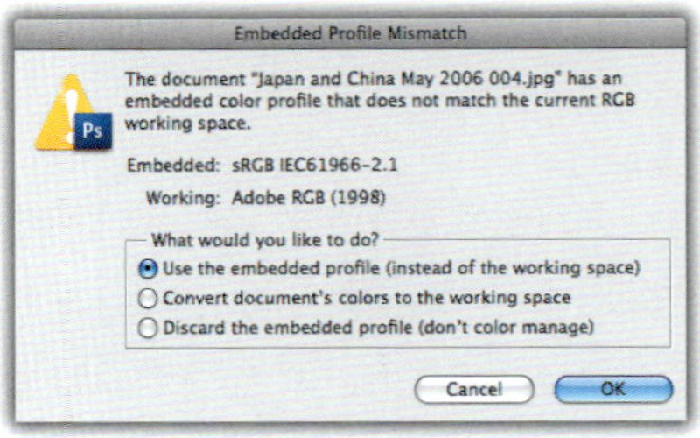

Before our image opens, we may or may not see an Embedded Profile Mismatch warning. A profile is just a color model and everything digital uses one. When we take a picture, our camera embeds its profile type (typically sRGB IC61966-2.1 which we'll just call sRGB). Working space, on the other hand, refers to the default profile that Photoshop is set to work in, Adobe RGB in this case.

The safest approach is to choose option 1, Use Embedded Profile. Photoshop changes its working space to conform to the image's embedded profile and everyone is happy.

But here's the rest of the story. We can define Photoshop's default Working Space under Edit>Color Settings>Working Spaces>RGB. We should choose sRGB if we plan to have our Photoshop'ed images printed out at our local camera store. Their printers almost always assume sRGB.

But if we are printing at home using Photoshop and our own printer, we may want to consider choosing Adobe RGB (1998) as our Working Space. This profile is a bit more robust and gives us a bit more color range. Of course unless we can set our camera for Adobe RGB (check its manual), we won't get the full benefit and we'll get a warning every time we open a file. Those warnings can be turned off but I recommend they be left on; there will be instances when we'll want to stick with the embedded profile.

So now our image is open in a new document window with a magnification chosen (by Photoshop) to fit our screen size. We can make the document window larger by dragging on the resizing handle in the lower right corner, creating gray borders around our image. Check out the first figure in Chapter 2 to see what I mean. Doing this helps us insure that we are seeing the whole image and that it hasn't been truncated by the document window.

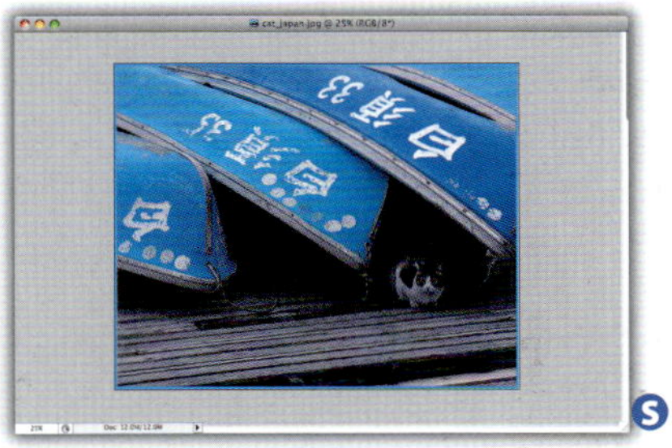

The header of the document window lists the name of the file we have opened (or untitled should it be a new untitled document), the magnification at which it is being displayed, and the color mode (which is different from color profile). We will discuss color modes later but our default is RGB (Red, Green, Blue) and we will stick with it. The /8 indicates we are in the default 8-bit dynamic range. (Photoshop can do 16-bit as well but we should stay in 8-bit until we have a compelling reason to move up.)

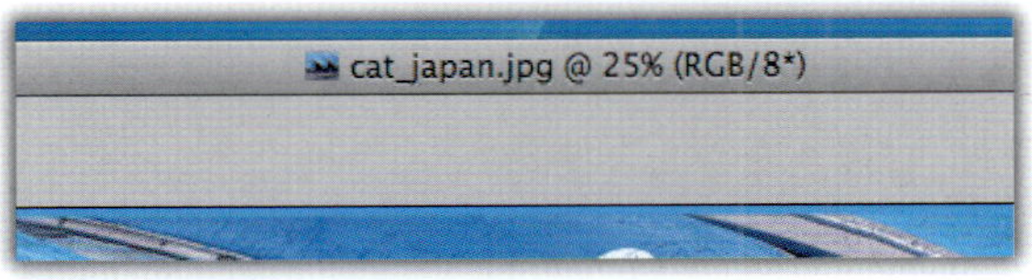

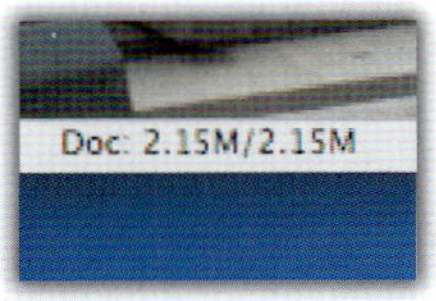

As described in Chapter 2, the status bar of the document window (the footer) shows the magnification as well. It also displays the total file size of this Photoshop document. Notice that the size has grown substantially from the JPEG we imported as we said it would. (There are actually two file size numbers. For now they are the same–2.15M in this example. Later, we'll actually have two different numbers. But that's later.)

Looking over at our **Layers panel** in the lower right of our workspace, we see that there is an item (a layer) called Background. (If this panel is not visible, click the tab called Layers. If that is not visible, select Window>Layers.) This background layer (denoted by italics and the little lock) has some special properties that can be confusing for those starting out (and even those who are experienced) so I suggest the following. Drag the word Background (which drags the layer) down onto the New Layer icon (the little tablet of paper) at the bottom of the Layers panel. This creates a copy without the special properties and keeps the original as an archive. We will learn more about this and what layers are all about when we get to the Layers chapter. But for now, believe it or not, this simple step will save us a lot of grief.

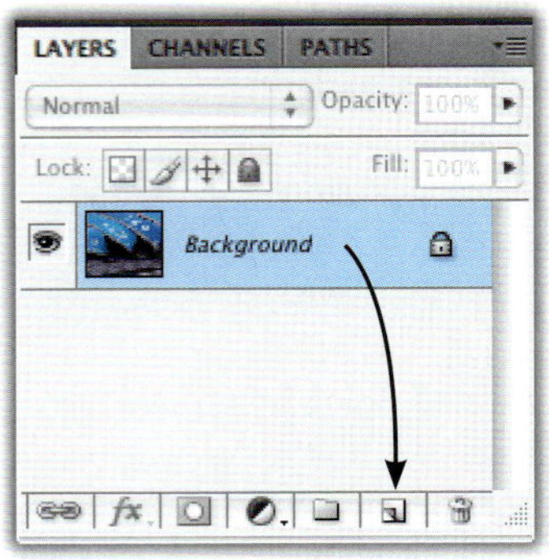

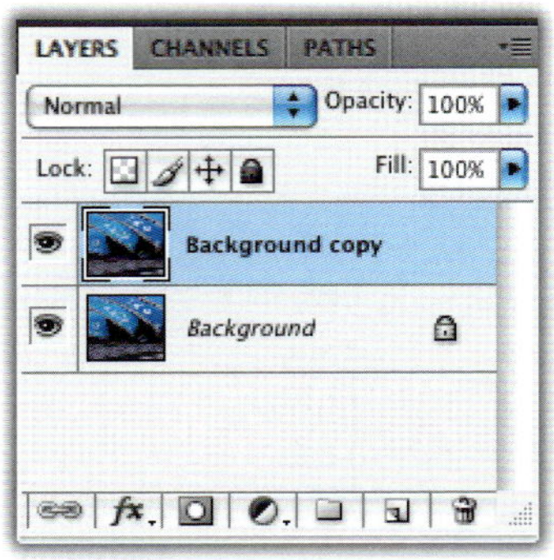

Later on, we will have a whole chapter on saving our work. But of course saving as we work is an excellent practice, so here's the short version. First, we choose **File>Save** (or **File>Save As)** from the menu bar to bring up the Save As dialog box.

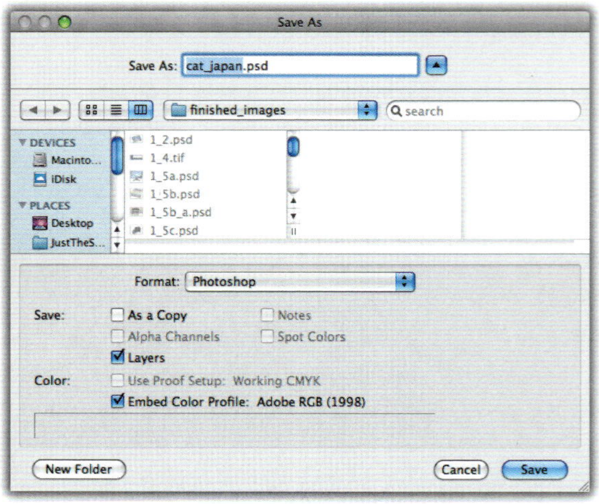

We name our file in the box at the top next to "Save As." If we followed my advice and created a Background Copy layer, Photoshop automatically adds its file extension ".psd". We now have a Photoshop file, not a JPEG. We use the dialog box to browse to a location to store the file and hit Save. There is no need to worry about any of the other settings or boxes. (If a Maximize Compatibility warning appears, just click OK. We will go over what this is a bit later.)

The Save As dialog box shown is for a Mac operating system–the PC has its own version. But they do the same thing.

Now if we were to open a JPEG and skip the duplicate Background step (maybe we are just doing a quick enhancement), Photoshop will maintain the JPEG extension, .jpg. (This is because we have yet to do anything with the file that makes it incompatible with JPEG.) As before, we use the dialog box to browse to a location to store the file and hit Save.

This time we get a new dialog box with JPEG options. Let's keep it simple for now. We just drag the slider all the way over to "large file" and finish by clicking OK. (In doing so, we are using the minimum compression and maximum quality setting.)

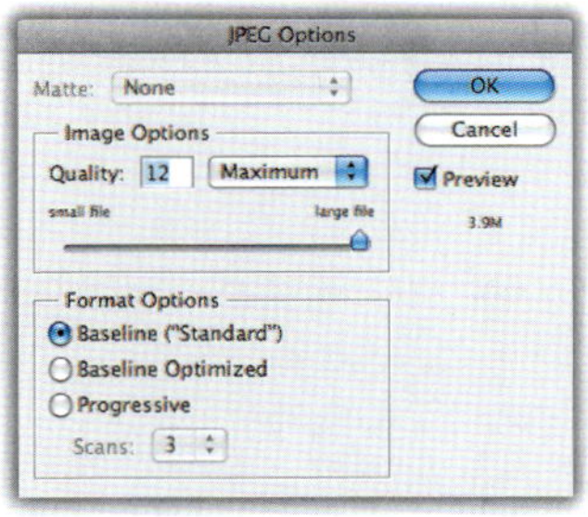

Let me mention one more thing that comes in handy for novice Photoshop users. It is pretty easy when we are poking around to inadvertently change a setting and not know how to reset it back. Making this more complicated is the fact that Photoshop's settings are sticky, meaning that if we close and reopen the program in hopes of fixing a problem, we will be out of luck; Photoshop will remember all of its settings. (This is great if we are continuing on a project but not so great if we've messed something up.)

What we can do in this case is to close the program and relaunch it, immediately holding down Cmd-Opt-Shift for the Mac or Ctrl-Alt-Shift for the PC. We release these when we get an ominous screen asking if we want to delete our settings. When we confirm, Photoshop opens, reverting to its default settings. Mind you, all settings (preferences included) revert, even those we may not have wanted to. So this is sort of a nuclear option. But it is great to have if you get completely stuck.

4. PANELS

Panels, introduced in Chapter 2, help us keep track of our work as well as perform modifications to it. There are a bunch of them. Some are immediately visible on our workspace, like the Color panel and the Layers panel. Some jump to the front when we click their tabs, like the Swatches panel, which is under the Color panel at the top of panel dock. And some, like the Navigator, Histogram, and Info panels, are completely hidden until we access them under Window in the menu bar.

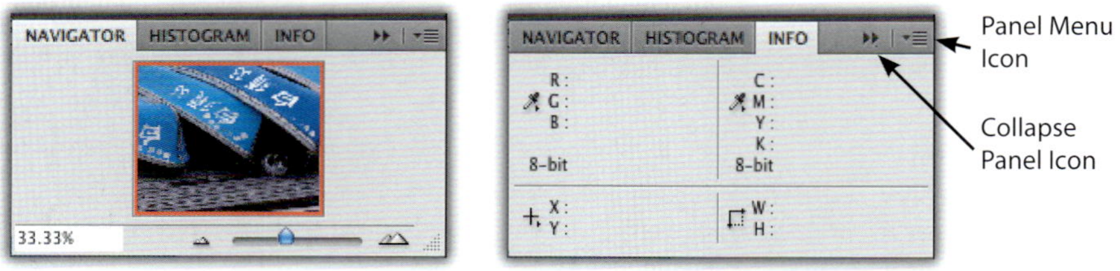

Clicking on the Info tab jumps the contents of that panel to the top of the stack.

All of the panels are useful and with time, you will use most if not all. Starting out, however, these will be the most handy:

- Navigator panel
- Color panel
- Swatches panel
- History panel
- Layers panel

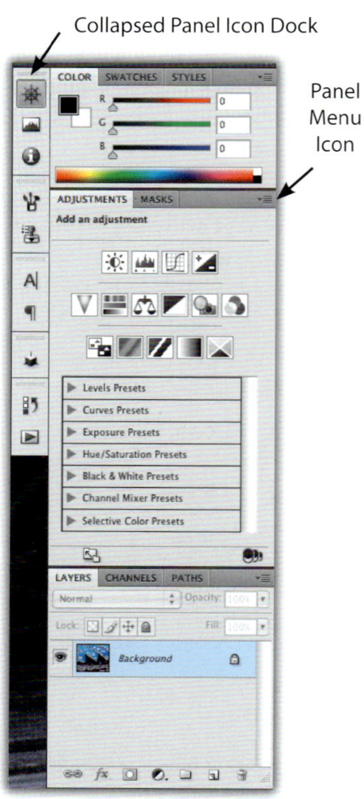

The Color, Swatches, and Layers panels are already visible as part of the standard workspace. The Navigator and History panels are accessed by selecting Window and then the panel name in the main menu bar. Once such a panel is open, if we click its Collapse Panel icon (see top figures), it closes but leaves an icon to the left of the panels with which we can easily reopen it. Notice that we also get icons for the other panels within a panel's group.

Each panel also has its own personalized panel menu, accessible by clicking on its icon in the upper right hand corner.

Open the **Navigator panel** by going to Window in the menu bar and selecting Navigator. It pops open along with the Histogram and Info panels (the panel group). Starting out, I found the Navigator panel to be both useful as well as a lot of fun. The slider at the panel's bottom allows us to zoom in an out on our image. Try it. (If your document from Chapter 3 is not still open, repeat those steps to get it open.)

As we zoom out, our image gets smaller relative to the document window. (Of course!) As we zoom in, on the other hand, the image can become larger than the document window and then only a portion of the image is visible. Look at the Navigator panel. The portion of the image that is visible is shown by the red rectangle.

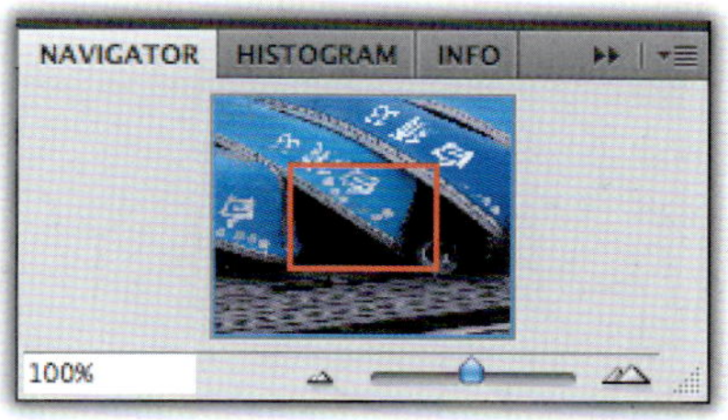

Click the smaller and larger icons to either side of the slider for preset zoom levels.

If we place our cursor over the rectangle, it turns into a hand tool. We can then click and drag the rectangle to reposition the image relative to the document window.

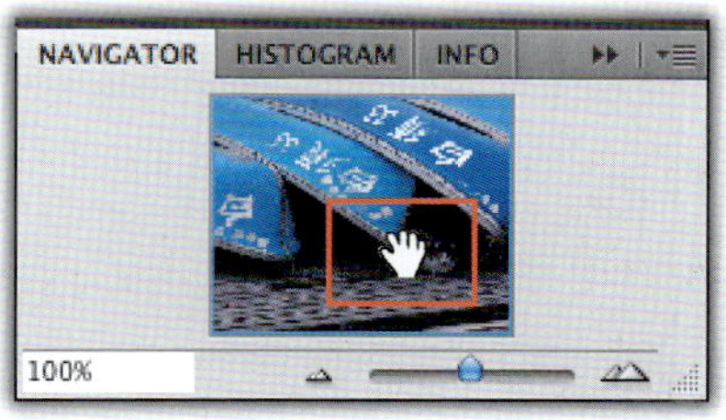

The **Color panel** is for choosing colors, something we will do quite frequently with Photoshop. We will discuss Color and the sliders later but for now we can play with those sliders to make different colors. As we move the sliders, the "foreground color box" updates, depending on R (red), G (green), and B (blue) values. (If your sliders look different, select the panel menu and choose RGB sliders.) For me, it's fastest to click on the color strip at the bottom to get close to the color I want and then fine tune with these sliders. Uncomfortable with that amount of flexibility? The Swatches panel (click its tab) affords us a simplified preset selection of colors.

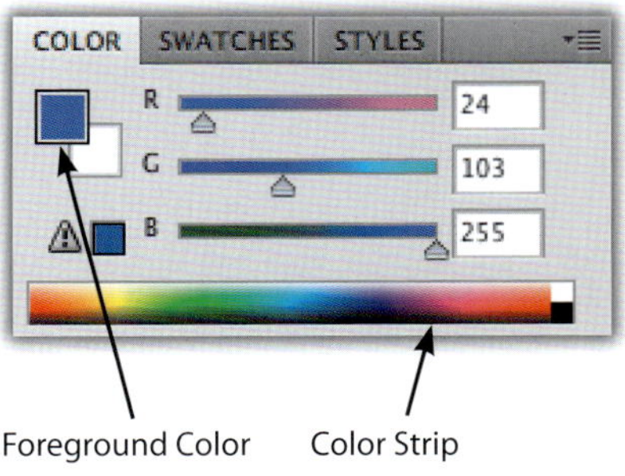

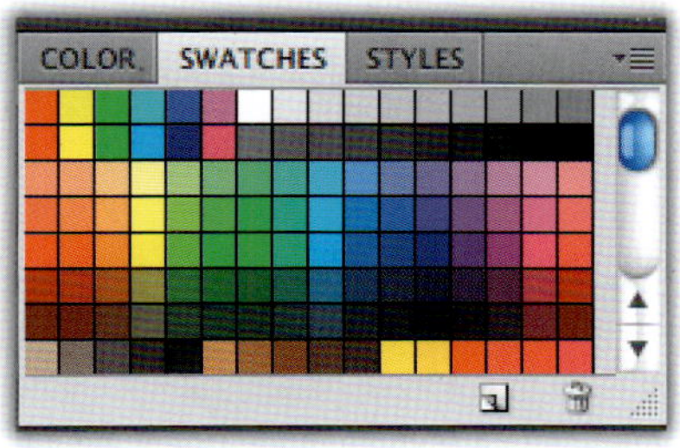

The **History panel** can be one of our best friends. There are times when we make a mistake or want to undo something we've done. (Maybe this doesn't happen to you, but it sure does to me.) If we just want to undo one step, we can select Edit>Undo (shortcut Cmd(Ctrl)-Z). But this only works on the last step–if we do a second Undo, it actually undoes the Undo, generally not what we had in mind.

The History panel is our way around this. Access it by selecting Window>History. It remembers the last 20 steps we have performed. With this panel, we can go back to any of these 20 steps and pick up our editing there as if that were our most recent step. Quite the time saver for the error prone. So let's check it out.

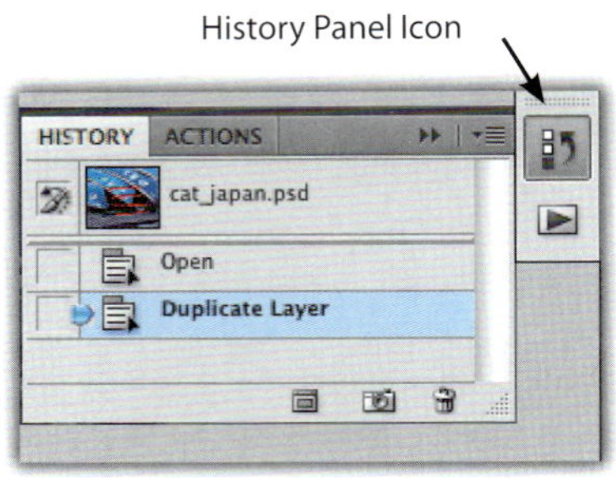

With our image still open, let's choose the Brush tool from the toolbox. In the options bar, we click the pull down menu icon to the right of the word "Brush," set the diameter to 30 px and the Hardness to 100%. Now we go to the Color panel or Swatches panel and choose a color; I picked red. Lastly, we draw four horizontal lines across our image by clicking and dragging left to right four times, each time underneath the last.

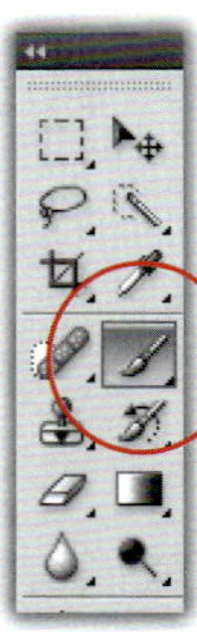

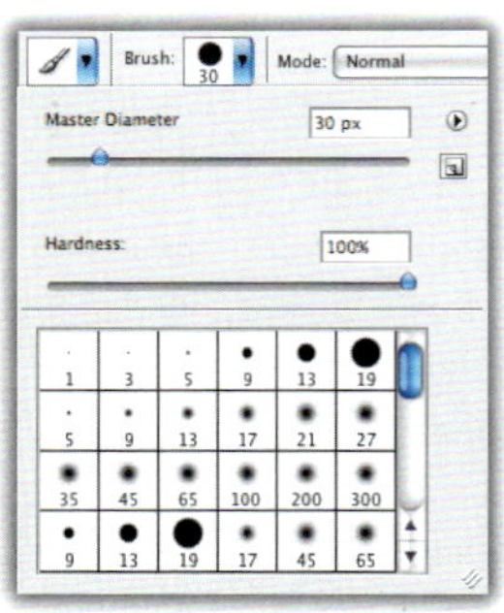

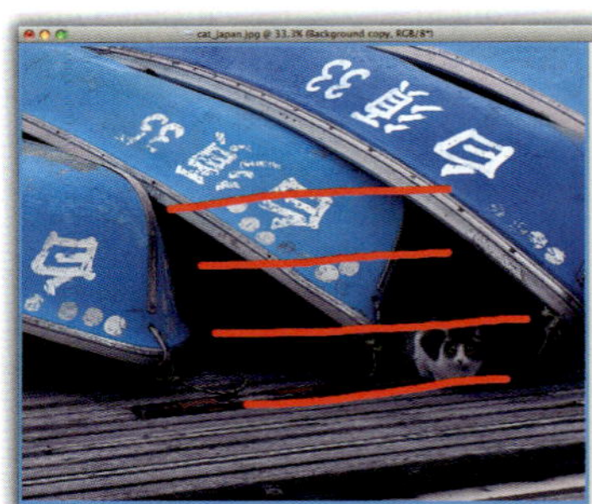

If we check out our History panel, we notice that our Brush tool actions are now listed. The most recent action is at the bottom of the list and is highlighted. We can also see, at the top of the list, where we opened our file and duplicated the Background layer.

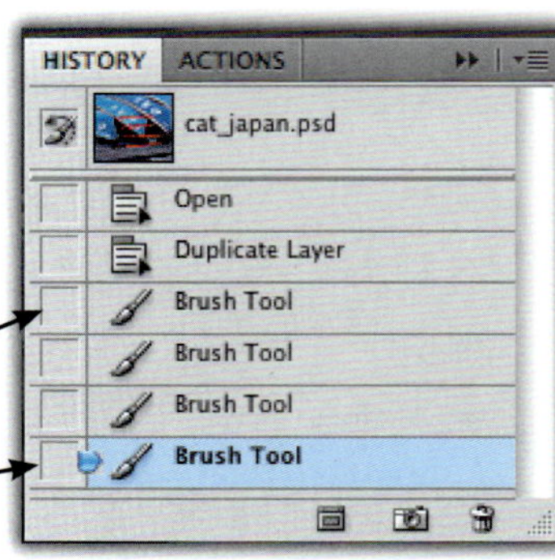

If we click on the line third from the bottom, we are moving back two steps–notice we now only have two lines. The steps corresponding to the last two lines are grayed out but are still there. We can click on the bottom step (most recent) to restore everything.

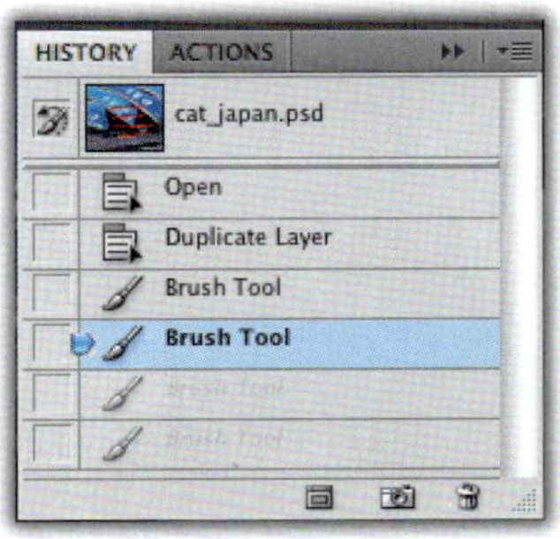

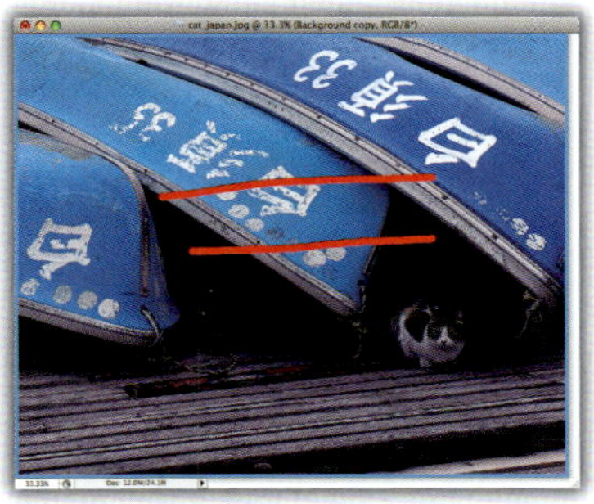

If we click on a past history point and begin to edit, however, all of the actions below it will be discarded and replaced by our new actions. We will have lost our ability to restore. Click the history line corresponding to our second line (third from the bottom). Choose a new color and draw some more lines to see this in action. Click around on the History panel to convince yourself.

Last but certainly not least is the **Layers panel**–we already touched on it briefly in the last chapter. We will use this panel more than any other in Photoshop.

When we open an image in Photoshop, the program loads the image's array of pixels into a layer and names that layer Background. When we make a copy of Background (Ch. 3), Photoshop creates a second layer identical to the first, naming it Background copy. We can see both of these layers in the Layers panel, stacked one on top of the other. The little thumbnail images clue us in as to what is on the layer. (Since my red lines were drawn on the Background copy layer, they can be seen on that thumbnail.) To edit a layer, we select it by clicking on it in the Layers panel.

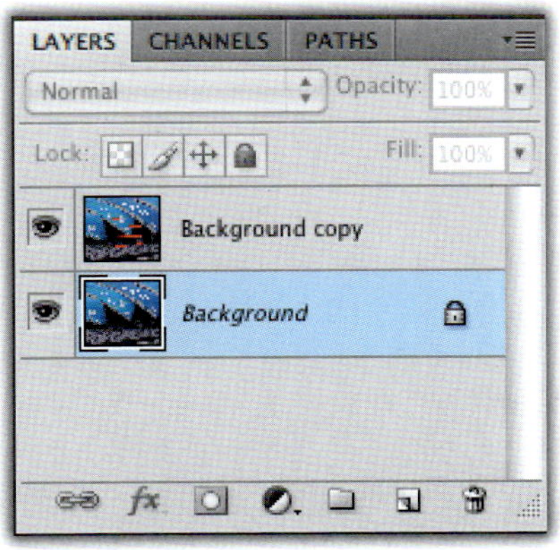

We really don't need to worry about layers at the moment, though. Two whole sections of this book are devoted to layers so there is plenty more to come. But at least for now, you know where the panel is and where the layer icons are.

5. IMAGE SIZE & RESOLUTION

This subject might be one of the more confusing to master for the novice user but together, you and me, we'll make it simple.

Imagine a 6Mp image that is 3,000 pixels wide by 2,000 pixels tall. If we wanted to print it on a printer at 250 dots per inch, where each dot was to correspond to a pixel, then our print would be 12" by 8". (2,000 pixels divided by 250 dots per inch equals 8 inches.) **Dots per inch**, or dpi, is a measure of resolution for the printer. The tighter the spacing, the higher the resolution. The looser the spacing, the lower the resolution.

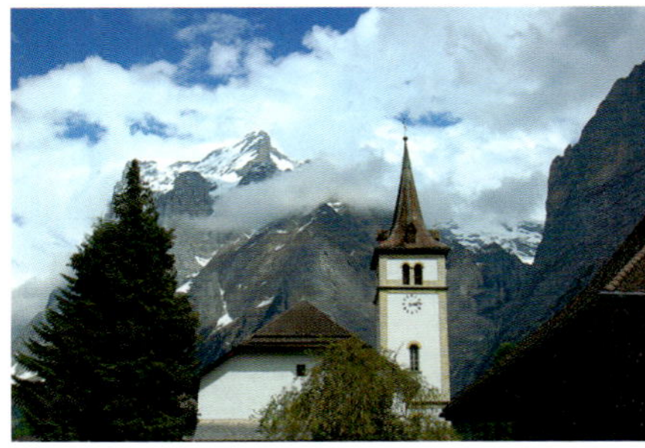

Now if we were to take this same image and display it on our computer monitor, how big would it be? Typical monitors display at 72 pixels per inch (or ppi) so at 100% (one camera pixel for one monitor pixel), the image would be a whopping 41.7" by 28.8". (Now you know why Photoshop has zoom in and zoom out controls.)

Pixel count, resolution, and size are forever linked. Change one and either one or both of the other two must change.

Let's open up any image in Photoshop (if you don't already have one open). Then select **Image>Image Size**. This screen has all of the information we have just been talking about (and then some, of course). My screen shot corresponds to the 6Mp, 250 dpi example from above. (But Photoshop thinks in terms of pixels, right? So it lists ppi (pixels per inch) instead of dpi.)

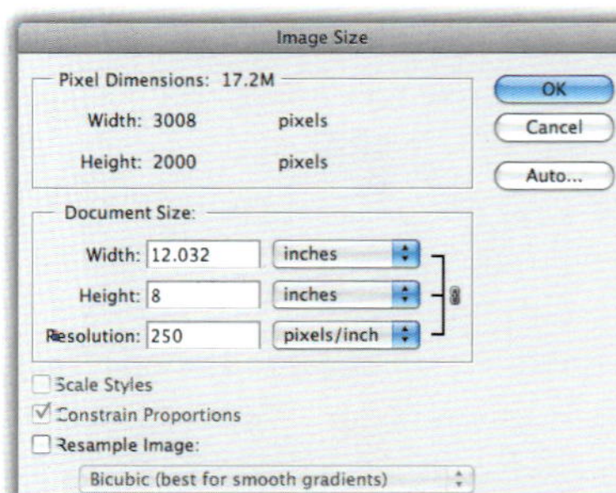

Check Constrain Proportions to maintain aspect ratio. Uncheck Resample Image, which freezes the pixel dimensions (count). If we then make changes to the resolution, the pixel count can't change, so the size changes. Or if we change size, resolution changes. Here I have changed the Resolution to 72 ppi.

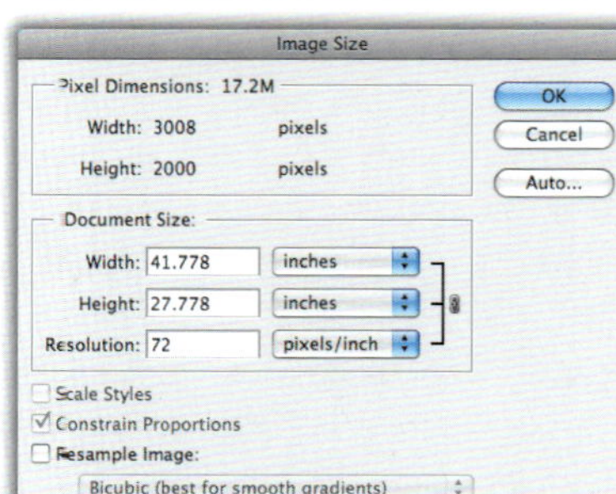

With Resample Image unchecked, changes to size or resolution only change how our image is displayed; the original pixel data is unaltered. Practically speaking, however, we usually want to specify both resolution and size. Then, because pixel count, resolution, and size are forever linked, pixel count will have to change. Let's go through that process.

When we want to size an image, our first consideration should be resolution. We can make it simple and say that if we are creating images to be viewed on a computer screen, say on the web, we choose 72 ppi for our resolution. If we want a higher quality print, at home on our inkjet or at a camera store, we choose 250 ppi and we'll be safe.

RESOLUTION RECOMMENDATIONS	For the Web.................72 ppi For Printing...............250 ppi

Next, we decide what size we want. But we don't want to change resolution; we just chose that (72ppi or 250 ppi). And this is where the Resample Image check box comes in. When we check it, we are telling Photoshop that when we change size, it should change pixel count ("Pixel Dimensions") and not resolution. And if we change resolution, it should change pixel count and not size. (We can also change pixel count directly if we want. Size, not resolution, will correspondingly change.) It is worth spending a few minutes playing with entries and watching the results.

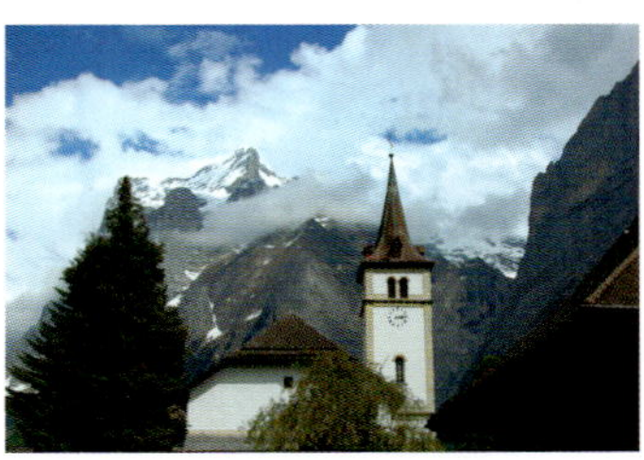

Cutting the pixel count in half cuts the size in half when Resample Image is checked.

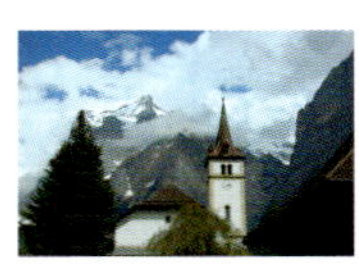

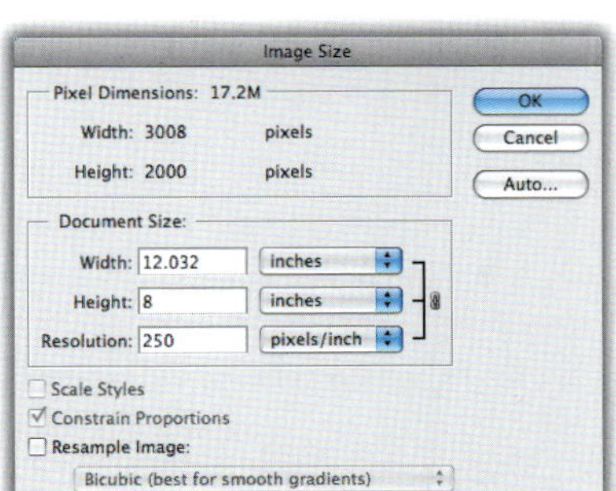

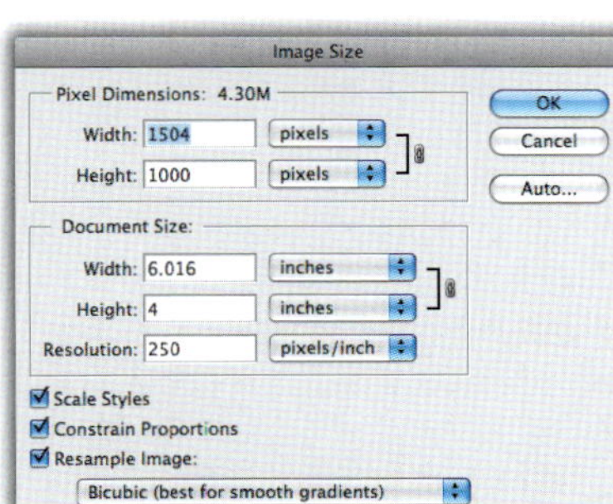

Okay, if Photoshop is changing the pixel count, isn't it changing the image? The answer is yes and this is a key concept to get under our belt. Photoshop changes the pixel count by "resampling" the pixels. When it resamples, Photoshop distributes our image over a different (larger or smaller) number of pixels. In our 6Mp, 250 ppi example, when we checked Resample Image and changed the size to 4x6, Photoshop resampled our image, resaved it if you will, using 75% fewer pixels.

This is called **downsampling** because the number of pixels is dropping. Keep in mind that we are losing data when we do this–some of the finer details in the image might be degraded. In these two images, the one on the right has been downsampled by a factor of four (2x in each dimension). When printed at the same resolution, they look similar in quality. If we blow them both up, however, we can see that detail has been lost.

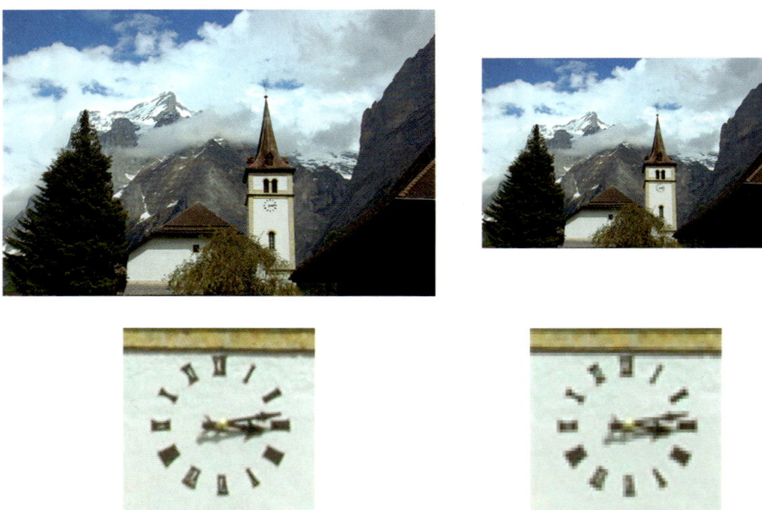

The image of the church steeple on the right has been downsampled by a factor of two in each dimension so it only has 25% as many pixels as the original (left). If we magnify the image, we can see that some of the detail in the original has been lost.

When we downsample to make a smaller image, the loss of detail is generally not perceived because the resulting image is smaller. But the detail is lost. And keep in mind, after downsampling, that detail is gone forever. A good plan of attack is to save our original and to create a copy to resize with downsampling. This way we will have our original higher quality image should we ever need it (like for an enlargement).

Making the image larger (that is increasing the number of pixels) is called **upsampling** and should be done with caution. When Photoshop downsamples, it does averaging to display the information over a smaller number of pixels. When Photoshop upsamples, it has to guess what to put in the extra pixels it is adding. It does this with a calculation called a smoothing algorithm.

In these three images, the one on the left is our original. The image in the middle is a downsampled version of the original (it has one ninth the pixels). Notice the image degradation; the platform edges are becoming jagged and detail is lost. The image on the right was upsampled from the middle image, back to the same resolution as the original. See how the "jaggies" were smoothed out but the image is still blurred. Upsampling can't add detail that isn't there; all it can do is try and fill in as best it can.

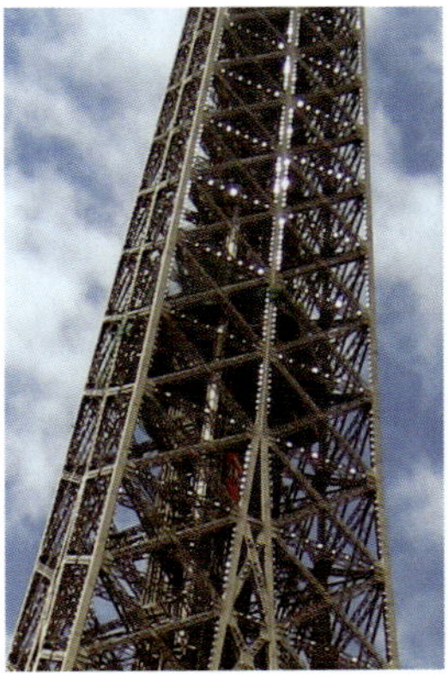

Image 1. This image is our original and has dimensions of 400 by 600 pixels.

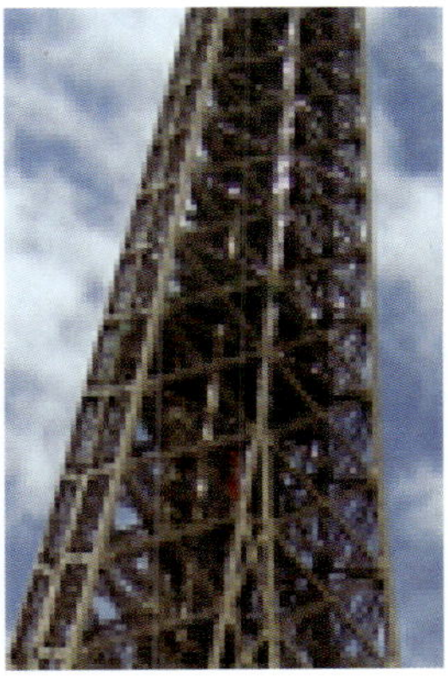

Image 2. This image is downsampled to 80 by 120 pixels and shows image degradation.

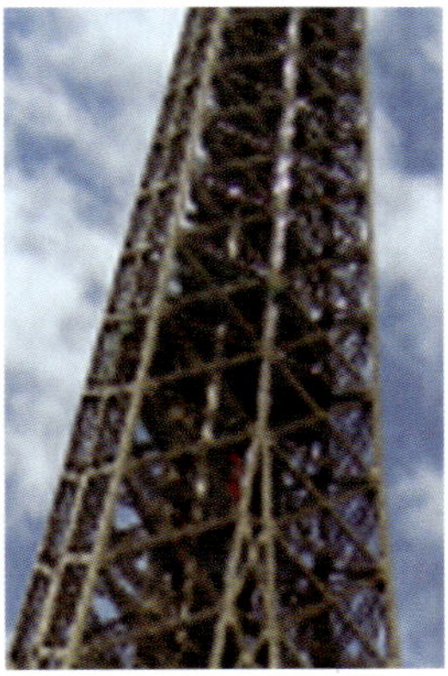

Image 3. This image was upsampled from Image 2 back to 400 by 600 pixels. But the lost detail doesn't return.

If we have to grow an image, a good rule of thumb is that we shouldn't try to do it by more than 10% to avoid visible degradation. Don't confuse any of this with the zoom (magnification) amount in our document window. When we zoom in and out, Photoshop is changing what is displayed to us but it is not changing the pixel count.

We have several resampling method options when we check Resample Image, all available in the pulldown menu by the check box. Choose Bicubic Sharper for downsampling and Bicubic Smoother for upsampling.

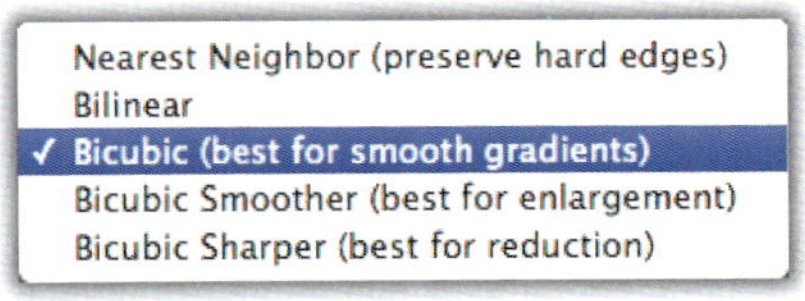

6. SELECTIONS–PART 1

When someone says that an image has been "photoshop'ed," they probably mean that it has been modified from the original. Perhaps the color of a car was changed. Or maybe a moon has been added. Or faces swapped! This is all made possible by selections and we are going to go through the basics of that now.

As we know, when we open up an image, Photoshop loads it as an array of pixels. This array of pixels is stored in a layer, called Background, shown in the Layers panel. Any changes we were to make now would be global, meaning that changes would affect all pixels equally. If we brighten the picture, we brighten everything, all pixels, equally.

But let's say we wanted to make changes to some pixels and not others? What if we could mask off the pixels we didn't want changed, much like a painter masks off a wall to paint the trim a different color? Well, that's what a **selection** does. When we "select" pixels, the "unselected" pixels are masked off and protected from any changes. (Believe it or not, this is the first step to swapping faces...)

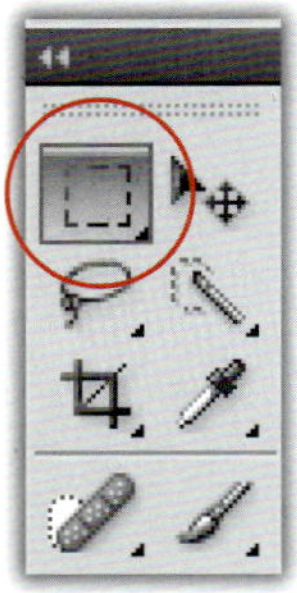

Open an image in Photoshop, but don't make a copy of the Background layer. Now select the **Rectangular Marquee tool** (check in the options bar that Feather=0 and Style=Normal) and click and drag to create a rectangle like I have shown below. The rectangle has a moving dashed border sometimes referred to as "marching ants." All of the pixels within the border of the marching ants are selected. Those outside are masked off.

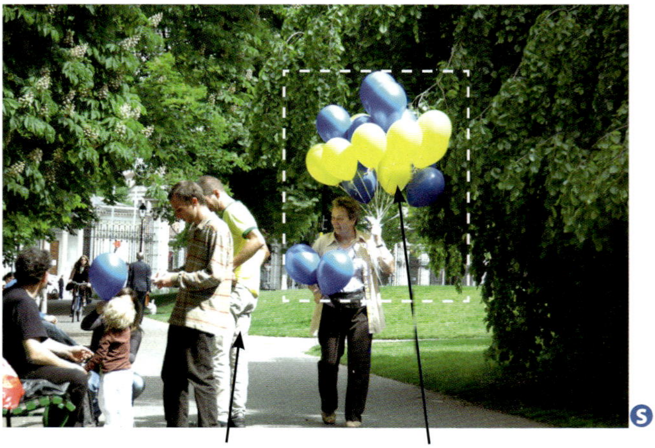

These pixels are outside of the marching ants box and are not selected.

These pixels are within the marching ants box and are selected.

Let's prove that. Select Image>Adjustments>Hue/Saturation. Then drag the Hue slider to the left or right, changing the color hue of the image. As we see, only the selected bits are affected. Those outside the marching ants are masked from the adjustment. It is not a big leap to see how this technique of selective changes might be somehow used to change the color of a car.

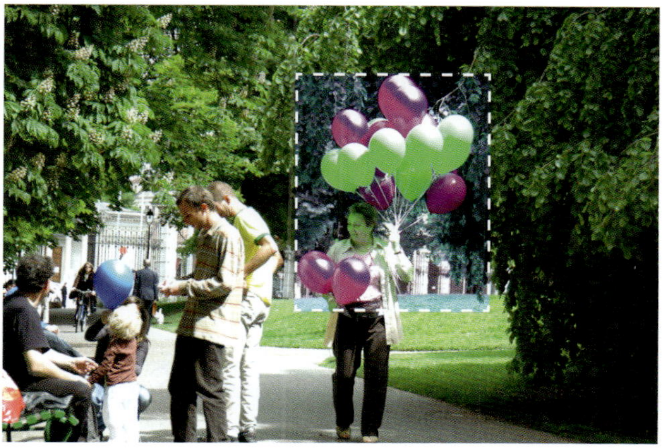

Next select the **Move tool** from the toolbox. This tool allows us to move selected bits around on the document. With the Move tool selected, we place our cursor within the marching ants and click and drag (the icon turns into scissors then a pointer). The selected pixels are moved, overwriting the pixels that get covered up by the move and leaving a hole where the moved pixels used to be. Are you starting to see how swapping faces might be done? We can reset our image by choosing File>Revert.

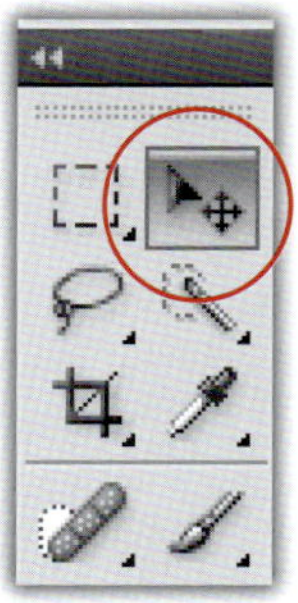

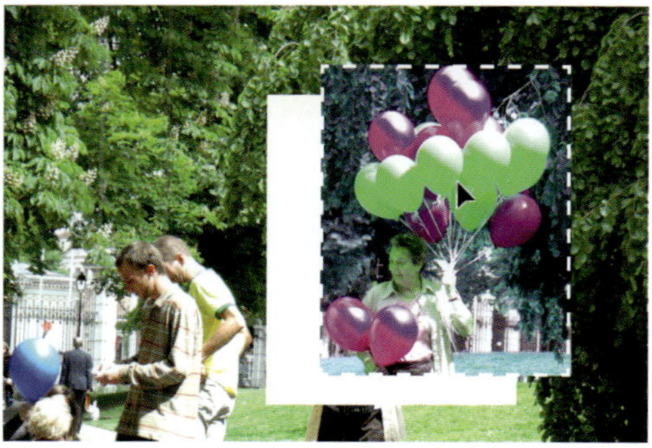

Now granted, selecting only in the shape of a rectangle is a little limiting. In the rest of this chapter, we will learn a few tools that will allow us to do more complicated selections. Later in this section, we will learn some additional techniques.

If we are selecting an object that is elliptical, we use the **Elliptical Marquee tool**. (The Elliptical Marquee is found behind the Rectangular Marquee; click and hold on the Rectangular Marquee and the list of tools behind it appears. Select the Elliptical Marquee and it jumps to the front on the toolbox and is selected.) For circles (and for squares when using the Rectangular Marquee), we hold down the shift key as we drag.

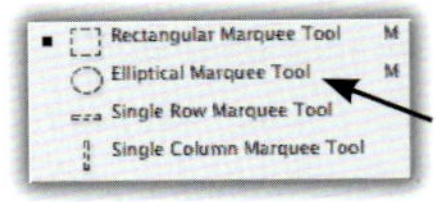

We won't always get the exact selection we want, especially with the Elliptical Marquee. But that's easily fixed. After we make our initial selection, we choose Select>**Transform Selection** and a bounding box appears with transformation handles. We click and drag on the corner boxes to scale our selection in two directions (shift maintains the aspect ratio); the handles on the sides and top and bottom scale in a single direction. (See below.) If we place our cursor within the bounding box, we can move the selection by clicking and dragging. Lastly, we can rotate our selection by hovering our cursor just outside the bounding box until we see the rotate arrows. Then we click and drag to rotate.

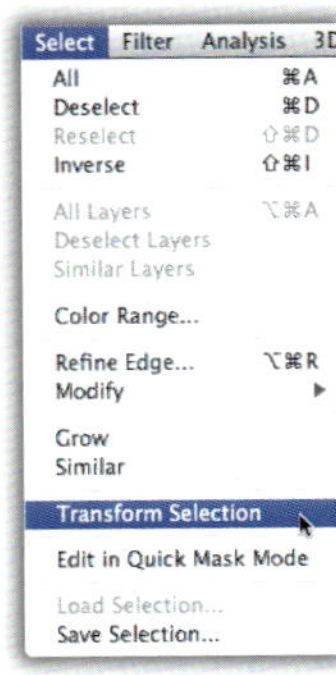

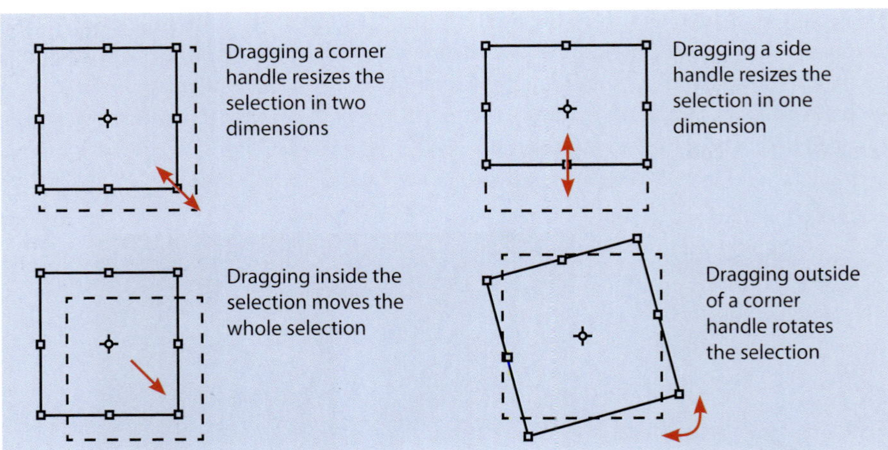

Once we have the changes we want, we need to accept them by either pressing Return/Enter or by clicking the Commit Transform check mark on the right side of the options bar. If we don't like the transform and want to reset, we click the Cancel button. And if we want to get rid of the selection altogether, we choose Select>Deselect.

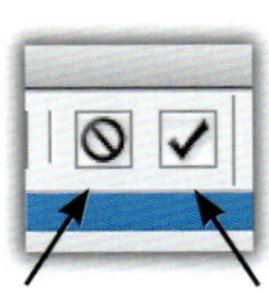

So what about irregular shapes? Well if we have an extremely steady hand, we can use the **Lasso tool** found right under the Rectangular Marquee. With it, we click and drag around the desired shape, releasing the mouse button over the starting point. (If we are exactly over the starting point, Photoshop will display a small circle by the cursor. If we release the button somewhere else, Photoshop will simply complete the selection for us from that point.)

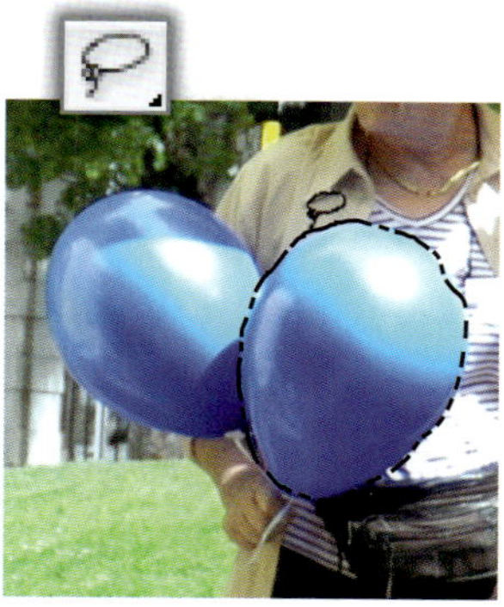

The right balloon is (loosely) selected using the Lasso tool.

For those of us with slightly less steady hands (yes, my lasso selection is lame), there is the **Polygonal Lasso tool**, nested under the Lasso tool. This tool creates the selection boundary by drawing straight lines between clicks. So click, release, move the mouse, click, release, move the mouse, etc. We close our selection by clicking over the starting point–Photoshop will again help out by displaying that small circle by the cursor when we are close. Alternatively, we can double click wherever we are to have Photoshop complete the selection.

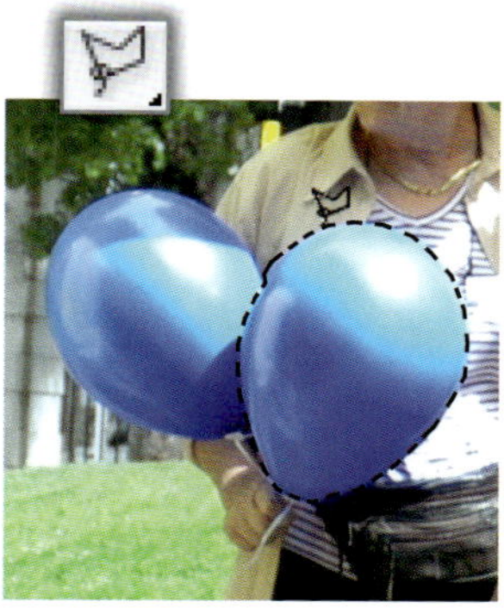

The right balloon is selected using the Polygon Lasso tool.

We can get remarkably accurate selections with this tool by working at higher magnifications, keeping the distance between clicks small, and exhibiting boundless patience.

Try the following. Select an irregularly shaped object using the Polygon Lasso Tool. Choose Image>Adjustments> Hue/Saturation and use the Hue slider to change the color.

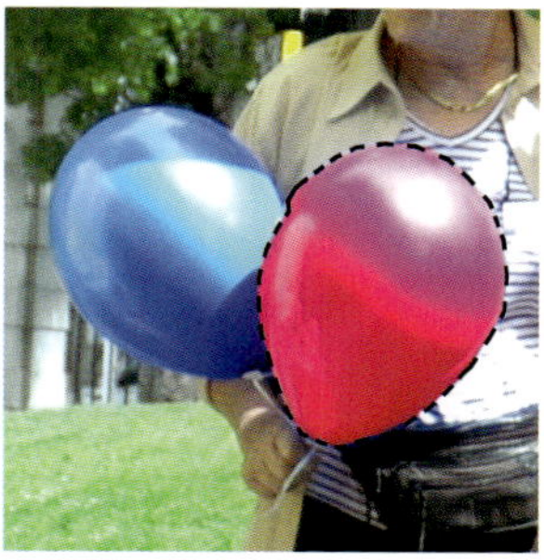

Changing the hue affects only the selected balloon.

There are more precise selection tools but this one works pretty well. Select>Deselect gets rid of the selection.

7. ZOOM AND HAND TOOLS

In Chapter 4 we discussed how the Navigator panel can be used to zoom in and out and move around within our image. Fun though that was, there are actually much more efficient ways of doing both of these functions.

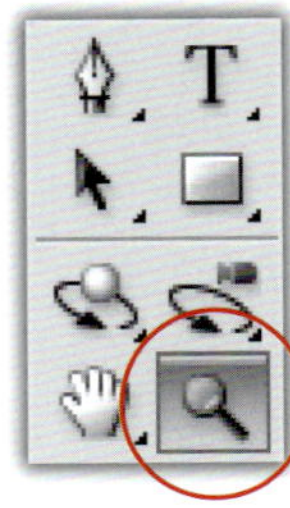

Let's start with zooming, which is short for increasing or decreasing the on-screen magnification of our image. With the Navigator, we did this with a slider or by directly entering a magnification percentage. The **Zoom tool**, which looks like a little magnifying glass and is located near the bottom of our toolbox, allows us to do much the same and more.

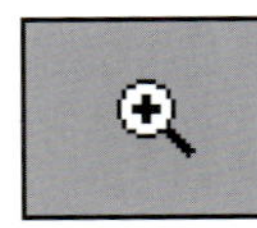

Let's open an image, choose our Zoom tool and move the cursor over our image. The cursor changes into the magnifying glass icon of the Zoom tool with an added plus sign in it. The plus means the tool is set to magnify, or zoom-in. Click the image and it magnifies. (Recall we can see the level of magnification in the lower left hand corner of the document window or in Navigator.) Click again and it magnifies again. Each click moves us up a step in magnification. The steps are preset.

Where we click within the document window is important as well. Photoshop will assume that the place we click is the place that we are most interested in and will do it's best to center that point in the magnified image. It can't always do this because the image edge won't pull within the document window border. But as I said, it will do its best.

The unseen parts of the image are not lost, they are just hiding outside of the document window. Remember the little red square we saw in Navigator when the image was larger than the document window? The red square indicated what was within the document window. Everything else was hidden.

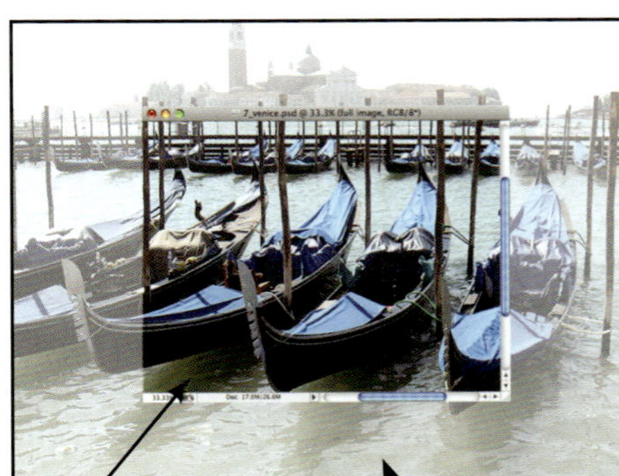

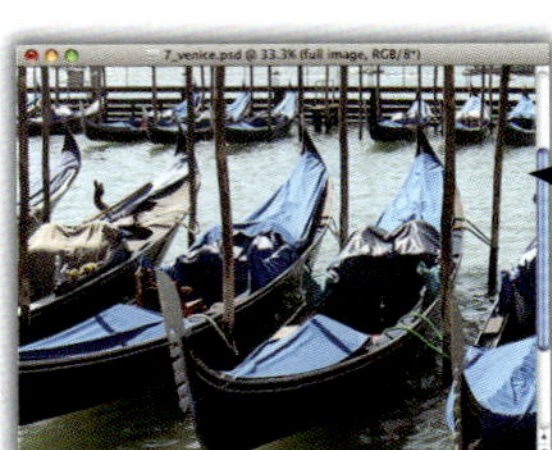

Perhaps we zoomed in too much. Up in the options bar for the Zoom tool, near the left we can see a magnifying glass with a minus in it. By selecting this, we put our Zoom tool in a demagnify, or zoom-out, mode. Note when we select it, our cursor changes to the magnifying glass with a minus. Now if we click on the image again, the magnification decreases. If we keep clicking, the magnification keeps decreasing. Of course going up to the options bar to switch back and forth can get a bit tedious so I'll show you a simpler method. In the options bar, let's switch back to the zoom-in mode (magnifying glass with a plus). Our cursor should now have the plus sign back. To temporarily go to the zoom-out mode, we can simply hold down the Opt(Alt) key and the zoom-in mode changes to the zoom-out mode. When we let go of the Opt(Alt) key, the zoom-in mode is back. And of course the cursor changes back and forth from plus to minus to signal which mode we are in.

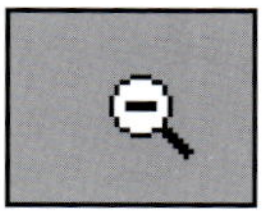

Zoom tool in demagnify mode.

What if we are all zoomed in on an image but want to look at a different part of it, one that is hidden outside of the document window? We could zoom out and then back in on a new location. But an easier way is to use the **Hand tool**, located right near the Zoom tool in the toolbox. The Hand tool works just like the hand in the Navigator panel, allowing us to move the magnified image around in the document window. With the Hand tool selected, we simply click and drag until the portion of the image we are interested in becomes visible.

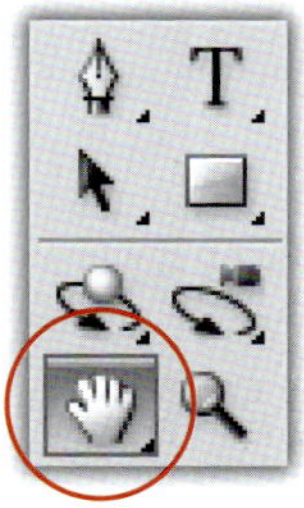

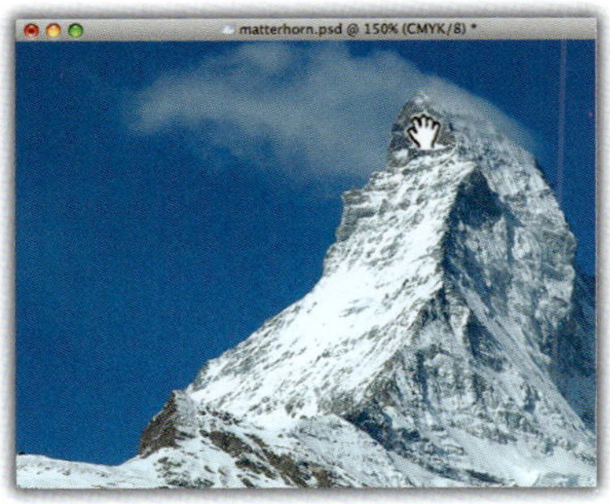

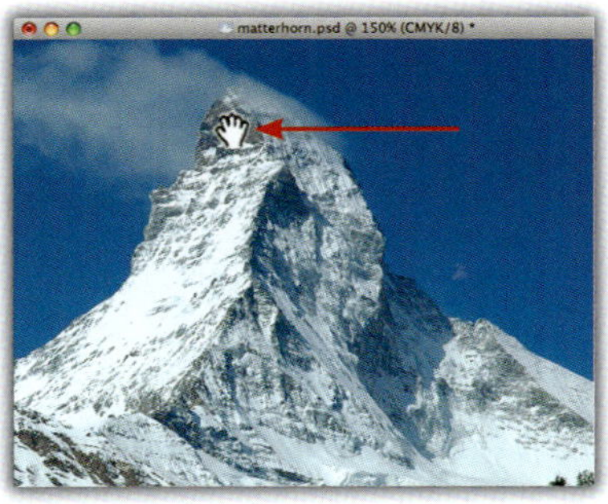

In this example, I am zoomed in so that there is hidden image area outside of the visible area. To see the area that is off to the right, I click with the Hand tool anywhere within the document window and drag from right to left (see the red arrow in the example). The image will move along with the hand as if the hand had grabbed it.

It gets even better. Here we have our image of the cat by the row boats. And let's say we would like to lighten up the cat a bit. To start, we'd probably like to zoom in on the cat to help our accuracy. Now we could click the Zoom tool to zoom in and use the Hand tool to move us over to the cat. And then maybe zoom again and move again. And so on until we got it just right.

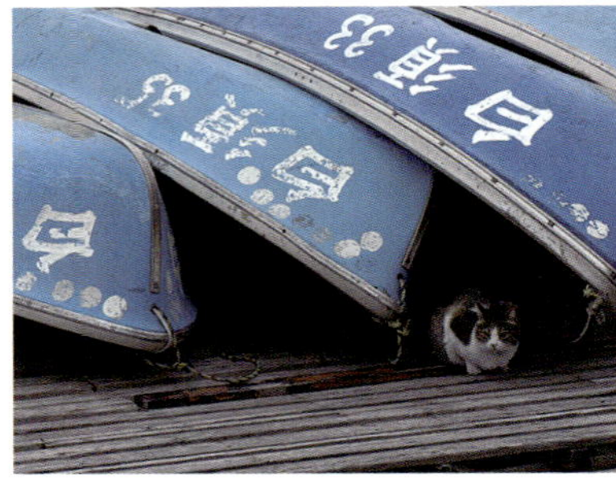

But watch this. Instead, we select the Zoom tool and click and drag a rectangle around our item of interest (in our case the cat) using the marching ants as a guide. When we let go, Photoshop blows up the image so that the area we selected fills up the Document Window. Pretty slick!

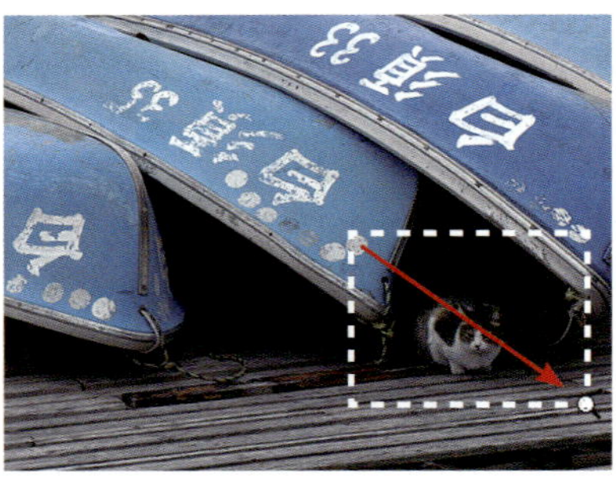

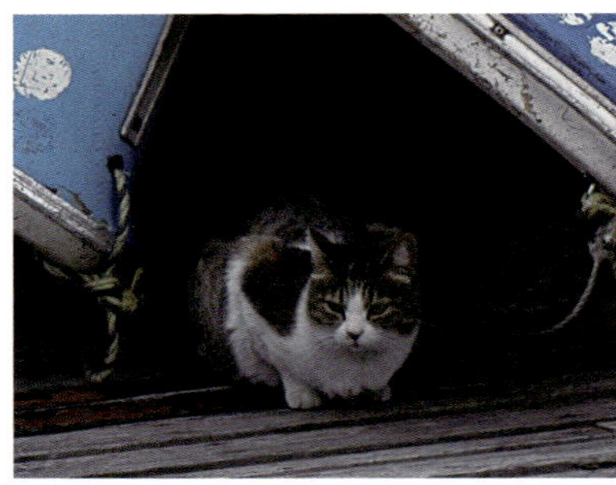

And if we are not exactly centered where we want to be, we can use the hand tool to move the image around in the document window. 99% of the time, this is how I zoom in.

By the way, in case you're wondering, there is no corresponding click and drag technique for zooming out. But there are other tricks. For example, if your mouse has a scroll wheel, you can use it with the zoom tool to zoom in and zoom out. To enable this behavior, choose Photoshop> Preferences>General (Mac OS) or Edit> Preferences>General (Windows) and select the Zoom With Scroll Wheel option. Then to zoom, you select your Zoom tool and zoom in and out with your scroll wheel.

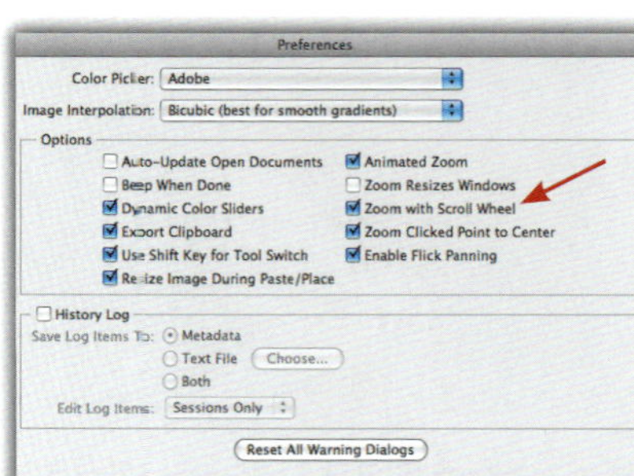

But we're not done. The designers of Photoshop realized that it would be very common for users to want to temporarily switch to the Zoom tool or the Hand tool. (We rarely use them for more than one quick change.) So they made an easy way to do this. Let's choose any other tool, like the Rectangular Marquee tool for example. We move it over our image and verify that we have the familiar cross hairs icon. Now with our left hand, we hold down both the Cmd(Ctrl) and Spacebar keys simultaneously. And voilà! The Zoom tool appears in zoom-in mode. Still holding those keys down, we click and drag over a small area on the screen and then release the mouse and then the Cmd(Ctrl) and Spacebar keys. The image zooms in, the Zoom tool disappears and the Rectangular Marquee returns.

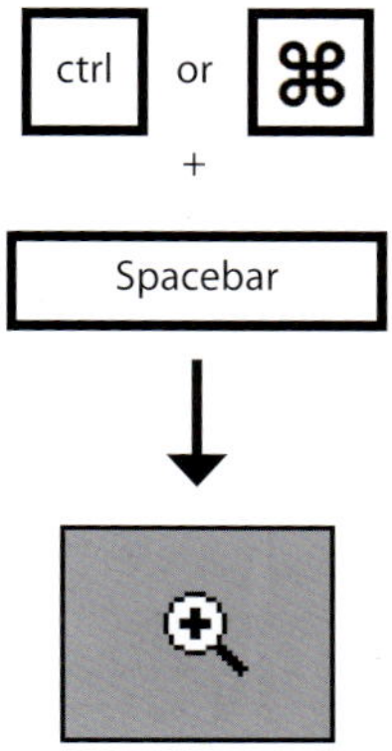

Practice this; you will use it a lot. I almost never select the Zoom tool from the toolbox. I always use this keyboard shortcut. It may feel funny at first but it becomes second nature.

A similar trick works with the Hand tool. If we are in any other tool and want to temporarily use the Hand tool, we simply hold down the space bar and we are temporarily switched to it. With the space bar held down, we use the hand to move our image around as usual. And then when we release the space bar, we are back in the tool we were previously using. You will use this a lot as well.

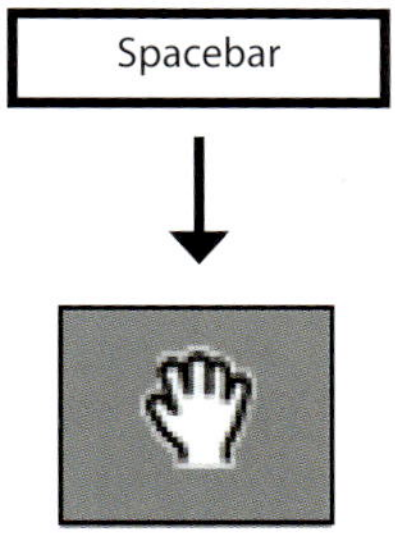

A couple of final tricks with the Zoom and Hand tools. If we double click on the Zoom tool, our image magnification automatically goes to 100% (which could be and probably is larger than our document window). If we double click on the Hand tool, our magnification adjusts so that our image just fills the document window, whatever size that is. The latter is a convenient way to get back to a full image after being at higher magnifications. One note, though. When we do this, we are left in whichever tool we double clicked. (And this can get annoying.)

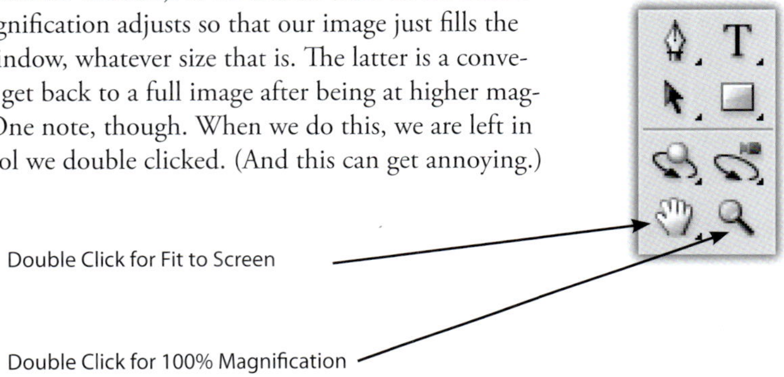

8. COLOR

We started our earlier discussion of pixels by describing how a camera's image sensor and the pixels on our computer manage color in RGB, varying amounts of red, green, and blue to store or display a desired color. Later in the Panels chapter, we saw how the Color panel had sliders for red, green, and blue, allowing us to create our own colors (in that case for the Brush tool). Let's revisit that panel for a moment.

Check out the numbers in the boxes to the right of the sliders. As we move a slider from left to right, the corresponding number varies from 0 to 255. So there are 256 shades of each color available. (Zero counts as a shade). The composite, or foreground, color is shown at the left. If we move all sliders to the left, that is set all to level 0, we get black. Moving all sliders to the right, that is, all set to level 255, gives us white.

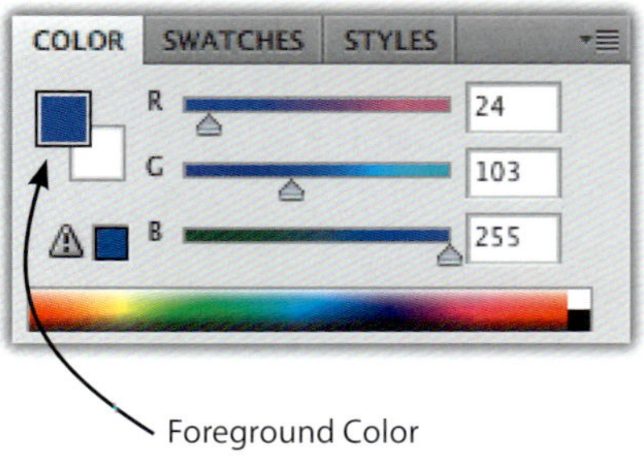

The color strip above each slider helps us to understand how our foreground color will change as we move the slider. Note also how moving one slider changes the color strips above the other two sliders. And remember the colorstrip at the bottom is for choosing an approximate starting color.

For those who don't think too well in RGB (and I am one of them), there is an alternative. Click on the Color panel menu icon and select **HSB sliders**. HSB stands for Hue, Saturation, and Brightness and is an alternative way to describe color. Hue is what we are referring to when we describe a color as red or magenta. Saturation is how pure the color is. And brightness is how light or dark it is. Play with the sliders to get a feel for how they affect the foreground color.

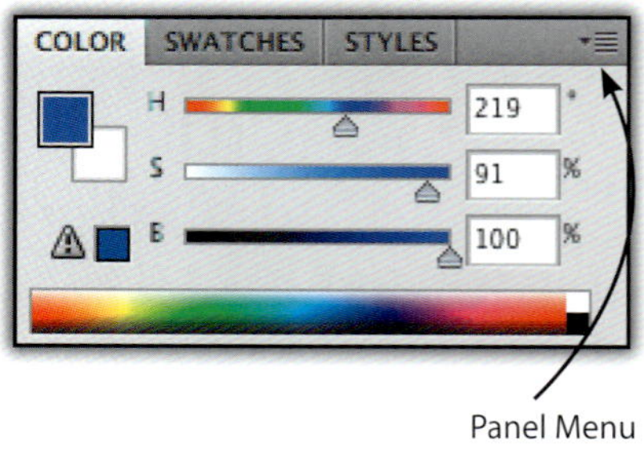

The saturation and brightness levels vary from zero to 100. This stands for 0% to 100%. Hue varies from zero to 360 because color is often represented as a wheel where hue varies as one goes around the wheel. Zero to 360 refers to degrees, an angular measurement around the wheel. (Zero to 360 makes one complete revolution so zero and 360 are actually the same hue, red as it happens.) I usually set the hue first and then adjust saturation and brightness to fine-tune.

There is an even more visual way to do the same thing. If we click on the foreground color box, we bring up the **Color Picker** dialog. The radio button by H, in the HSB group, must be selected to make your Color Picker look like the one shown below. Clicking H puts the Color Picker in HSB (but RGB levels are listed as well). The vertical slider in the middle of the box selects Hue. The left hand box displays an array of all the possible saturation and brightness combinations for the chosen hue. Click, or click and drag, in that box to choose. (If we had clicked the radio button for S or B, that characteristic would have become the vertical slider with the other two attributes in the box. But choosing H works best for me.) Similarly, we could select R, for red, putting the Color Picker in RGB, red in the vertical slider and green/blue combinations in the box. I still find HSB the more useful. (I'll discuss Lab and CMYK in a moment.)

The Color Picker is more than just a more visual Color panel; we'll see that it has a lot of extra features. One is obvious right away. It shows us before and after colors (or current versus new). This is really useful when fine tuning a color.

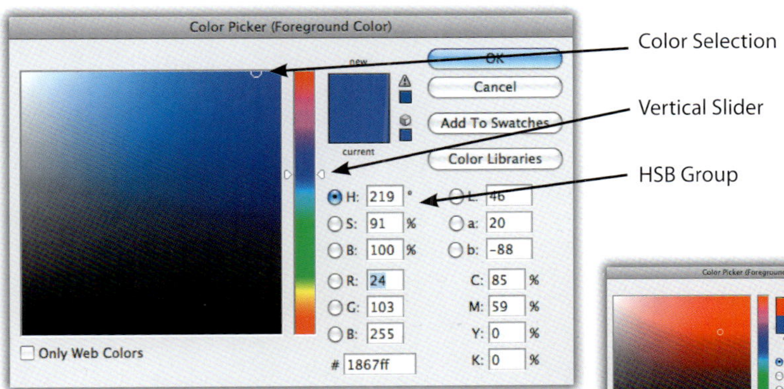

Maybe the most useful capability of the Color Picker and one not found in the Color panel is its ability to sample. Open a picture if you don't already have one open. (Maybe use File>Open Recent...) We open our Color Picker by clicking on the foreground color in the Color panel. Now we take our cursor and click and drag it over the image. The cursor changes into the **Eyedropper tool** (a color sampler) and, as long as we keep the mouse button down, continuously samples colors from the cursor location. When we release the mouse, the last color sampled is locked into the Color Picker. This way we can grab a color from an image and use it for text, as an example. Neat!

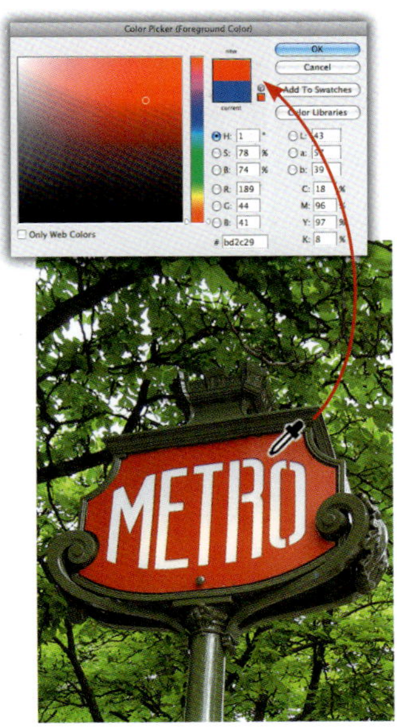

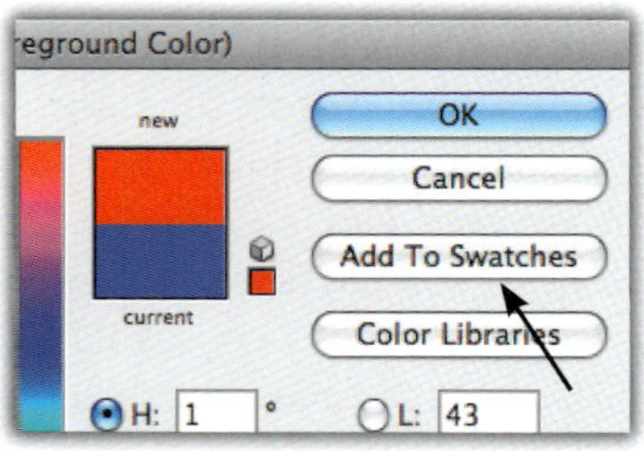

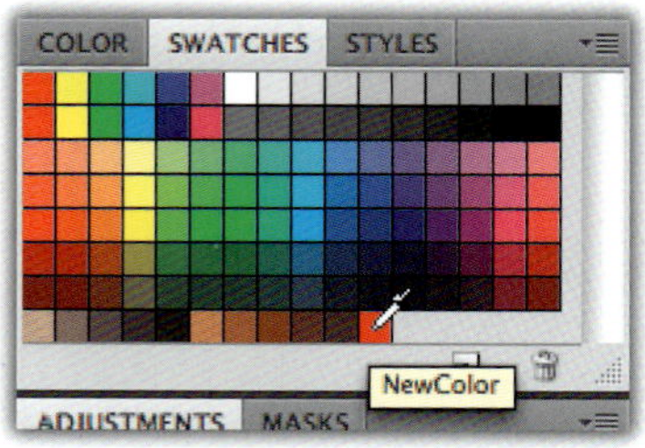

One other nice capability that the Color Picker gives us is the ability to save a color as a **custom swatch**, by adding it to our Swatches panel. Let's say we have an image open and have sampled a color from it for later use, maybe with text. On the Color Picker dialog box, we see a button labeled Add To Swatches. With our color sampled (or with one we have created), we click Add To Swatches, name it when prompted (I'll use NewColor), and click OK. Now if we go back to our Swatches panel and look at the bottom row, there it is. If we hover our mouse over the new swatch, the color name we gave it is displayed.

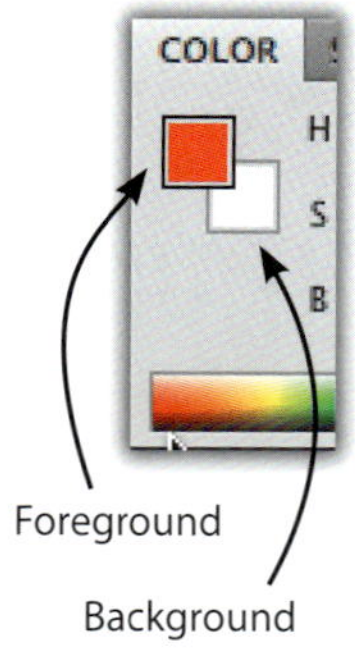

We have been referring to the color box in the Color panel as a foreground color. But there are actually two boxes there, right? The color box in back is called the background color. For now, just think of it as a second color we can define in reserve. Click in its box and the sliders now refer to it. Click again and the Color Picker dialogue box comes up, but now it is referring to the background color.

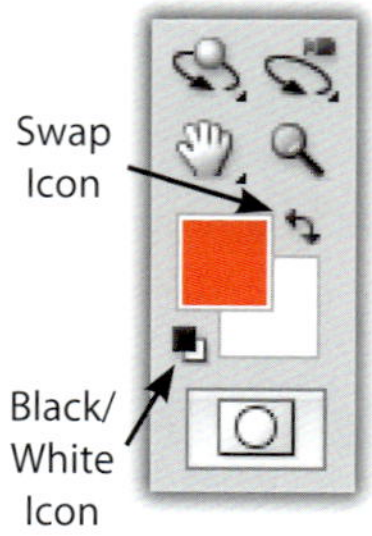

Maybe you have already noticed, but the foreground, background color boxes that are in the Color panel are also at the bottom of the toolbox. As we make changes in the Color panel, the toolbox colors follow right along. In fact we can make our changes there if we like, clicking on those foreground or background color boxes to bring up the Color Picker. But there are a couple of additional features in the toolbox color boxes. The little icon with arrows at each end allows us to swap our foreground color with our background color. This is an easy way to switch back and forth between colors when painting, for example. And since black and white get used a lot, Photoshop allows us to default to them by clicking on the little Black/White icon.

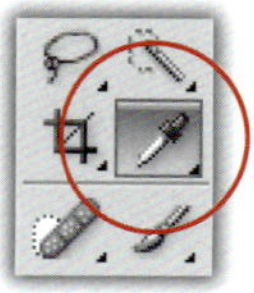

Remember the Eyedropper tool from the Color Picker? That same Eyedropper tool is available in the toolbox, near the top. This is a shortcut way to sample colors. We can select this tool and sample a color to our foreground color without ever opening up the Color Picker

Now is a good time for us to briefly touch on **color modes**. A color mode is a way for us to describe color mathematically (the only way a computer will understand us). The most well known color mode is the **RGB mode**, which breaks down color in terms of its red, green, and blue components. We could actually spend most of our adult Photoshop lives in RGB and be just fine. But let's at least touch on some of the others.

With an image open, if we select Image>Mode, we should see RGB Color and 8 Bits/Channel both checked. As I said, this is where we will commonly work.

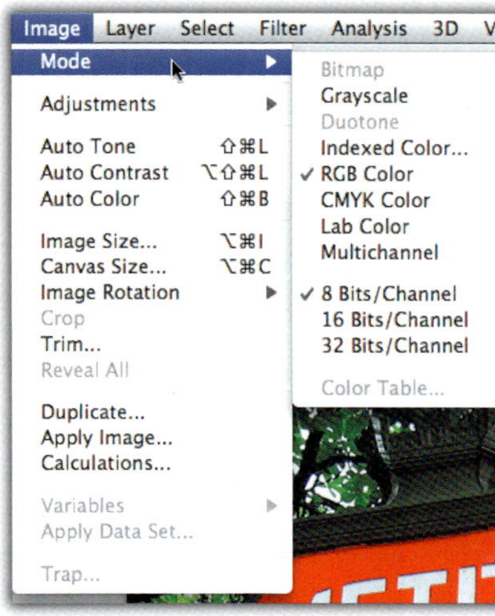

Immediately under RGB is **CMYK**, which stands for cyan, magenta, yellow, black and is used by commercial printers. Cyan, magenta, and yellow are the color compliments of red, green, and blue. But the important thing for you to remember is that only commercial printers use this color mode. At home or with photo finishers, RGB is what you want. Even if your home printer uses C, Y, M, K cartridges, stick with RGB. More on this in Chapter 43.

Under CMYK we see **Lab Color**. The "L" stands for luminance and "a" and "b" for obscure color channels. In this mode, the image intensity is separated onto the L channel and the colors onto the a and b channels. There are a number of interesting tricks that can be performed in the Lab color mode but that's outside the scope of this book.

The **Indexed Color Mode** is interesting only because if you open up an image saved in the GIF (graphics interface format) format, it comes up in Indexed Color Mode and much of Photoshop gets disabled. So if you open up an image and nothing seems to be working right, choose Image>Mode and see if Indexed Color is checked. If so, select RGB Color instead. Then life will be good again.

Since we have popped open the Image>Mode menu, let me make a quick comment about 8-bit versus 16-bit. Stick with 8-bit!

Too quick? Okay, here's why. At 16-bit, our file sizes double, making editing and manipulation more difficult. At 16-bit, a number of Photoshop functions are disabled (they only work at 8-bit). At 16-bit, Photoshop has more dynamic range but our original image was most likely captured at 8-bit anyway. As I said, stick with 8-bit.

9. HISTOGRAMS

When we get to the section on Image Adjustments (coming right up, by the way), we will see that fixing contrast is one of the most effective ways to improve an image. To best understand that, we need to first spend some time discussing **histograms**.

Go ahead and open an image in Photoshop. Open the Histogram panel (Window>Histogram), and the image's histogram is displayed.

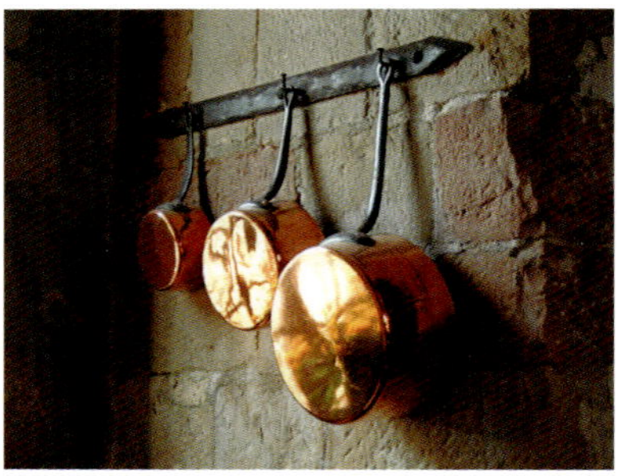

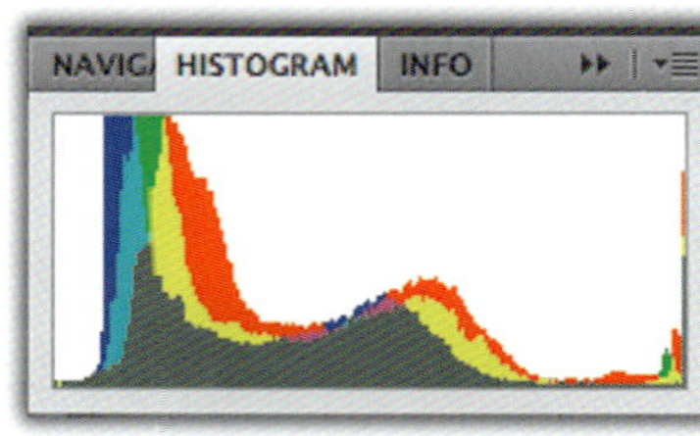

So what exactly is a histogram? It is a plot of the number or count of something versus some measure of that something. An example will make this more clear. Let's say we go into a classroom of 30 students and measure their heights and list them in a table. To simplify the results, we can create a second table that counts the number of students whose heights fall in discrete ranges between the high and the low; in the example, I created six ranges. Then to visualize this, we can plot the number of students in a certain height range on the vertical axis versus that height range on the horizontal axis. This type of plot is a histogram and gives us a visual look at the distribution of heights. In this example, we can see the average student is just over four feet tall.

Student	Height	Student	Height
Student1	3'6"	Student16	4"0"
Student2	3'9"	Student17	4'2"
Student3	4'1"	Student18	4'1"
Student4	3'10"	Student19	3'8"
Student5	4'0"	Student20	4'1"
Student6	4'3"	Student21	4'4"
Student7	4'5"	Student22	3'9"
Student8	3'11"	Student23	3'7"
Student9	3'7"	Student24	3'11"
Student10	3'10"	Student25	4'2"
Student11	3'3"	Student26	3'10"
Student12	3'11"	Student27	4'0"
Student13	4'0"	Student28	4'3"
Student14	4'1"	Student29	3'11"
Student15	3'8"	Student30	4'2"

Height Range	Count
3'6" - 3'7"	3
3'8" - 3'9"	4
3'10" - 3'11"	7
4'0" - 4'1"	8
4'2" - 4'3"	6
4'4" - 4'5"	2

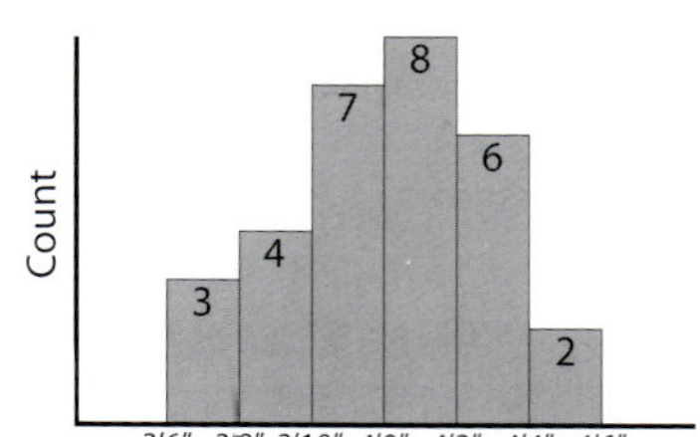

Now instead of students, let's say we have an array of squares filled with ten different shades of gray; so we have white, black, and eight shades of gray between. Let's number those shades from 0 to 9 with 0 being black and 9 being white. (There are still ten shades; we are just counting from 0 to 9 instead of 1 to 10.) If we count up how many squares are 0's, how many are 1's, etc., and plot that against the shade number, we get a histogram of the shading. (Black or zero is to the left and white, or 9, is to the right on the horizontal axis.)

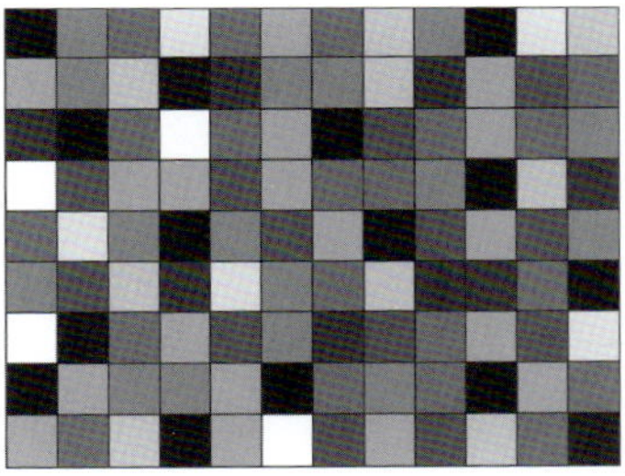

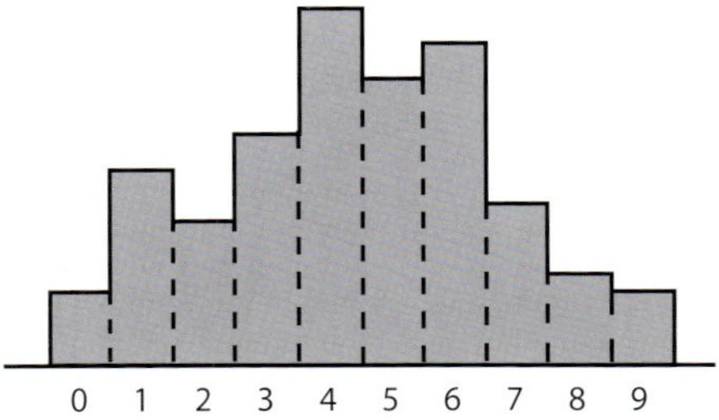

Now imagine that instead of 10 different shades of gray, we have 256 shades of gray (and we number them 0-255), still ranging from black to white. And instead of around 100 squares, we have millions of them, say around 6 million. Well, this is pretty much what a Photoshop histogram is. An 8-bit black and white image has 256 shades of gray and a 6 Mp image has 6 million pixels (or squares). This is exactly the same as our checkerboard example above; there is just more of everything.

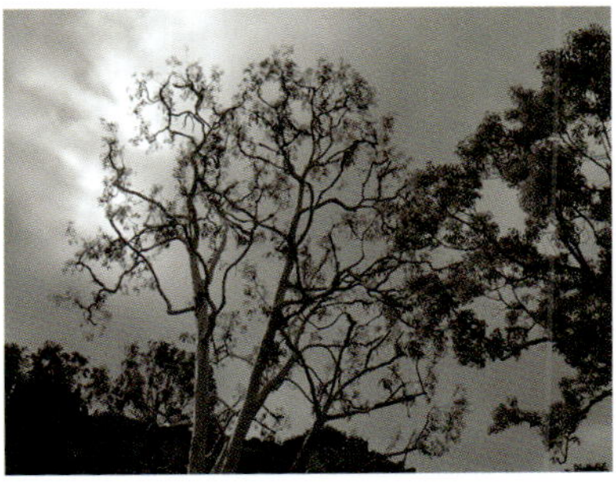

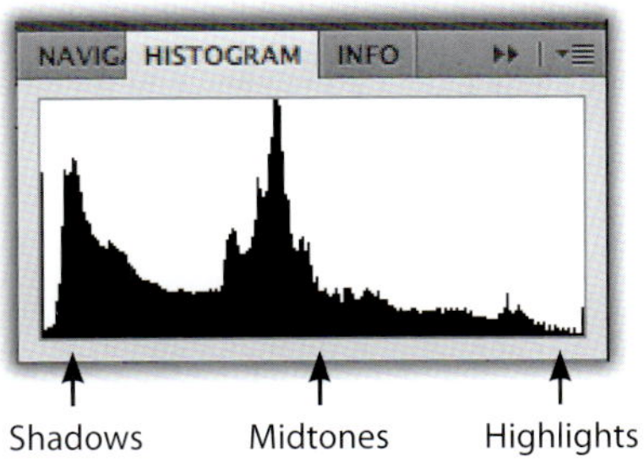

This histogram displays our 256 shades of gray on the horizontal axis versus the number of pixels with a particular shade on the vertical axis. Black, or zero, is still on the left; this end of the histogram is referred to as Shadows. White, which is now 255, is on the right. This end is called Highlights. The middle is called Midtones. Looking at our image, we see that there are not a lot of white pixels. This is validated by the histogram, where the highlights distribution is low. The histogram also shows peaks in the midtones (the gray background) and the shadows (the silhouette) as we see in the image.

But what about color? Well, Photoshop breaks down our image into red, green, and blue (assuming we are in RGB mode) and then displays a separate histogram for each of those colors. Where the colors overlap, the histogram shows the resulting blended color. So where red overlaps green, we see yellow. I personally find this too much information and prefer a composite black and white histogram. See the tips at the end of this section to learn how to convert to that mode. But for now, onward.

The two images to the right help us begin to explore the power of histograms. This image has information that extends all the way from black to white. The darkest parts of the image are pretty black, if not totally black, and the whites are nearly white. This picture has good contrast; there is a nice range between the darkest and brightest parts of the image. And it is visually pleasing (I hope) as a result.

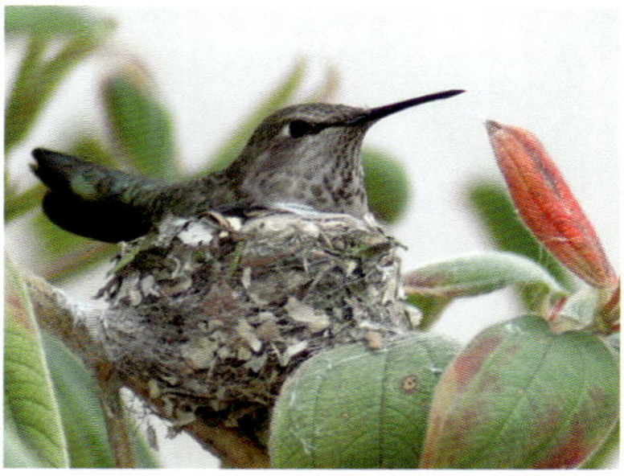

Good Contrast

Compare that to this second image, taken at the same time, but with less zoom. The exposure is such that the darkest areas are not so dark (certainly not black) and the lightest areas are almost gray (and certainly not white). This picture has poor contrast; there is a smaller range between the darkest and lightest parts of the image. And as a result, the image looks a pretty flat, less visually pleasing than the first example.

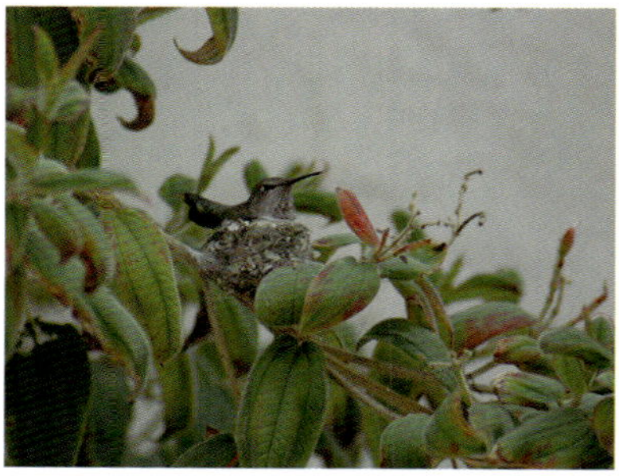

Poor Contrast

Now look at the histograms for each of these examples. The good contrast image histogram stretches most of the way from black to white (0 to 255) while the poor contrast image histogram is a narrower, tighter distribution. This is just what we would expect.

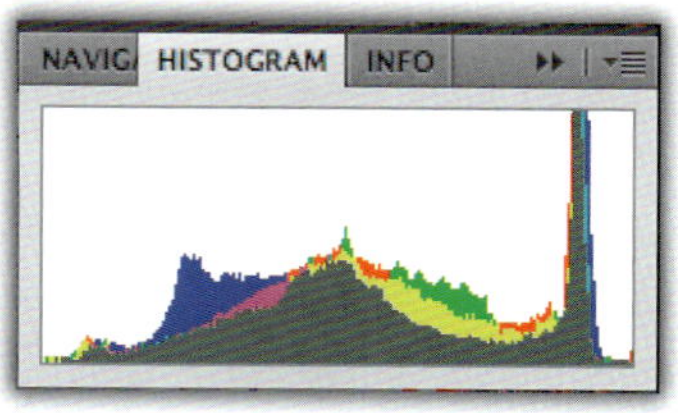

Good Contrast

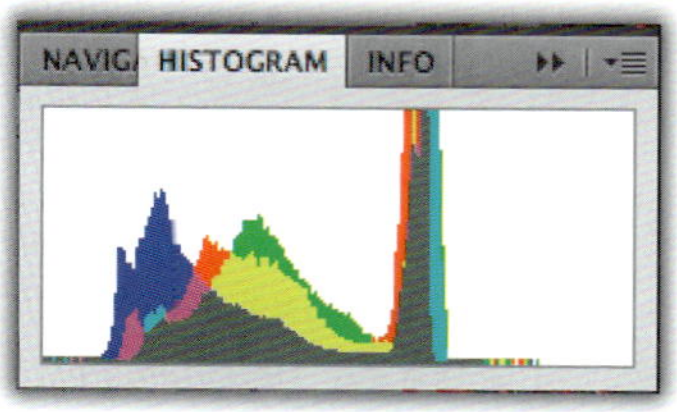

Poor Contrast

The power of the Photoshop histogram is that we have the capability to use it to take a low contrast image and turn it into a much more visually pleasing high contrast image. More on that in Section 2. For now, when you open up images, have a quick look at the Histogram panel and get used to noticing its correspondence with the image.

We've just looked at examples of histograms for a high contrast image and a low contrast image. Here are a few more examples of "reading histograms."

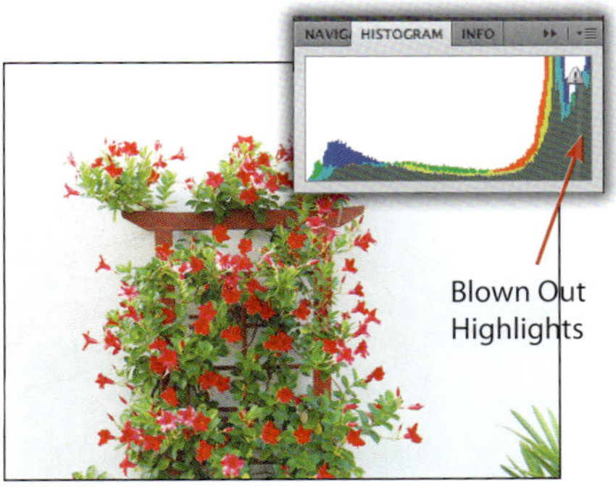

This image is over exposed. Notice how the histogram is bunched in the highlights. This is called blown out.

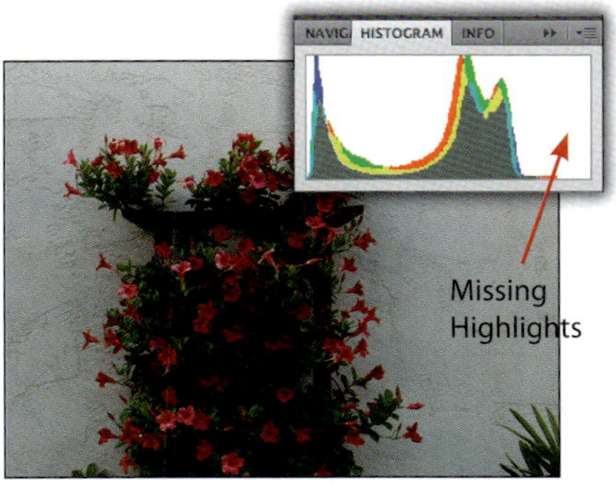

This image is under exposed. Notice how the highlights distribution is missing and more of the image is in bunched in the shadows.

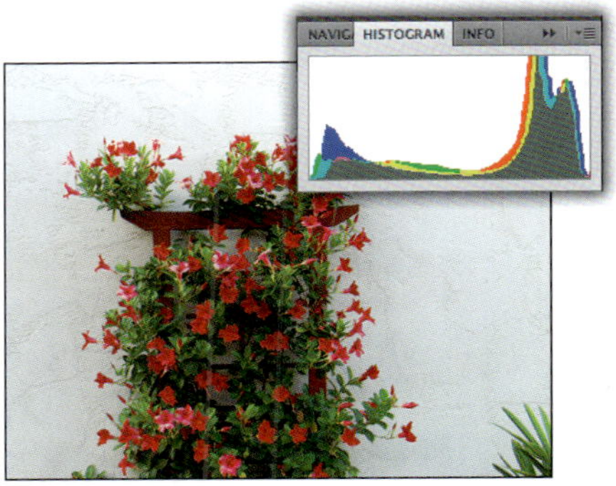

This image has been correctly exposed. It is centered nicely with no content loss.

Many of the newer digital cameras have histogram capability built right in so we can get our exposure right at the time of taking a shot instead of having to fix it later. I highly recommend using this if is available on your camera. You will probably still end up optimizing with Photoshop but it's better to start with a good exposure.

10. FILE FORMATS

So far we have opened up some images and used them as vehicles to understand a few of the basic concepts in Photoshop. And while we haven't created anything worthy of saving, that comes next. So it is time that we learn which format to save in.

Let's start by reviewing the most ubiquitous of graphics file formats, the **JPEG.** JPEG stands for Joint Photographic Experts Group, and is pronounced "jay-peg." JPEG, the word, is actually used in two contexts. JPEG compression is a compression methodology that shrinks file size by simplifying data. JPEG also means a picture that has been saved with JPEG compression. JPEGs have the file extension .jpg.

JPEG compression is lossy. It simplifies an image by replacing similar colors with an average color and then using mathematical models to store that new information very efficiently. The slight differences are thrown away, lost. Hence the term "lossy." But the resulting file requires much less memory to store. For these images (magnified so we can see actual pixels), the file size of the JPEG compressed image is one fourth that of the original image.

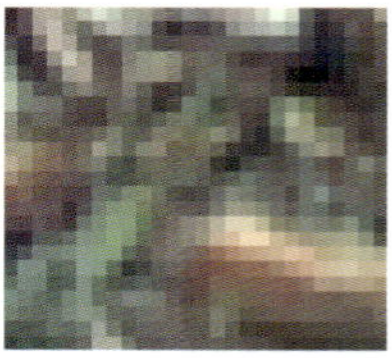

Original image, magnified and uncompressed

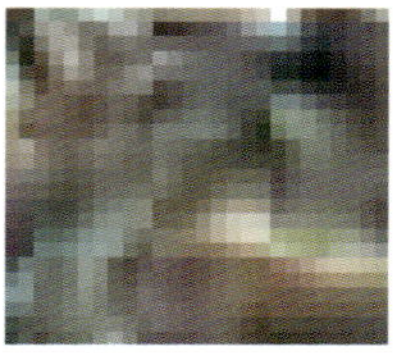

After JPEG compression

Our digital cameras usually save images as JPEGs. When we choose a quality level in our camera settings, we are actually setting the level of JPEG compression. High quality means less compression, less loss and bigger files. Low quality means higher compression, more loss, and smaller files. My recommendation is to always save at the best quality. Memory, both on your memory card and in your computer, is cheap. And when you snap that picture of a lifetime, you'll be glad you captured it with the best quality.

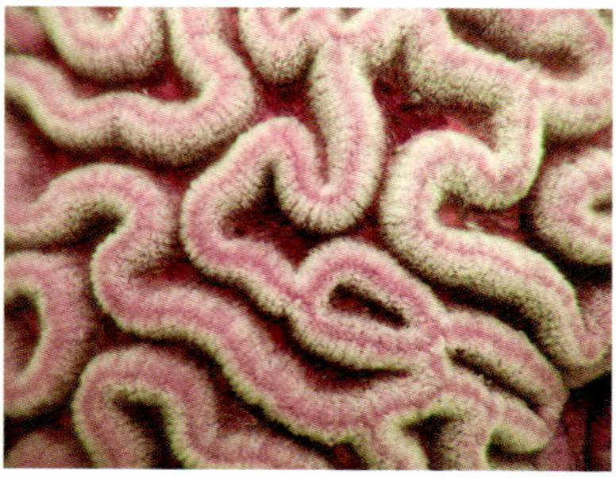

High Quality (Low Compression)

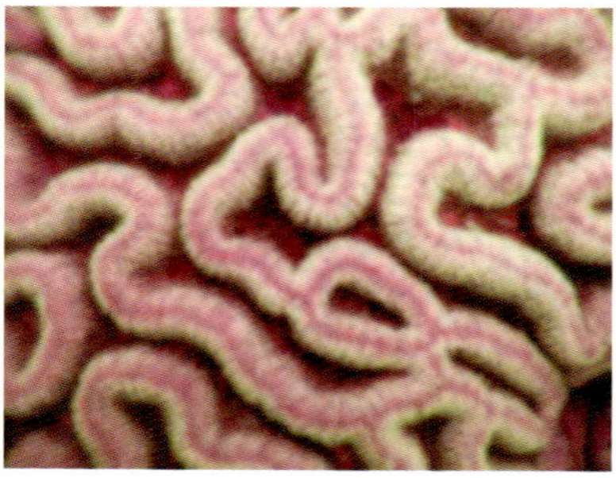

Low Quality (High Compression)

Once we open our image in Photoshop, it is no longer a JPEG. The compression, that mathematical model, is undone and the image is converted back into an array of pixels. It becomes uncompressed. (But the detail lost in the original compression has not and cannot be recovered.) After enhancing our image, we will of course want to save our work. And then we'll need to decide what format to save it in. As we see in the Save Dialogue Box, there is a wide assortment of choices. Most are a bit esoteric and beyond our scope. But here is the rundown on the major ones.

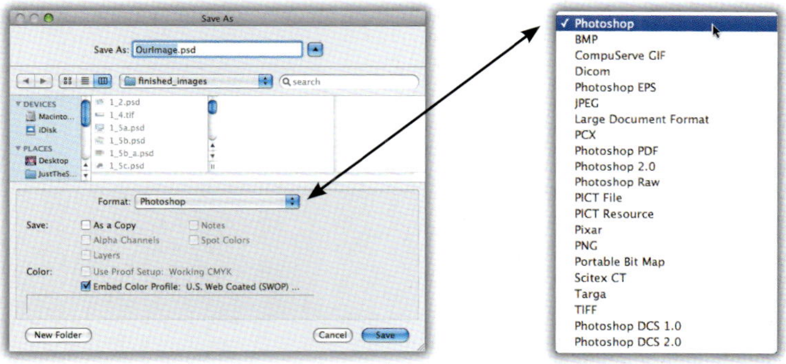

JPEG

Our image started as a JPEG and we can resave it as a JPEG. In fact, this a very probable scenario. Whatever our intended application, whether it be printing, emailing, or importing into another program, it will likely be compatible with JPEG. Certainly it is a good choice for email, the web, or when printing at a photo service. To save in JPEG, we select File>Save As and choose JPEG under file format.

JPEG ATTRIBUTES

- Digital Camera Standard
- Common on Web
- Lossy Compression
- Small File Sizes
- No Support For Layers

A JPEG Options dialog box pops open allowing us to specify a quality level between 1 and 12, with 12 being the best. (Note as we change quality level, Photoshop displays the new projected file size.) Choose 12, the highest quality, for print applications. Lower quality may be better for email. But remember, we are still recompressing and therefore losing even more precious data.

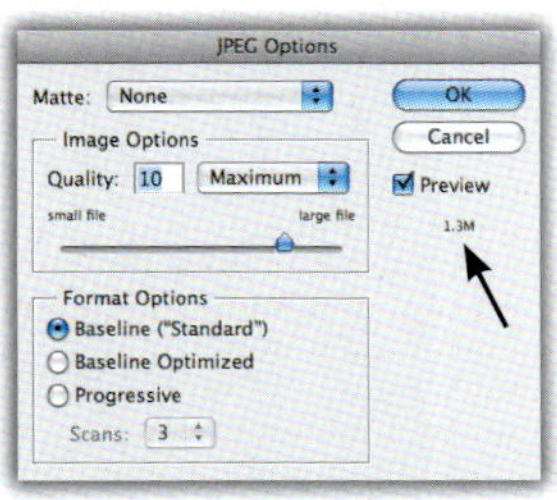

Photoshop PSD

The native file format for Photoshop is the .psd. It is uncompressed and very large as we have previously noted. But if file size is not an issue, this is the best way to store our images. We can print our PSDs directly from Photoshop. And PSDs can also be imported into many other applications (although checking is advisable). The biggest advantage to PSDs is that we can always save out a copy as a JPEG later should we need a smaller file. In the meantime, we won't have already sacrificed any quality. As we advance in Photoshop, we will also start employing layers which cannot be saved as JPEGs. So why not get used to PSDs right now?

PSD ATTRIBUTES

- Native PS Format
- Common for Print
- Never on Web
- No Compression
- Large File Sizes
- Support For Layers

TIFF

TIFF (rhymes with "if") is yet another graphics file format used primarily for professional printing applications. TIFF stands for Tagged Image File Format and has a .tif file extension. Like PSDs, TIFFs are generally uncompressed (although that option is available), so they don't sacrifice quality. But uncompressed, they are very large files.

TIFF ATTRIBUTES

- Common for Print
- Never on Web
- Optional Lossless Compression
- Large File Sizes
- Support For Layers

TIFF is a favorite format for professional photographers but may not be the best choice for you. While it is very compatible with most other applications and does support layers, my opinion is that you are better off just sticking with Photoshop's PSD. At least for now. But if someone asks you for a TIFF, now you know what it's all about.

CompuServe GIF

GIF ATTRIBUTES

- Common on Web
- Lossy Compression
- Small File Sizes
- Best Suited for Graphics
- No Support For Layers

GIF stands for Graphics Interchange Format (CompuServe originally owned the format) and has the file extension .gif. Some pronounce with a soft "g" and others (like me) with a hard "g." Like JPEG, it uses compression, but of a different nature. GIFs are really well suited for logos or other graphics that don't involve a lot of colors. They are often found on the Web because their file sizes are quite small and they have less visual distortion than JPEGs.

Recall that we introduced GIFs previously in Chapter 8, when we were reviewing color modes. GIFs don't use RGB like JPEGs; they use the Indexed Color Mode. When we do a Save As and choose GIF, an Indexed Color dialog box shows up. For now, all of the defaults will be fine.

The Photoshop Save As dialog box has tons of different options for us over and above the file format. But after choosing a name for our file and a location where it is to be saved, we can be comfortable accepting all of Photoshop's other default settings. And as I said above, we are also good to go with the default settings on the option dialog boxes that may show up for a particular file format. The one exception is the quality setting on the JPEG Options dialog box.

We are going to get back to a detailed discussion on saving later in Chapter 41. But for now, I will note just one more thing. When we save as a PSD, we may see an ominous warning dialog box regarding **maximizing file compatibility**. It's fine to click OK. I will go over what this is specifically in Chapter 41, but for now, go to Photoshop>Preferences>File Handling (Edit>Preferences>File Handling on the PC). In the File Compatibility box, change "Maximize PSD and PSB File Compatibility" from Ask to Always. Then you won't be bothered by this warning anymore.

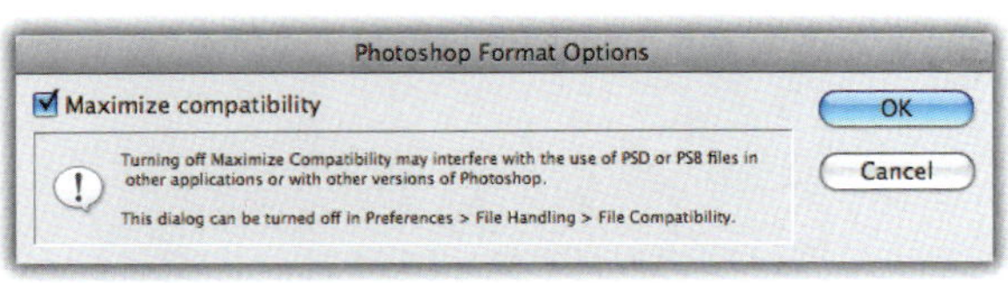

11. THE BRUSH TOOL

We will be discussing drawing in Photoshop in Section VI but it will help us to spend a few minutes right now discussing Photoshop's Brush tool; the look and feel of this tool shows up in many places.

Artist's brushes (the handheld kind) are tools for making strokes, by dragging across a canvas, or for making dots, by dabbing on the canvas. They come in different sizes, making lines and dots of varying widths. And they come with various tips; some are round and some are flat; some have hard edges and some have soft edges. Brushes in Photoshop have all of these same attributes. We can click and drag with them to make strokes or just click to make dots. In the options bar, we can control the tip diameter, the extent to which it is hard or soft, and the shape. But unlike the artist's brush, the Photoshop brush can paint with effects as well as colors.

Let's open something we can play with. Select File>New and under Preset in the New dialog box, select Default Photoshop Size. I'll name my document BrushTrial and click OK. Size the document window and magnification to a comfortable setting. A blank canvas of white awaits. Lastly, press the D key to set Photoshop to its default colors (black foreground and white background). Our Brush tool always paints with the foreground color, in this case black.

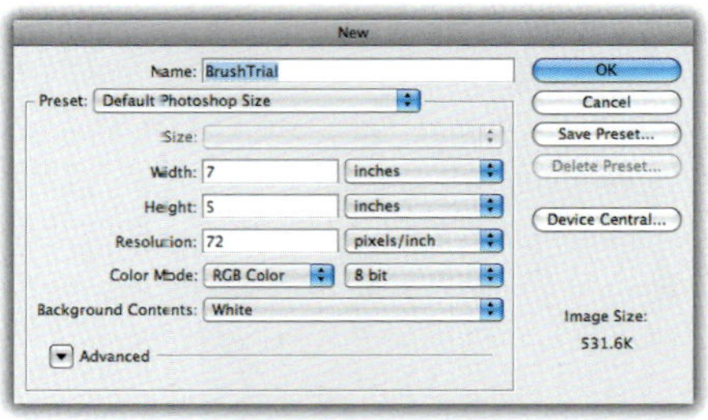

In our toolbox, select the **Brush tool**. In its options bar, make sure Mode is Normal and that both Opacity and Flow are set to 100%; then pull down the Brush Preset Picker menu. Here we have sliders controlling diameter and hardness, with 100% being hard and 0% soft. We will return to descriptions in a second but for now, set hardness to 100%. And set the diameter to 50 pixels.

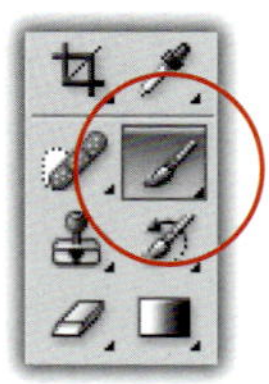

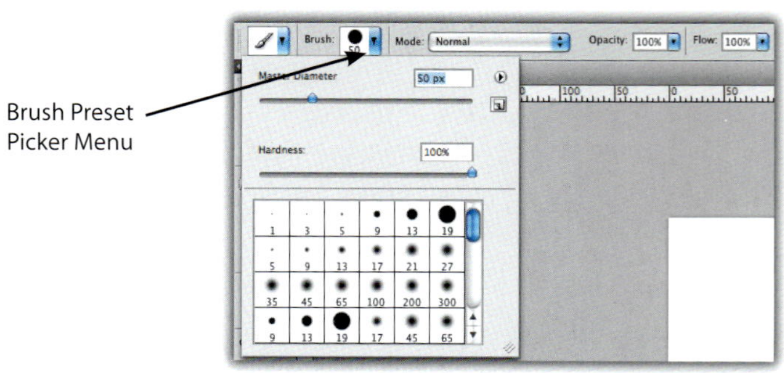

When we move our cursor over the blank canvas, it turns into a circle with a diameter equal to our diameter setting. Let's pick a spot near the upper left of the canvas and click our mouse once. The Brush tool creates a black circle equal in diameter to the cursor. If we slide our cursor a little to the right and click and drag towards the right, the Brush tool flows black along the path of our mouse until we release.

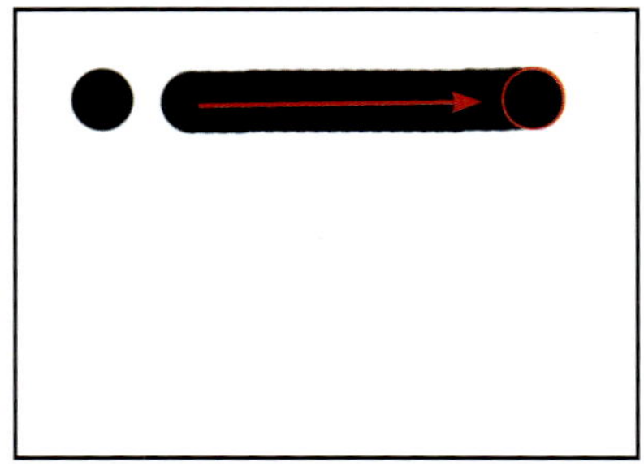

Now let's go to the Brush pulldown menu in the options bar and set hardness to 0%. This corresponds to a soft edge. If we move our cursor back to our document and hover over our first dot, we notice that the diameter appears smaller. Now move the cursor under that first dot and click to see what this soft edge (also called a feathered edge) looks like. Center the cursor over the new dot you just made and notice that the color not only drops off inside the edge of the cursor but also extends outside the edge as well. The cursor diameter corresponds to where the color intensity drops to half of the center amount (50% gray in this case). That's why it appears to be smaller. Click and drag to make a line.

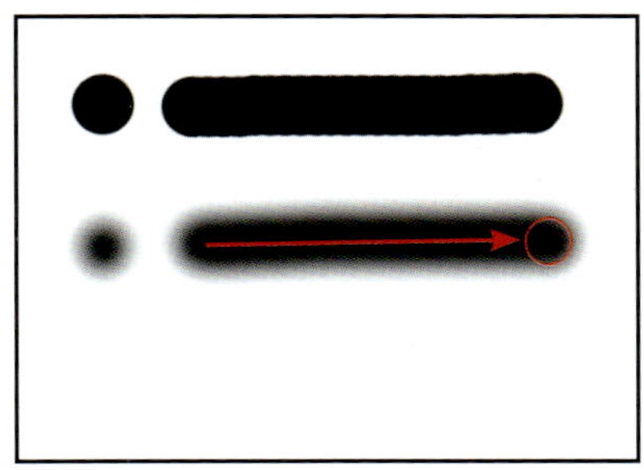

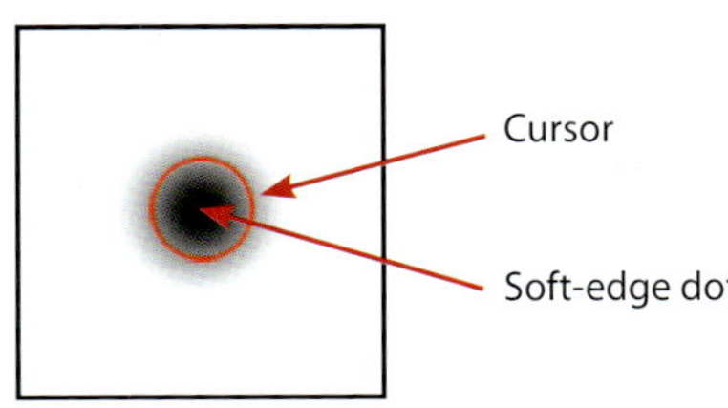

The Brush pulldown menu, in addition to having sliders for diameter and hardness, also has a rather extensive list of presets, including diameter, hardness, and tip shape. It is worth exploring around a bit.

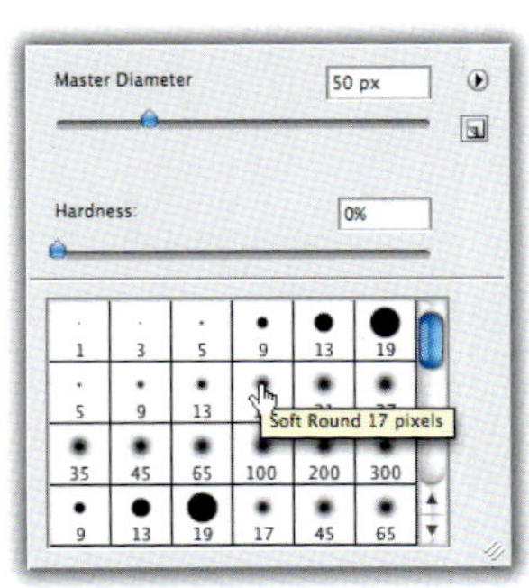

A more useful control for right now, though, is **Opacity**, found in the options bar. Setting this to less than 100% causes the brush's paint (or effect) to be semitransparent. Less opacity means more transparency. It is a great way to soften an effect.

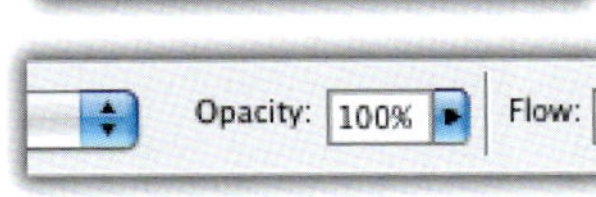

These brush concepts, diameter, hardness and opacity, show up in a number of different Photoshop tools. Most of the time, these tools will be used to paint an effect (like locally lightening or healing defects) as opposed to a color. When using soft edges with these tools, it is the effect that gets feathered. For example, putting a soft edge on a brush-style tool that lightens would create a smooth transition at its edge, softening the border between lightened and unlightened areas. Notice how much more realistic my soft-brush lightened cat looks. (We'll do this together in Chapter 17.)

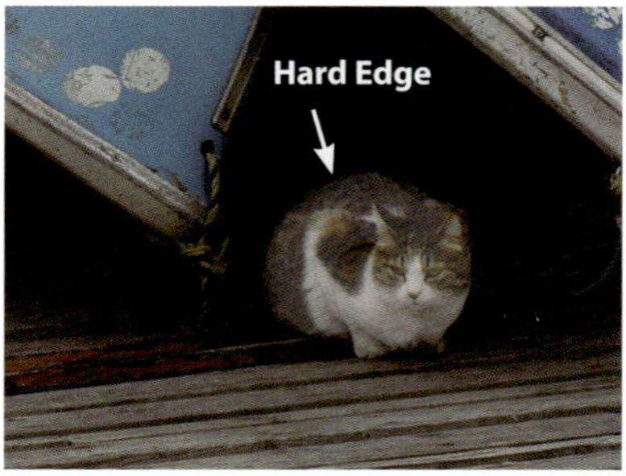

Cat lightening with a hard brush

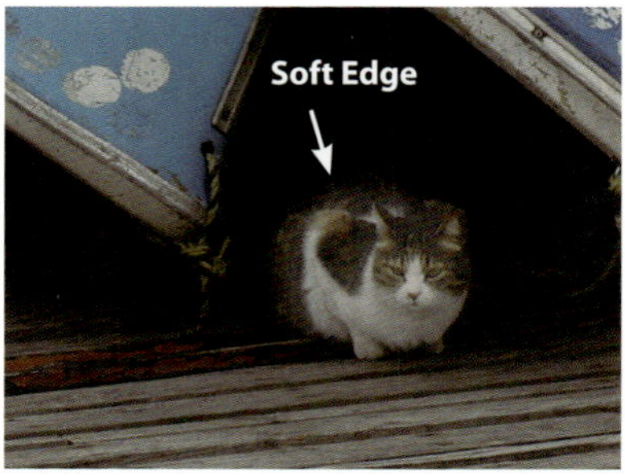

Cat lightening with a soft brush

The Brush tool's counterpart is the **Eraser tool**. Think of the Brush tool as painting color or effects into pixels while the Eraser tool removes color or effects from the pixels.

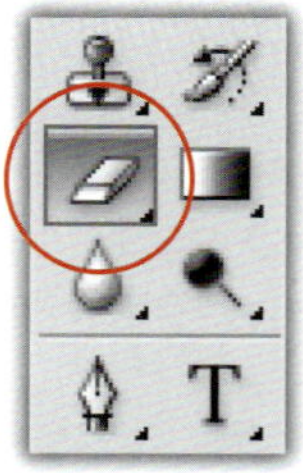

The Eraser tool options bar is virtually identical to that of the Brush tool. Diameter, hardness and opacity will be our primary controls. If your brush example from above is still open, change to the Eraser tool and set the diameter to 50 pixels. Leave hardness and opacity at 100%. Now we can click and drag down vertically through the lines we created with our brush and see what happens. As expected, the black disappears where the Eraser crosses it and the erasure has a hard edge.

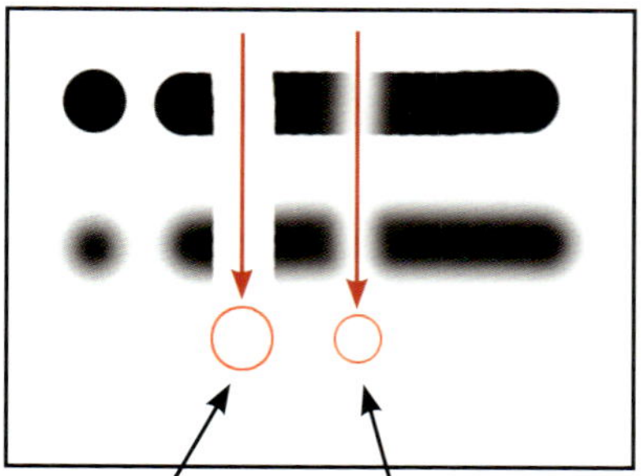

If we reset the Eraser hardness to zero and click and drag again, the edges of the erasure are softened; there is a smooth transition between black and white.

If we lower opacity in the options bar, then the erasure effect is not complete. At 100% opacity, the erasure is complete, leaving 0% of the pixel information. It's all gone, erased. But if we lower opacity to 60%, then 40% of the pixel information will be left. Soft edges and opacity are great for graphics but really come into their own in helping us soften the effects of brush-like image enhancement tools. We will learn about these tools in the next section.

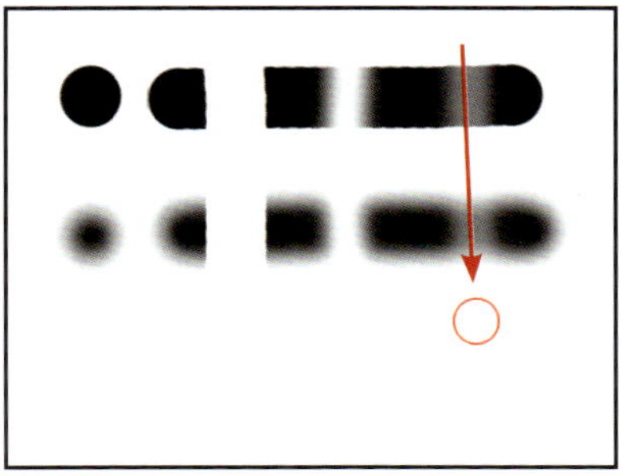

Eraser opacity set to 60%

Changing diameters and hardness is something we will do frequently. We can do it using the menu but it is much easier to do it with the keyboard. Here's how. We use the left and right brackets, [and], to move the diameter down and up. And we use the left and right brackets with Shift depressed to move the hardness down and up.

If we wanted to erase the background from behind our little cat, we would need to change the diameter of the eraser as we moved in and out of regions with greater and lesser detail. I would have my left hand on the keyboard brackets and my right hand guiding the mouse as I work in order to always have an optimally-sized eraser. I would use Shift with the brackets to change hardness/softness, choosing a small brush with a soft edge near the cat.

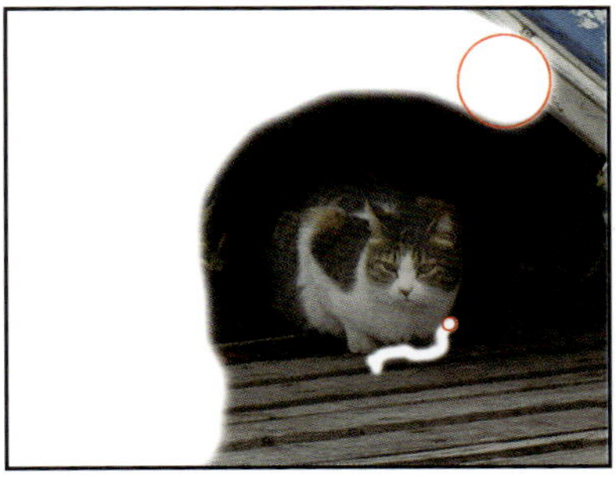

One of the huge advantages of using this method is that we can see the cursor diameter change as we adjust it with the keyboard, allowing us to make it just the right size. After all, we want the diameter set according to what we are seeing visually with the image; the exact pixel diameter is really of no consequence. Jumping to the options bar to set a diameter and then back to the image to check cursor size gets old really fast. With the bracket keys, we can adjust the size real time.

As I said in the preface, to keep things as simple as possible, I am not giving you too many keyboard shortcuts. But this one, like others I've mentioned, is such a huge time saver that it makes the cut.

12. SELECTIONS—PART 2

Before we leave our Basic Concepts section, let's revisit selections. Recall from Chapter 6 that when we perform a selection, we are selecting which pixels will be active and which ones will not be active (i.e. will be masked) from any action we then take. We learned that we could use the Marquee tools to select geometric shapes and the Lasso tools to select more free form shapes. In this chapter, we will learn a few more techniques and tools for creating selections.

First up is **feathering**. In our last chapter, we learned that brush-based tools utilize a hardness setting to control how hard or soft their edges are. Soft edges smoothed out, or blended, the borders of the brushed area. Photoshop has included this same hardness control with all of its selection tools and it works in exactly the same way. With selections, the control is called feathering. When a selection is feathered, there is a smooth transition between 100% selected and 100% masked pixels. In between, the pixels are partially selected and whatever we do to them is only partially done.

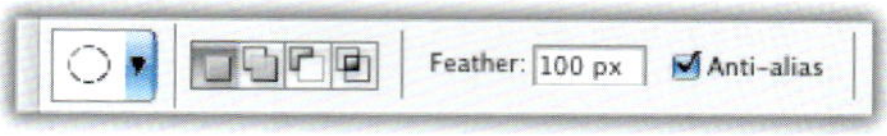

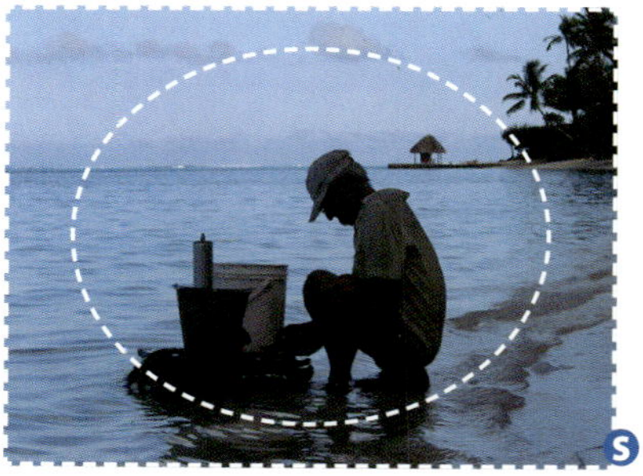

I'll open an image (it happens to be 1000 px by 750 px) and select the Elliptical Marquee tool. In the options bar, I'll set the feather to 50 px and make an elliptical selection. This selects the pixels in the ellipse (with a soft edge) and masks off the outer ones. For reasons that will be clear in a moment, I next choose Select>Inverse. This inverts the selection, masking off the pixels within the ellipse and selecting those outside of it. (Note the border.) Because the edge is feathered the marching ants represent the 50% selected pixels.

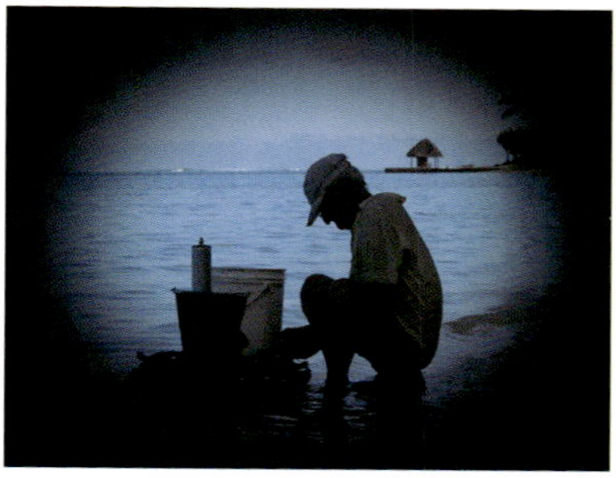

If I now choose Edit>Fill and choose black under Contents/Use, when I hit OK, the selected pixels are painted black and the unselected pixels are left untouched. The partially selected pixels near the selection border are partially painted and partially left untouched, creating a very popular vignette effect. There may be a bit of trial and error to get the ellipse size and softness just right for a particular image but that's why we like having the Undo function (Cmd(Ctrl)-Z).

Feathering is a common control and can be found in the options bar for most of the selection tools. But it must be set prior to making the selection. If we want to feather an existing selection, we have to do it by choosing Select>Modify>Feather.

Speaking of selection tools, let's expand our repertoire. We talked about the Lasso and Polygonal Lasso tools but there is a third lasso tool, the **Magnetic Lasso tool**. Tucked underneath the Lasso tool in the toolbox (click and hold on the Lasso), the Magnetic Lasso is particularly helpful for selecting items with high contrast edges.

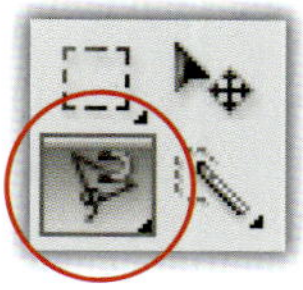

To use the Magnetic Lasso, we click and release where we would like to begin our selection and then move (not drag) our mouse along the intended path. The tool will try to follow the edge, dropping anchor points (little squares) as it goes. We complete the selection by returning to the starting point (watch for a little closed loop icon by the cursor) and clicking. The path turns into our familiar marching ants.

On Track

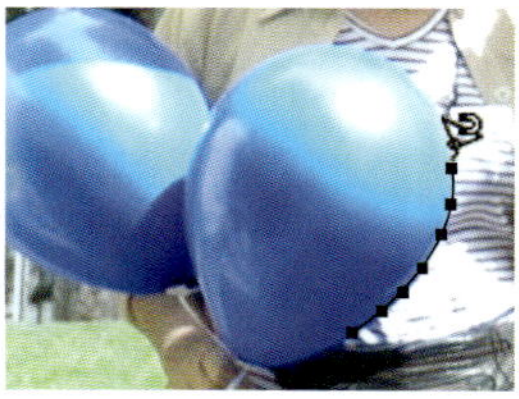

Off Track

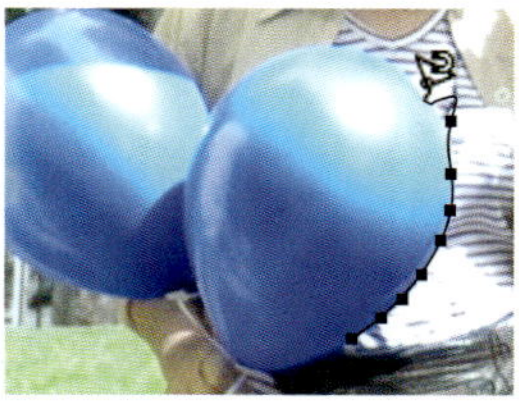

Back On Track

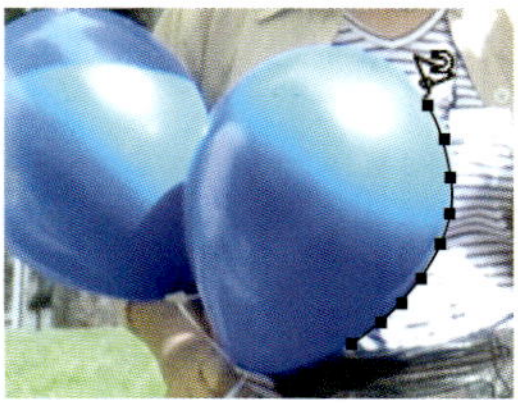

Unfortunately the Magnetic Lasso tool can get confused and head off in unintended directions. If it is off our intended path but has yet to put down an anchor point, we can coax it back with our mouse to the desired path and click once. This will force down an anchor point and hopefully get the tool back on track. If an off-path anchor point has been placed, we simply hit our Delete(Backspace) key and it will be removed. Then we coax and click as above.

The Magnetic Lasso tool looks for variations in contrast, not color, so what looks like a sharp edge to you may not appear as such to the tool. But there are a number of settings in its options bar that we can use to fine tune the tool for the job at hand. Play with them to see how they work or check them out in Photoshop Help. Search on Magnetic Lasso Tool and read "To Set Options for the Lasso, Polygonal Lasso, and Magnetic Lasso tools." This tool is fun and works well. So give it a try and see what you think.

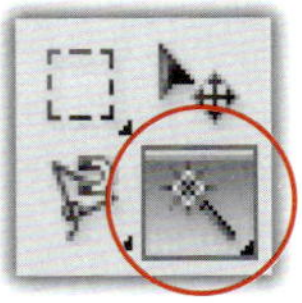

Another popular and easy to use selection tool is the **Magic Wand** tool, nested under the Quick Selection tool. This tool can make short work of selections if there are large areas of uniform color in either the area to be selected or the area to be masked.

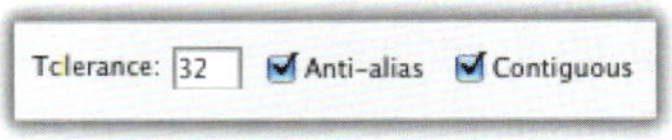

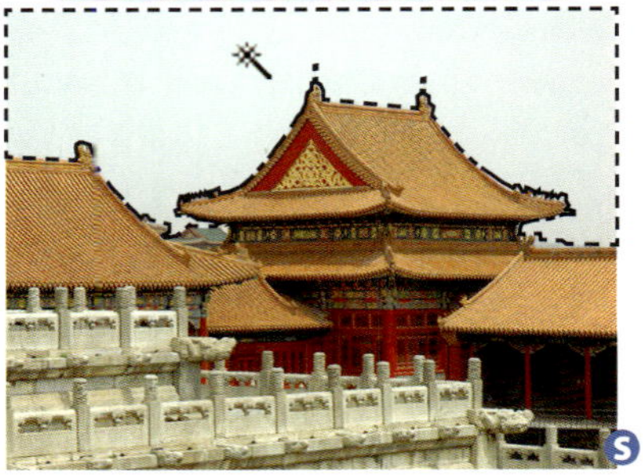

In this example, we want to remove the hazy white overexposed sky and replace it with a more comfortable blue. (Later we will learn how to replace it with a real sky.) We choose the Magic Wand, make sure that Contiguous is checked, and click anywhere in the sky on the image. Because Contiguous is checked, Photoshop selects all pixels with a color similar to the clicked location and that are continuously connected to each other. Not bad for a single click.

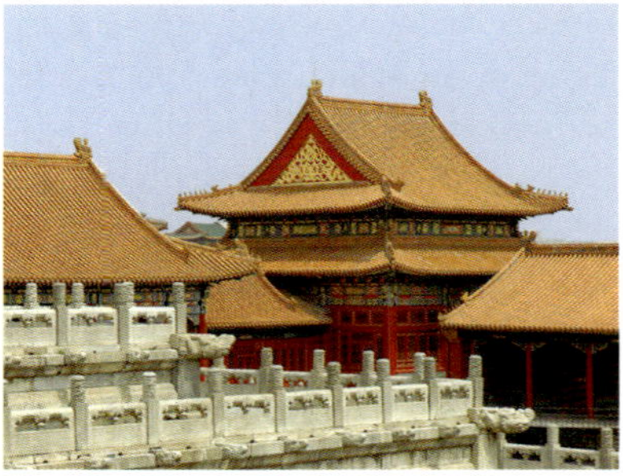

With the selection made, we set the Foreground Color to a pleasant light blue (using the Color Picker) and choose Edit>Fill using the Foreground Color. Select>Deselect removes the selection. (The Magic Wand does not have a feather control. To feather, use Select>Modify>Feather after making the selection.) The result isn't perfect but it is pretty good for just one click.

We already mentioned Contiguous in the Magic Wand options bar. What about Tolerance and Anti-Aliasing? Tolerance defines what "similar" means when the Magic Wand is selecting "similar" pixels. The smaller the number, the more similar the color must be to be selected. Trial and error works the best here. Choose a tolerance (I chose 32) and see how it does. If you don't get everything, set the tolerance higher and try again. Anti-aliasing creates a smoother selection; I recommend leaving it checked.

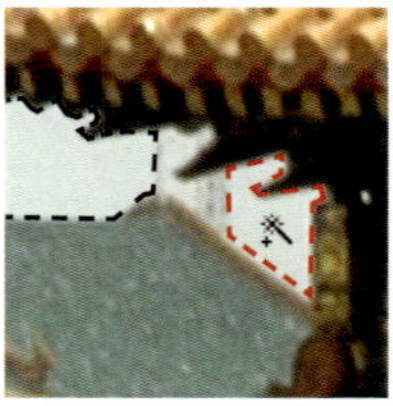

Sometimes with Contiguous checked, there will be little unselected areas that we really wanted selected. Check out under the eave; some faint poles in the background blocked the selection. To fix this, with the original selection still active, we hold down Shift and click with the Magic Wand in the missed area, creating a new selection (shown in red) that is added to the original selection (shown in black).

This brings us to the last selection method we will cover for now, and one of my favorites, the **Quick Mask**. With the Quick Mask, we can see which pixels are selected and which are masked off; Photoshop actually displays the mask. But more importantly, we can adjust our selection by modifying the mask with our Brush tool.

Here is an image with a selection already done. In the toolbox, we choose the Edit in Quick Mask icon. When we do, the pixels that are masked by the selection get covered by a red, semitransparent overlay. The selected pixels remain clear, unchanged. The selection itself hasn't been altered. Only how we are viewing the selection has changed.

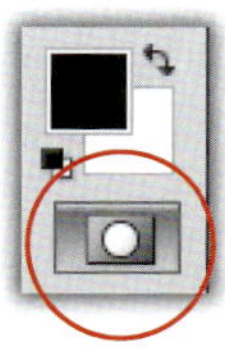

Edit in Quick Mask

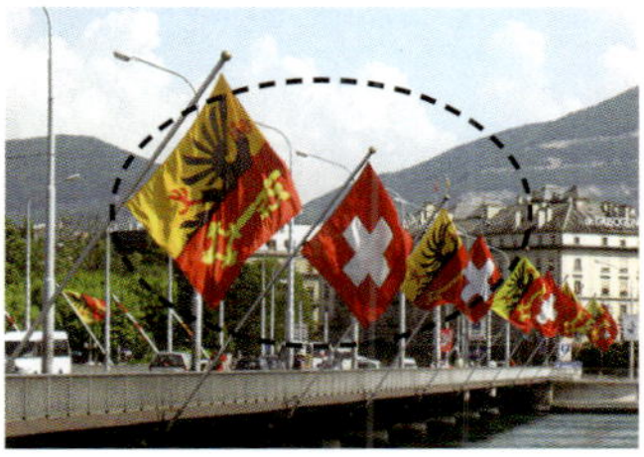

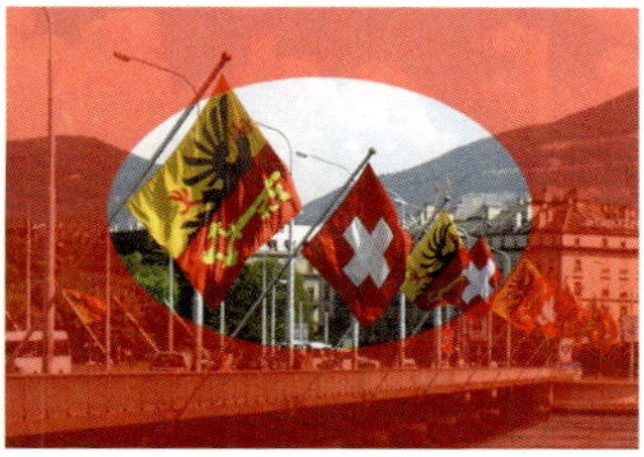

The power of Quick Masking is that it is easily editable. We can use the Brush tool to refine our selections by either painting with white to add selected pixels or with black to add to the masked pixels. In the example below, I used the Magnetic Lasso to select the first flag. When I switched to Quick Mask, I could easily see that part of the selection was off. Still in Quick Mask, I chose a small diameter brush and painted with black (adding red overlay), subtracting from my selection and covering the boo boo. Back in Standard Mode (by toggling off Quick Mask), the selection is corrected.

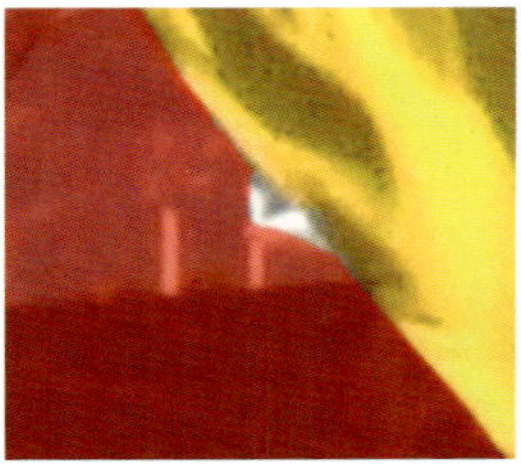

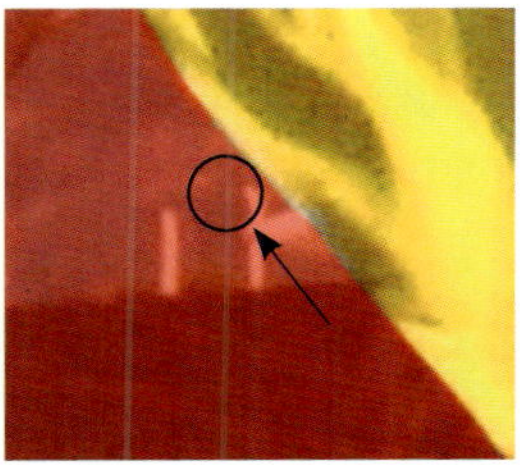

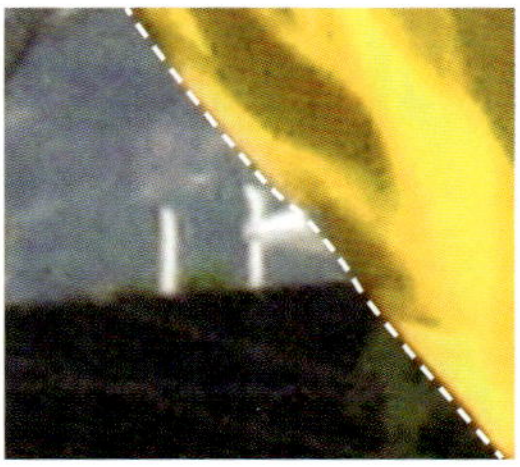

If I inadvertently overshoot and paint some of the flag with black (excluding it from the selection), I can just switch my foreground color to white and paint away the mask where necessary. Painting with white on a Quick Mask creates selected pixels; painting with black on a Quick Mask creates masked pixels. (Hard to remember, I know. Trial and error does it.) Plan to use soft brushes to match the feathering in your original selection. This can often make the difference between a realistic image versus what appears to be a hack job.

Toolbox: For those users of versions prior to CS4, your toolbox will look a little different from the CS4 version shown in this book. All of the tools we discuss are present, however, but some are in slightly different locations. The Eyedropper tool, for example, which is shown near the top of the toolbox in CS4, can be found in earlier versions just above the hand and zoom tools near the bottom of the toolbox.

Application Bar: The CS4 workspace has added a so-called application bar right underneath the main menu. Here you can quickly switch to Bridge, adjust magnification, and select the hand and zoom tools among other things. Most of this is duplication of other, more intuitive ways to do things.

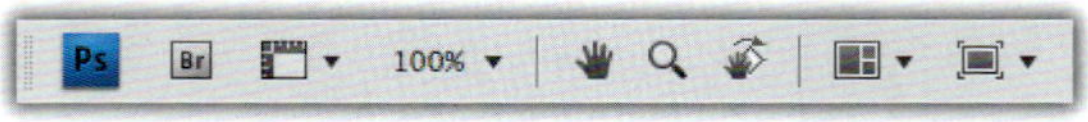

Application Bar

Histogram Panel: In versions prior to CS4, the Histogram panel displayed in black and white only and was a composite of all of the red, green, and blue information, all mixed together. With CS4, as we discussed, it now displays a histogram for each color blending the three histograms together.

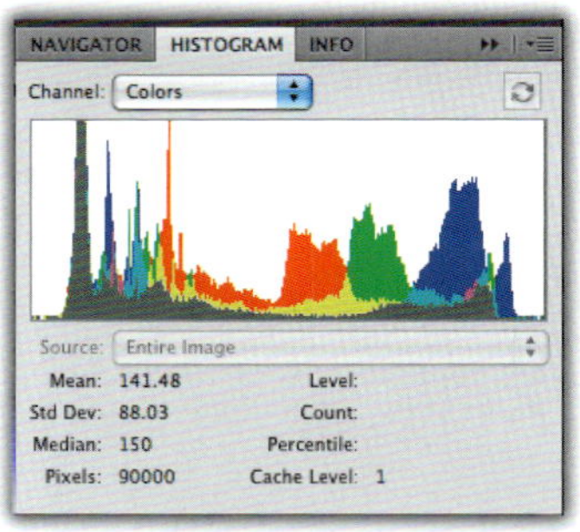

Histogram panel with Colors

Maybe it is just what I am used to, by I find the black and white version a little less busy and easier to work with.

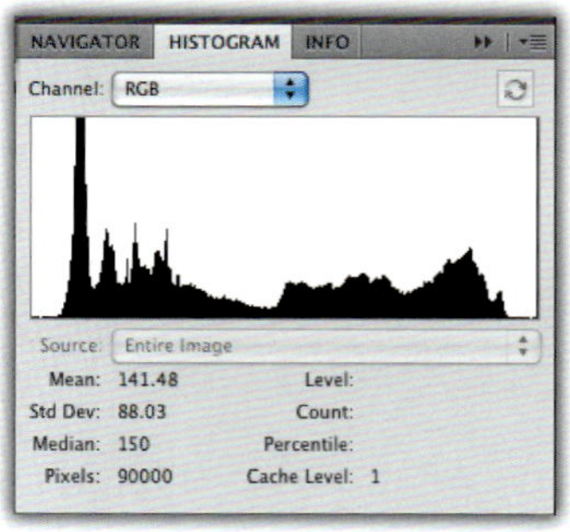

Histogram panel with Composite RGB

Switching back and forth is not a huge deal. First, we go to the Histogram panel menu and choose Expanded View. (These screen shots are in that expanded view.) Then, under Channel, we select RGB for a composite (displayed in black and white) view or Colors for the existing technicolor view. If we want the panel's original smaller size back, we can go back to the panel menu and reselect Compact View. Our channel choice will stick.

SECTION

II

IMAGE ENHANCING

In the last section, we learned a bit about how our digital images are constructed, how to get them into Photoshop, and what a Photoshop environment looks like. Now let's start to put it all together by learning the basics of using Photoshop to enhance our images.

Sad to say, most of the images we take need help. This is certainly true of the images I take. Sometimes we need to do things like removing a tree branch that appears to be growing out of someone's head. And we will get to that type of editing in a later section. But more often, we are looking to improve the general attributes of the photo–the lighting, the colors, etc. This will be the focus of this section.

We will start by reviewing basic image adjustment, where we will learn to optimize our image contrast (making blacks blacker and whites whiter) and our color saturation (how strong are the colors). I think you will find that with just these two enhancement techniques, your images will improve dramatically.

We will also learn how to crop our images, useful for both improving composition as well as adjusting proportions for fixed print sizes (like 4x6 versus 8x10).

Then we will start to explore the real power of Photoshop–the ability to make localized changes within our image as opposed to changes to the entire image (sometimes called global changes). Perhaps you want to brighten a flower's bloom while leaving the rest of the image untouched. Or maybe remove little blemishes, like dust spots or wrinkles. Just a little taste of what's to come.

13. IMAGE ADJUSTMENTS

Adjustment commands are commands for adjusting the look of our image. This is where we go to correct contrast issues, color issues, and white balance issues to name a few. These commands are mostly geared towards enhancing appearance as opposed to altering content. Two of these adjustments, Levels (for contrast issues) and Hue/Saturation (for color issues), are so fundamental to my recommended image enhancement workflow that they will get their own chapter. But let's take a quick look through the menu of commands first.

Image adjustment tools are found under Image>Adjustments. But before we go there, notice there are three automatic adjustment commands: **Auto Levels, Auto Contrast, and Auto Color** within the Image menu itself. Auto Levels and Auto Contrast improve an image's contrast. (Between the two, Auto Contrast seems to do a better job.) Auto Color improves color balance. I actually recommend against using any of these. The manual counterparts to these one-click adjustments allow us to optimize the image to our taste, not that of the computer. But they are a quick solution.

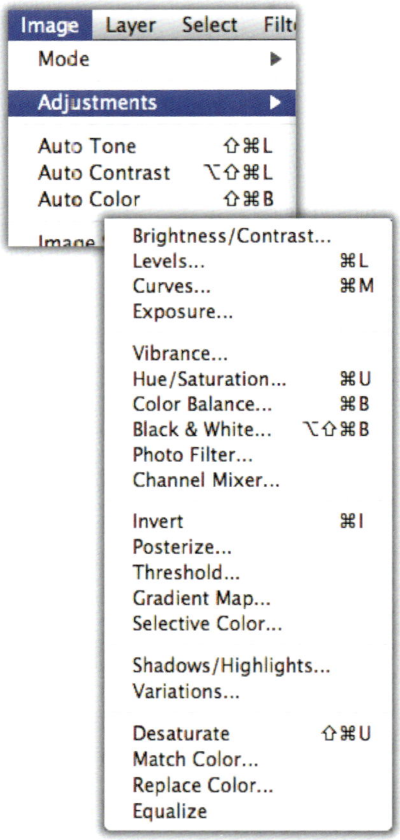

So back to the tools under Image> Adjustments. As you play with the various commands, you may be struck by the degree to which they have overlapping functions. (The same is true almost everywhere in Photoshop!) In many cases, this is because Adobe developed better tools with new releases but kept the old ones around; there are those people (and you know who you are) who are quite attached to certain commands and would stir up a ruckus if a favorite one were to disappear, even if it was replaced by something better.

So we are skipping the Levels and Hue/Saturation adjustments because they get their own chapters and we are skipping the auto adjustments because we'd rather have more control. So let's start out by having some fun with a few one-click (or almost one click) commands that yield immediate results (but with admittedly varying degrees of value).

Open an image in Photoshop if you would like to follow along. I've chosen an image of two seagulls, one of which seems to be getting a lecture. Remember from Chapter 3 that it's a good idea to go into the Layers panel and drag the Background layer onto the New Layer icon to create a copy.

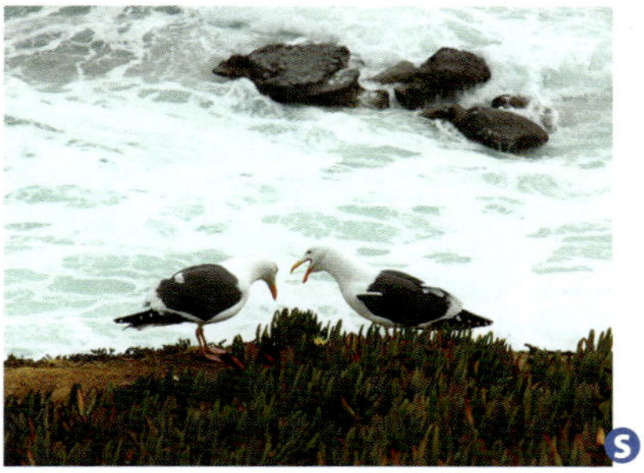

Image>Adjustments>**Posterize** is sort of a special effect that gives our image more of a graphic appearance. Select Posterize and play with the levels to check it out. If we choose four levels, for example, our image is rendered with only four tonal levels of red, four of green, and four of blue. The fewer the tonal levels, the more posterized our image becomes.

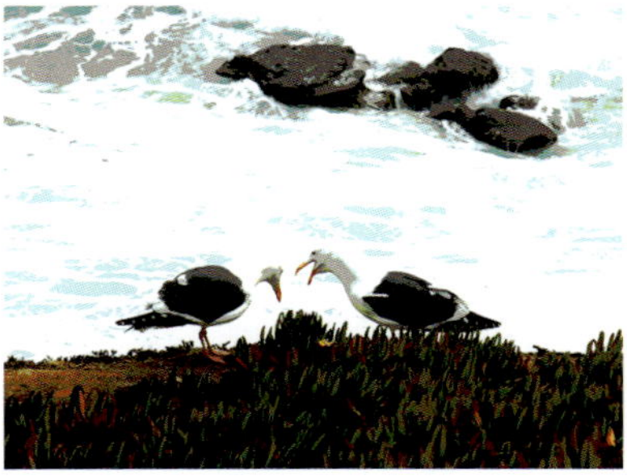

If you are playing along, undo the Posterize adjustment (Edit>Undo), and choose **Invert**. Invert creates a color negative of our image. It does so by making bright pixels dark and dark pixels bright and replacing each color with its compliment. It's like a color negative. There are some advanced usages for this particular adjustment but for now, just enjoy the cool effect.

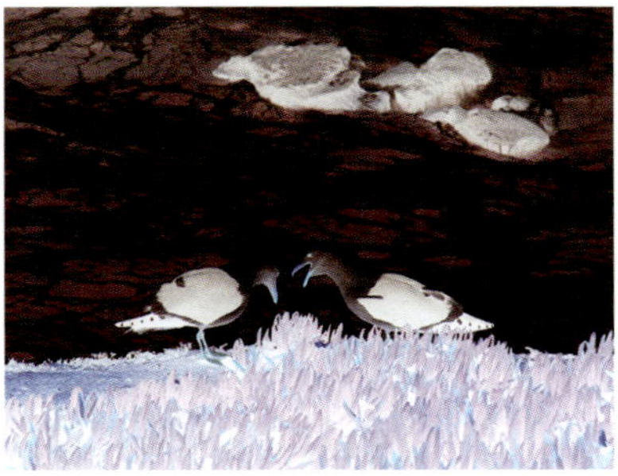

Image>Adjustments>**Black & White** (new to CS3) is a quick but effective way to create a black and white image from a color image. Undo Invert and choose Black & White. In the pop-up dialog box, we can click Auto, to have the program optimize the adjustment, or we can manually optimize the conversion using color sliders. Each slider controls the contribution of the associated color to the final black and white image. Just play with it to get a feel for it.

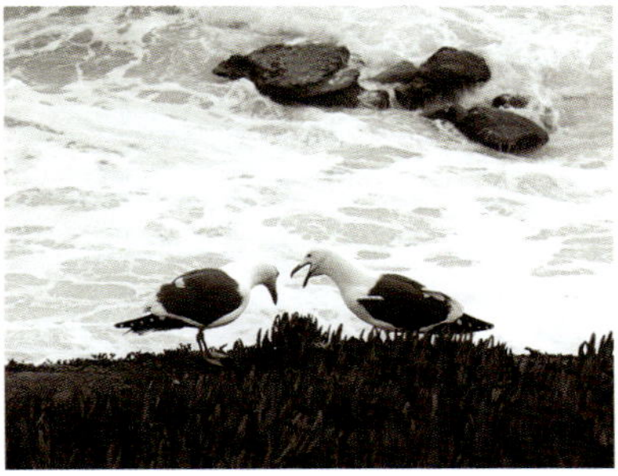

Before we move on to the chapters on Levels and Hue/Saturation, I would like to describe the **Variations** adjustment in some detail because I think it is very useful when just starting out. Often times, when an image doesn't look quite right, it's because it has a color cast. Maybe the exposure was off or the lighting was funny. But while we can sense something is amiss, our eye may not yet be adequately trained to know exactly what. Oh, we could click Auto Color but then we would never learn anything. A better place to start is with Variations, which creates six color adjustments for us.

When Variations opens, our existing image is shown in the center and is called Current Pick. Around it, variations are shown that correspond to more or less red, green, or blue (where less red is more cyan, etc.). While it is obvious in this case that my original is too green (it was taken underwater), we will have many images where the problem is not so obvious.

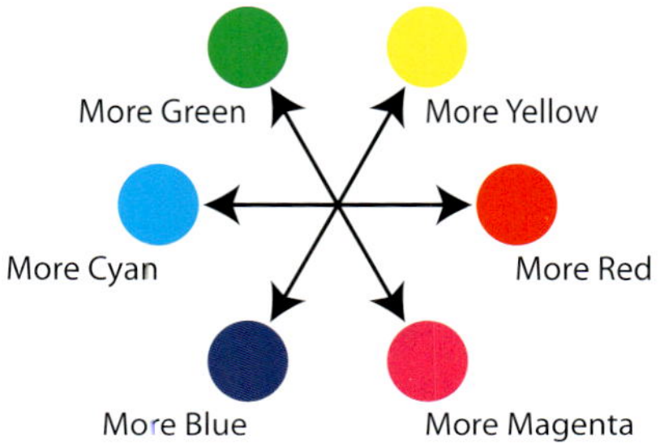

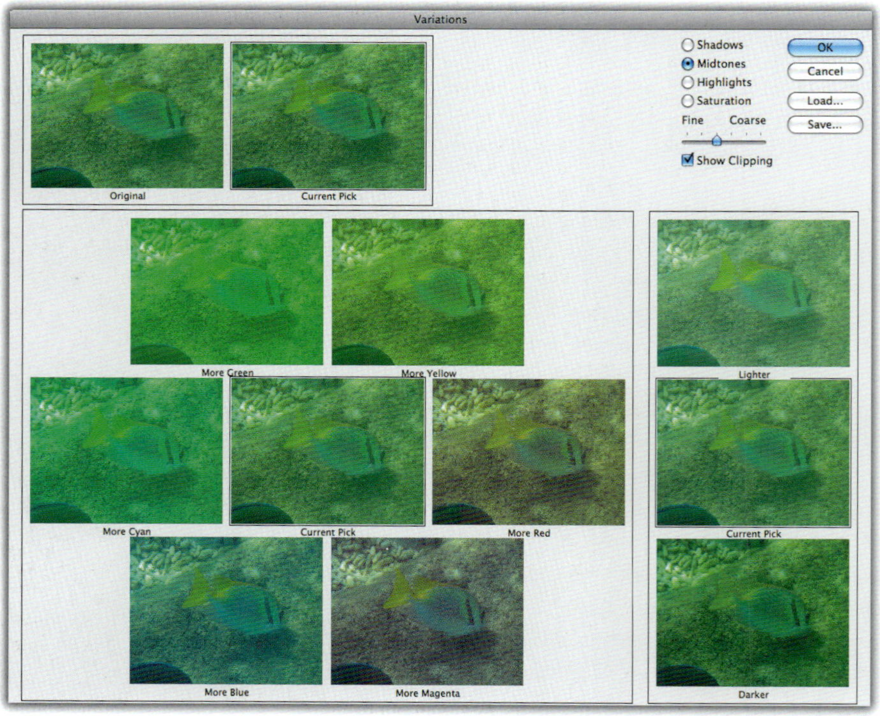

The Fine/Course slider determines how dramatic these variations are. Radio buttons focus the changes on the Shadows, Midtones, or Highlights; Midtones will generally produce the best result. To the right, brighter and darker variations are shown as well. If we were to choose the More Magenta variation (counteracting the greenish tint) by clicking on it, that variation then becomes our Current Pick and a fresh set of variations around it is generated. We might even need more magenta. We can keep clicking to get to an optimum result. In the upper left, we can compare our original to our then existing Current Pick. And if we have gotten a little off track, we can just click on the original image to reset. This tool works well because while our eye may not tell us what is wrong with an image, it will generally recognize when the problem is fixed.

If we pick the Saturation radio button, we get variations of more or less color saturation. Over saturating can cause some pixels to max out; they are called clipped because further increases in saturation won't change them. This is not good for our image and should be avoided. Make sure the Show Clipping box is checked so you can see what is getting clipped with increasing saturation. Here the orange and purple regions indicate that information is getting clipped.

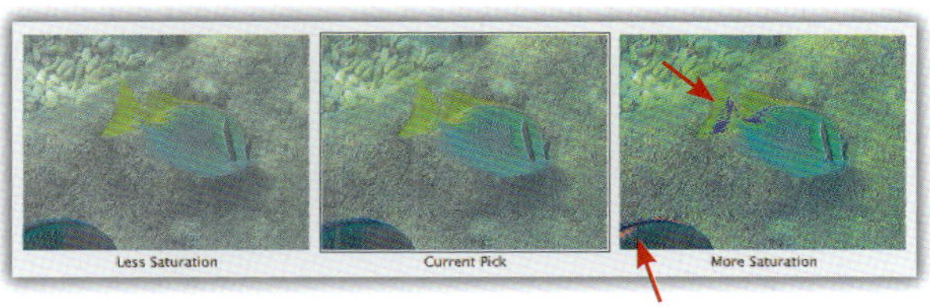

The Variations adjustment is a fun tool, especially when you're just starting out. As your eye gets better attuned, you will gravitate to more advanced tools with more sensitive controls. So here are the before and after images. (The tint in the original, by the way, is the result of having taken the picture underwater. Water partially filters out yellows and reds from natural light resulting in pictures that have a blue, green appearance.)

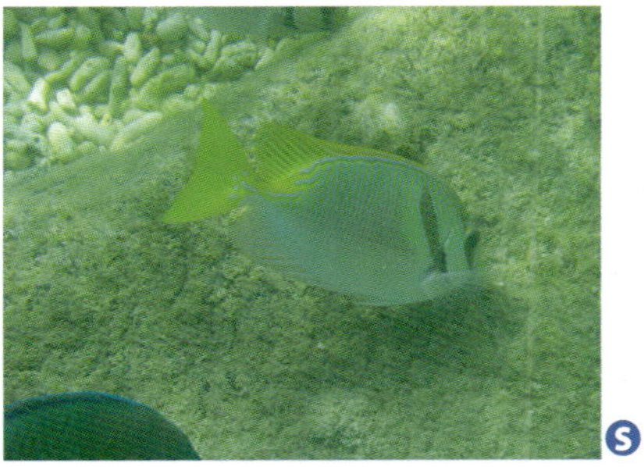

Before

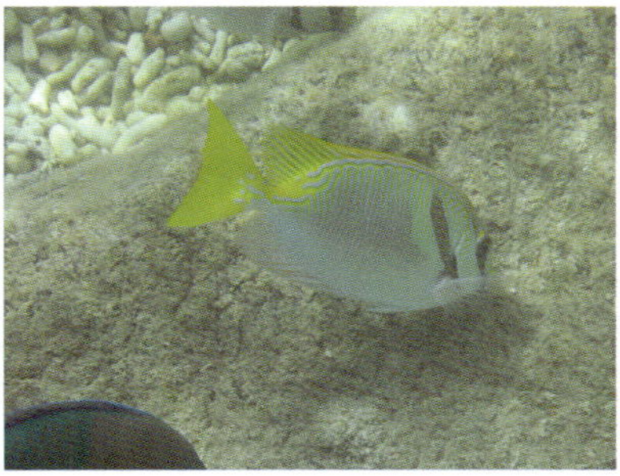

After

In the last chapter, I recommended against using Auto Levels. For one thing, it doesn't do a great job. But the other reason is that doing **Levels** manually is fun and very rewarding. Perhaps the easiest way to jazz up an image is to improve its contrast, exactly what Levels (regular Levels that is) allows us to do. If we open an image in Photoshop and select Image>Adjustments>Levels, the Levels dialog box pops open. (Recall from my introduction that I am avoiding lots of short cuts in order not to overwhelm you. I'll break that rule (again) because we will be using Levels so much. Open Levels in a snap by pressing Cmd(Ctrl)-L.) The dialog box should look somewhat familiar because it is dominated by a histogram of our image. We learned about histograms back in Chapter 9.

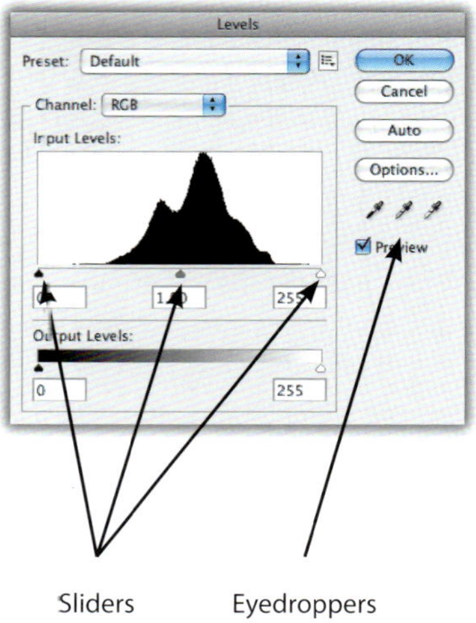

Underneath the histogram in the Levels dialog box we see three sliders. The left slider is the black point (shadows), the right slider is the white point (highlights), and the middle slider is the neutral gray point. Recall that a picture with poor contrast has a histogram that does not extend to either end; the darks are dark gray, not black, and the whites are light gray, not white. With these sliders, we can fix all that.

Here is an image of a seawall with poor contrast (unfortunately I had many different examples from which to choose). The associated histogram shows that the pixels don't extend to either end, exactly as we would have expected. This is the type of image we might get on a hazy day–it basically looks washed out. There's no vibrancy. Let's see how, with these sliders, we can vastly improve the image contrast.

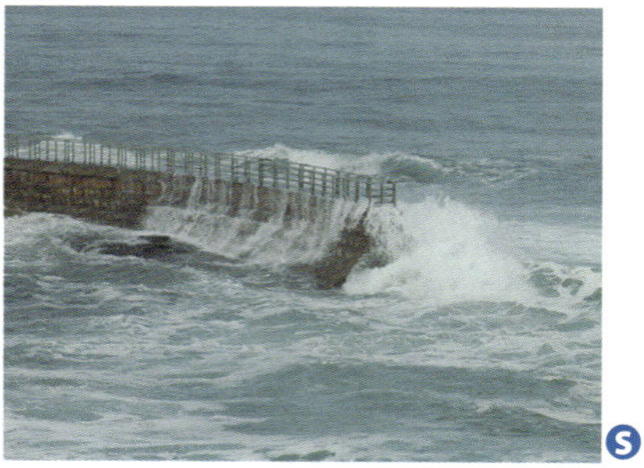

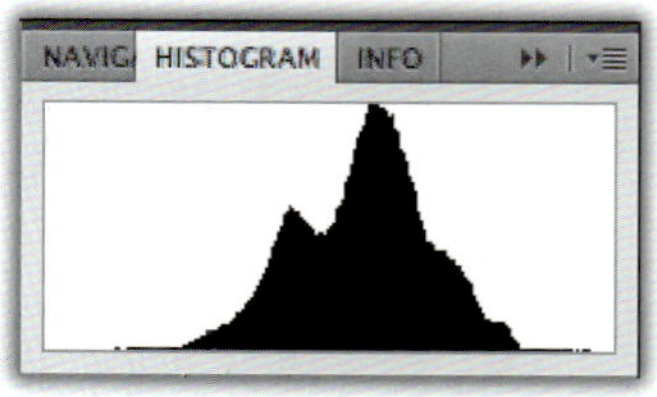

Note: I'm displaying my histogram as an RGB composite instead of in colors as discussed on Page 50. Easier to see what is going on.

First we slide the black slider to the right to just where the first image data starts in the histogram. This tells Photoshop to make that point (and everything to the left of it) black, or level zero, and to stretch out the remaining pixels between levels zero and 255. The Histogram panel updates in real time and we can actually see both the before and after histograms. The after histogram has been stretched to the left, increasing dynamic range, i.e. contrast. The little white vertical bars are gaps that Photoshop has inserted to stretch out the distribution. They look scary but are normal. If we have the Preview box checked, our image updates to reflect our changes. The image has darkened because we "reset black." (These changes don't become final until we click OK.)

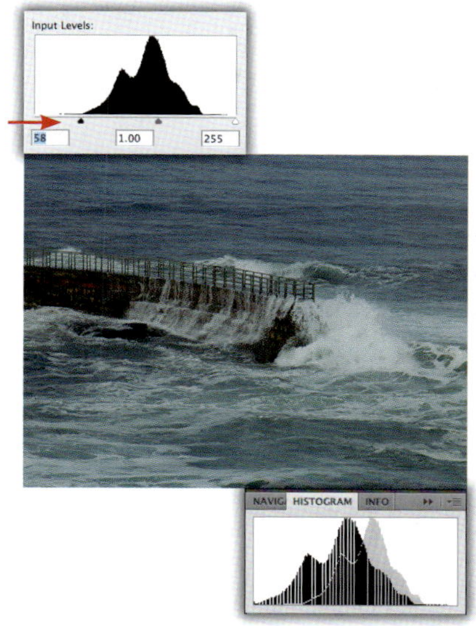

Now let's do the same thing on the white side. We move the white slider to the left just to where the first image data starts. This tells Photoshop to make that point (and everything to the right of it) white, or level 255, and to stretch out the remaining pixels between levels zero and 255. More gaps show up but that's normal, right? As we can see, we have made a huge improvement. The image data now extends the full width of the histogram, increasing the dynamic range, enhancing the contrast. The colors are even more vibrant.

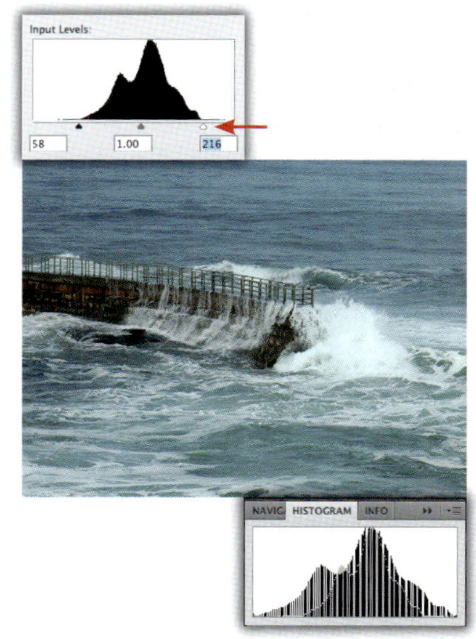

This is why I usually start image enhancement projects with a Levels adjustment.

In this example, we moved our black and white sliders to the edges of the original distribution. But we're not stuck doing that. In practice, move each slider to that point and then, watching the image, not the histogram, adjust left and right. Choose the setting that looks most pleasing and realistic. This is the power of manual adjustments.

So we have improved the overall contrast. But what is the middle slider for? Well, if we slide it to the left, our image gets lighter; sliding it to the right makes the image darker. As we move it, we are telling Photoshop to make the new location the midpoint of the histogram while keeping the black and white points where they are.

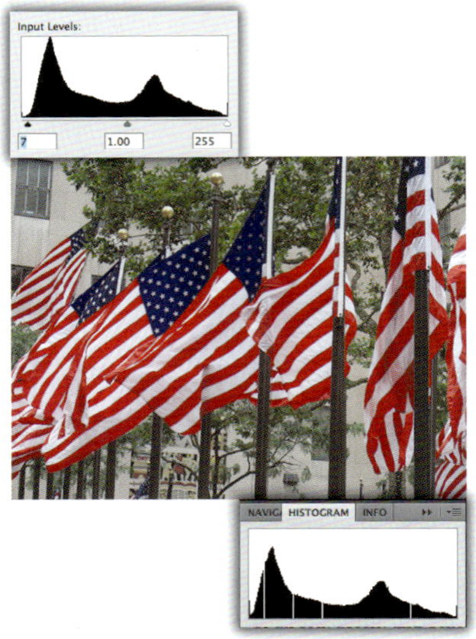

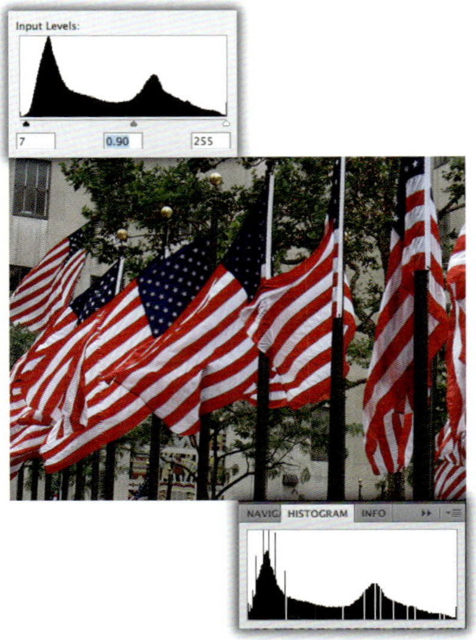

This before and after shows the effect. The starting image has pretty good contrast. I have already moved the black slider over just a bit as shown, creating the few histogram gaps. The after image has been darkened slightly by moving the middle slider to the right. Notice how the gaps have increased on the right (the distribution has been stretched) and little spikes have shown up on the left (the distribution has been squeezed). Again, this is normal so not to worry.

A word of caution, however. Those gaps and spikes don't create noticeable effects in our image as long they are here and there. But lots of stretching, i.e. big gaps and spikes, may result in some visible artifacts. So watch out for this and try not to overdo it.

The black and white levels boxes below the sliders give us the numerical value for associated slider location. In the seawall example, the level 58 in the original image was redefined to black (level 0). Level 216 was redefined to white (or level 255). The number in the middle box doesn't correspond to a level. It is something called gamma and has a default of 1.0. As mentioned above, it sort of defines the midpoint of our histogram. This is sometimes referred to as neutral gray point. In our flag example, we changed it to 0.9 which darkened the image slightly.

Recall that a histogram is a composite of all red, green, and blue information. With Levels, we can see the individual histograms for each. They are accessed by changing the Channel selection from RGB to either Red, Green, or Blue. Go ahead and check out the differences. Here are the composite and red, green, and blue histograms for the flag example.

I will suggest that you stick with the RGB composite, though, until you get more advanced. For now, just note that the three channels are different and imagine the fun of playing with each independently.

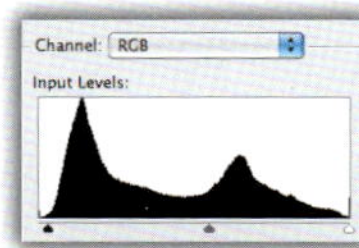

RGB Composite

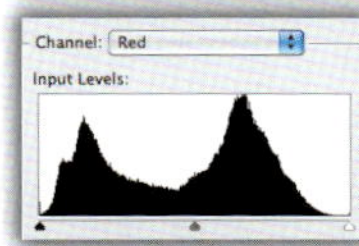

Red

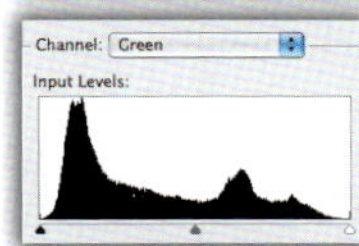

Green

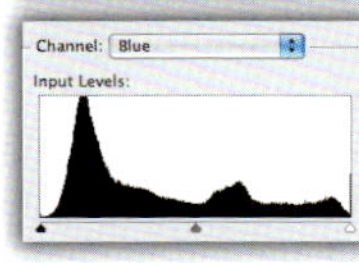

Blue

At the bottom of the Levels dialog box are Output Levels. Don't plan on using these for now–they actually do the opposite of the Input Levels, reducing contrast. I only use them on images with a really bright feature, like a sunrise with the sun just above the horizon. Shifting the white slider a bit to the left would tone down this brightness.

The **Eyedroppers** in the lower right corner are interesting tools–they do levels and more. There are three of them. From left to right they are black, neutral gray, and white. If we select the white eyedropper and click a spot on our image, Photoshop adjusts Levels to make that location white. Not just level 255, but level 255 for each color. Each of the color histograms is separately adjusted to make that point RGB = 255, 255, 255 = white. Black and neutral gray work similarly. So if we have a location in the image with known black, known white, or known gray, we can actually correct color casts with a simple click. (Only use one of the eyedroppers.) Then we can use our sliders to optimize contrast.

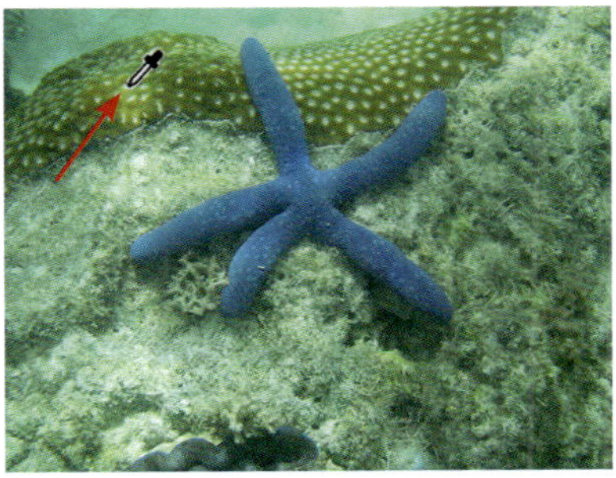
Before white eyedropper sampling...

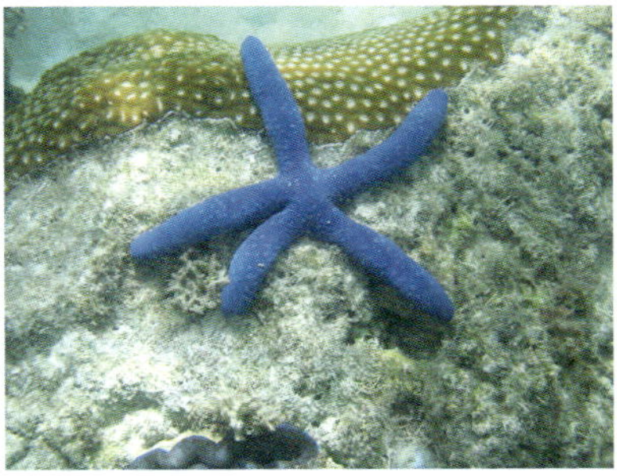
After!

15. HUE/SATURATION

Having fixed our contrast issues (and maybe some color cast issues) with Levels, we next take on our colors with **Hue/Saturation**. Find it under Image>Adjustments> Hue/Saturation. Like Levels, Hue/Saturation will likely become a standard part of your workflow. So you may want to use the keyboard shortcut Cmd(Ctrl)-U to bring it up. Open an image if you like and open Hue/Saturation. I will use the seawall example (after levels optimization) from the previous chapter.

The first thing that we notice in the Hue/ Saturation dialog box is that it offers adjustments for Hue, Saturation, and also Lightness. This should remind you of the HSB model we discussed in Chapter 8. (Refer back to that chapter if the terms need refreshing.)

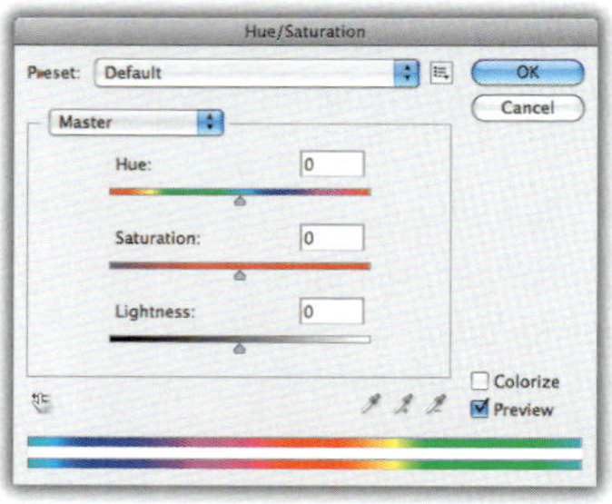

Let's start with **Lightness**, because that will be quick. Don't use it, at least not much. Lightness shifts all of the pixels in our histogram either left or right and since we just optimized all that with Levels, we don't want to mess with it. If you can't resist, very, very small adjustments are okay. But I rarely touch it.

Next we go to **Saturation**. I find that many images benefit from a little boost in Saturation. Photography purists are probably blanching at this but adding saturation to our colors makes them pop a bit more. Try sliding up +10 or +15. We can toggle the Preview Box on and off to do a before and after comparison. Be careful not to overdo it. The saturation slider affects all colors and the image can become unrealistic quickly.

After I have adjusted Levels, a saturation adjustment is always the next step in my image enhancement process.

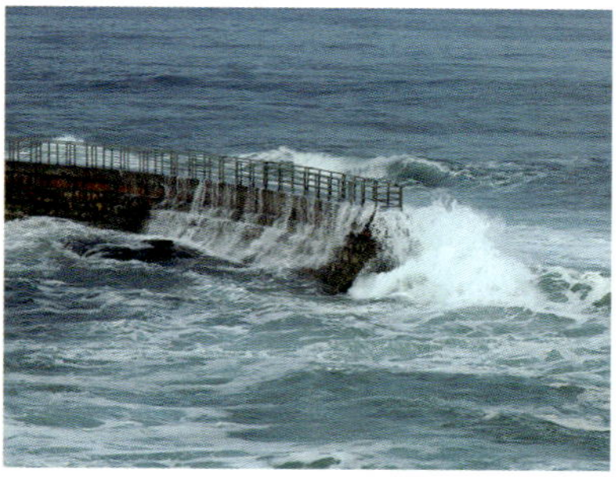

Before Saturation Adjustment

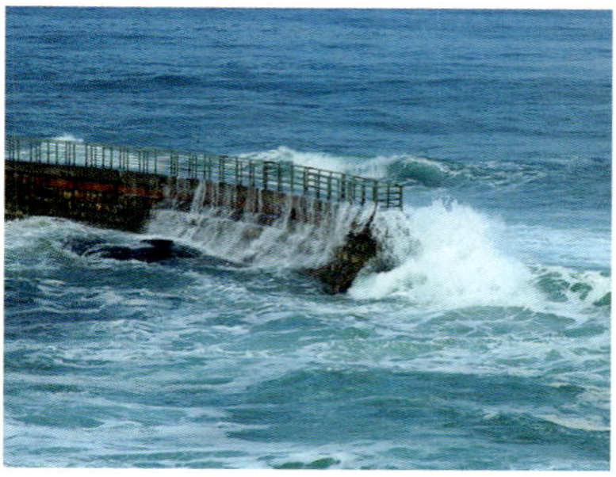

After +20 Saturation Adjustment

This leaves the **Hue adjustment** and at first blush it doesn't seem very useful. As we move the slider in either direction, the hue of all of the colors shifts. The two color strips at the bottom help us see how the colors are changing; the bottom strip shifts in concert with the slider. The way to interpret this is to say to ourselves "If this existing color is this," and then pick a color on the top strip, "it will become that" and look at the corresponding color directly below on the bottom strip. In this example, red became yellow/green. Doesn't seem too useful, does it? But play with it or look at my example to at least make the concept clear. I will make it worth your while in a moment.

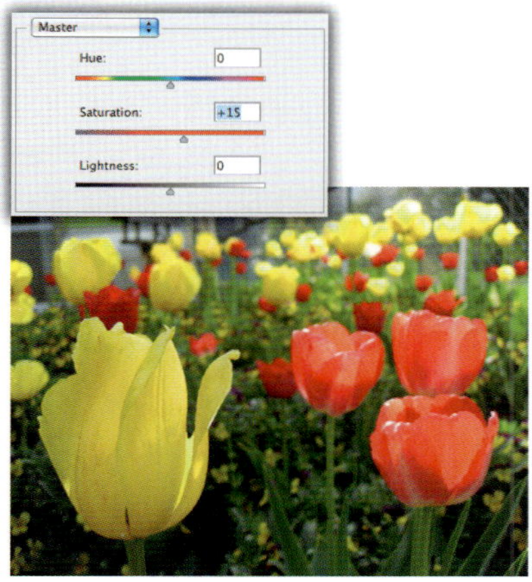

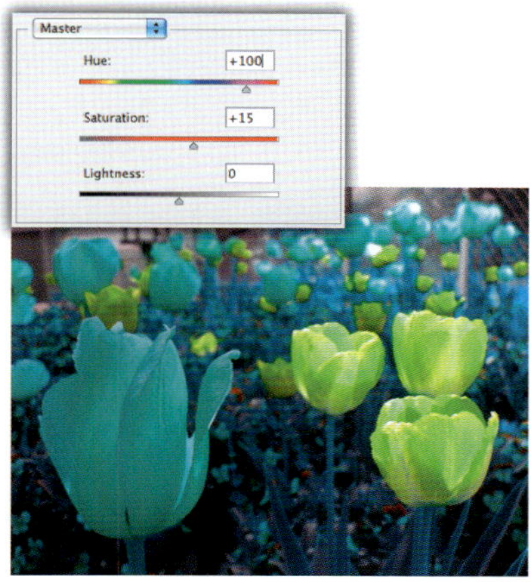

In the right hand corner of the Hue/Saturation dialog box, there is a check box for **Colorize**. If we check that, our image gets converted into sort of a duotone (an image made up of two inks, black and our chosen hue). The hue can be changed by adjusting the Hue slider. The bottom color strip now reflects the chosen hue. Saturation and Lightness both work as before and can be adjusted to your taste. The original image determines the luminosity (light and dark). There are more effective ways to create duotones but none that are quicker than this.

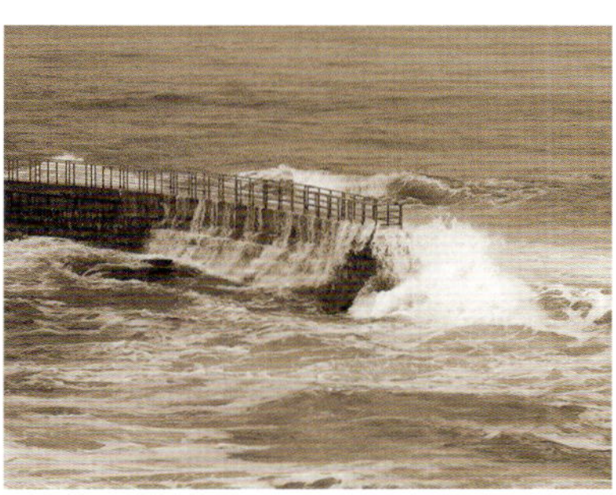

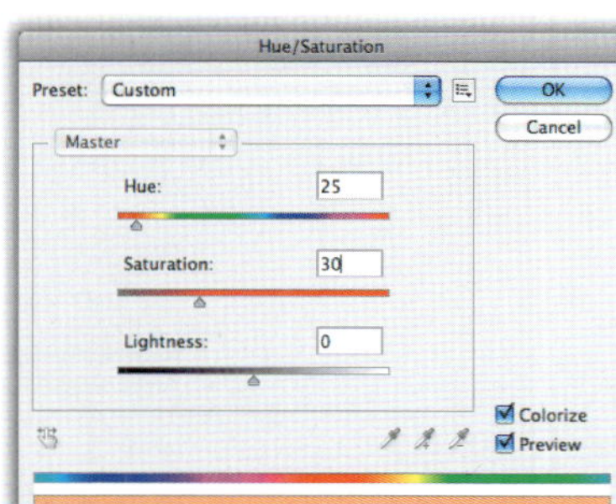

On the lower right of the Hue/Saturation dialog box we see some grayed out **Eyedroppers**. These eyedroppers, as it turns out, unlock the real power of the Hue/Saturation adjustment. But first, in the upper left, there is a box called Edit; Master is currently selected, meaning the whole composite image. If we click on that menu, we see that we can also select specific colors: reds, greens, blues and their compliments cyans, yellows, and magentas. By choosing one of these, let's say Reds, we restrict the effects of the sliders to only reds.

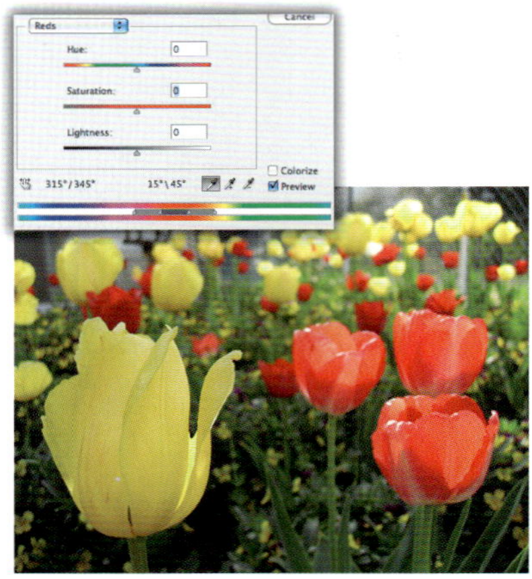

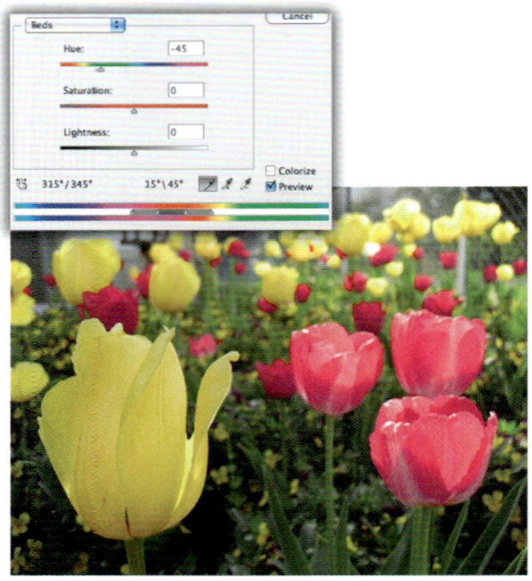

The reason the menu says "Reds" and not "Red" is because it actually shifts a family of reds. If it were only to affect a single red, it would be of limited value. A red jacket in an image, for example might have many shades of red in it due to the lighting. We can actually see the spectrum of affected reds by looking at the little addition (it looks like a Band-aid to me) to the color strips at the bottom of the dialog box. All of the colors above the darker central band are the colors that will get shifted with the slider. Those in the lighter gray regions to the left and right are affected but to a lesser extent (this is to keep our color transitions looking smooth). If we move the slider now, the bottom color strip shows us the how color is shifting, but only for those colors within the Band-aid.

The little blocks delineating the light and dark gray regions of the Band-aid are actually sliders also, so if we feel adventuresome, we can tighten or loosen up the distribution of affected colors.

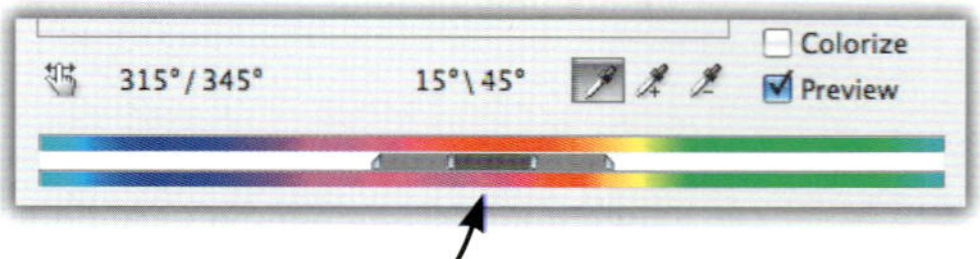

Color Distribution (Band-aid)

Okay, so back to the eyedroppers. Note that when we change Edit from Master to any of the other colors, the eyedroppers are no longer grayed out; they've become active. If we choose the eyedropper on the left and click on a specific color in our image, the hue slider will now affect only the hue of that color (within the little range around it). So we are not restricted to reds, greens, etc. We can target any specific hue in our image that we want. (The plus and minus eyedroppers affect the distribution of affected hues and seem difficult to control. I use the Band-aid sliders instead.)

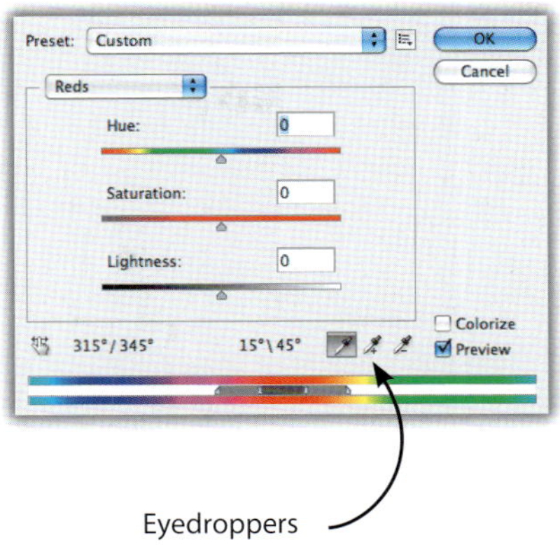

So let's say we wanted to shift the hue of the jacket in the picture below. In the Hue/Saturation dialog box, we choose Reds (anything other than Master) to turn the eyedroppers on. With the left most eyedropper, we sample the jacket's hue.

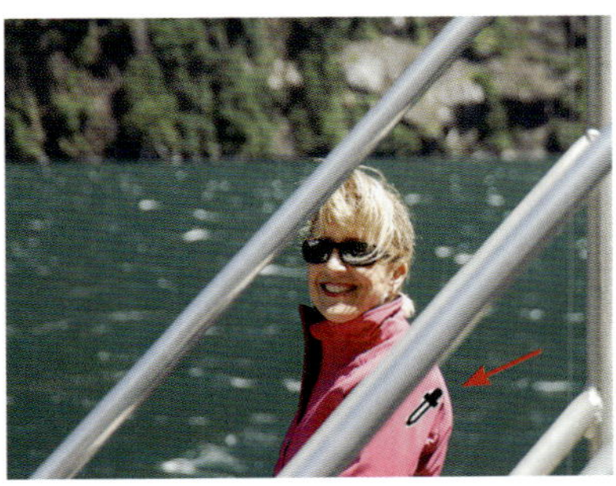

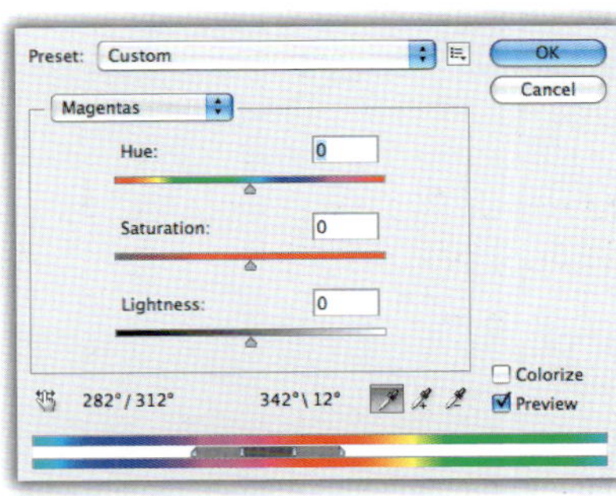

Now we can slide the Hue slider left or right, fine tuning the jacket hue to our satisfaction. Beware that if there is other content within the image that had the same hue as the jacket, it is going to change as well. We can get around this pretty simply, though, by first creating a rough selection around the jacket so that only its pixels would be affected.

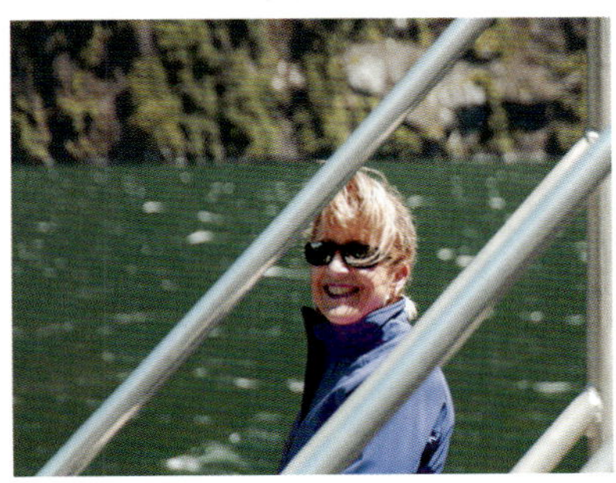

CS4 added a new adjustment called Vibrance that is similar to the Saturation adjustment but with some special attributes. See the tips at the end of this section for more.

16. CROPPING

The last major enhancement we will use frequently is **cropping**. I refer to cropping as an enhancement because we usually do it to improve an image. With cropping, we can possibly improve our composition or remove edge intrusions. The ability to crop is a good justification for upgrading to a higher megapixel camera; the more pixels we start out with, the more we can crop and still print a decent-sized image.

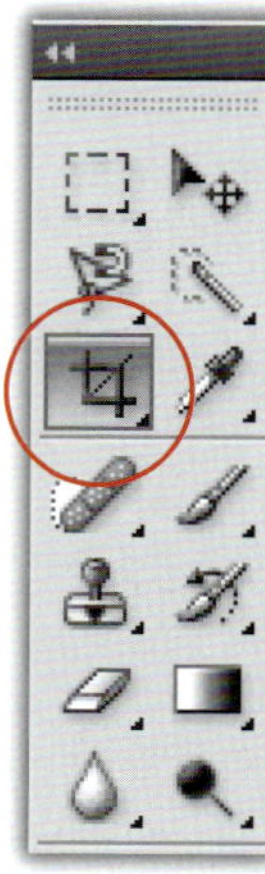

The basics of cropping are simple but can be frustrating. Open an image and adjust the zoom so that you have a gray border around the image in the document window. Find the Crop tool in the toolbox near the top. The crop tool works kind of like the Rectangular Marquee in that we click and drag to select the cropping boundary. First, make sure that height and width in the options bar are blank. After we drag and release the mouse, the cropping boundary is marked by marching ants with transformation handles and the portions of the image to be cropped are darkened (just on the display to make viewing easier). On the right side of the options bar, we see a Stop icon (cancel) and a Commit icon (accept) have shown up. We click Commit, or hit Return(Enter), to complete the crop.

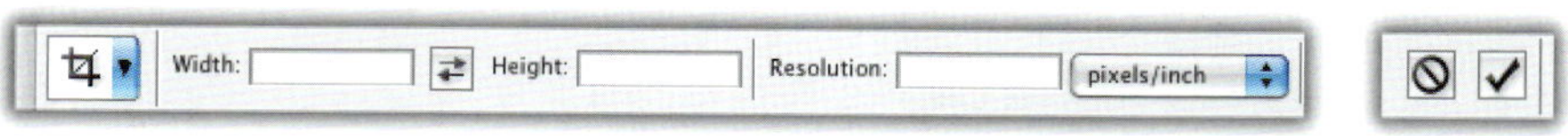

Crop Tool Options Bar

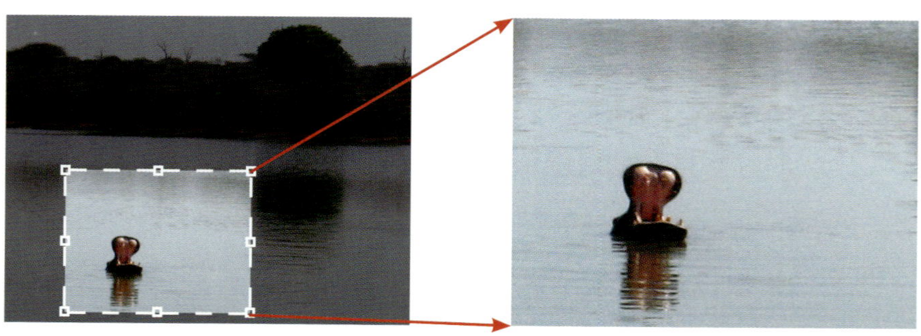

We have to either accept or cancel the crop in order to get out of the crop mode. (There will be times we forget and wonder why Photoshop feels locked up.) Accepting throws away the pixels that are outside the crop boundary; the image dimensions change accordingly. I usually like to save out a copy of the original prior to doing this. Canceling removes the crop boundary (but leaves us in the crop tool), with the image untouched.

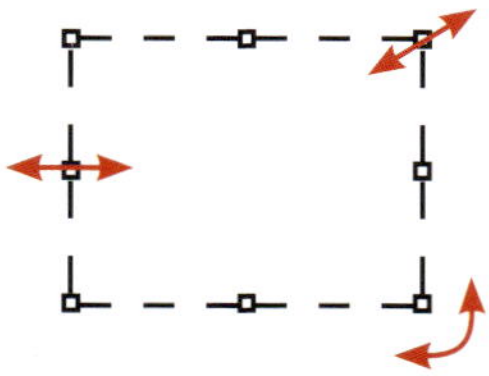

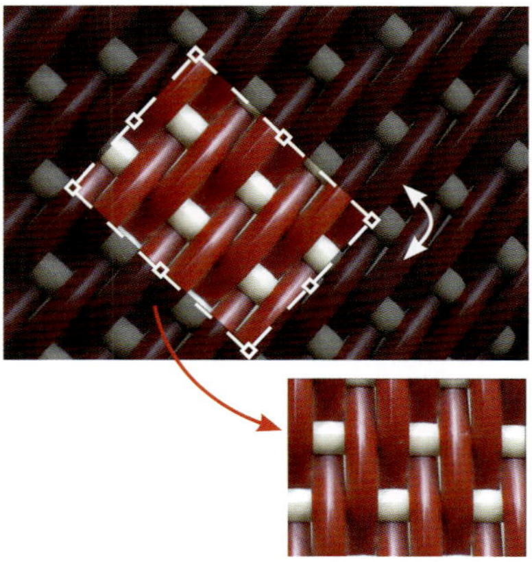

After we first click and drag with the Crop tool, we'll probably want to modify the selection before accepting it. This is the purpose of those transformation handles. The handles on the top, bottom and sides move their respective edges. The corner handles move the two edges defining that corner. As with other applications, holding down the SHIFT key while moving a corner handle maintains the aspect ratio of the border. Click and drag within the crop boundary to move the entire selection. The crop boundary can also be rotated, great for straightening images. To do this, we hover the cursor just outside the marching ants and, when the cursor becomes the rotate icon, we click and drag. Accepting the crop both crops and straightens the resulting image.

We can also crop to a specific aspect ratio, like 4 by 6 or 8 by10, as long as we are a little bit careful. With the Crop tool selected, we look in its options bar and see boxes for Width, Height, and Resolution. If we wanted a 4 by 6 image, we would type 6 for the width, 4 for the height, and (for now) leave resolution empty. Photoshop will add "in" for inches into the height and width but just ignore that for now. (If you are seeing px for pixels, go to Preferences>Units & Rulers and set the ruler units to inches.) The Swap button swaps width and height in case they were entered backwards.

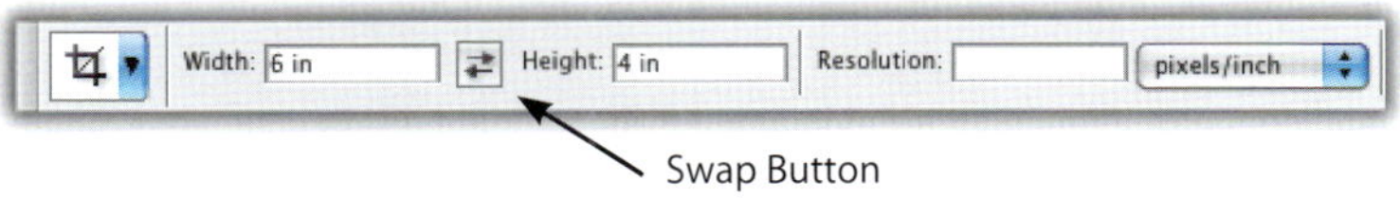

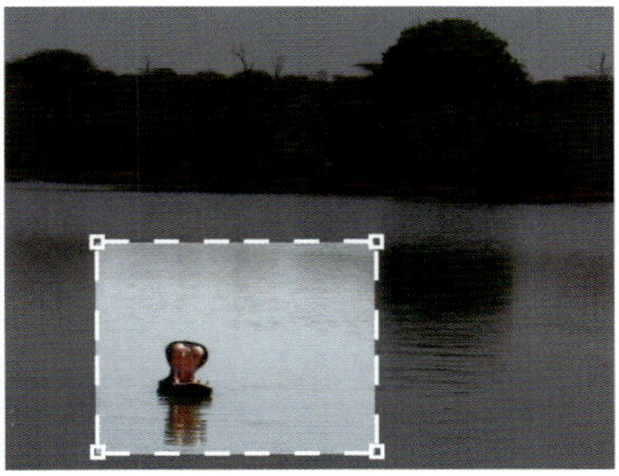

Now when we click and drag with the Crop tool, our marching ants boundary only has corner handles; this is because we have constrained the crop to a fixed aspect ratio. We can size the box, or move it and rotate it all as before. Just no aspect ratio changes. Hit return to accept the crop.

I mentioned being careful regarding fixed aspect ratios because of the Resolution box. When it is empty, Photoshop does not resample our image when it crops. (This is kind of like having the Resample Image check box in the Image Size dialog box unchecked.) The pixel count within the crop boundary stays fixed, independent of the size we may have requested.

If we do specify a resolution along with a size, however, Photoshop resamples our image to achieve the requested size at the requested resolution. To do this, it may have to downsample, which is probably not a problem. Or it may have to upsample which means that our quality will suffer. (Review Chapter 5 if this is unclear.) This is why we need to be careful.

Let's show this with an example. The image to the right was taken with a 6 Mp camera so it is approximately 3000 pixels wide by 2000 high. If we wanted a portrait-style close-up, we could crop as shown in an 8x10 aspect ratio with the resolution box empty for now. The cropped area shown is 1440 by 1800 pixels; if we printed this at 250 dpi, the resulting image would be 5¾ by 7¼ inches. This is the maximum image size we can achieve without upsampling.

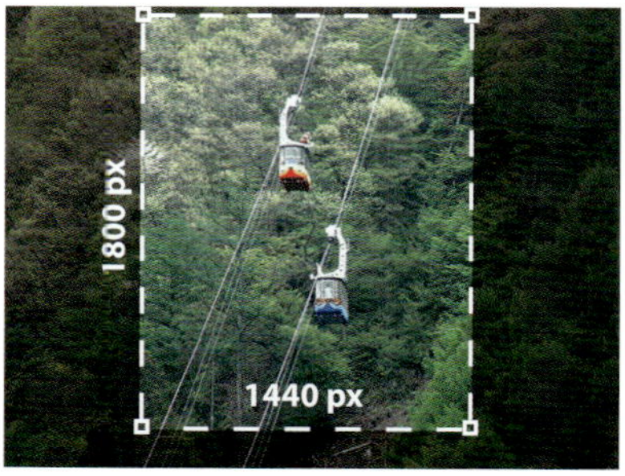

If we had told Photoshop to crop 8 inches by 10 inches but with a resolution of 250 dpi specified, it would have complied by upsampling to create an image that was 2000 (8 inches x 250 dpi) by 2500 pixels (10 inches x 250 dpi)–larger than the original–with a corresponding loss of quality. Now we may want to do this; we just need to understand what we are doing.

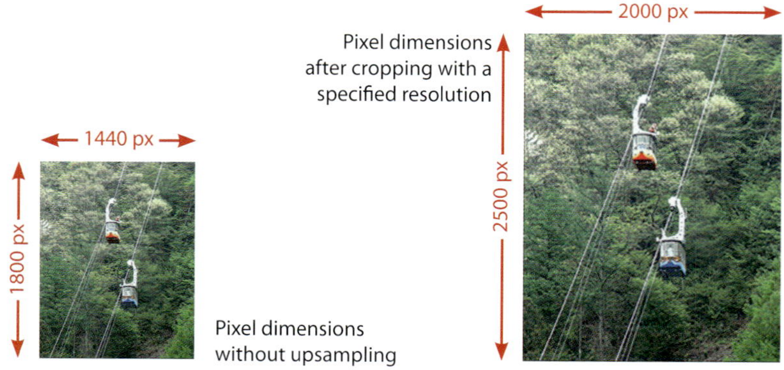

If we're good with numbers, we can pretty easily determine if downsampling or upsampling is going to occur. But there is a more straightforward way. To maintain control, we first crop our image to our liking with the resolution box empty. Then we select Image>Image Size and use that dialog box to set size, resolution, and pixel count as was discussed in Chapter 5. Here, I am upsampling but under better control...

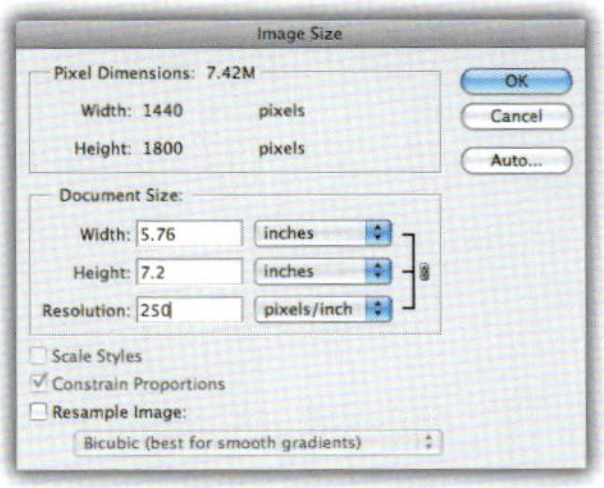

Image Size Dialog Box after crop

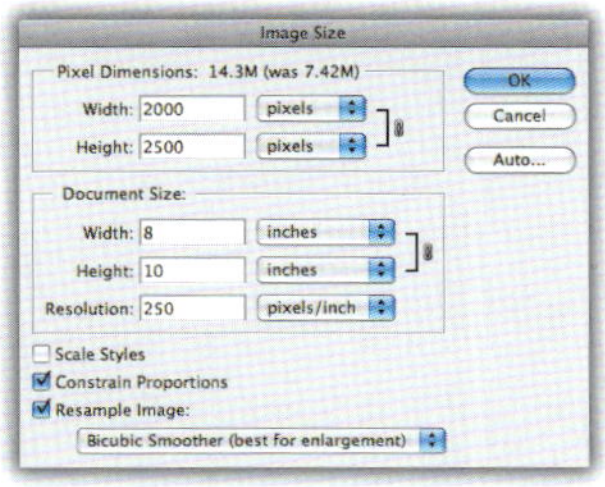

Controlled resampling using Bicubic Smoother

We may not need this next cropping feature very often but, when we do, it is invaluable. There will be times when we have a picture taken at an angle, either up and down or left and right, that adds perspective to what would have otherwise been a rectangular shape. In this example, the framed picture is obviously rectangular, but not when taken at an angle. To crop to the frame and at the same time remove the perspective, we create a loose cropping boundary around the frame and then, before accepting, we check the now visible **Perspective** in the options bar. With Perspective checked, the cropping boundary is no longer constrained to a rectangular shape; each handle can move independently of the others. So we move each handle to its respective frame corner and hit return. Presto! (This is a great way to take pictures of pictures without reflections. At the angle I took this, the picture was reflecting a blank wall.)

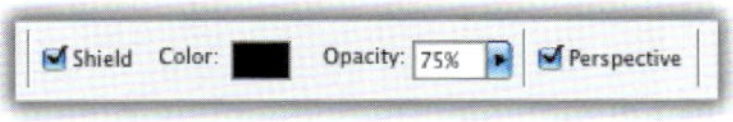

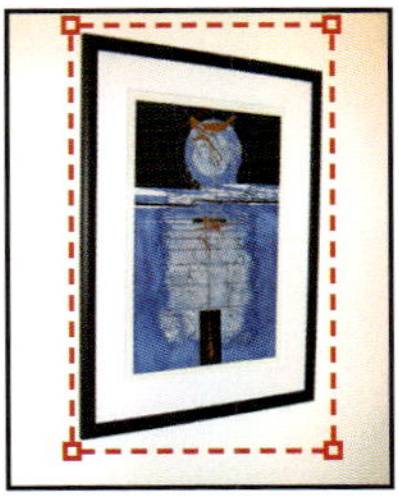

Loose selection...

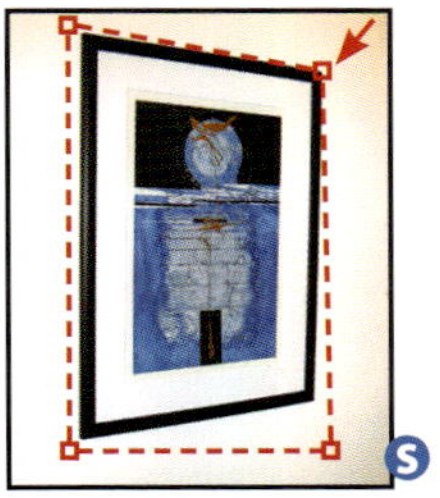

Check Perspective and drag in corners

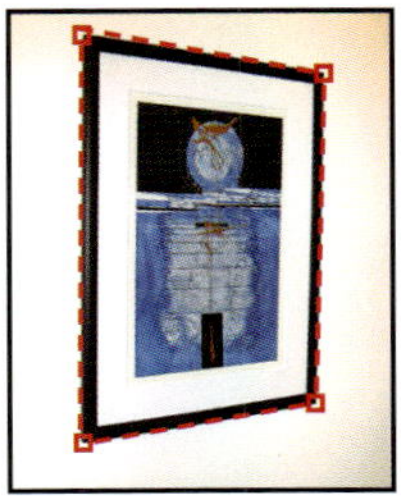

Finished crop boundary

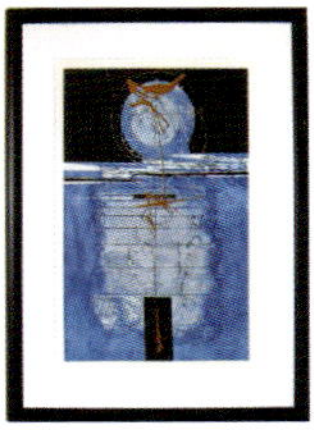

Finished crop

In summary, cropping is a powerful way to improve images. The old adage in photography is that closer is better. By framing our picture in the camera a little larger than necessary, we can use the Crop tool back at home to carefully perfect our composition.

17. LOCALIZED ENHANCEMENTS

Thus far in this section we have been making mostly global changes to our images, changing most or all of the image's pixels at once. Now we will attack making more localized enhancements. We will look at a total of six, count'em six, different tools. But as we'll see, they all work pretty much the same way so once we have mastered one of them, we've mastered them all. They all look like brushes, but apply effects, not color.

Let's start with the **Dodge tool**, which has the effect of lightening. With an image open, we select the Dodge tool from the toolbox. In its options bar, we see the familiar Brush pull down menu along with selections for Range and Exposure. For now, let's set Range to Midtones and Exposure to 30%.

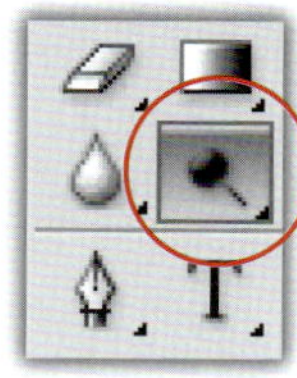

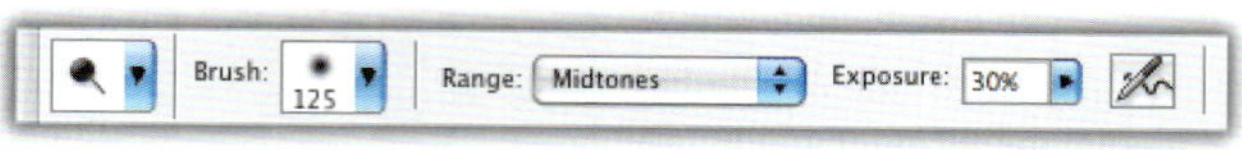

Recall in Chapter 11, I lightened up a cat underneath a rowboat. We didn't discuss it back then, but the Dodge tool was the tool I used to do it. With the diameter set to around the size of the cat's face (remember to use the brackets, [and]...) and the Hardness set to zero (the softest edge possible), we click and drag over the cat. If the effect is not strong enough, we can repeat it for additional lightening. If we go too far, we can undo or use the History panel to go back. Try it on your image.

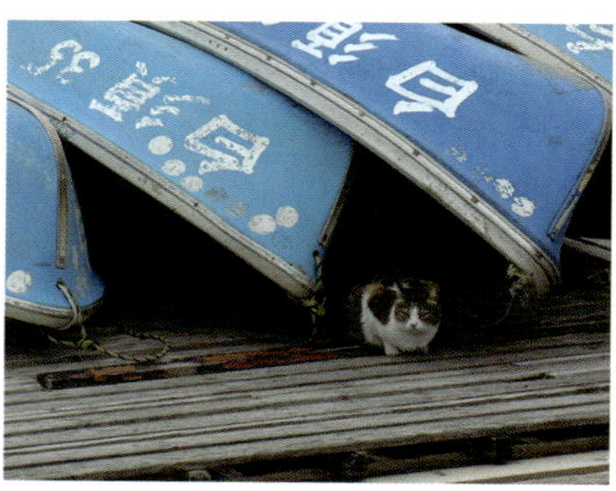

Original image. I would like the cat to be a little lighter.

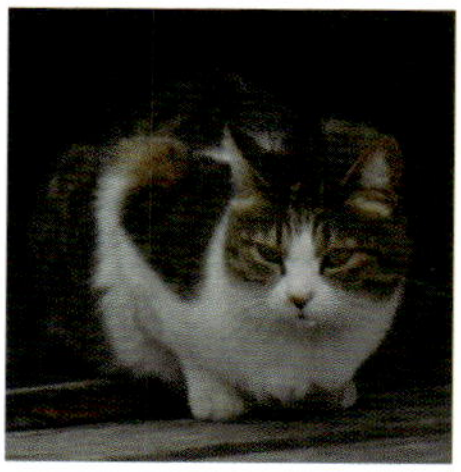

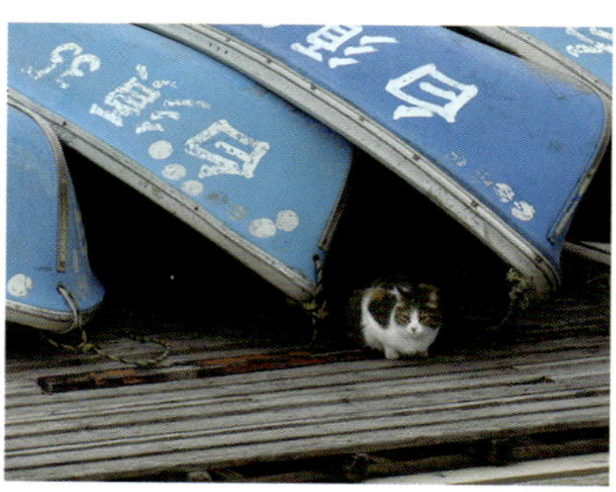

Completed image. I lightened up the cat with the Dodge tool, mostly on its white fur.

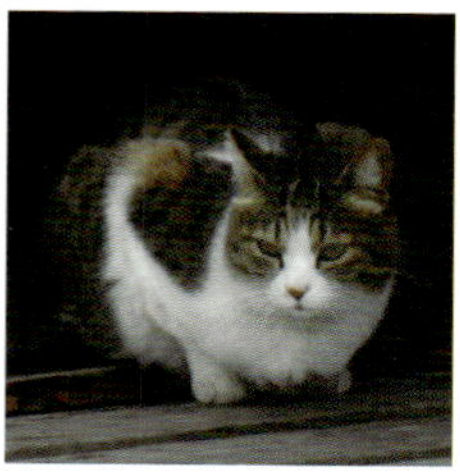

The Range setting allows us to target midtones, shadows, or highlights. So we can separately lighten neutrals, blacks, or whites as we wish. For my cat, I Dodged with midtones and with highlights, the latter to bring out more of the whites. The Exposure setting controls how much of a change each Dodge operation makes. Since we are generally looking for subtle results, a low number like 30% is good. We can always go over a spot more than once. Selecting Airbrush icon allows for the lightening to compound as we hold the mouse key down.

Also recall that we set our Hardness all the way down to zero. With all of the tools in this chapter, we will be looking for subtle transitions between affected and unaffected areas. A soft edge on the brush creates this softened border.

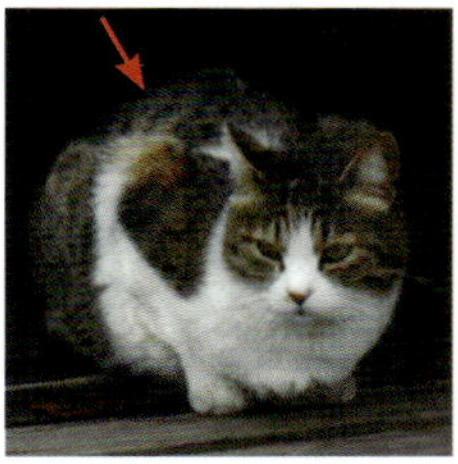

After Dodge tool with
100% Hardness

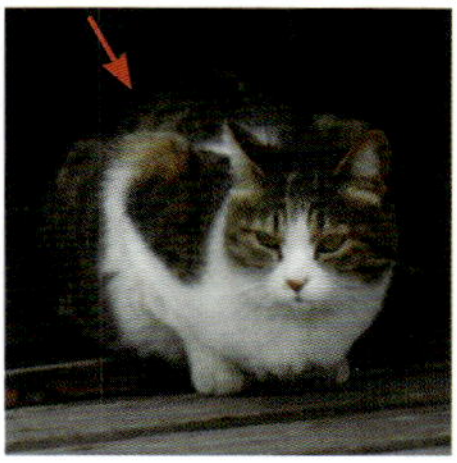

After Dodge tool with
0% Hardness

Nested under the Dodge tool in the toolbox (click and hold), we find the **Burn tool**. The Burn tool works exactly like the Dodge tool but it darkens instead of lightens. All of the controls work the same so I won't repeat them here. By the way, Dodge and Burn are photography darkroom terms for tools that do the same thing, localized lightening and darkening. In the example below, the bloom is in the sun and a little too bright. With the Burn tool, I was able to tone that down a bit.

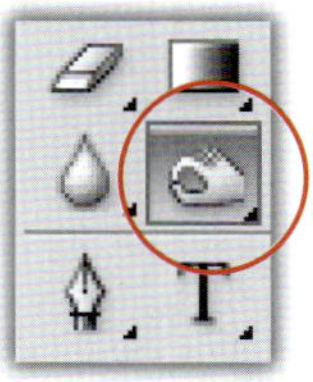

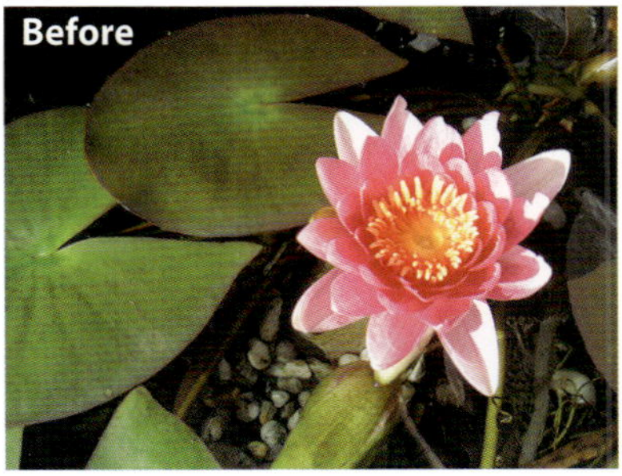

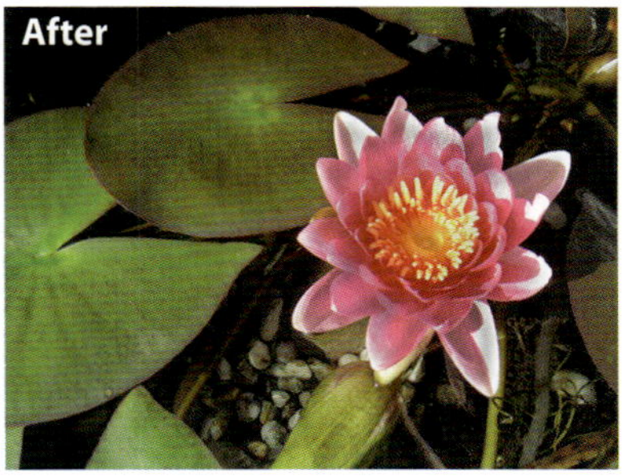

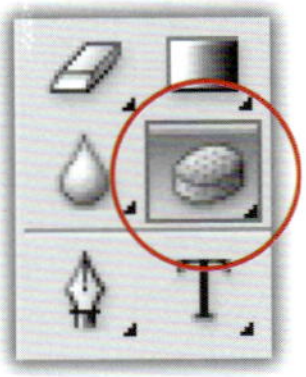

Also nested behind the Dodge tool, we find the **Sponge tool**. This tool allows us to modify color saturation. The options bar is pretty similar except that now we get to choose Mode, either Saturation or Desaturation. The saturation mode increases saturation while desaturation lowers it. Flow behaves very much like exposure did for the Dodge tool, setting the rate at which the saturation changes. A typical application for this is shown below where I wanted to have the bloom color pop a bit more without boosting saturation of the background. (I dodged a bit also.)

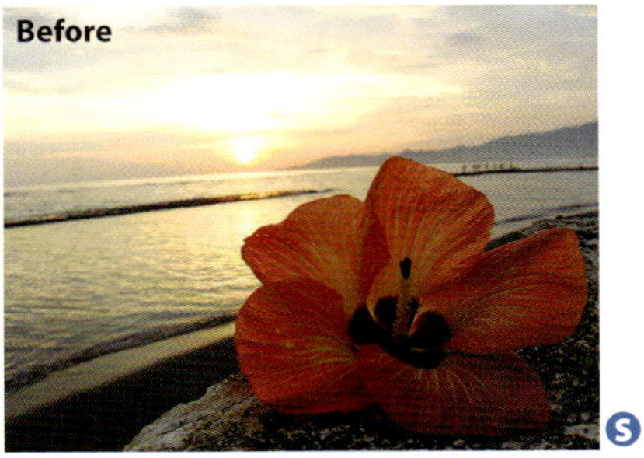

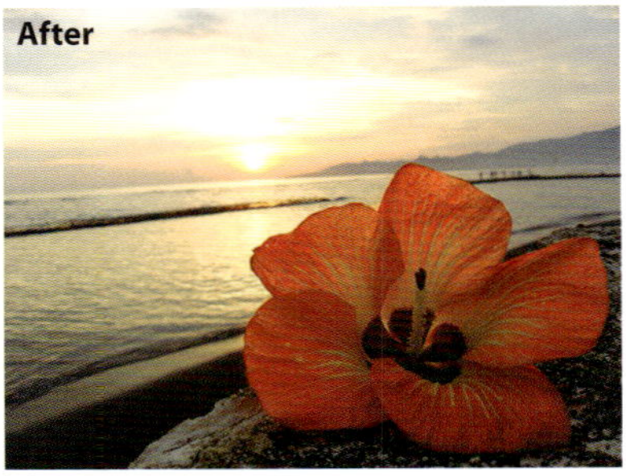

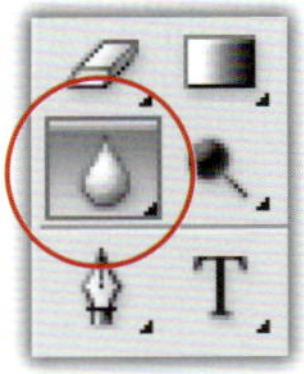

Back to our toolbox, let's select the **Blur tool**, located just to the left of the Dodge tool. The Blur tool has the effect of, well, blurring. The options bar looks pretty much the same; leave the mode on Normal and set Strength to 50%. As before, use a Hardness setting of zero. We use this tool to soften things, like a subject's complexion in a portrait, or a background.

Here is our image of the blossom on the lily pads. The crisp background has some particles in it and doesn't really add to the picture; if anything, it is distracting. By blurring the background just a bit, it recedes from our attention. (Notice that in all of these examples I am making very slight changes; this keeps the image realistic.)

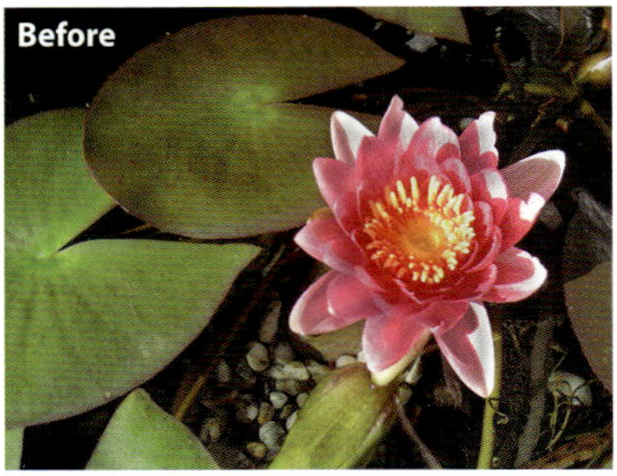

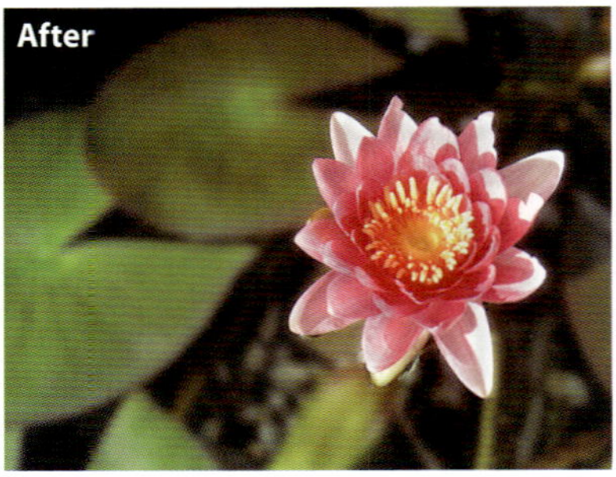

Underneath the Blur Tool is its counterpart, the **Sharpen tool**. This tool has the effect of making affected areas look sharper, more in focus. Later, when we discuss filters, we'll go through how this works. But for now, imagine that you have a portrait that has a lovely soft appearance but you would like to make the subject's eyes really pop out. You might want to lighten the highlights with the Dodge tool and then sharpen with the Sharpen tool. In the example below, I have sharpened up my favorite little cat. The effect is subtle but stare at it and you'll see a difference.

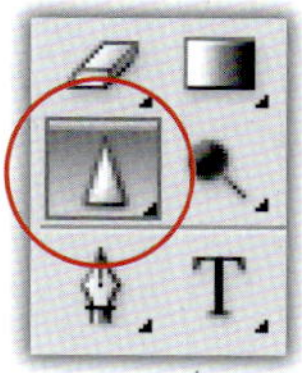

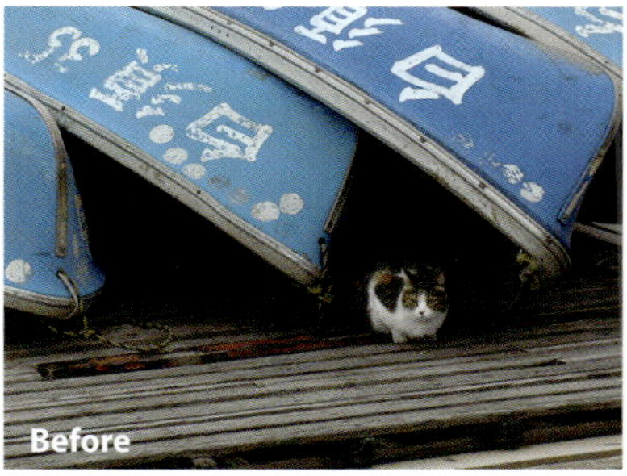

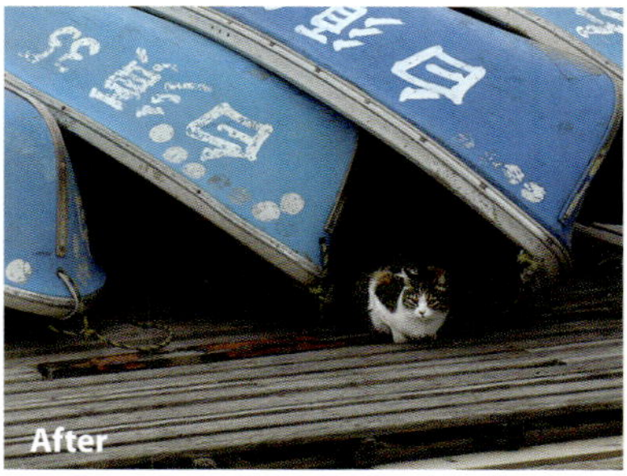

Last on our list, and at the bottom of the group nested under the Blur tool, is the **Smudge tool**. This tool, as its icon suggests, is best described as a finger painter; it smooshes pixels around as we click and drag across our image. Mode should be Normal and Strength should be set according to our needs. The bigger the brush, the bigger the "point of your finger." And as with the other tools reviewed in this chapter, the softer the brush, the more the effect will be feathered at the brush edge.

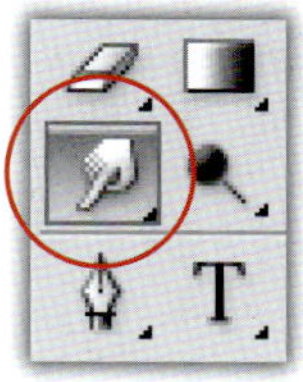

I don't have many applications for this tool to suggest (other than occupying your children) but we will put it to good use in Chapter 45.

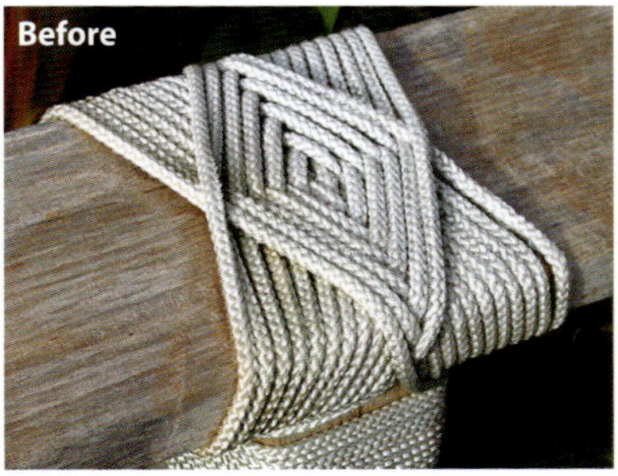

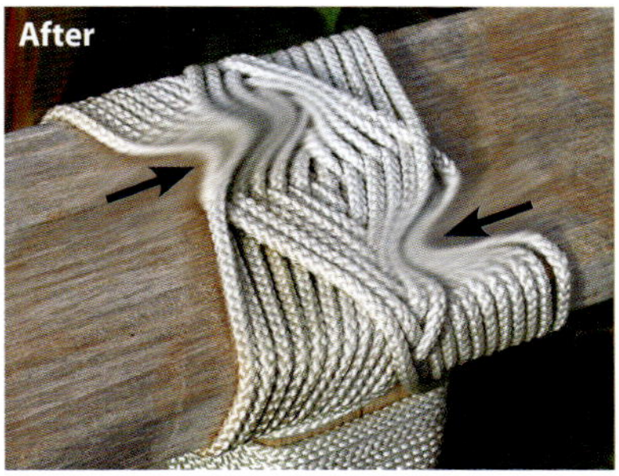

18. FIXING DEFECTS

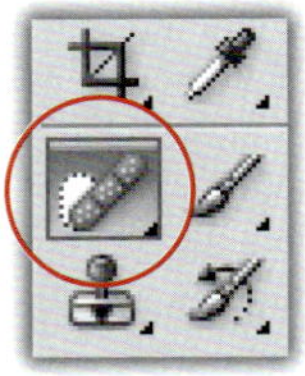

This chapter deals with getting rid of small defects in our images. (One could argue that this is image alteration as opposed to enhancement but I'm leaving it in this section anyway.) We will start with the Spot Healing Brush tool. (The other tools we'll discuss in this chapter, the Healing Brush, the Patch tool and the Red Eye tool, are all nested underneath the Spot Healing Brush). All of these tools help us deal with imperfections in our images, from dust particles to scratches to pimples to red eye.

The **Spot Healing Brush tool** is designed to help us eliminate simple defects or blemishes in our images. In the example below, we can see where a (huge) dust particle has landed on my image sensor and has created a black dot in the image. To correct this, we select the Spot Healing Brush tool and, using the options bar, open the brush pull-down menu. Hardness should be set to the maximum and the Spacing to minimum. (Angle should already be set to 0, Roundness to 100%, and Size to Off.) Lastly we set a diameter just larger than the defect we want to correct. This is the last time I'll mention using the left and right bracket keys, [and]. In the options bar, we make sure that Mode is Normal and Type is Proximity Match. Lots of settings!

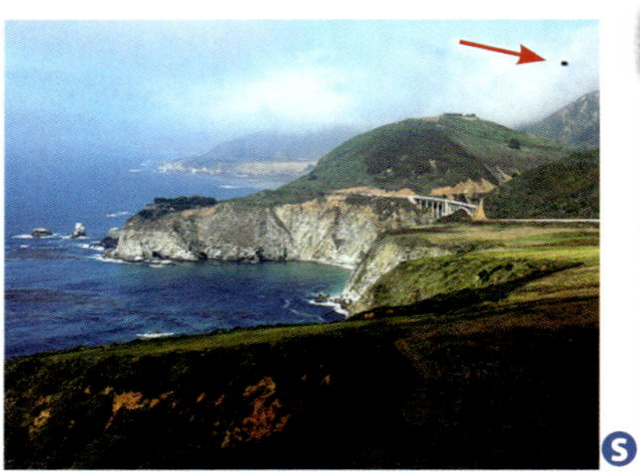

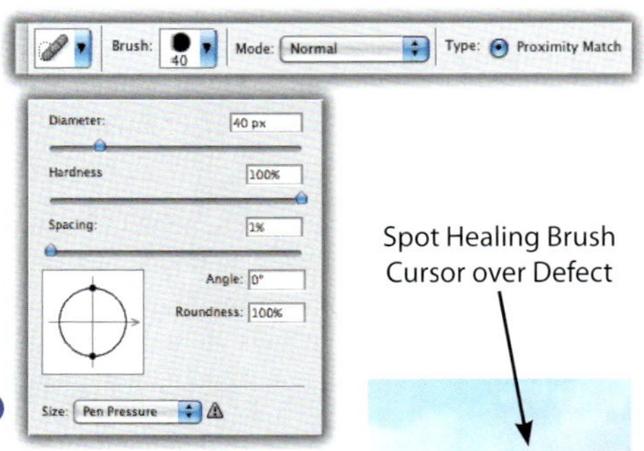

Spot Healing Brush Cursor over Defect

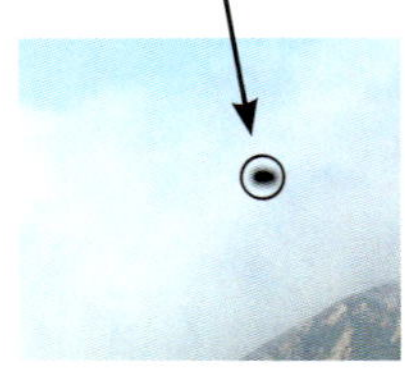

Ready to Click...

Positioning the Spot Healing Brush over the dust spot, we click once and the spot disappears. What the tool did was to look for out-of-place pixels within the brush cursor and then replace them with pixels sampled from the proximity. This works really well for defects on a fairly uniform background.

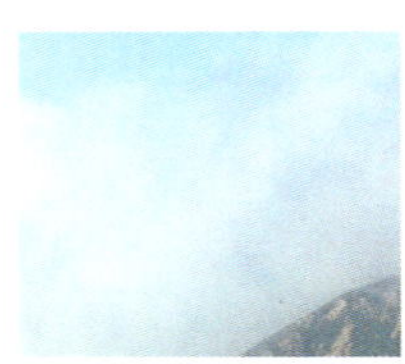

And Presto!

A brush can click and drag as well, right? So can we remove wrinkles and scratches? But of course. We select a diameter just bigger than the width of the wrinkle or scratch and click and drag along its length. As we drag, the brushed area turns dark but once we release the mouse button, the repair takes place and the wrinkle or scratch disappears.

The Spot Healing Brush can run into problems if the background is not uniform because it has trouble distinguishing what's really out of place. Remember, it samples all around the defect. Here I've simulated a defect just above this house on the hill. When I use the Spot Healing Brush, it grabs some pixel information from the house and weaves it into the replacement pixels, creating unwanted artifacts (a white splotch).

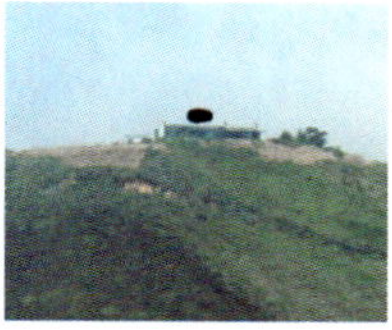

With Spot Healing...

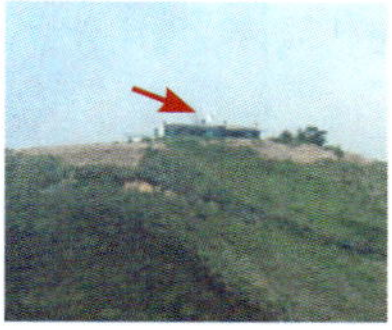

We can get artifacts

Enter the **Healing Brush tool**, nested under the Spot Healing Brush. Its options bar is very similar to that of the Spot Healing Brush. Set the brush options as before. Keep Mode set to Normal and set Source to Sampled.

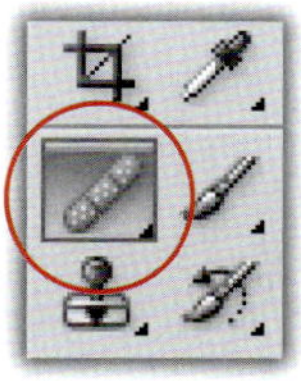

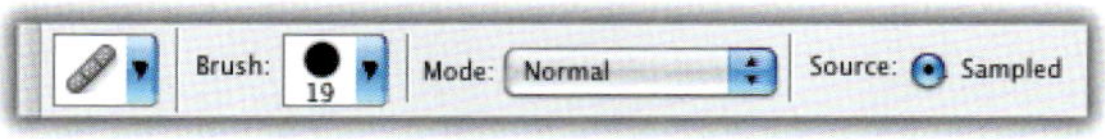

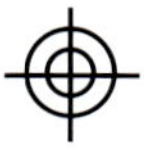

Cursor when setting the source.

Instead of sampling pixels around the brush cursor for the healing process, the Healing Brush has us identify another source for this sampling, from anywhere in the image. We do this by choosing another location with a background and texture similar to the area to be healed and then make it our "source" by holding down Opt(Alt), clicking on it and then releasing. (Notice how the cursor changes into a little target when we depress the Opt(Alt) key.)

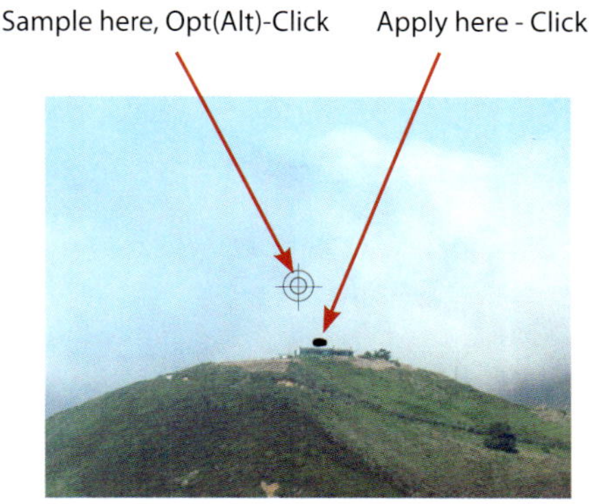

Now when we click (or click and drag) on our defect, the healing brush samples from the source point and melds those pixels into the area to be healed. This brush does not copy pixels over, it actually blends the sampled pixels into the texture and lighting of the area to be healed so that it all matches. I find this truly magical.

Since our defect is oblong and placed right up close to the house top, I opted to make a oval brush to better fit it. To do this, use the Roundness control in the Brush menu.

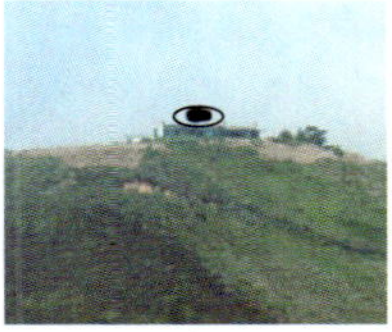

Oval Healing Brush

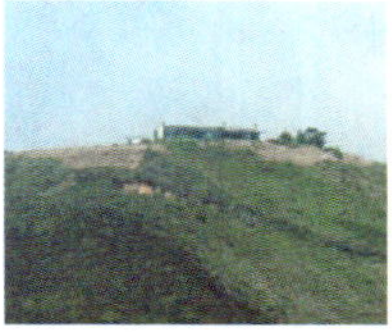

A Clean Result

The **Patch tool**, nested third in the list underneath the Spot Healing tool, takes a little getting used to but it worth the effort. It combines the power of the Lasso Selection tool (see Chapter 6) with that of the Healing Brush to allow irregularly shaped areas to be healed. Let's say we want to get rid of the long shadow in the lower right hand corner of the image below. We select the Patch tool and, in the options bar, make sure that the New Selection icon and Source radio button are selected.

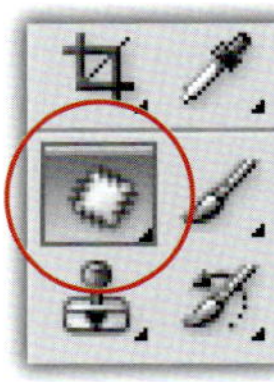

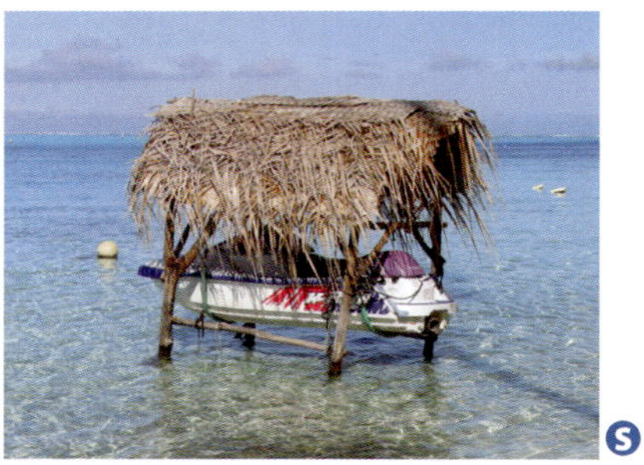

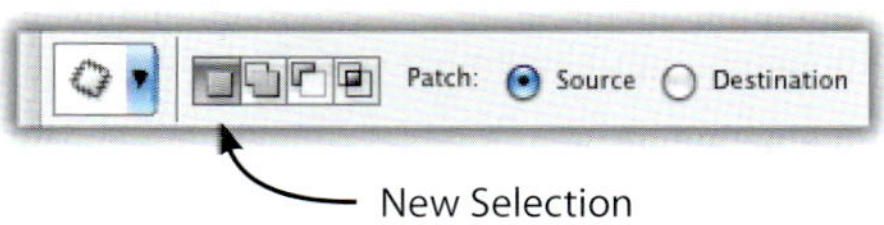

Next, we drag the cursor around the area to be healed, releasing when the selection boundary is closed. This is a standard Lasso selection. We then click within the selection and drag it to another location in the image that is similar but defect free. When we release the mouse button, Photoshop thinks a moment and then melds the area we dragged to into the originally selected area, matching texture and lighting. This is just like the Healing Brush.

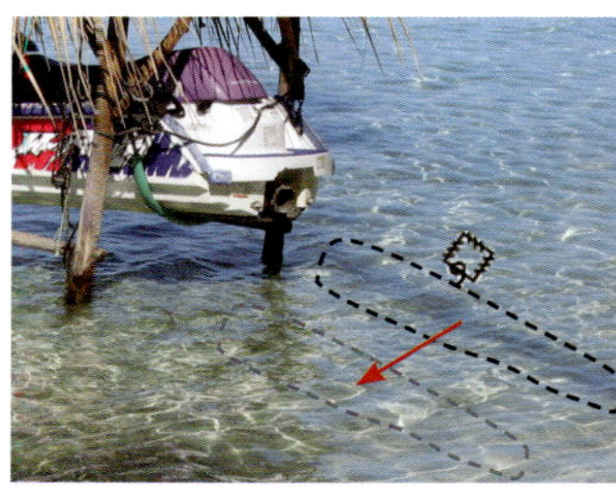

Select then click and drag...

By choosing Source in the options bar, we told Photoshop to replace, or patch, the originally selected area, the source, with information from the area we dragged to, the destination. This can be reversed by choosing Destination in the options bar. But I find using Source to be the more intuitive of the two.

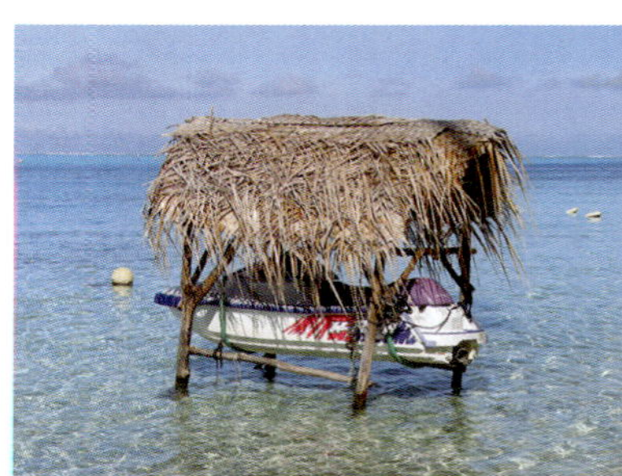

And the shadow disappears

This leaves the last tool, the **Red Eye tool**, the final tool nested under the Spot Healing Brush. We have all seen this defect; light from our camera's flash reflects off our subject's retinas and is recorded as red by the camera, giving our subject red pupils. Many cameras have a "red eye mode" which flickers the flash prior to the main flash, causing the subject's pupils to close down. This helps but doesn't always eliminate the problem. Red Eye tool to the rescue.

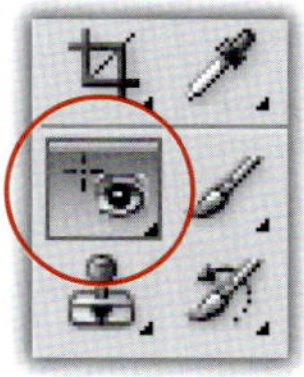

The first step is to blow up our image so that we can see what we are working with. With our Zoom tool (or the Cmd(Ctrl)-Spacebar shortcut), we drag a marquee around the villainous eyes to magnify them on our screen. Then we select the Red Eye tool from the toolbox. A simple click in each pupil will probably adequately fix the problem.

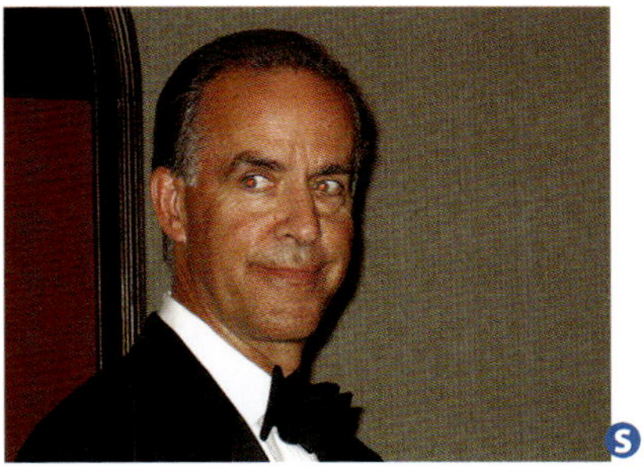

There are a couple of settings for us to play with that can create even better results. In the options bar, we see a box for Pupil Size and a box for Darken Amount, both with a default of 50% (or the last value used). Pupil Size refers to how large a dot the pupil should be in relation to the surrounding iris and Darken Amount allows you to change the shade of gray used to replace red color. If our subject has light colored eyes, we might consider using a lower Darken Amount, maybe 30%. (If it doesn't look right, we choose Edit>Undo and try again with a different amount). For a subject with brown eyes, perhaps we would choose 70%.

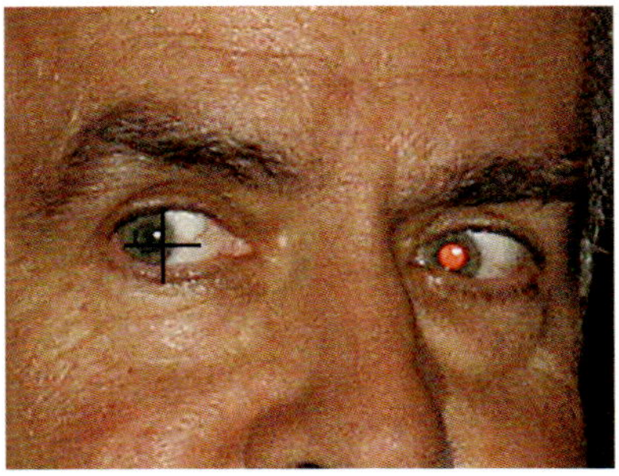

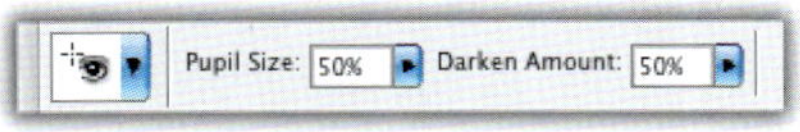

It is generally a good idea to complete all levels and hue/saturation enhancements prior to attempting these healing techniques. The reason for this is that slight artifacts introduced during the healing process can get aggravated during the levels and hue/saturation steps. If healing is saved for last, this won't happen.

Vibrance Adjustment: New to CS4 is a vibrance adjustment. This adjustment gives us an effect very similar to what we see with a saturation adjustment but with a subtle, but important, difference. In fact vibrance, found under Image>Adjustments> Vibrance, is so similar to saturation that a saturation slider is included in its controls.

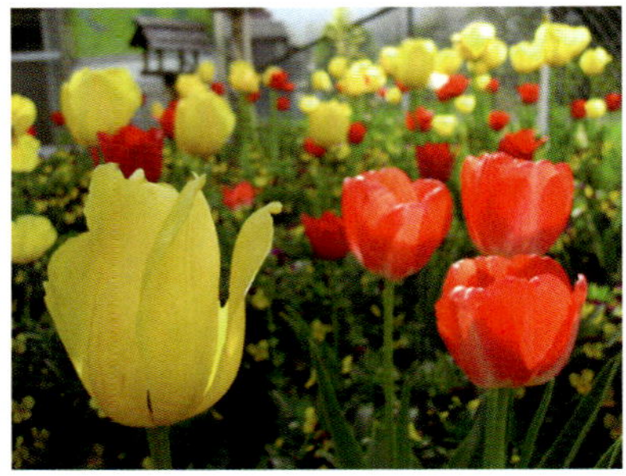
Original

When we do a saturation adjustment, Photoshop boosts the intensity of all colors uniformly. So pixels with colors that are already pretty saturated get pumped up as much as pixels with colors that are low in saturation. What this means is that colors that are already saturated may get completely maxed out.

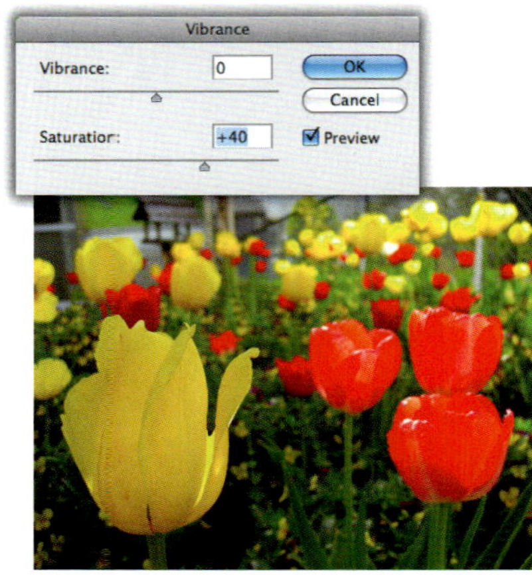

After saturation adjustment

In our examples to the right, the red in the tulips is already pretty saturated. If we open the vibrance adjustment and apply a +40 to the saturation slider, we see that much of the red detail begins to disappear. It has been maxed out. The greens and the yellows look okay because they were not very saturated to begin with.

Now what if we were to make the same adjustment using the vibrance slider. We see that the greens and yellows have been punched up as before but now the reds have been largely left alone. Vibrance adjusts the saturation shift according to the existing saturation. Pixels of low saturation get the full adjustment. But highly saturated pixels may hardly be changed. Vibrance protects the detail in the image, giving us a better result.

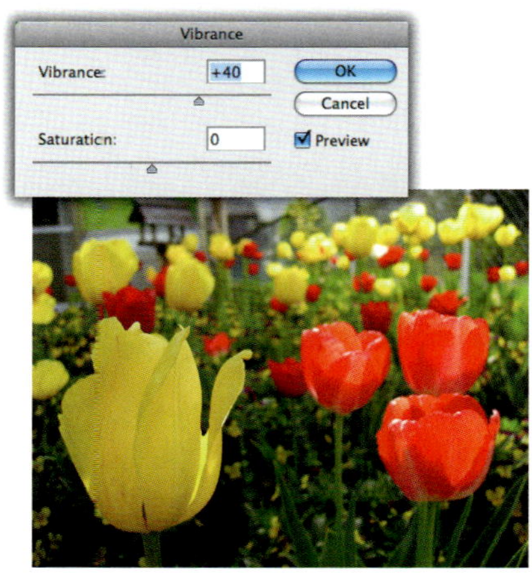

After vibrance adjustment

Vibrance is a great adjustment and I now almost always use it in place of saturation.

SECTION III

INTRODUCTION TO LAYERS

So far, so good, right? So now it's time to kick it up a notch.

This section is about layers, the real powerhouse of Photoshop. With layers, we can merge different images together into a single image, we can float text anywhere we want on an image, or we can extract an item from one image and place it in another. In fact, the number of things we can do with layers is only limited by our imaginations. They are that powerful.

We've actually already been working with layers. Well, at least with one of them. When we open up an image, it loads into a layer–the Background layer. The array of pixels is a layer. Photoshop allows us to have multiple layers. (We saw this when we made a copy of the Background layer.) The individual layers are stacked on top of each other and what we see on our screens is a composite of those layers. But I'm getting ahead of myself.

In this chapter, we will learn about layers–how to create them and how to manage them. We will also learn about adjustment layers, a special type of layer that performs image adjustments similar to those we studied in Section II. Then we will introduce layer styles, our first venture into Photoshop special effects. And as if all this wasn't enough, we're also going to learn how to work with text in Photoshop.

Enough with the preliminaries. We took nice little test drives in Sections I and II but now it is time to buckle up.

19. LAYERS

Let's start by building a simple Photoshop document with four layers; I will call it Triad for purposes of discussion. Here's what we'll make and how to do it.

As you can tell by the Sample Image icon, Ⓢ, this example file is included with the downloadable images available to you at www.JustTheSkinny.com/support.html. Consider making your own copy, however, per the directions below. The sooner you get going with the Layers panel, the better off you will be.

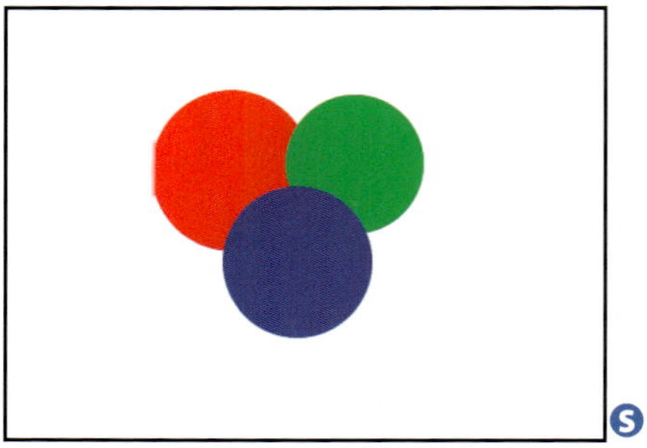

1. Choose File>New, making sure Default Photoshop Size is selected and click OK. Choose File>Save, name the document Triad, and save it somewhere.
2. Choose Layer>New>Layer and name it Red. Click OK. Notice this new layer has shown up in the Layers panel (Chapter 4) above the white Background layer. (If the Layers panel is not visible, select Windows>Layers.)
3. With the Elliptical Marquee tool (see Chapter 6), and with Feather set to zero in the options bar, make a circle like the red one shown above. Remember you can use Select>Transform Selection if you need to resize or reposition your selection.
4. Click on the Swatches panel (see Chapter 8) and select a red color by clicking on it. Your foreground color is now red.
5. Choose Edit>Fill, Use Foreground Color and click OK. The circle selection fills with red. Choose Select>Deselect.
6. Choose Layer>New>Layer and name it Green. Click OK. Notice the new layer has shown up in the Layers panel, just above the Red layer.
7. With the Elliptical Marquee tool and holding down the shift key, make another circle to the right of the red circle and partially overlapping it as shown above.
8. Click on the Swatches panel and select a green color. The foreground color becomes green.
9. Choose Edit>Fill, Use Foreground Color and click OK. The circle selection fills with green. Choose Select>Deselect.
10. Choose Layer>New>Layer and name it Blue. Click OK. Notice this new layer has also shown up in the Layers panel, above the Green layer.
11. With your Elliptical Marquee tool and holding down the shift key, make a third circle, below the first two and partially overlapping both as shown above.
12. Choose a blue color from the Swatches panel and Edit>Fill the circle. The last circle is now blue. Choose Select>Deselect.

Recall that when we load an image into Photoshop, it stores as an array of pixels, where each pixel contains a variety of information like color, intensity, etc. That array of pixels is called a layer and is by default named Background. (We will discuss the Background layer in a moment as it has special properties.) But the power of layers is that there can be more than one. Each layer is its own unique array of pixels (but all layers in a single document have identical resolution and dimension). And, except in special circumstances, each layer is independent of the others. Our example has four layers.

A **layer** is like a transparent plastic sheet with something (like our colored circles) printed on it. If we have three plastic sheets with red, green, and blue circles on them and stack those sheets with red on the bottom, green in the middle, and blue on top, the blue circle would cover parts of the green and red circles and the green circle would cover part of the red one. From the top, it would look just like our example.

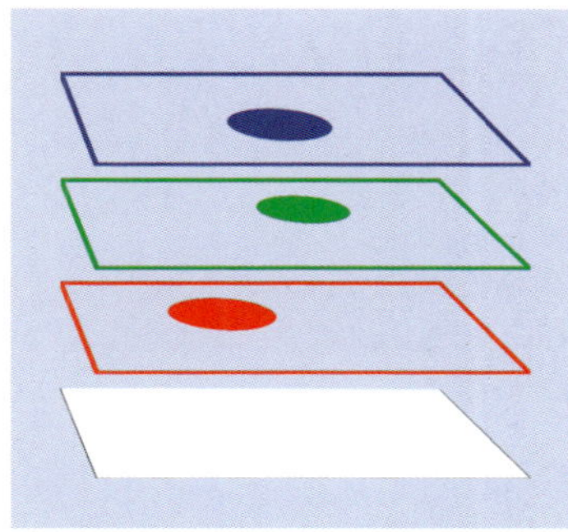

If we look over in the **Layers panel**, we see the stack as I have described it. Each thumbnail visually represents its layer and they are stacked on top of each other, red on the bottom, green in the middle, and blue on top. (Background is below everything.) We can also reorder the stacking. Click and drag the Red layer up until the line between the Green and Blue layers is highlighted and release. The stacking order changes to Red above Green, both in the panel and on the image.

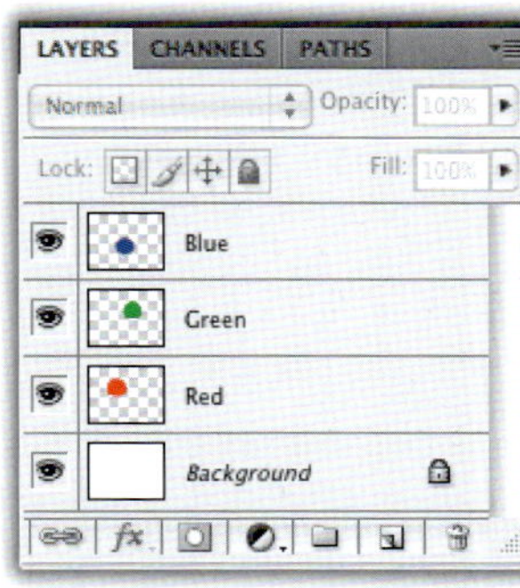

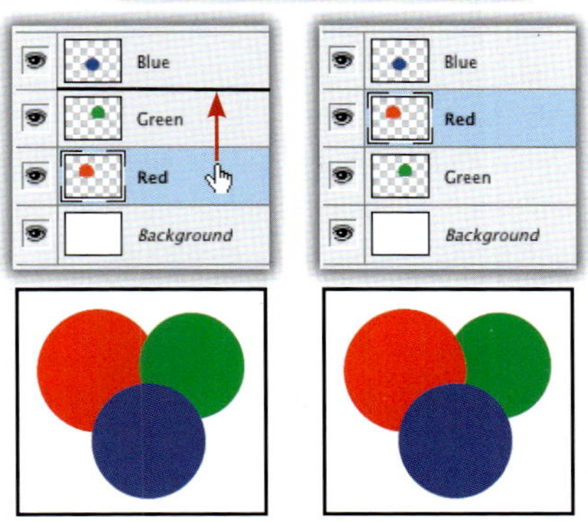

Before reordering After reordering

The eyeball icon to the left of each thumbnail indicates that the layer visibility is "on." It's often useful to hide a layer; clicking this icon will toggle that layer's visibility off and on. Toggle Green off and on and note the effect. Now toggle Background off, hiding the white background. The light checkerboard pattern you'll see indicates transparency (i.e. the clear plastic sheet).

Let's study the Layers panel in a little more detail. We just talked about the stack and the stacking order. When we click on a layer, it turns light blue, indicating it is selected. The concept of selecting a layer is extremely important because if we want to make edits on a layer, we must first select it. In fact, when Photoshop is giving me unexpected results, I almost always look first to see if I am on the right layer. Except in special cases, Photoshop works on one layer at a time.

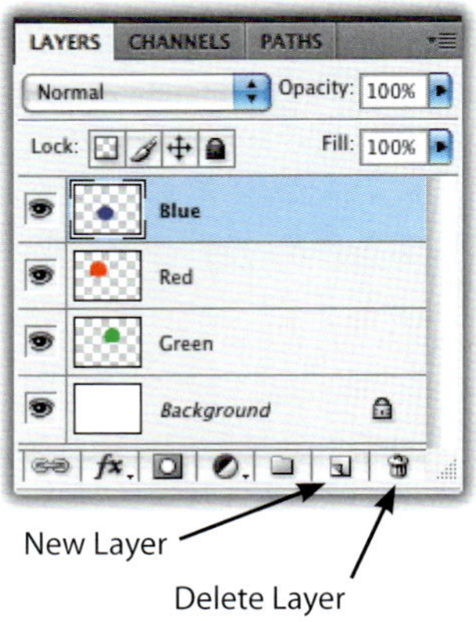

The box near the top with Normal in it refers to blending modes; leave it set on Normal for now. Opacity controls a layer's transparency. Select the Blue layer and set the opacity to 50% to see it in action. Opacity makes a layer's content semitransparent but keeps it visible and editable. (Visibility completely hides it.) Opacity is useful as a special effect or for allowing us to see what's beneath a layer without having to totally hide it.

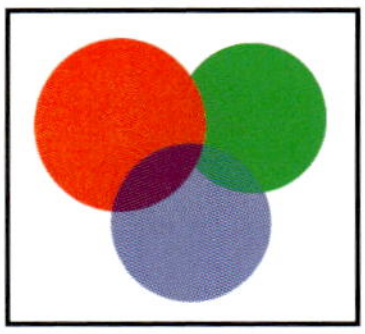

The Lock icons allow us to keep a layer visible but lock it from editing. Each icon locks different aspects of the layer but the padlock on the right locks everything. That's the one to use in the beginning. Ignore Fill for now.

At the bottom of the Layers panel there is another series of icons related to layer management. For now, let's focus on the two icons on the right. The trash can at the right is for deleting layers; clicking it with a layer selected deletes that layer. Alternatively, we can drag a layer on top of it for deletion. To the left of the trash can is the New Layer icon (it looks like a little tablet). Click on it and a new layer appears on the stack above the currently selected layer, or at the top if no layer is selected. (This is the same as choosing Layer>New>Layer). If we drag an existing layer on top of this icon, we get a copy of that layer, not a new layer. This is the easiest way to duplicate a layer.

Naming our layers with meaningful names is an extremely important practice. Photoshop has inventive names like Layer 2 and Layer 3 Copy. A month from now, they won't mean much to us. To rename a layer, double click on its name and type the new (much more meaningful) name.

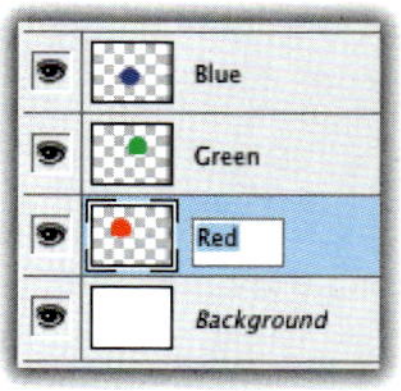

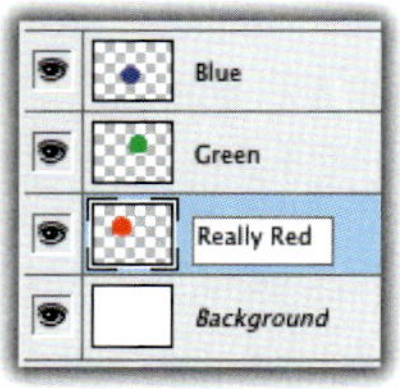

On more than one occasion, I have mentioned a special layer called Background. The time has finally come to learn about it. The table below summarizes the differences between a normal layer and the special **Background** layer.

Background	Normal
Always at the bottom of the stack	Anywhere on stack except below Background
Erased pixels become the background color	Erased pixels become transparent
Only 100% opacity	Can have varying opacity
Only one	As many as we need

Think of Background as a blank canvas as opposed to the transparent plastic sheet analogy I used above. Like a canvas, it is always at the bottom. (We always draw on top of the canvas, right?). If we have something drawn on a canvas and erase it, we get the color of the canvas, the background. The same is true of Background except that when we erase on this layer, we get the then current background color (the box under the foreground color), not necessarily the white default.

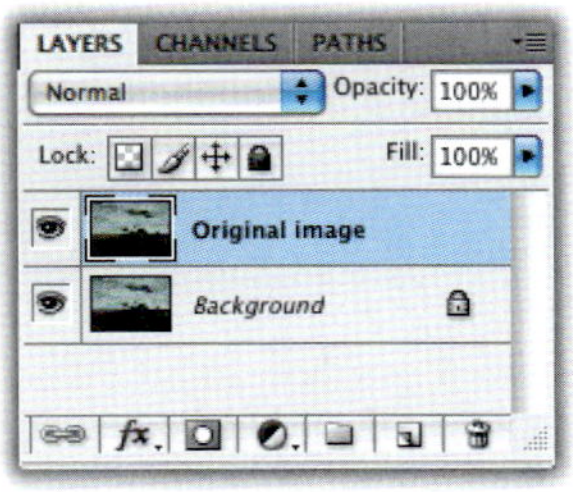

When I open a new image, I almost always first drag Background onto the New Layer icon thus duplicating it to a normal layer named Background Copy. Then I rename Background Copy something more meaningful. After that, I never touch Background. In this way, I maintain a layer with a completely unedited, original image.

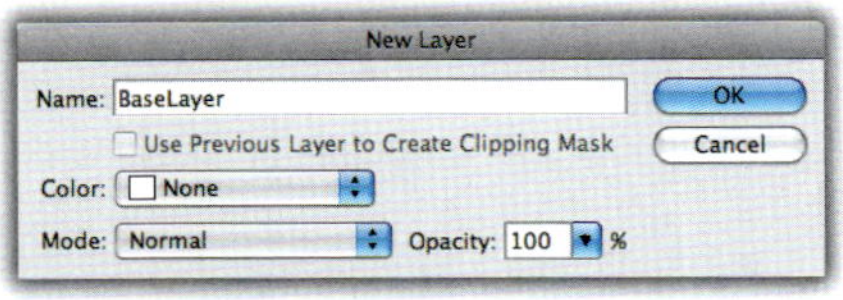

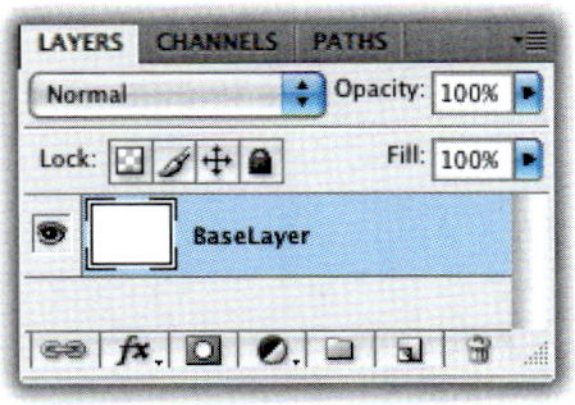

If I'm starting a new project from scratch, I actually find Background an unnecessary hassle. We could create a Background Copy, rename it, and then delete Background. A quicker way, though, is to double click on Background. This opens up a New Layer dialog box where we can rename the layer. When we click OK, Background assumes the new name and is converted into a normal layer.

I know we are at the end of the chapter but there is oh so much more to learn. Since I'm not willing to break my maximum-chapter-length-of-four-pages rule, we're just going to have to continue in the next chapter.

20. LAYERS ENCORE

Let's pick up where we left off in the previous chapter, but enough with the discussion. Let's have a little fun with an image from Paris.

First we'll open the image, duplicate Background by dragging its layer onto the New Layer icon, and rename the copied layer, ET (for Eiffel Tower). Next, we'll hide Background, select the ET layer and then choose the Eraser tool. With the Eraser tool we erase everything on the layer but the Eiffel Tower, using a small diameter for the nooks and crannies and a larger diameter for the rest. We just extracted the Eiffel Tower pixels–all of the other pixels in the layer are empty, transparent. Notice the change to the ET layer thumbnail.

After copying Background

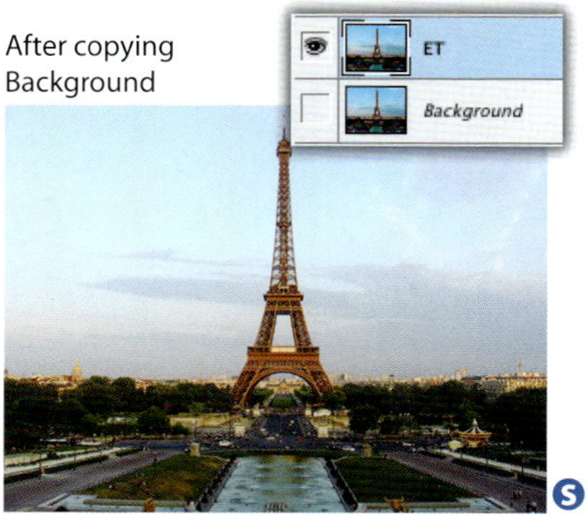

After extracting the Eiffel Tower

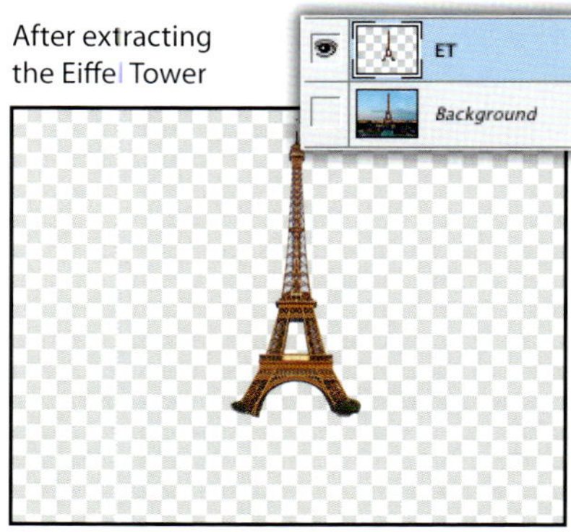

Our next step is to unhide the Background layer so that it is visible to us again. Then, with the ET layer selected, we choose the Move tool (Chapter 6) and drag the extracted Eiffel Tower to a new location on the image. Only the Eiffel Tower pixels on the ET layer have content, the rest are transparent. So now it appears as if there are two identical Eiffel Towers in our image (which would shorten the wait to go up). This gives us a feel for the power of layers.

Moving extracted Eiffel Tower

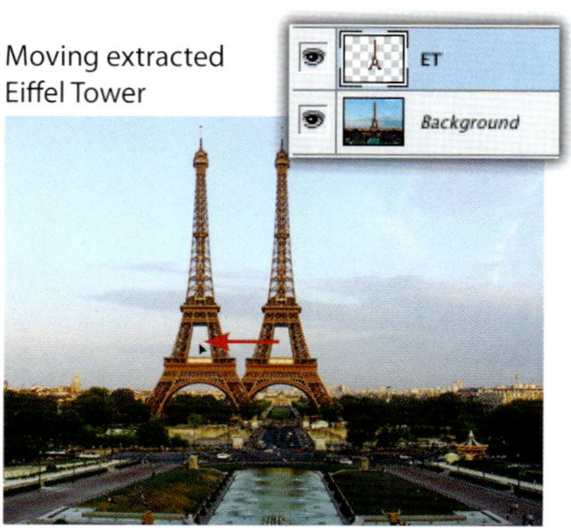

Final image

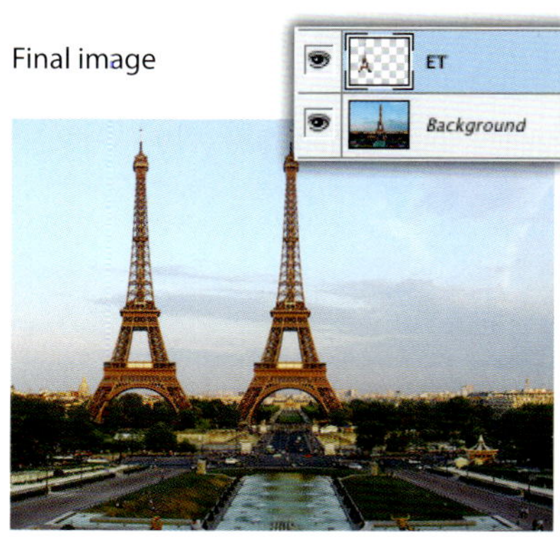

This method for extracting an object works okay but there are much better ways. Instead of copying the entire Background layer and then erasing the pixels we don't want, what if we only copied the pixels we did want on to the new layer. This is easily done using the selection techniques we discussed in Chapters 6 and 12.

We open our original image and, with the selection tool of our choice, make a selection around the object we wish to extract. We then choose Layer>New Layer>**Layer Via Copy**. Done! Only the selected pixels are copied to the new layer. (I do this so much that I'll mention the keyboard shortcut. It is Cmd(Ctrl)-J. Think of J for Jump.) If there were no pixels selected, by the way, the entire layer (the layer selected) would be copied, just as if it were dragged onto the New Layer icon in the Layers panel. (In my example, I jumped the Eiffel tower and then erased the section of sky in the middle.)

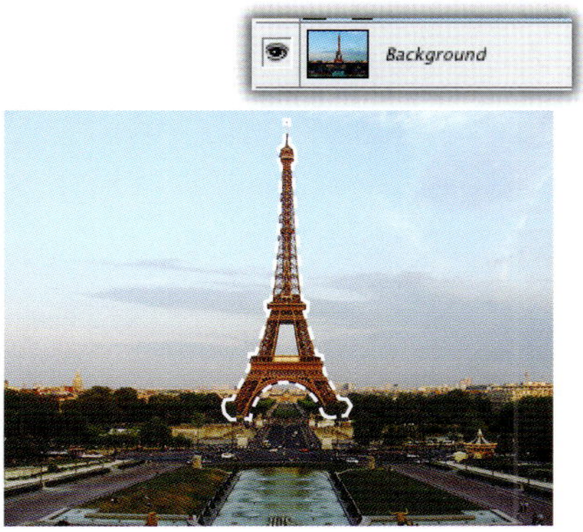

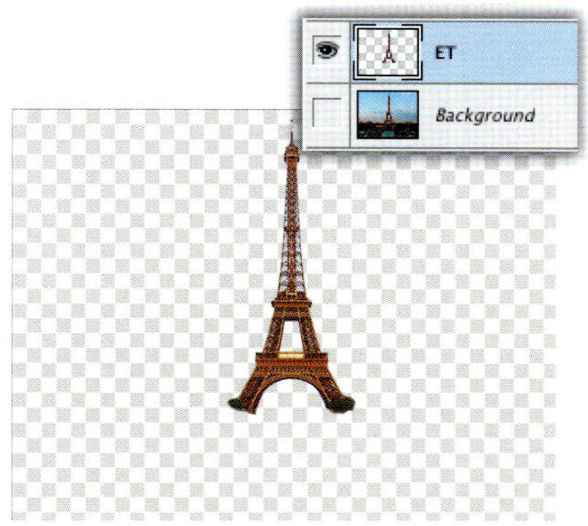

Let's spend a couple of moments reinforcing our understanding of the **Move tool**. We first used it in Chapter 6 to move selected pixels on a layer (our only layer at the time) elsewhere in the image. In doing so, because we only had one layer, the moved pixels permanently replaced the existing pixels. We just learned that to avoid this, we simply jump the selected pixels to a new layer and then move them. The moved pixels cover the preexisting pixels, but being on a new layer, they do not replace them. (We can verify this by turning off the visibility on the upper layer.)

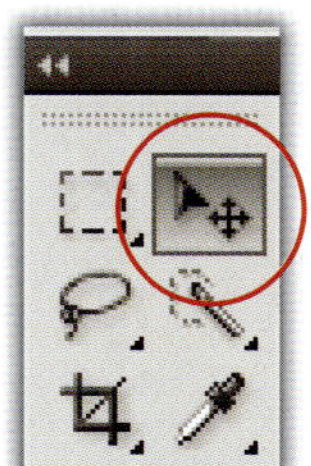
The Move tool

When we jumped our pixels to the new layer, our selection disappeared. But there's no need to reselect the jumped pixels. With nothing selected, the Move tool moves all pixels on that layer. By the way, if for some reason we did want our selection back, we can easily get it back by holding down Cmd(Ctrl) and clicking on the thumbnail for the jumped layer in the Layers panel. Photoshop selects all of the nontransparent pixels on the layer.

Next let's look at sharing layers between different documents. In the example above, we extracted an object and copied it to a new layer within the same document. What if we wanted to place it in a new document, on a new background? It's easy, of course.

After we extract the Eiffel Tower onto its own layer, as described above, we open a separate image, the one that will serve as our new locale. Now Photoshop has two document windows open, our original and the new one. The document window for the new locale is on top of the Paris original and is the active document window.

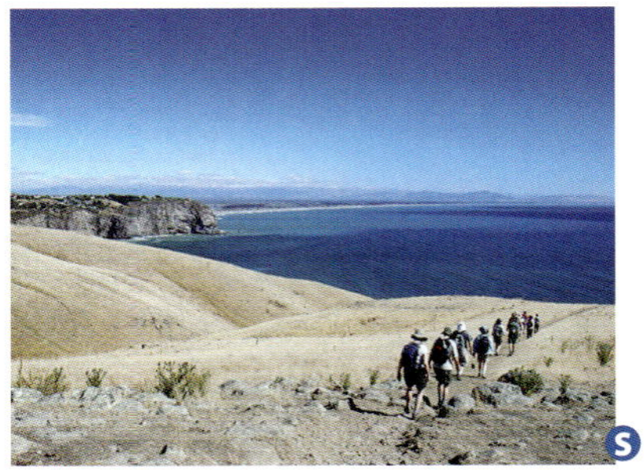

Now we do the following. We choose Window in the menu bar and at the bottom of the menu, we select the original Paris document. This makes our Paris document with the extracted ET layer the active document and brings it to the front. With the extracted ET layer selected, we open the Layers panel menu and select **Duplicate Layer**.

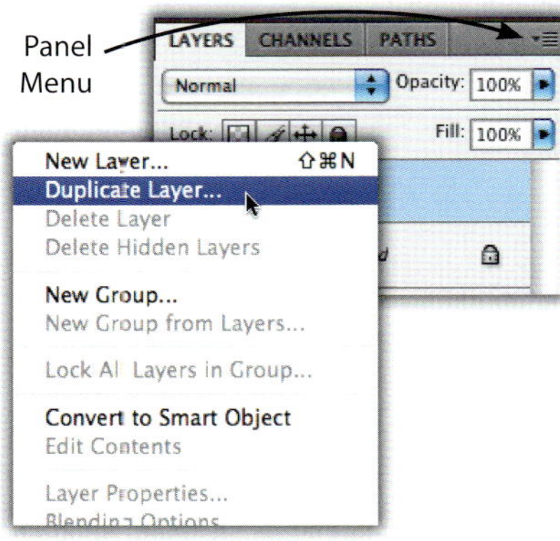

This brings up a Duplicate Layer dialog box. Here we can rename the copy we are about to make but more importantly, we can choose a destination for it. We click on the Destination/Document pulldown, and choose the new image (NewLocale) document. (The NewLocale document must be open for it to be available here.) When we click OK, the ET layer is copied into the NewLocale document as a new layer and with the name we just chose.

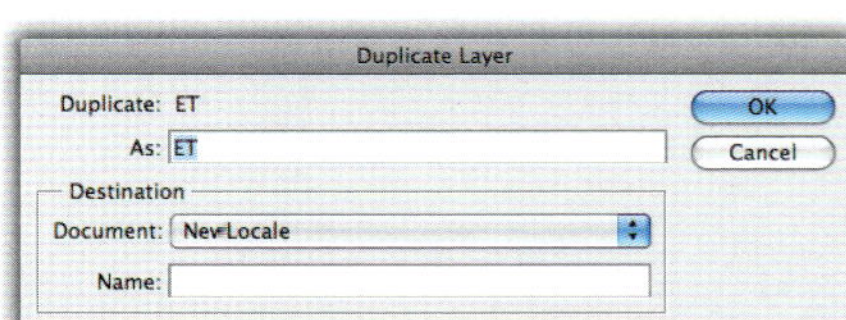

The original document is still open so we either need to close it or shift to the NewLocale document via the Window menu. There's the ET layer copy. Now we need only select the Move tool and, with the ET layer selected, reposition it to our liking.

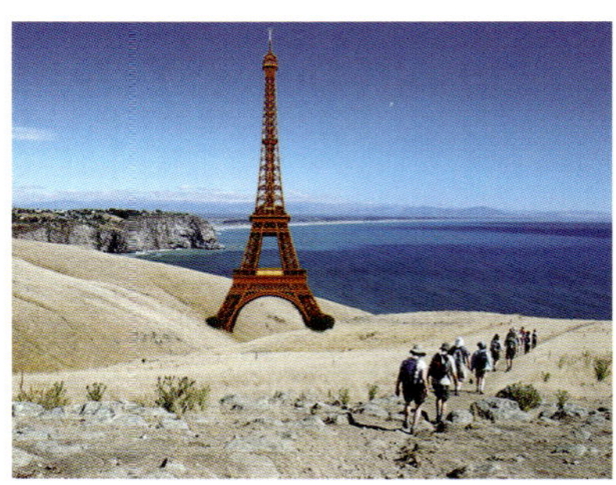

Let's do another example, one with a slightly different wrinkle to it, just to make sure we have the hang of it. We'll return to the Forbidden City image from Chapter 12 that needed a better sky. This time, let's give it an actual new sky. We first use our selection tool of choice to select the foreground. (I actually used the Magic Wand to select the sky and then inversed the selection.) We then choose Layer>New>Layer Via Copy (or Cmd(Ctrl)-J) to create a new layer with just the building on it.

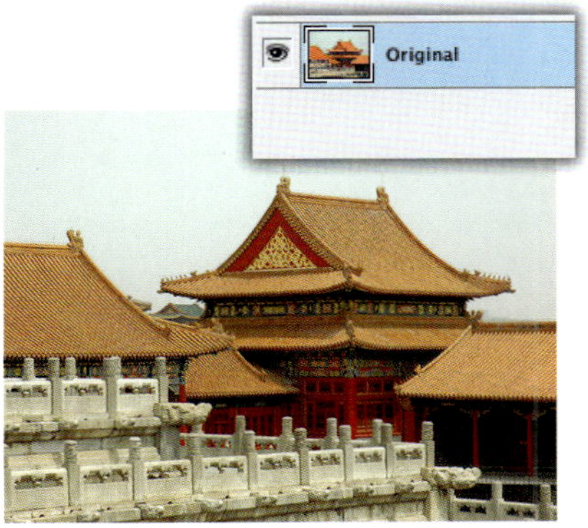

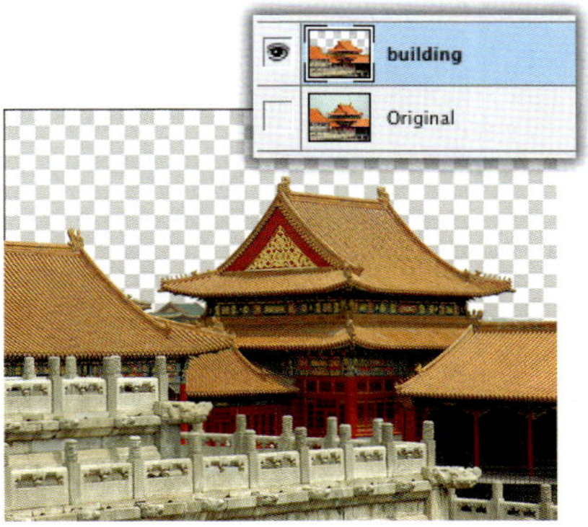

Now we find a new image, one with an pleasing cloudy sky, and open it. As before, we go back to our original document (select it under Window), choose the building layer and, using Duplicate Layer from the Layers panel menu, duplicate that layer with the cloudy sky document as the destination. (It will copy in above the sky.) Switching back to the cloudy sky document, we see we have what we want, a cloudy sky behind our building. A quick adjust with the Move tool if necessary and we're done.

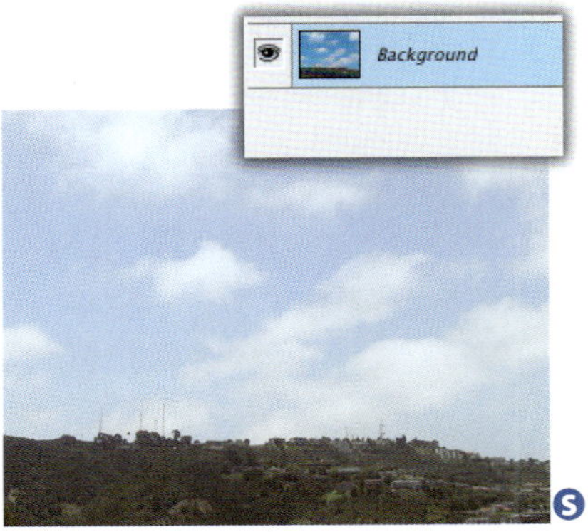

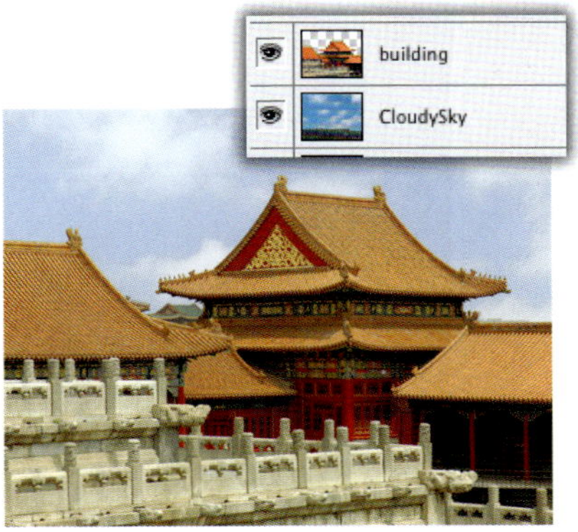

Trouble will arise when our original and destination images are very different sizes. We'll learn to fix this kind of problem with the Transform command in an upcoming chapter. Patience please.

Back in our section on Image Enhancing, we learned several techniques for improving images. We learned how to use Levels to refine contrast. We learned how to use Hue/Saturation to adjust color. And then there was Dodge and Burn and a host of other tools. One attribute that all of these tools share is that they are not modifiable once we hit the OK button. **Adjustment layers**, the subject of this chapter, give us a better way to perform these enhancements along with many of the others in the Image>Adjustments menu. They are better because they are modifiable at any time.

First I'll show you how to make adjustment layers and then I'll explain how they work. At the bottom of the Layers panel there is a New Adjustment Layer icon, the half-filled circle. With an image open, clicking this icon brings up a menu of all the possible adjustment layers. Levels is there, as is Hue/Saturation, and a bunch more.

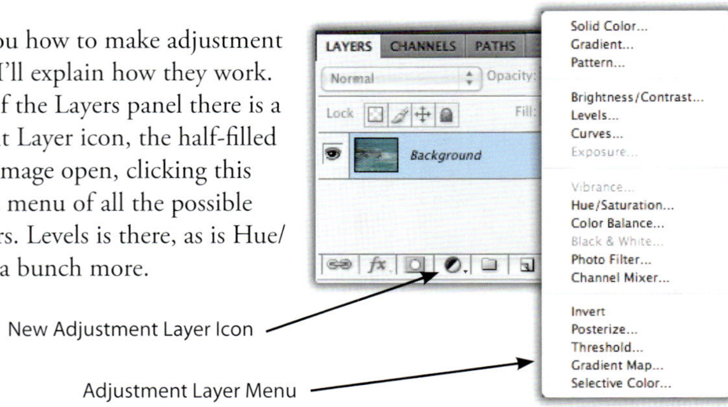

If we choose Levels, a familiar Levels dialog box is brought up for us to play with. It appears in the Adjustments panel (new to CS4) just above the Layers panel. We make our adjustments and click OK and see an improvement in contrast just as if we had used Image>Adjustments>Levels. See more on the new Adjustment panel in the CS4 tips at the end of this section.

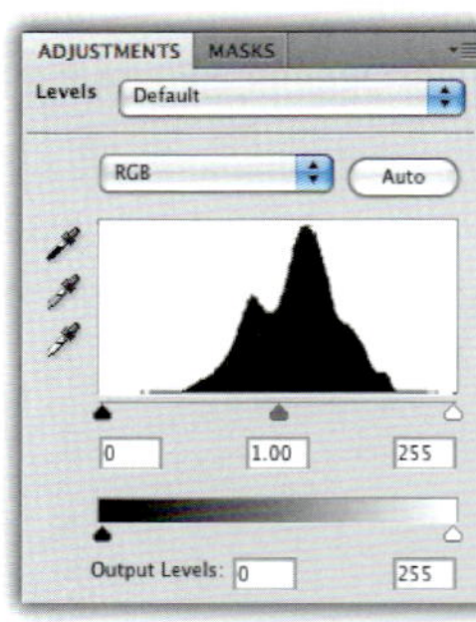

One difference, though, is that if we look over in the Layers panel, we see that a new layer has been created above our image; it's been named Levels 1. This is an adjustment layer, our very first. Congrats! Notice that the thumbnail looks like a little histogram, our visual clue that it is a Levels adjustment layer. Next to the histogram thumbnail is another thumbnail, a white box. Ignore that for now–we'll discuss it in a bit.

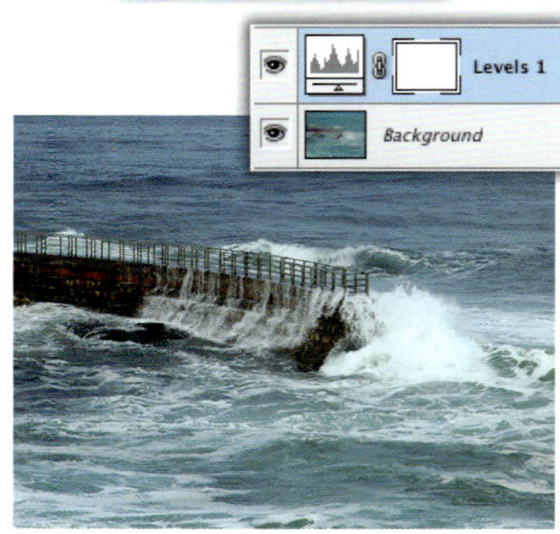

Now here's the magic. If we double click on the Levels 1 layer thumbnail, the Levels dialog box pops up again with the adjustments we just made still intact, available to be changed if we so desire. At any time we want, right now, or a year from now, we can make changes or even restore the original (by resetting, hiding, or even deleting the adjustment layer all together). With adjustment layers, if we adjust Levels and then Hue/Saturation, we can still go back and fine tune Levels.

Now you might be wondering why this is different from just doing multiple Image>Adjustment>Levels steps. It's a good question. The answer is that every time we perform an Image>Adjustment, we create a brand new adjustment. And each time we do an adjustment, we change pixels and lose some of the original detail. Doing multiple adjustments just compounds this problem. With adjustment layers, we re-edit the original adjustment; we're not doing multiple adjustments. And with adjustment layers, we are not even touching the original pixels.

When Photoshop modifies an image via the Image>Adjustments menu, it physically changes the pixels on our image layer per our instructions. The original pixels on the image layer are overwritten, replaced by the modified pixels. But when Photoshop creates an adjustment layer, it creates a layer of effect, or instruction, instead of a layer of pixels. The effect layer modifies how we see the pixels, not the pixels themselves.

Imagine a semi-transparent blue plastic sheet superimposed over a photograph–it turns the photograph blue, right? Well, actually no, it doesn't. It changes our perception of the photo, making everything look more blue. But the underlying photograph is actually untouched; it looks just like it always did.

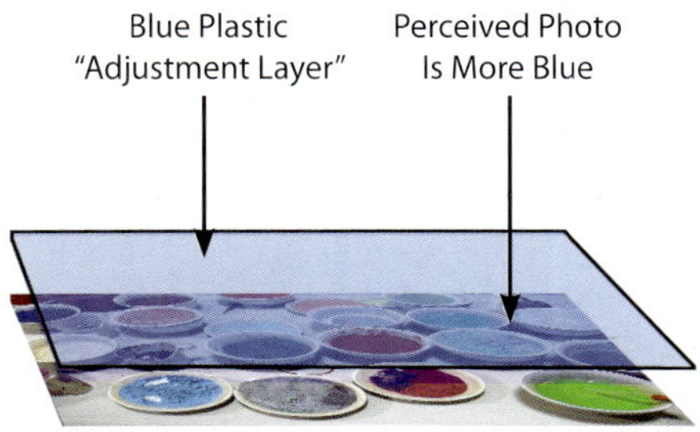

An adjustment layer works the same way. It doesn't change the underlying pixels, only how they are perceived.

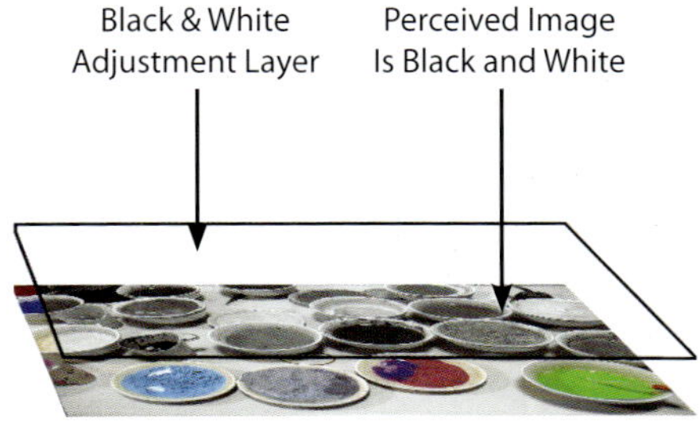

The last step is to realize that while colored plastic can change hue, adjustment layers can create all of the effects in the adjustment layer menu. And all without touching the underlying pixels. The Black & White adjustment layer, for example, makes it appear as if all color has been removed.

We can have as many adjustment layers as we want, all stacked on top of each other. Here is a Layers panel after a typical basic image enhancement. Background has been duplicated, as we have discussed, so as to maintain an unedited version. Then I've added a Levels adjustment layer followed by a Hue/Saturation adjustment layer. (The Hue/Saturation thumbnail looks like a little Color Picker with saturation picked.)

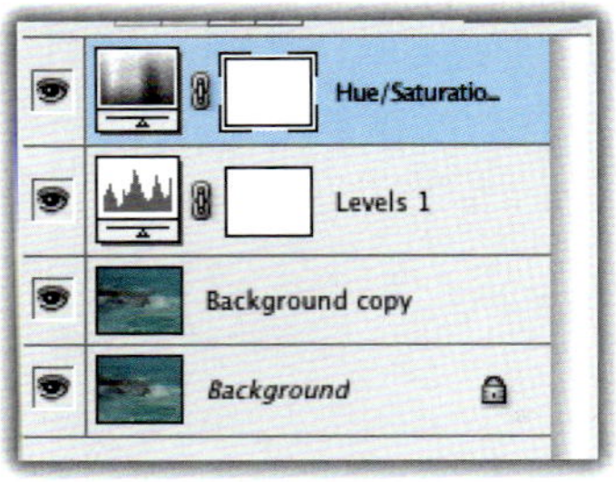

The stacking order is important. Each adjustment layer affects everything below it (just like a camera filter would). So the Levels adjustment layer affects the image layer only. But the Hue/Saturation adjustment layer affects both the Levels 1 and image layer. This is equivalent to having done Image>Adjustments>Levels followed by Image>Adjustments>Hue/Saturation.

We manage adjustment layers much as we manage ordinary layers. For example, we can toggle an adjustment layer's visibility on and off by clicking on the eyeball to the left of its thumbnail. This is a handy way of double-checking the effect of the adjustment. And we can rename it by double clicking on its name. (You might wonder why you would ever want to do this but, as we will see in the next chapter, there may be times when we will have multiple adjustment layers of the same type. Renaming them can make it easier to distinguish their purpose.)

Adjustment layers can also be copied from one document to another, using the same techniques we learned in Chapter 20. Suppose we took a number of pictures that were very similar in content and we wanted to apply the same image adjustments to all of them. We could open them all up at the same time, perform adjustments on one of them, and then duplicate the adjustment layers into the other documents. (By the way, if we select multiple layers by shift clicking, we can duplicate all of those layers at once with the Duplicate Layers command in the panel menu. (Note how the menu changed from "Layer" to "Layers.")

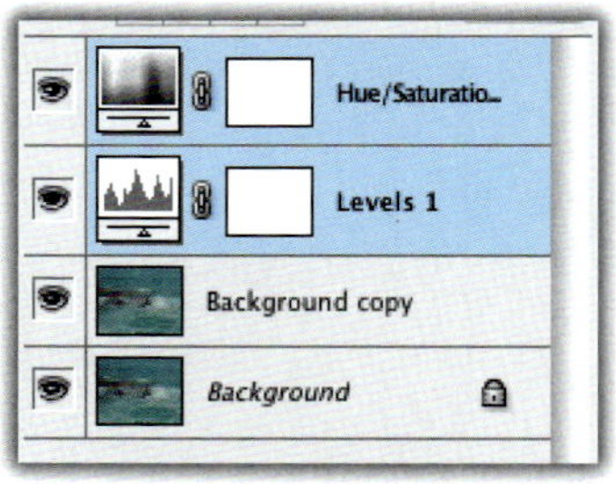

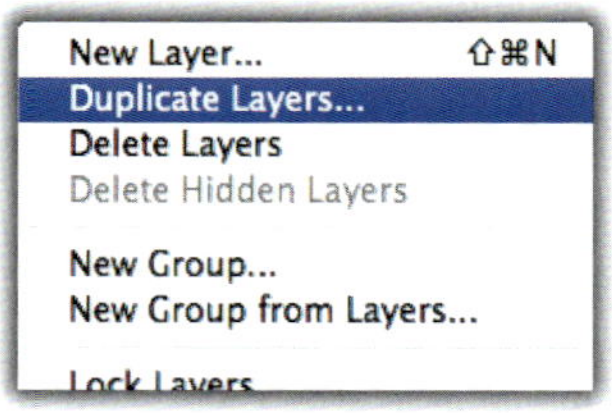

Since it is a layer, an adjustment layer can also have its opacity varied. This turns out to be a very valuable technique to fine tune adjustments as we add them. Recall in Chapter 19, we discussed how for a normal pixel layer, changing the opacity changed the layer's transparency. At 100% opacity, the pixels were fully opaque; at 0%, they were completely transparent and we could see right through them. Since an adjustment layer is an effect, 100% opacity now means that the effect is at full strength. 0% opacity means that the effect is essentially turned off; there is no effect. 50% opacity on an adjustment layer means that the effect occurs at half strength.

Here is an image that came out too warm or yellow. I tried to cool down with a Photo Filter adjustment layer, but the Blue Cooling (80) filter made it a bit too bluish. By backing the adjustment layer opacity down to 50%, I got what I was looking for.

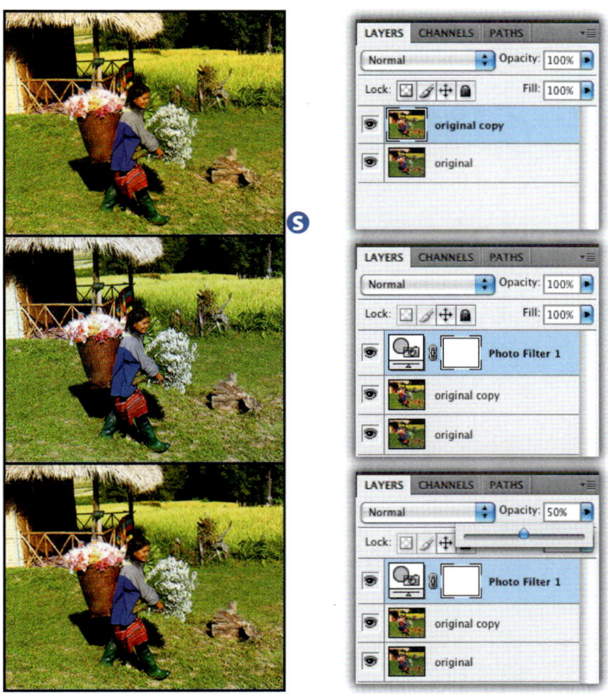

Original image is too yellow.

A Photo Filter adjustment layer is too blue. The field in back has lost its vibrance.

Changing the Photo Filter adjustment layer to 50% opacity is just right. The field looks good.

I've gone on and on about how wonderful adjustment layers are and you might be asking yourself what the downsides are. The biggest is probably that our file size grows. That and our Layers panel gets a bit more complex. From my perspective, though, these are pretty minor negatives compared with the huge advantages we get with adjustment layers. And actually, the best is still to come. In our next chapter, we will learn how to use adjustment layers to make adjustments to localized areas in our image.

So far, everything we have done with adjustment layers has been global, meaning that the entire image was affected equally. But back in Chapter 17, we learned some techniques for applying localized enhancements that were pretty useful. Wouldn't it be nice if we could marry the ability to do localized modifications with the many advantages of adjustment layers? Of course it would. And we can.

The secret lies in the little white box to the right of the adjustment thumbnail, the one we ignored in the last chapter. It's called a **Layer Mask** because it can be used to mask, or turn off, the effect of the adjustment layer. Think of it like an imaginary stencil underneath the adjustment layer that only allows the effect through its opening.

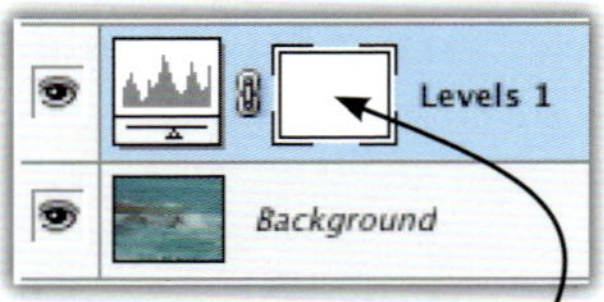

This layer mask thumbnail comes automatically with adjustment layers.

The layer mask thumbnail is just that, a thumbnail, a representation. The real layer mask is invisible to us. But the thumbnail allows us see what it looks like. We will learn to edit them in a moment but here's one that I've made look like a plus sign.

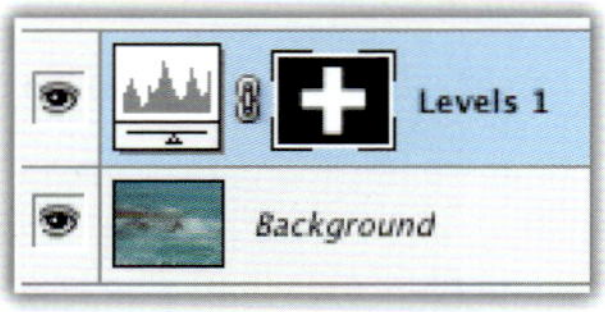

And here's is the imaginary stencil that would correspond to that plus sign layer mask. Where the layer mask is white, the stencil is open and the effect of the adjustment layer is allowed to interact with the underlying pixels in the image. Where the layer mask is black, the stencil is solid and blocks the effect of the adjustment layer on those underlying pixels. Only the adjustment layer effect is blocked, not our visibility of the underlying image.

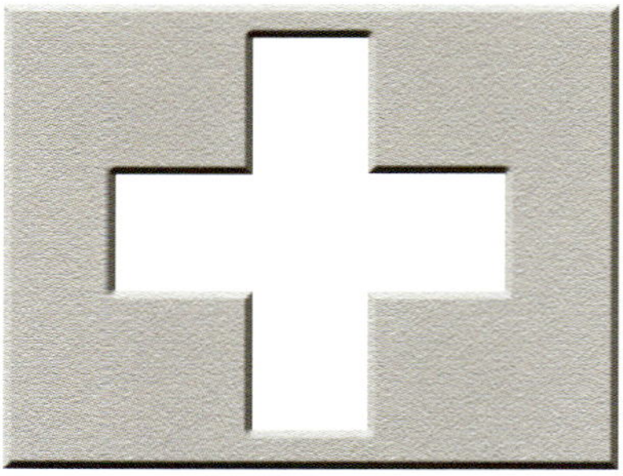

Let's use our sea wall from the previous chapter. We had used a Levels adjustment layer to pump up the contrast. Now, just as a demonstration, I have added that plus sign layer mask to its Levels adjustment layer. As we see, the contrast is enhanced within the plus sign (the white area on the layer mask) and untouched outside of the plus sign (the black area on the layer mask).

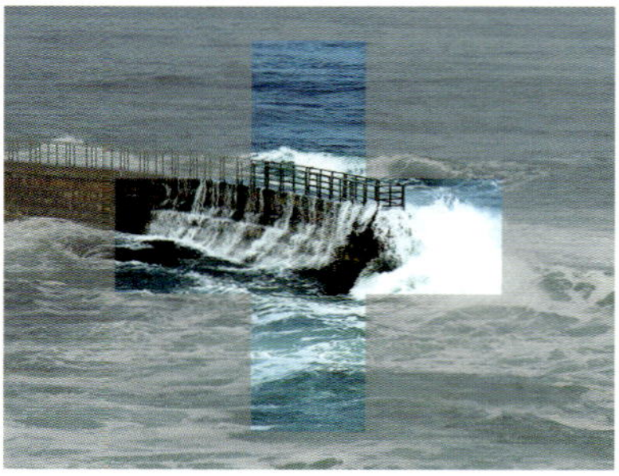

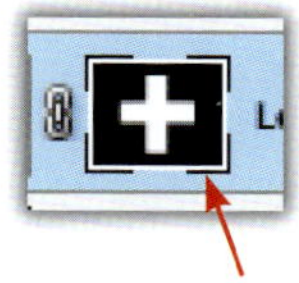

We edit a layer mask by selecting its thumbnail (the little brackets are our visual clue that it is selected) and then by painting black, white, or even gray. If we use our brush to paint black on our image in the document window, the black is painted on the mask, not the image, and the effect gets correspondingly blocked.

This is sufficiently important and non-intuitive that I will repeat it. With the adjustment and its corresponding layer mask thumbnail selected, painting on the image with black does not paint black on the image, it paints black on the mask. Within the image, then, it will appear as if we are painting away, or blocking, the effect of the adjustment layer.

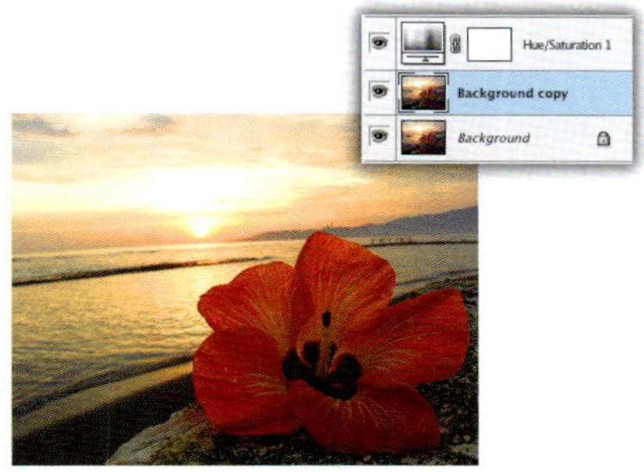

Let's try an example. In Chapter 17, we used the Sponge tool to brighten a bloom on a sunset scene. Let's do the same thing with an adjustment layer. I open the image, duplicate Background, and then make a new Hue/Saturation adjustment layer, pumping up both saturation and lightness. Our layer mask is all white by default. So the entire image is currently affected.

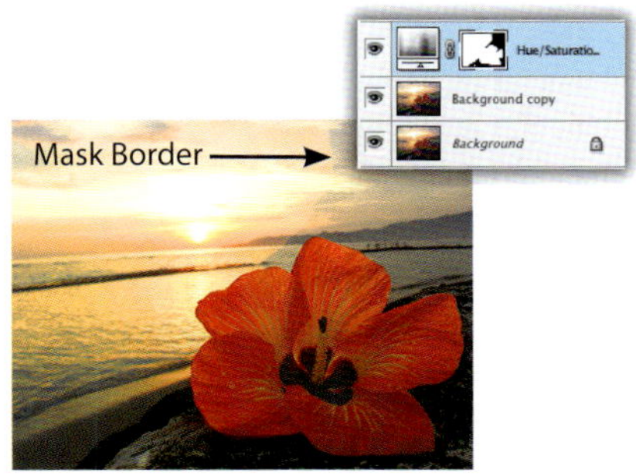

With the adjustment layer selected, I choose the Brush tool. With a foreground color of black and varying the brush diameter as I go, I "paint away" the extra saturation from everywhere except the bloom. Here, I am about half done. Note that the mask thumbnail reflects the painting I've done so far. I've masked the adjustment layer along the upper right and the bottom.

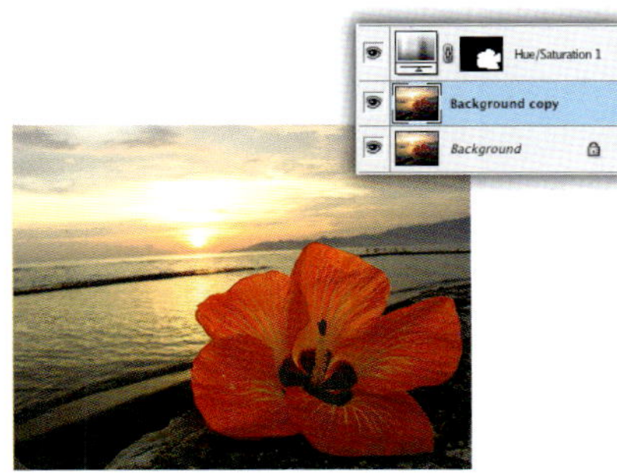

I keep painting with black until I am satisfied with my mask. The layer mask thumbnail now reflects the completed mask. And I can double click on the adjustment layer and, in the Hue/Saturation dialog box, fine tune the saturation to just where I want it. This is much more flexible than the Sponge tool.

If we would like to actually see a full size view of the layer mask, we can Opt(Alt)-Click on its thumbnail and it displays in our document window. This is a good way to make sure we have totally blackened the regions we had intended. If we see some stray white, we can simply paint it away with our black brush.

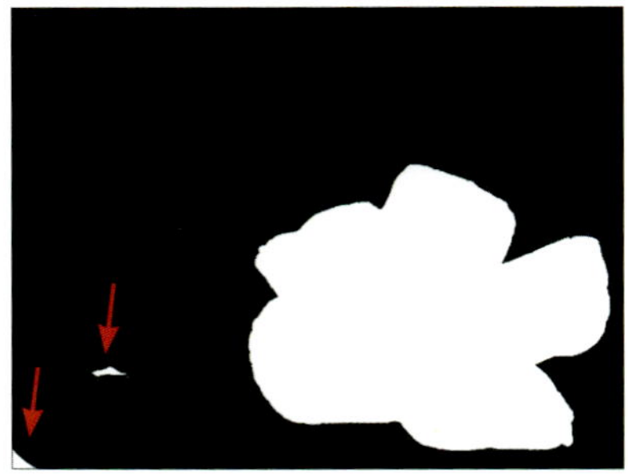

We can paint white as well as black on a layer mask, allowing more of the effect to show through. Let's say when I was creating the mask for the background, I inadvertently overshot and got some of the mask on the bloom. I can easily fix this by changing my foreground color to white and then brushing over the part of the mask that overshot the petal. (This "black hides" and "white shows" behavior is just like we saw with the Quick Mask.)

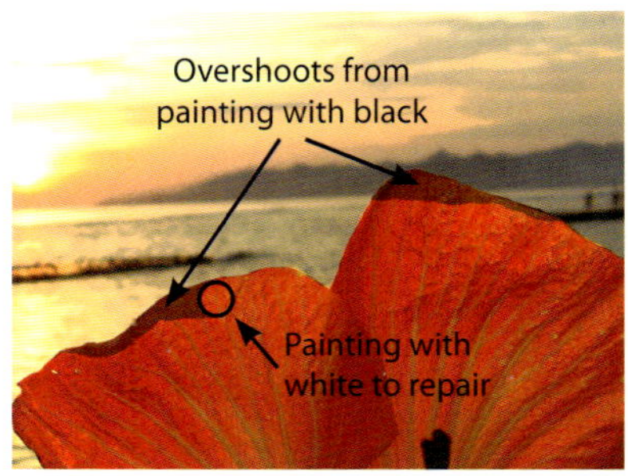

Perhaps it would have been easier to start with a black layer mask and then add the effect over the bloom with white. This is very easy to do as well. We create our adjustment layer and make adjustment settings as before. Then, with the adjustment layer still selected, we choose Edit>Fill and under Use, choose Black. The mask becomes totally black, hiding the effect completely.

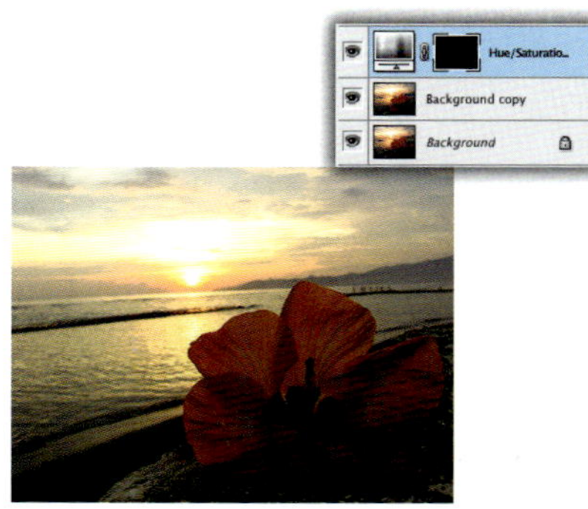

Now with a white foreground color, we can use the Brush tool to paint in the effect on the bloom. Here I am about half done. I have the Hue/Saturation pumped way up so we can see it easily. Once the mask is complete, we can dial it back to our liking by double clicking on the adjustment layer and adjusting the saturation slider.

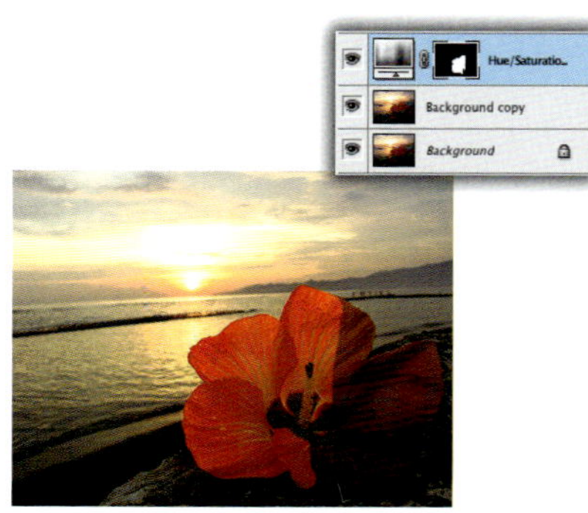

I've likened the layer mask to a stencil and told you that white transmits and black blocks. But now I have to break the analogy a bit and tell you that gray partially transmits and partially blocks. The closer the gray is to black, the more it blocks. And the closer it is to white, the more it transmits. 50% gray pegs the adjustment effect to 50% strength.

So where might we use this? Well, what if I used a soft edged brush to paint in my bloom in the previous example? The resulting mask would have a softer transition between the oversaturated bloom and the background. It would be just like using a soft-edged Sponge tool. Compare the resulting image with its associated layer mask.

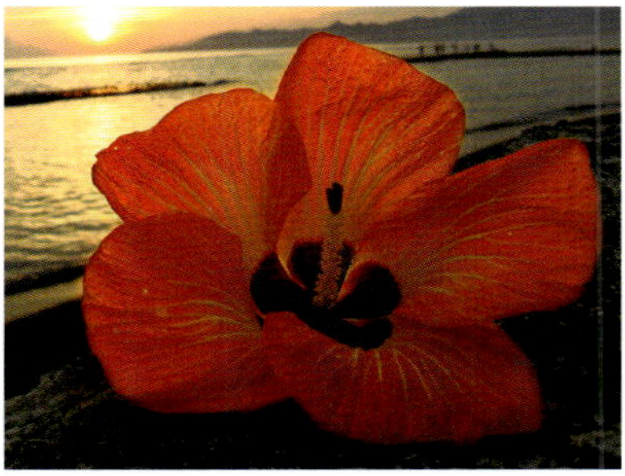

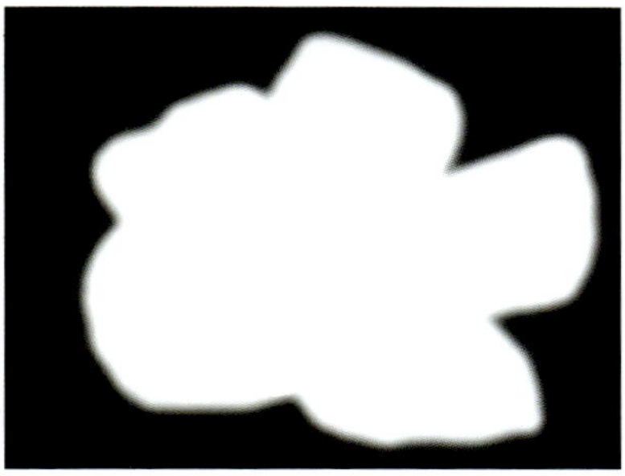

Here's one last way to create a layer mask for an adjustment layer. It is similar to the technique that we used in Chapter 20 to jump selected pixels up to a new layer. When we make a new adjustment layer, if there is an existing selection in the document window, Photoshop automatically turns that selection into the layer mask, with the selected area white and the remaining area black.

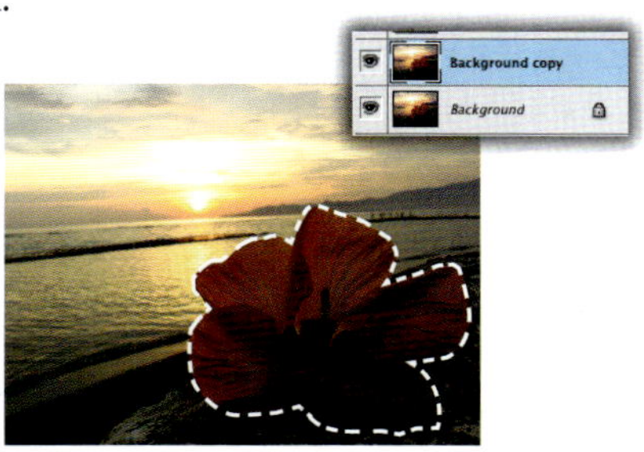

Let's try this with our bloom example. We open the image and duplicate Background. Using one of the techniques we learned earlier, we make a selection around the bloom. Next, we click on the New Adjustment Layer icon and choose Hue/Saturation. The Hue/Saturation dialog box pops open but more importantly, the selection has been imported into the adjustment layer as a new layer mask. Now we can just make our Hue/Saturation settings and we are done. And don't forget, we can do our selection with feathering in order to get that softer edge.

Layers panel after choosing a New Adjustment Layer with the pre-existing selection

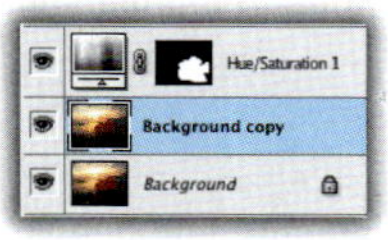

23. TEXT

This section on layers might seem an odd place to insert a chapter on text but there is some method to my madness. Whenever text is created, you see, it goes on its own individual layer.

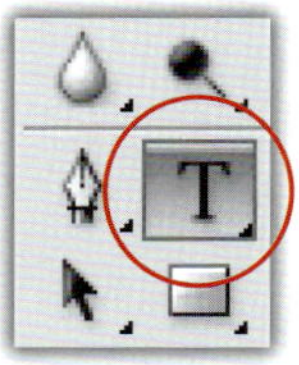

The **Horizontal Type tool** resides in the toolbox. When we select it, the options bar displays a set of options similar to what we would find with a word processor. From left to right we can pick our font, font style, font size, anti-aliasing, alignment, and color.

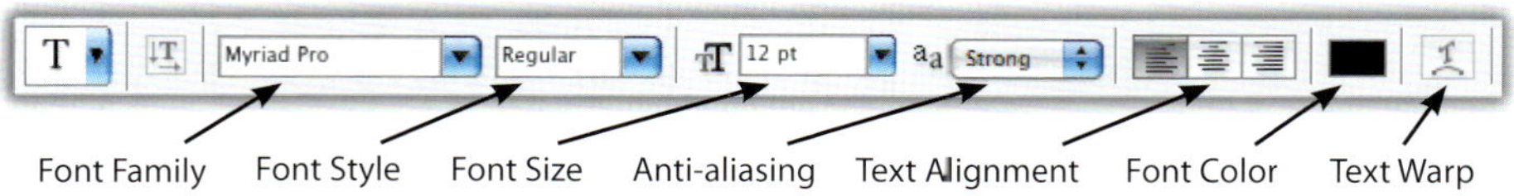

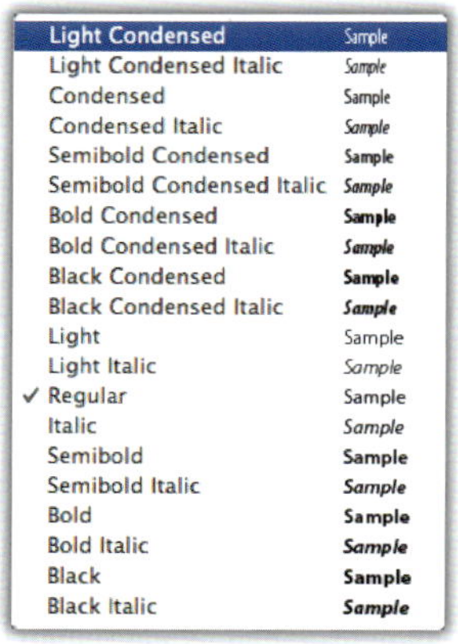

There are a few things to keep in mind. Unlike a word processor, the font styles available to us can change from font to font, depending on what is available for that font. We'll review why in a moment but don't be surprised if some styles are missing. And in some cases, like with this Myriad Pro example, we get even more options. Many more. Anti-aliasing helps make our text appear to have smoother edges–choose Strong. Choose text color by double clicking on the text color box and using the color picker. And we'll come back to Text Warp.

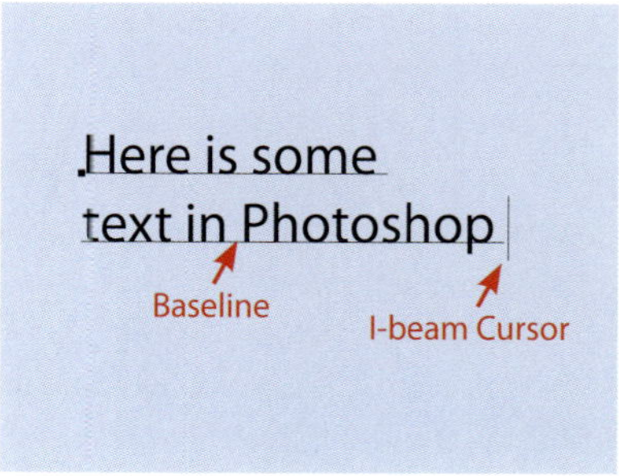

Once we have set our options, it is time to start typing. We just click in our document window where we would like our text to appear, bringing up an I-beam cursor, and start typing. The Return(Enter) key gives us a carriage return. The text we type is displayed on a baseline. When we are done, we click the Commit check mark on the right side of the options bar (or we click Cancel to start over). Don't forget to hit Commit; Photoshop is quite unforgiving on this and Return(Enter) doesn't work.

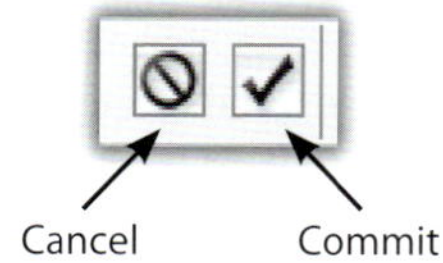

Over in the Layers panel, note that Photoshop has made us a new layer at the top of the stack. The thumbnail has a T in it indicating that it's a text layer. And the first part of the text we typed has been used as the name of the text layer.

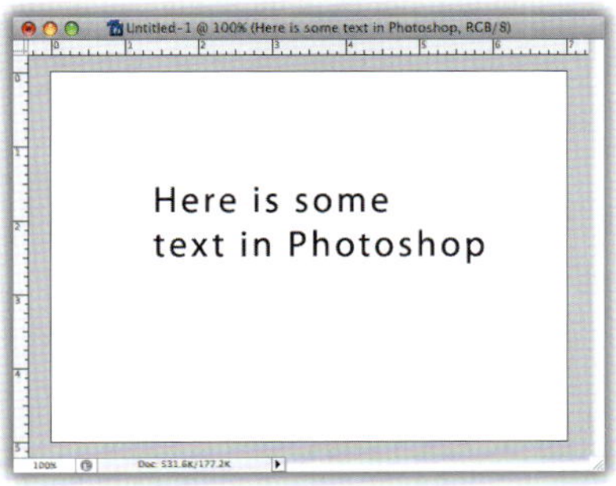

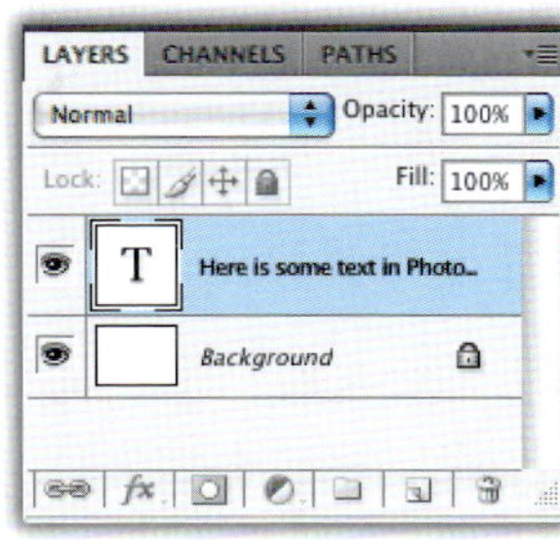

No doubt our text is not exactly where we want it. To move it, we make sure the text layer in the Layers panel is selected, choose the Move tool in the toolbox and then simply drag the text to exactly where we want it.

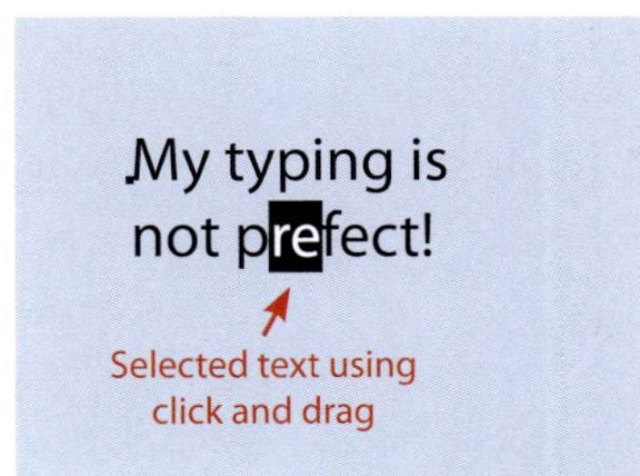

Typing mistakes are easily rectified as well. We choose the Horizontal Type Tool (if not already selected) and click anywhere in the text we wish to modify. This selects the appropriate text layer (if there are more than one) and inserts an I-beam cursor in the text. Then we click, drag, and modify exactly as we would with a word processor.

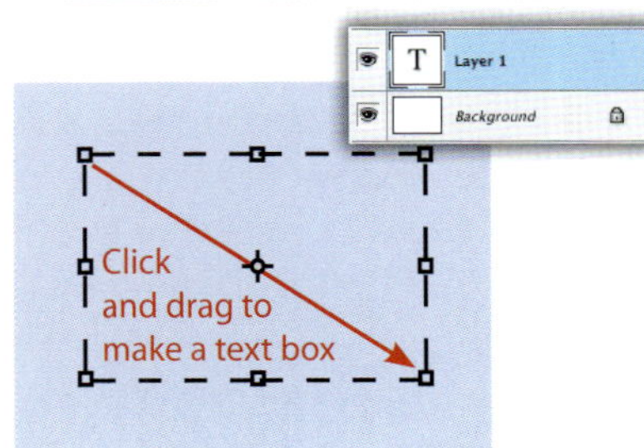

There is another variation on creating text. If we click and drag with the Type tool, we create a new **Text Box**. Then as we type, our text fills the new box. If we try to click and drag over text to edit without clicking first as explained above, Photoshop creates a new text box on a new layer instead of selecting our text. If this happens, just drag that newly created layer onto the Layers panel trash icon to get rid of it and go back to your original text and click inside it before trying to edit. Trust me, this will happen to you–we've been trained to click and drag to select text, not to click first.

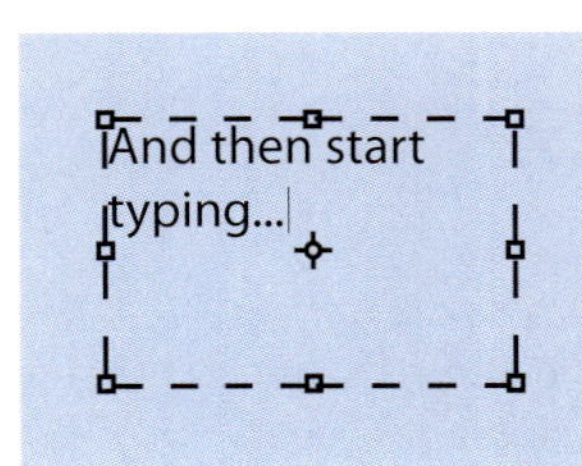

This is all great. But if that was all there was, I would think more than a few of you would be disappointed. After all, this is Photoshop we're talking about. Well of course there is more... A lot more. Start by selecting Window>Character to bring up the **Character panel**. Here (and behind it on the Paragraph tab) we have access to fully-featured typesetting capabilities.

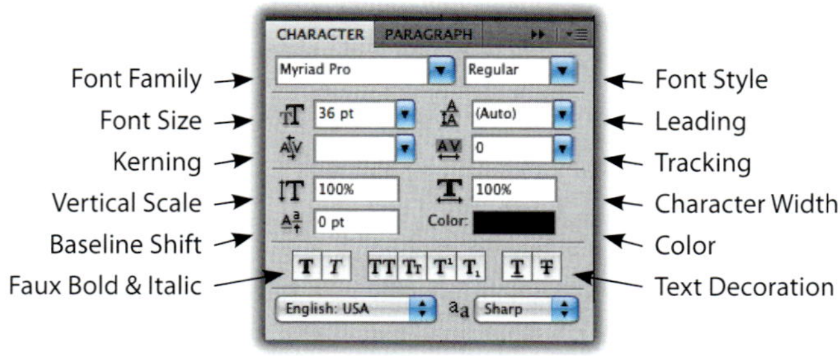

Font/Size/Style:	The same list of fonts as we have on the options bar.
Kerning:	Controls the spacing between two adjacent selected characters. We use this mostly for stylizing titles, not for general text.
Vertical Scale:	Allows us to vertically stretch or squeeze selected text.
Baseline Shift:	Allows us to offset text from the baseline, up or down.
Leading:	Fancy name for line spacing.
Tracking:	Controls the spacing between characters of selected characters. This can be used for general text.
Horizontal Scale:	Allows us to horizontally stretch or squeeze selected text.

The Faux options are interesting so let's take just a moment to review them. Not all font sets are created equal. If a font includes italic, the font designer has created a complete, unique set of italic characters consistent with the master font. If they did not, when we select that font, we will notice that italic is not on the list of styles. The same holds true for bold. But how come our word processors always seem to have italic and bold? The reason is that they cheat, just slanting the font for italic or bloating it for bold. Not to be outdone, Photoshop allows us these options as well. But it is up-front about it, referring to them as Faux Italic and Faux Bold.

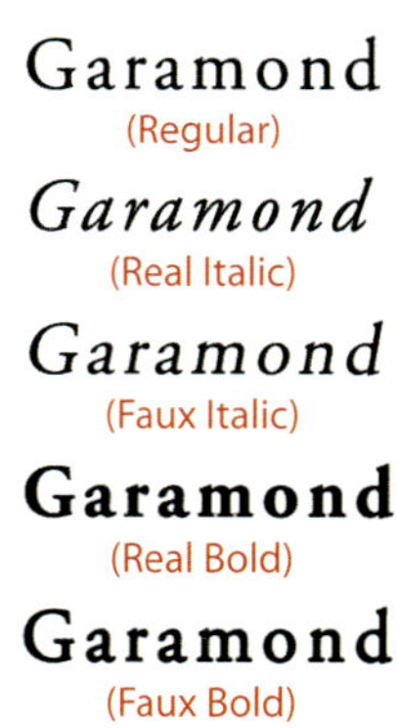

All of the other options at the bottom of the Character panel, as well as those on the underlying Paragraph panel, are pretty self-explanatory. Hover your mouse over any of them for a tool tip.

Impressive as all of this is, I don't suggest using Photoshop to input lots of text into a document. For this, use a word processor or page layout program instead and then transfer the text into a text box by copying and pasting. By the way, imported text will take on the formatting set in the options bar when the text box was opened.

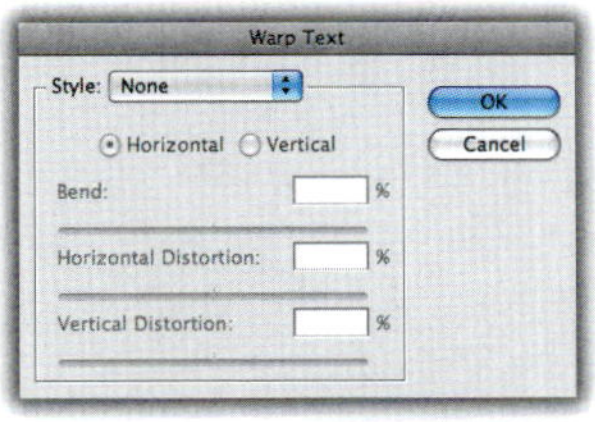

The Character panel is nice and has lots of options but what if we want something a bit more jazzy? In the next chapter, we'll learn how to make effects like drop shadows. For now, though, let's play with the **Text Warp** icon at the right of the Text options bar. Select it and up pops a dialog box with all sorts of phantasmagorical effects.

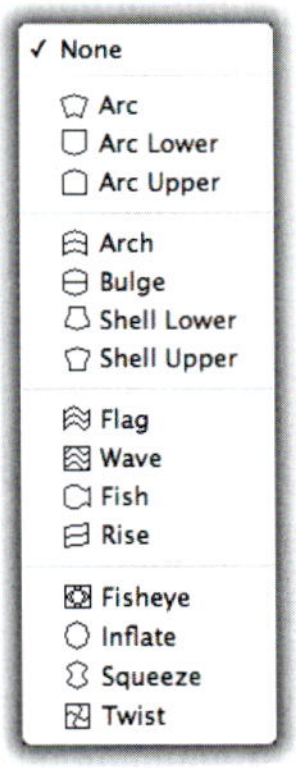

If we pull down the style menu, we see that we have quite a few choices. The names are not all particularly explanatory but most of them make some sense after you play with them. As with many other Photoshop's tools, warping is best learned by playing with it, seeing what the various controls do, and then probably sticking with your favorites. A word to the wise, though. Warping is fun and has its place but a little can go a long way. Just be careful not to overdo things.

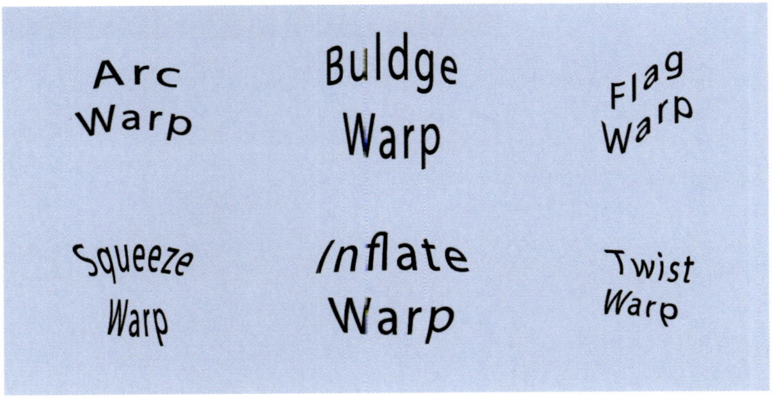

There is still much more that can be done with text but, alas, we have run out of time. One of the more interesting techniques is typing on a path. We won't learn about creating paths until Chapter 40 but you still might want to check out Photoshop Help on this subject. Search on "Create and edit type on a path."

24. LAYER STYLES

In the row of icons at the bottom of the Layers panel is the **Layer Style** icon, an "fx" in CS3, CS4 and an "f" inside a circle in earlier versions. We use layer styles to create layer effects, like drop shadows or embossing. These effects apply to the entire contents of the layer and can really jazz up appearance. They are especially suited to layers with a lot of transparent regions, like text layers (our last chapter) or layers with shapes on them, like logos.

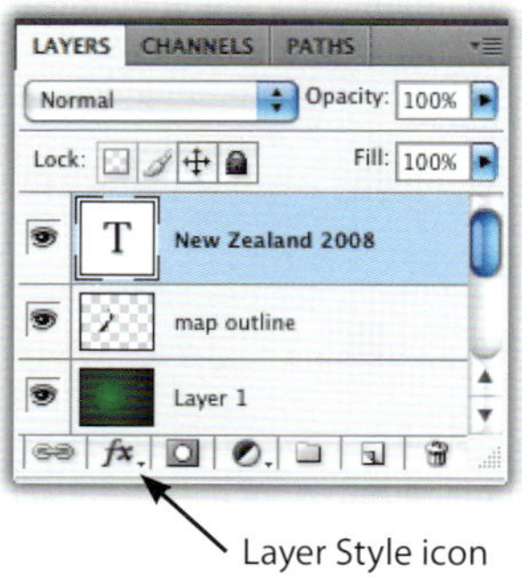

Here is an image that I made for a New Zealand family vacation slide show. The glow effect on the map (which was on one layer) and the drop shadow on the text (which was on another layer) are both layer styles. Very easy to do and they really dress up our text and graphics.

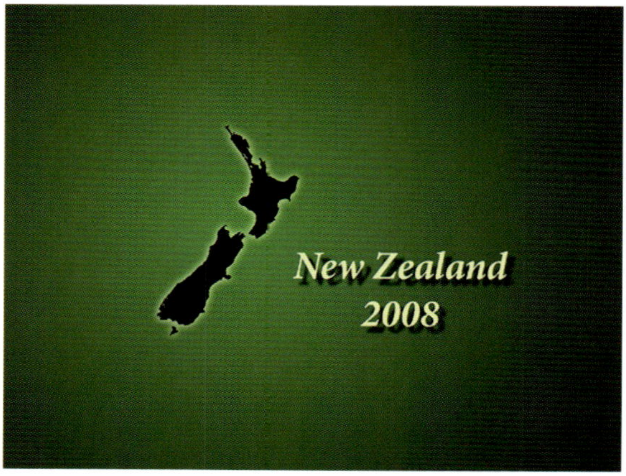

To create a layer style, we select the layer where we wish to apply the style and then click the layer style icon at the bottom of the Layers panel. A little menu pops up with our style choices. To apply a style, we click on it and up pops the Layer Style dialog box (opposite page).

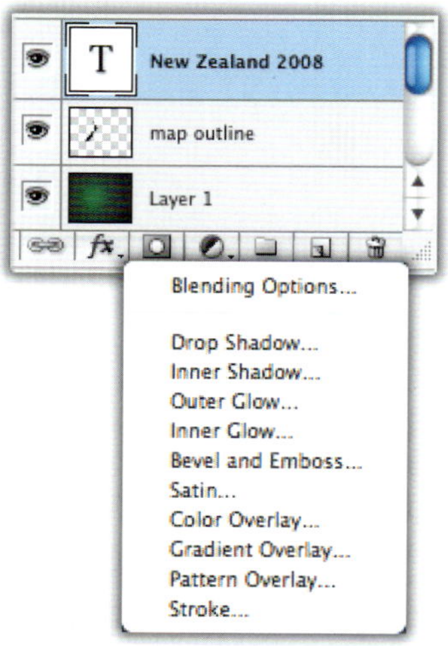

This dialog box is actually a one-stop-shop for all of our style needs but it pops open set up for the style that we just chose. As we will see, however, we are not limited to one style on a given layer. Once we have popped open the layer style dialog box, we can apply styles to our heart's content.

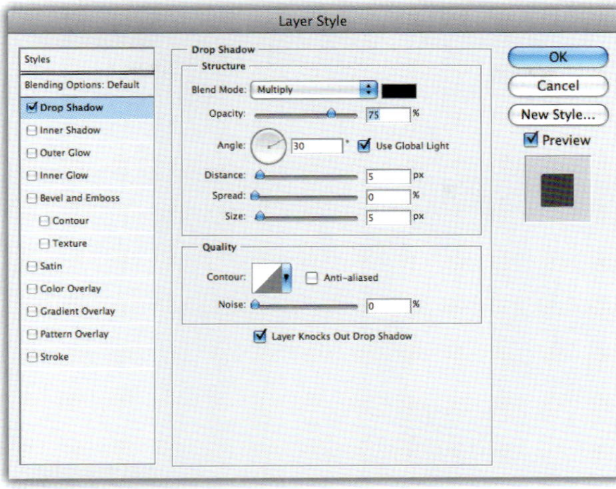

This dialog box was opened after I selected the Drop Shadow layer style. Notice that all of the styles are listed in the left column, but only Drop Shadow is checked and selected. The check mark indicates the style is applied, the highlight that it is selected. The middle section displays all of the controls for the drop shadow effect. And on the right are the dialog box controls along with a nifty little effect preview.

Each of the styles has a unique set of controls but there are a few general guidelines I will give you. For now, stay away from Blending Modes and all the controls in the Quality section; there's some neat capability here but save it for later. Definitely do play with controls like Opacity, Distance, Spread, Size and similar ones for other styles. These controls fine-tune the style instead of making radical changes. The best way to see how they work is to open a new document, add a text layer and start playing. A click is worth a thousand words. (And that's like a whole chapter in this book!)

The reason that all of the styles are listed in the layer style dialog box is because a given layer can have as many styles applied to it as we wish. So after making a Drop Shadow, for example, we can select Bevel and Emboss and adjust those controls. Again, the blue highlight indicates which style is selected. Here is a **BIG WARNING**, though. If we click the Bevel and Emboss check box instead of selecting the style, the Drop Shadow style remains selected and its controls stay visible. But the Bevel and Emboss style is nevertheless applied with whatever settings were there, settings that we can't see! Nasty! So make it a habit to click on the style name to select and apply it. Only use the check boxes to see which styles are applied or to turn one or more of them off.

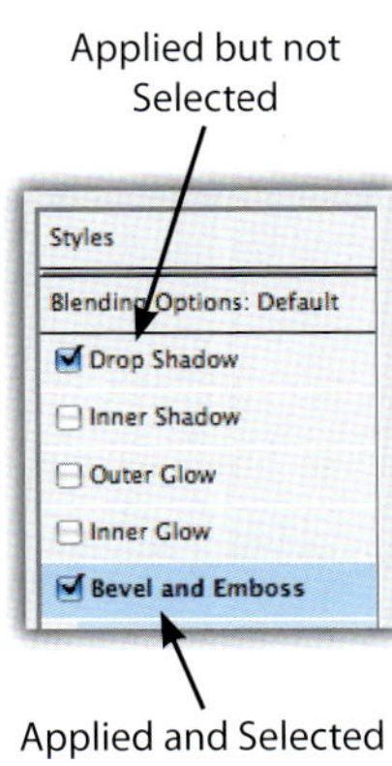

The layer styles that I find myself using the most often, either alone or in conjunction, are **Drop Shadow**, **Outer Glow**, and **Bevel and Emboss**. Here is an example of each along with the control settings I used to create the effect.

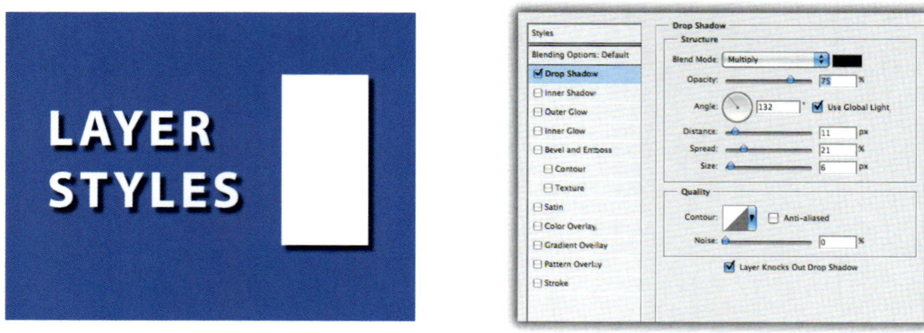

Drop Shadow

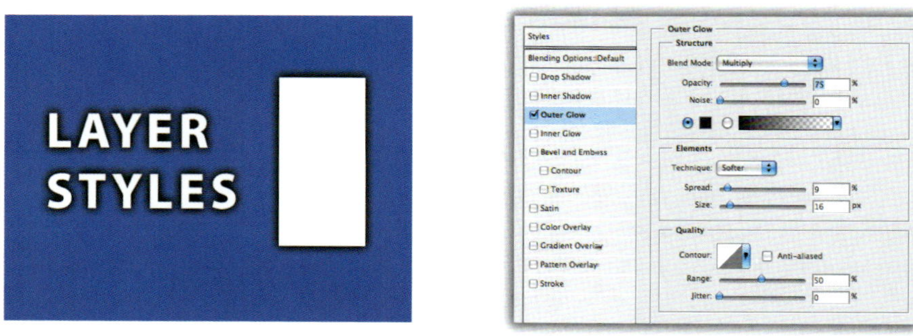

Outer Glow

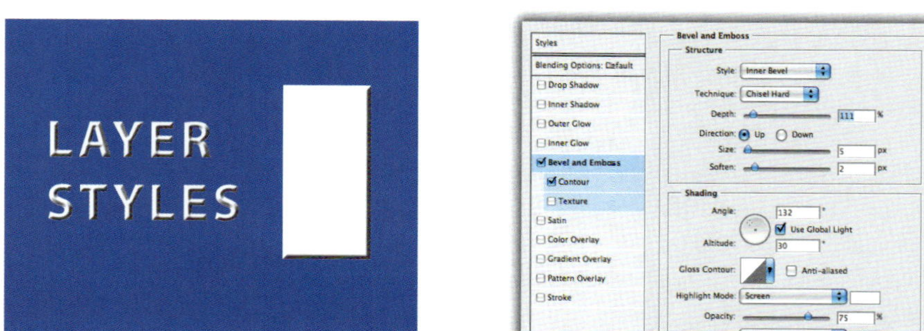

Bevel and Emboss

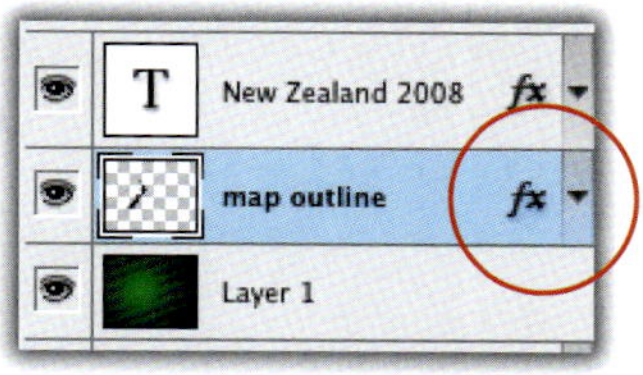

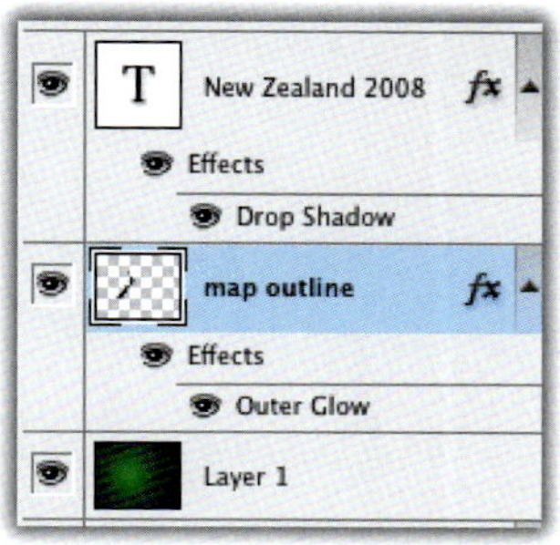

Once we have created a layer style, it becomes part of the layer to which it was applied. And again, a layer style can be made up of multiple effects, whatever has been checked off in the layer style dialog box. To help us remember that a layer style has been applied to a layer, Photoshop puts a copy of the layer style icon on the layer itself, to the right of the layer name.

Notice also that the layer style icon on the layer comes with a disclosure triangle. If we click on it, Photoshop expands the layer to include a summary of all of the layer styles that have been applied.

What if we decide that we want to make a change to a layer effect? No problem. All we have to do is to double click on the layer style icon on the layer and our familiar layer style dialog box will pop open with all the applied styles checked. From that dialog box, we can see all of the styles that have been applied to that layer as well as the settings for each. We can make any changes we want, editing existing settings, deleting styles all together (uncheck the box), or adding new ones.

Opt(Alt) Drag

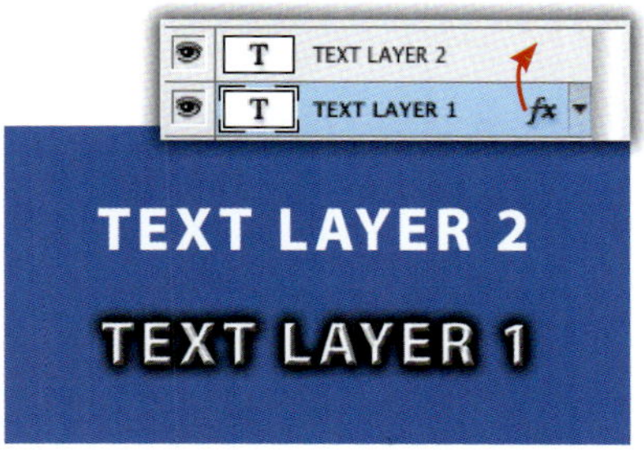

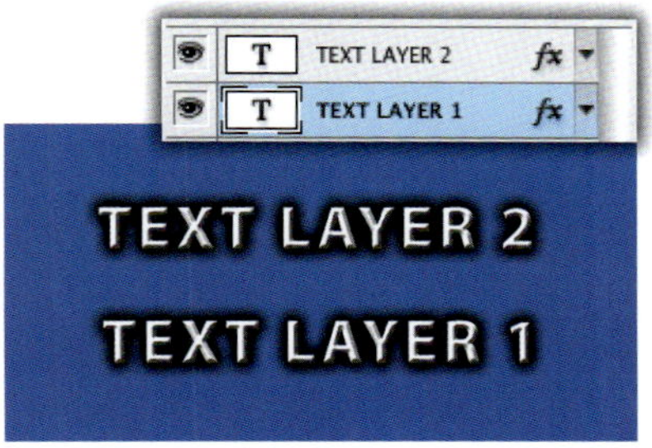

So now let's say we have a document and it has several different text layers on it. With one of our text layers selected, we click on the layer style icon and, with the methods described above, create a very pleasing set of layer styles. What if we would like to duplicate that style on other text layers? Do we have to do everything all over again?

Fortunately not. We can just copy the layer styles we created to the unstyled layers. Here's how. We Opt(Alt)-Click and drag the layer style icon from the styled layer to the layer where we would like it applied. Bingo, it copies. We then repeat the process for any other layers needing the same style. Here I copied the effects from Text Layer 1 onto Text Layer 2.

Multiple Open Documents: CS4 incorporates a revised system for handling multiple open documents. In CS3 and earlier, when we opened a second or third (and so on) document, Photoshop would create a new document window on top of any previous ones, generally offset down and to the right a bit. With CS4, the interface has been changed to a much more convenient tab system, similar to how browsers now handle multiple open windows. To switch documents, we simply click on the appropriate header.

Click here to select Paris.psd

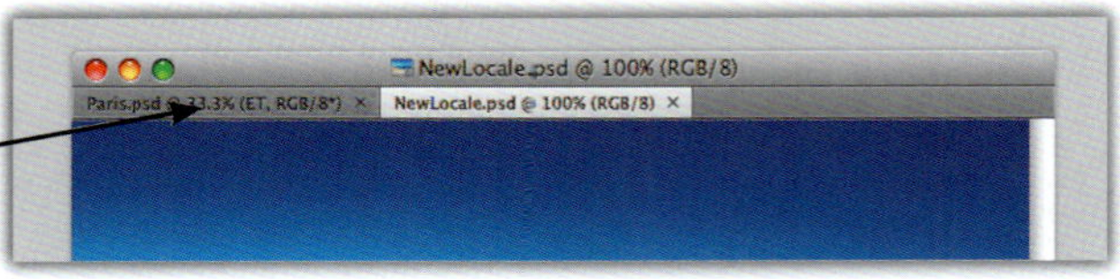

New Adjustments Panel: Perhaps the biggest change to the CS4 interface is the new Adjustments panel. Now instead of using the half-filled circle icon at the bottom of the Layers panel (although that still works), all we need to do is select an icon for an adjustment layer in the Adjustment panel and, presto, it appears in the Layers panel. The Adjustments panel then changes to display the controls for that specific type of adjustment. It is the same functionality, although not all adjustments are represented here. What's new is that we now also have a set of presets (predefined settings) to choose from. If later we want to make changes, a single click on the adjustment layer brings up its settings. Once you insert an adjustment layer, select the back arrow in the lower left of the panel to return to the main panel.

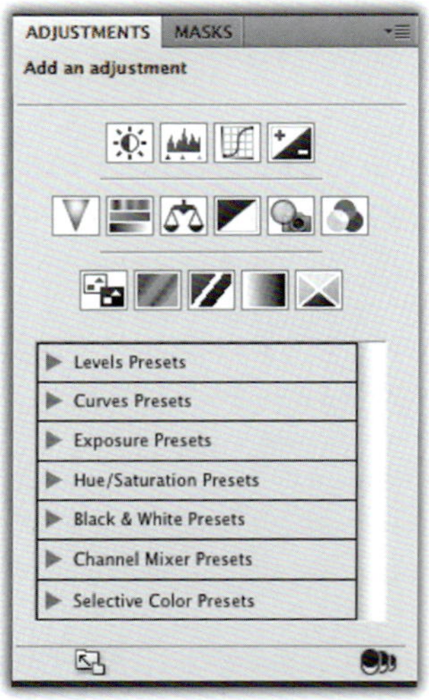

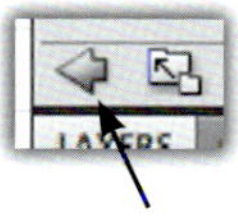

New Masks Panel: Behind the new Adjustments panel, we have a new Masks panel, accessed by clicking on its tab. It's controls become activated when we've selected a layer with a layer mask. The main sliders allow us to change density and feathering. And then there are more advanced controls. Play with it if you'd like but we will review more detail on this panel in the Section IV CS4 Tips.

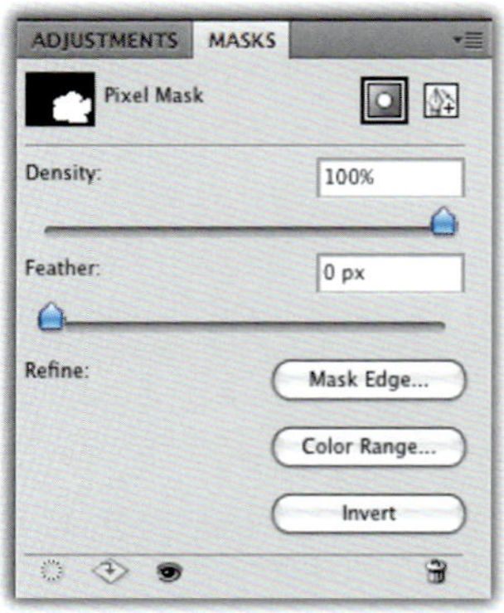

SECTION

IV

MORE LAYER CONCEPTS

Layers are pretty sweet, but there is a lot to learn. So welcome to another section on the subject.

Much of what we do in this section will be with an eye towards compositing (the fancy name for merging elements or objects from different images into a single, new image. We will learn how to transform objects so that they are appropriately sized when placed in a new image. We will learn new and more powerful extraction techniques. And we will explore a variety of different ways we can make layers interact with each other.

Another theme of this section is non-destructive editing. Adjustment layers were our first introduction to this technique. Recall that with adjustment layers, none of the underlying pixels are modified (i.e. destroyed) and we have the ability to go back and modify the adjustment at any time. Even if we do flawless work, never having an error to correct, non-destructive editing will still come in handy when we want to edit a completed project for some new purpose.

Topping the list of useful non-destructive editing methods is layer masking, a new application of the masking technique we discussed in relation to adjustment layers. In this section, we will apply those masks directly to regular layers.

Finally, we will pull everything together with a compositing example, step by step. So stay in your seats and hold on. The thrill ride continues.

25. LAYER MASKS

In Chapter 22, we learned about layer masks in conjunction with adjustment layers. We discussed how they worked kind of like a stencil and how a big advantage to them was that they were editable–at any time we could go in and modify the stencil.

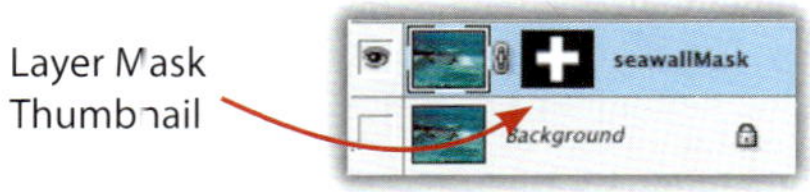

Now let's learn how to apply these same layer masks to ordinary pixel layers. With adjustment layers, the layer mask determined where the adjustment was applied and where it was not. With an ordinary layer, a layer mask determines where pixels are visible and where they are not. Here is our sea wall again from Chapter 22 but with the "plus" layer mask on the image layer. Where the mask is white, the image is visible and where it is black, the image is transparent. (Background visibility is off.)

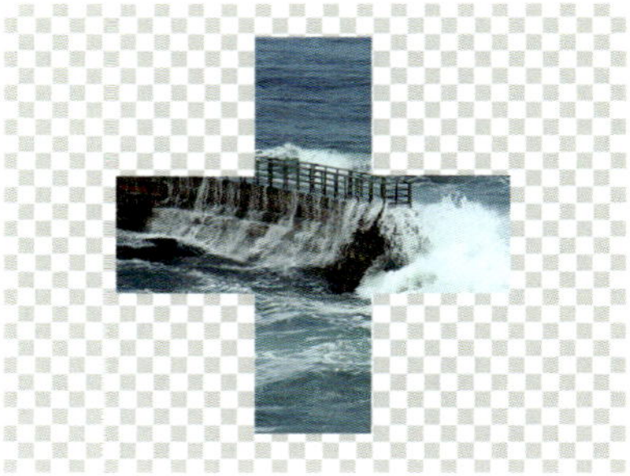

Unlike adjustment layers, ordinary layers do not automatically come with layer masks. But they're easily added. With our layer selected, we click on the Add Layer Mask icon at the bottom of the Layers panel and a layer mask thumbnail is inserted.

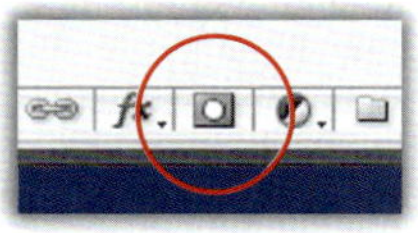

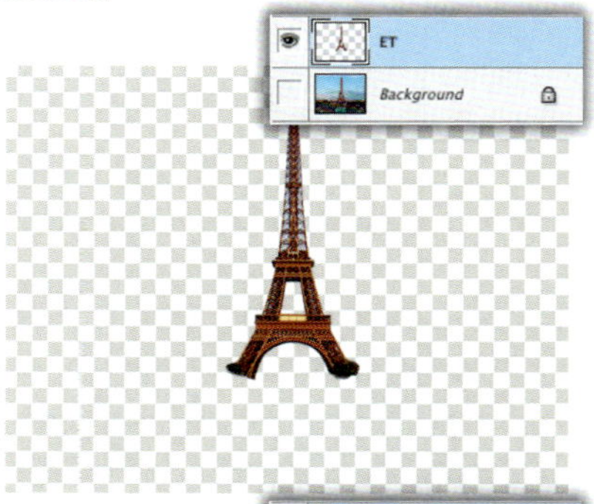

We edit layer masks for ordinary layers just as we did for adjustment layers. We paint with black or white to define regions of transparency or visibility respectively. And we can also use selections to automatically define our mask. Here's how.

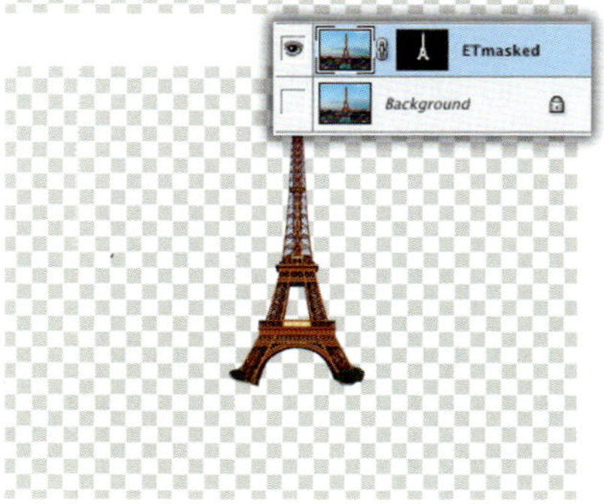

In Chapter 20, we performed an extraction of the Eiffel Tower by selecting it and jumping it to a new layer. The top image to the right repeats that result. Now we will do it with layer masking. We start by copying the background layer and then selecting the tower as before. Then we click the Add Layer Mask icon in the Layers panel and our layer mask is created from the selection. Just like that. The tower appears extracted, but the real case is that everything else is just hidden by the layer mask.

Now here's the point. If I jump my tower pixels to a new layer (the previous method) and later see that I had done a bad selection job, I'd need to start from scratch. With this layer mask technique, I can just go to the layer mask and fix my problem, using the Brush tool with black (to hide) or white (to show). Everything is reversible.

To make these edits, there is just one little gotcha. And trust me, it will getcha. When we made edits with our Brush tool on an adjustment layer mask, the Brush tool knew to paint on the layer mask. Actually, that was its only choice. But if we have an ordinary layer with a layer mask, how does the Brush tool know whether we want to paint on the layer mask or on the layer itself? The answer is that we have to tell it.

We do this by selecting (clicking on) either the layer image thumbnail or the layer mask thumbnail on the layer in the Layers panel. The selected thumbnail will have a dashed border around it. (The layer image thumbnail is selected by default.)

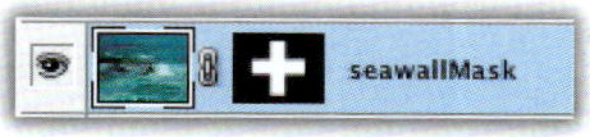

Layer Selected

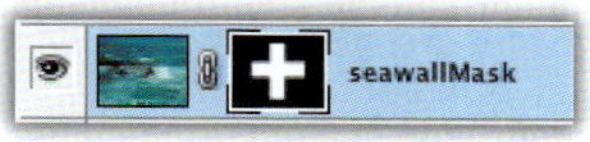

Layer Mask Selected

If we try to edit a layer mask and end up with a black or white brush stroke on our image instead, it's because our layer thumbnail is mistakenly selected. Just Cmd(Ctrl)-Z to undo the brush step, select the layer mask, and carry on.

Let's see this editing in action. We'll use our Eiffel Tower example from the previous page and say that we've now decided that we would like to add back in the scenery that is under the arch. If we had extracted the tower by our earlier methods, we would have to start from scratch. But since we have used a layer mask this time around, the fix is a snap.

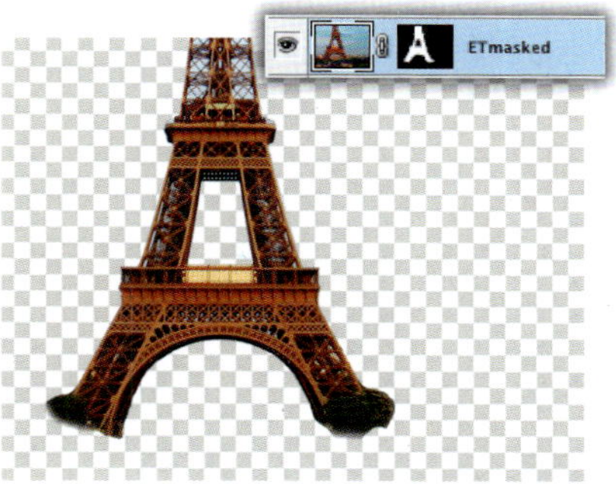

With our layer mask thumbnail selected, we choose our Brush tool (I used a soft edge) and set the color to white. With our brush, we paint back in the pixels that we want to show. If we reveal too much, we can switch our color to black, and paint away the excess. Quick, easy, and editable. But remember, the layer mask thumbnail must be selected.

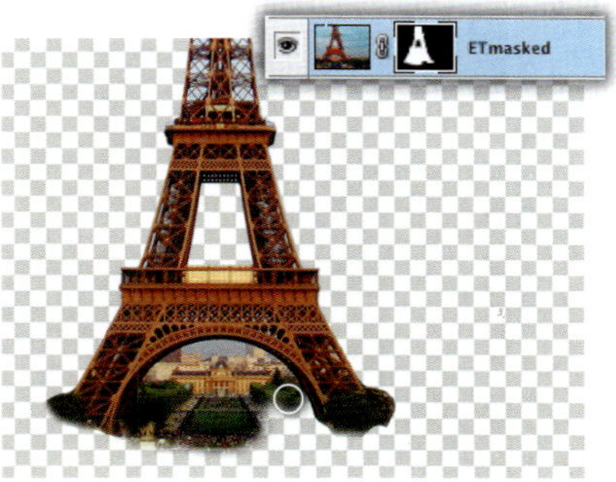

As another example of the power of layer masks, let's redo the vignette effect from Chapter 12. It's really easy with layer masks. First we open an image and duplicate Background. Then we make a new layer, choose Edit>Fill, select Black and hit OK. Finally we drag the black-filled layer under the image copy (but above Background). Now we are set up. With our image copy layer selected, we choose the Elliptical Marquee tool and set feathering to 30 (this number may vary depending on image size). Then we drag an elliptical selection (the vignette) and hit the Add Layer Mask icon. Done!

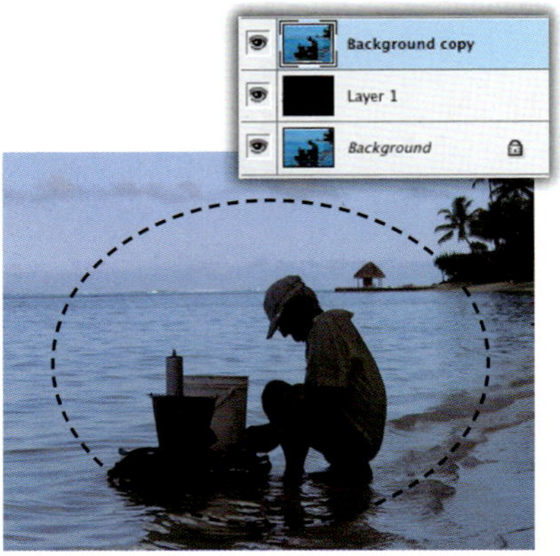

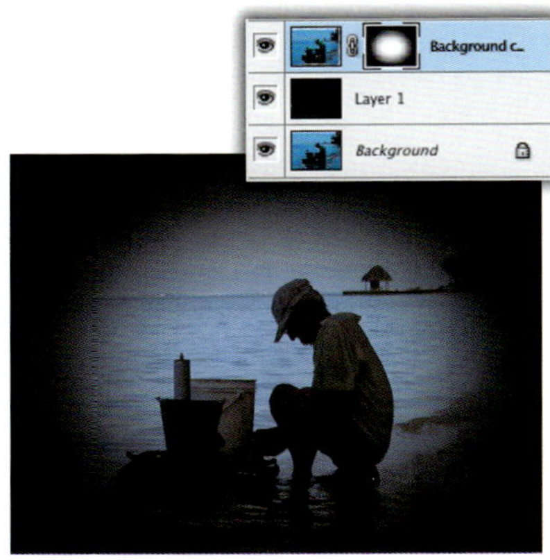

But wait! There is an even better way to do this. We repeat the exact same steps as above but with the Elliptical Marquee feathering set to zero. I know… Now we have a hard edge on the vignette that is not all that pleasing.

To fix it, we select the layer mask thumbnail and choose Filter>Blur>Gaussian Blur. With Preview checked in the dialog box, we move the Radius slider to the right and (after some number-crunching lag) our vignette effect updates. The Gaussian Blur filter (I know we haven't discussed filters yet but bear with me) has blurred the ellipse in the layer mask, giving us the exact same effect as did the feathered selection. But now, if the feathering is not to our liking, we can move the slider to refine it. No trial and error.

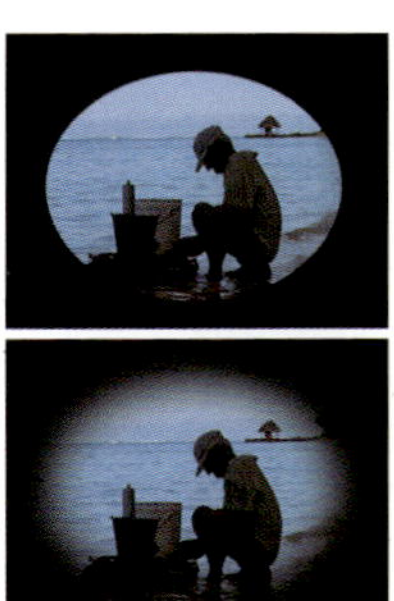

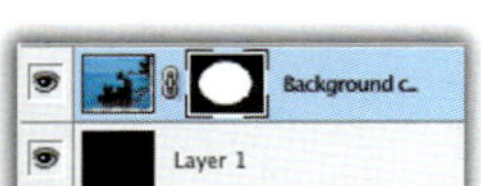

Before Gaussian Blur Filter

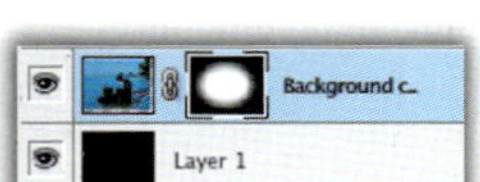

After Gaussian Blur Filter

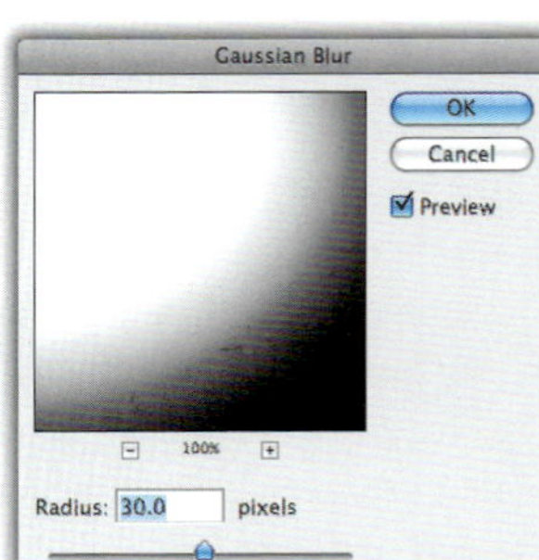

Very powerful, very quick, very neat! Now let's take care of a few nits and nats regarding layer masks to finish out the chapter.

As with adjustment layer masks, there will come a time when we want to have a look at the layer mask itself, a better look than the little thumbnail affords us. As before, we simply Opt(Alt)-Click on the layer mask thumbnail and our image in the document window is replaced by the layer mask itself. And as before, a second Opt(Alt)-Click reverses the process, restoring the image.

Sometimes we may want to unmask a layer, perhaps just temporarily, without throwing away the mask. Not a problem. If we right click (or Ctrl-Click for a one button mouse) on the layer mask thumbnail, we get a contextual menu and can choose Disable Layer Mask. This doesn't erase the mask, it just turns off its effect. The layer mask thumbnail fills with a red "X" to let us know it is disabled. Want it back? Right click on it again and choose Enable Layer Mask. And it is restored, good as new. This same menu allows us to delete the layer mask altogether if we so desire.

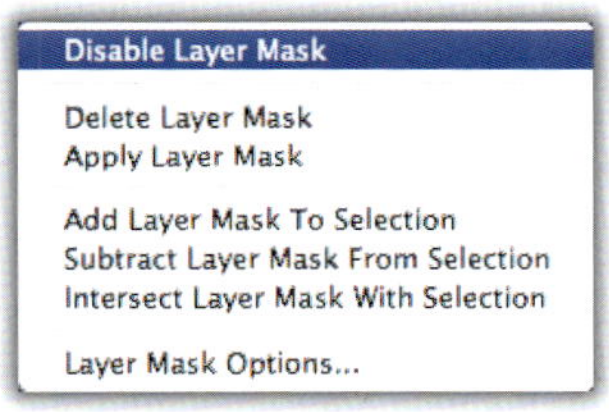

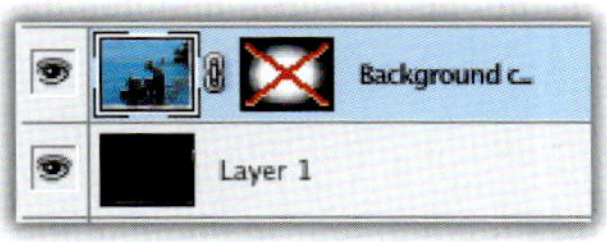

Layers and their layer masks are, by default, linked together so if we were to use the Move tool to move a layer, the layer and layer mask move in unison. If we want to unlink the two, we simply click the little link icon on the layer. We might want to do this, for example, to reposition an image relative to a vignetting mask. After repositioning, click between thumbnails to reset the link.

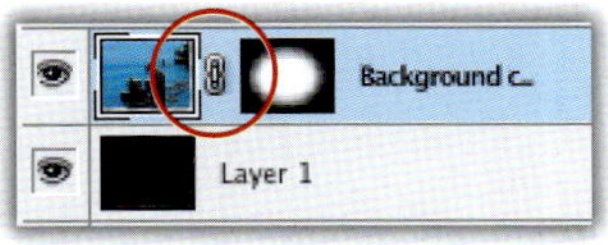

Linked

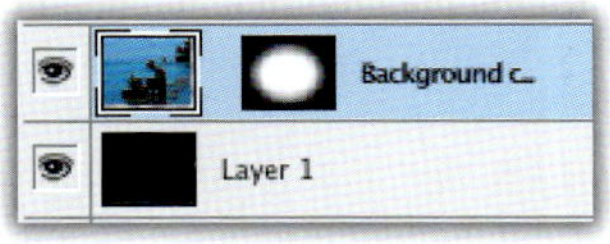

Unlinked

One last thing to keep in mind. In Chapter 20, we learned how to copy layers from one file into another. Our first foray into compositing. You will be glad to know that our use of layer masking doesn't affect that at all. If we duplicate a layer that has a layer mask from one document to another, the layer mask follows right along without a problem. So feel free to create a vignette with a layer mask and drag the whole shebang into another image.

26. THE GRADIENT TOOL

It has been a while since we learned a new tool and there is one in particular, the **Gradient tool**, which is very useful with layer masking. So let's spend some time on it.

The Gradient tool generates smooth blends between colors, allowing us to create a number of interesting effects. As with other tools, it's in the toolbox and has its own unique options bar.

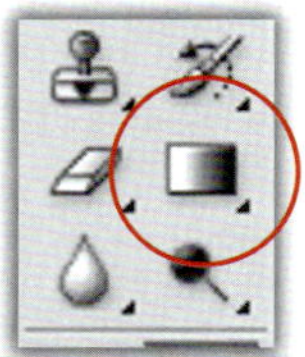

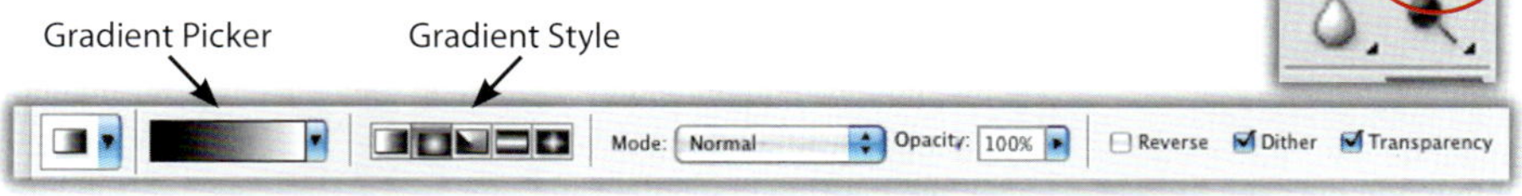

Let's click the **Gradient Picker** pull down menu and choose Black,White from the top row. (Each of these boxes represents an existing preset gradient; Photoshop also allows us to create our own custom gradients.) Let's also select the linear gradient, the left most of the gradient styles.

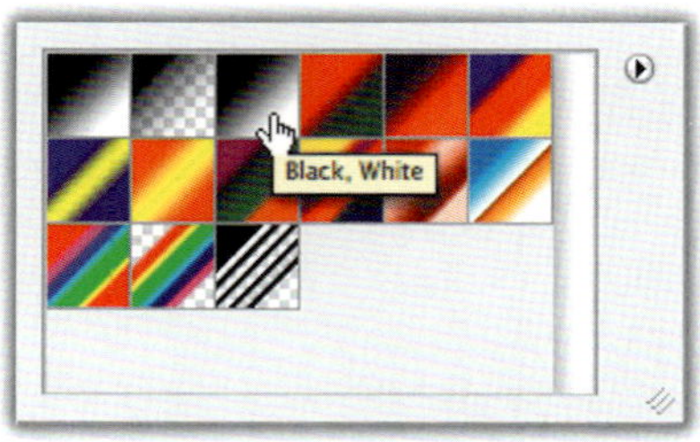

Now let's open a new Photoshop document, selecting the default size preset and a white background. With our Gradient tool selected, we click and drag our mouse from the left to the right as shown below. When we release, the gradient appears.

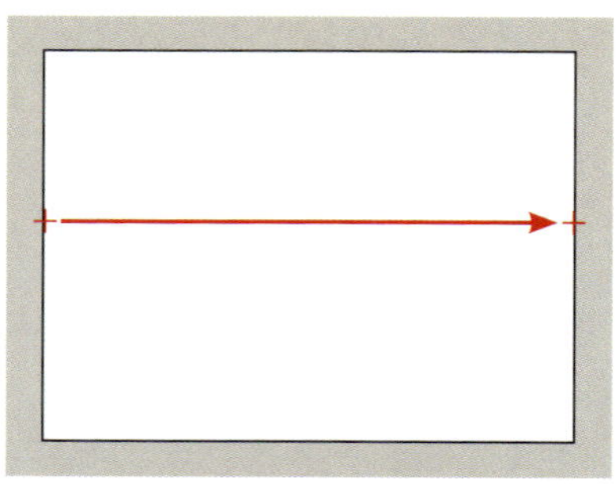

The pixels have been painted with the left most being black, the right most being white, and with all pixels in between being a continuous blend from black to white. This is called a linear gradient because the tonal variations are in one dimension only, from left to right in this case. There are no tonal variations in the up/down direction.

Note also that the gradient completely fills our document window. This will always be the case unless we have an active selection, in which case the gradient would fill only the selection. More on this in a moment.

The left hand color on the Gradient Picker is applied where we make our starting click; the right hand color is applied where we release. In between, we get the blend. So if we had dragged right to left instead, the gradient would have been reversed. If we hadn't dragged edge to edge, the pixels to the left of the starting point would have been black, those to the right of the ending point would have been white, with the blend extending only from the starting point to the ending point. Last, there is nothing that says we have to drag horizontally. We can drag vertically or at any angle we like.

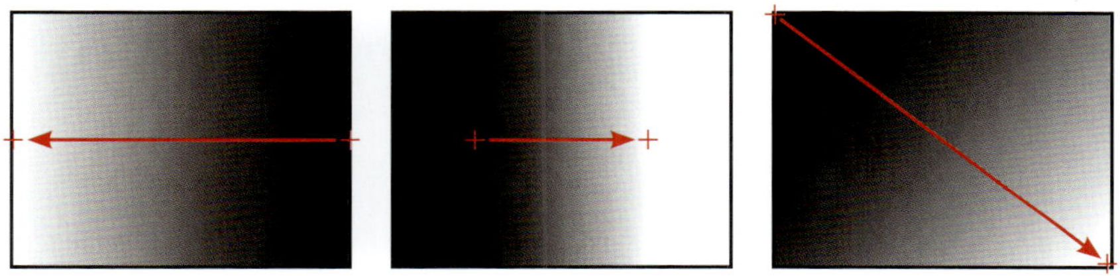

We can even drag outside the boundaries of the canvas if we want to have a softer gradient (dark gray to light gray). Or, if we have a selection in place and drag across it, only the selected pixels are affected. In both cases, the gradient is constructed based on the click and release points, even if they are outside the active drawing area.

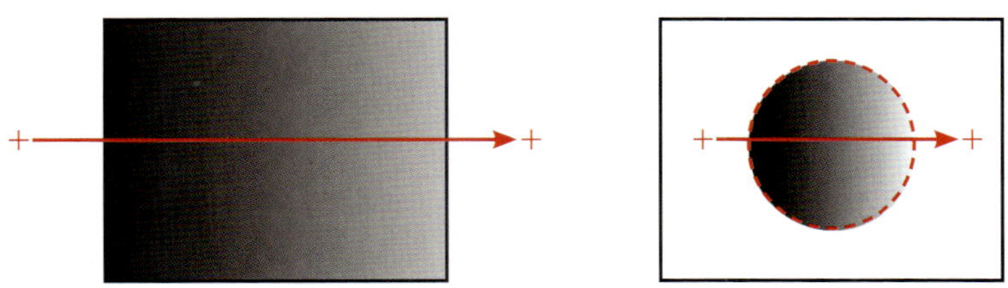

In the options bar, we see that in addition to the linear gradient, there are four additional gradient types. Let's choose radial, which creates a circular pattern, and see what it does. For this example, we'll check Reverse in the options bar, giving us White,Black gradient instead of Black,White. On a blank document, we create a circular selection with the Elliptical Marquee and then, with the gradient tool, drag as shown. Instant ball!

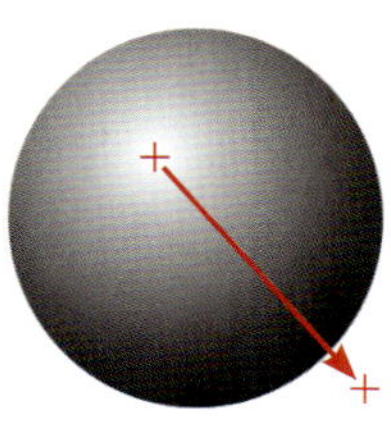

Earlier we saw that there were a number of preset gradients in the Gradient Picker (we chose Black,White). When we see the little gray checkerboard, it indicates transparency. So the second preset in the top row, for example, indicates black (actually it's the foreground color) blending to transparency. To learn how to create your own customized gradients, go to Photoshop Help and search on "Create a smooth gradient."

Gradients can be used to create all sorts of interesting effects, but for now, let's focus on their usefulness with layers and layer masks. That's the subject of this section after all. We'll start with a very common photographic problem when there is a bright window and the exposure is uneven. In the example below, the window on the right is very bright and the room to the left is dark. The challenge is how to lighten up the dark room without further lightening the window area. If we do a Levels adjustment layer (Chapter 21) for example, we can fix the room but then the window totally blows out.

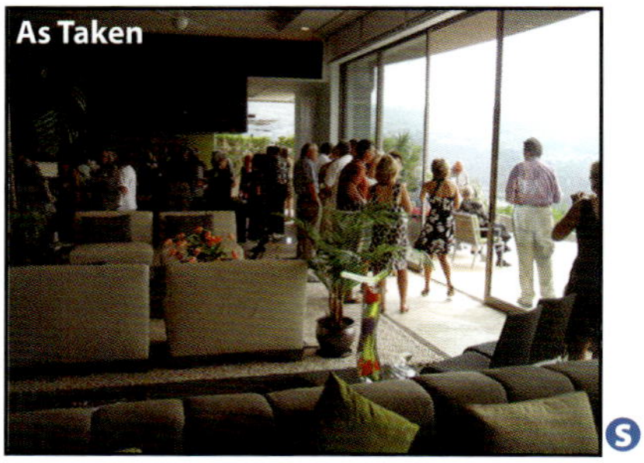

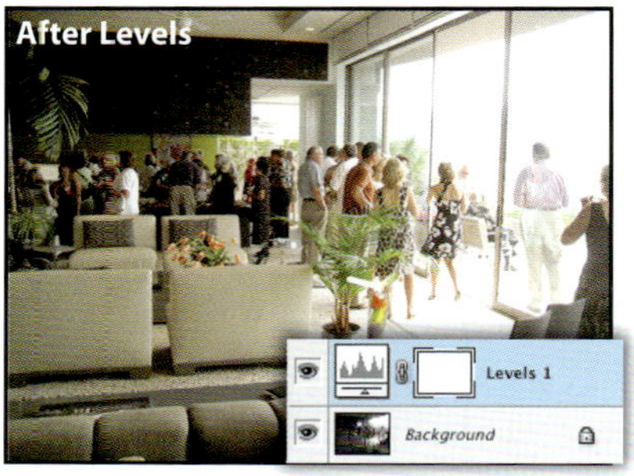

Now we could edit the adjustment layer mask to mask off the window but it is not too obvious where to stop and start. So we'll do something easy instead, using gradients. We go ahead and do our Levels adjustment layer, fixing the room at the expense of the window. Then we select our Gradient tool, choose Black,White and, with the adjustment layer still selected, we drag our Gradient tool from right to left as shown.

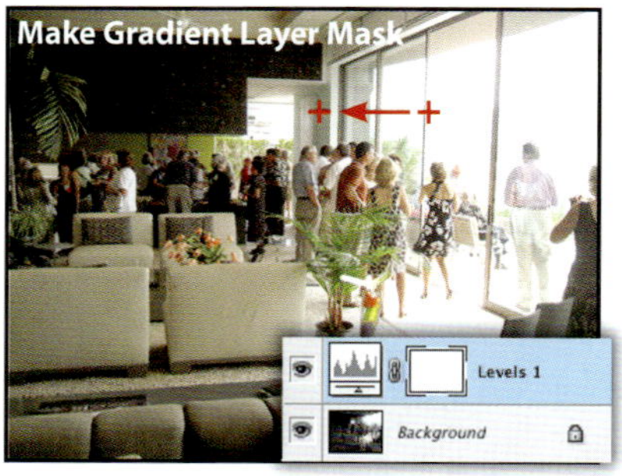

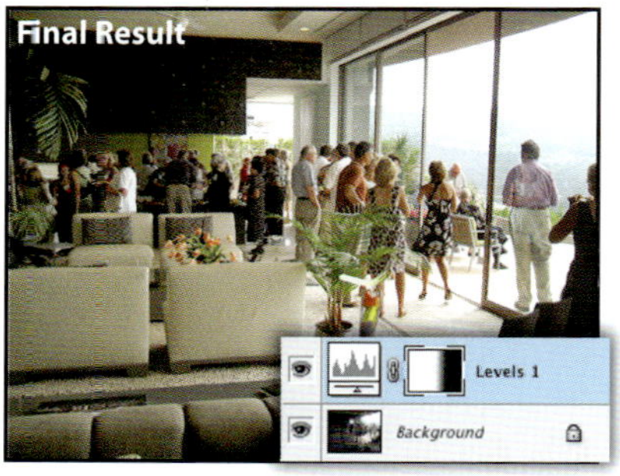

A gradient has now been painted onto the layer mask for the adjustment layer. Check out the thumbnail. The Levels adjustment layer effect has been masked out on the right side of the image but completely active on the left side. Exactly the effect we were looking for. And the beauty of this technique (aside from its simplicity) is that if our gradient if off a little bit, as long as the adjustment layer is still selected, we can just keep redrawing it (varying the start and end points) until it looks right. Each successive gradient paints completely over the previous one. Way cool!

A similar technique can be used to improve this sunrise picture. In this picture, I'd like the city lights to stand out more, as if they were overexposed. I could create a selection of the sky and then use it to create a layer mask to mask off the sky. But a quick and dirty (and very effective) method is to use the gradient tool instead. We create our adjustment layer as before and, with it selected, choose the Gradient tool (Black,White), dragging upwards to make the mask. With a judicious choice of start (where we click) and stop (where we release) points right near the horizon, we get a pretty darn good result. We even get a bonus glow over on the right side.

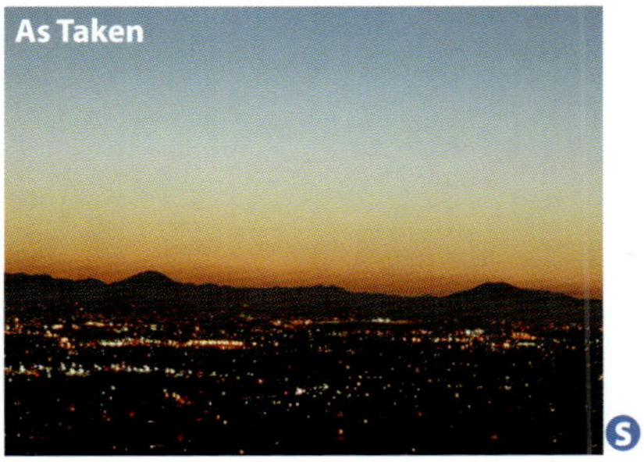

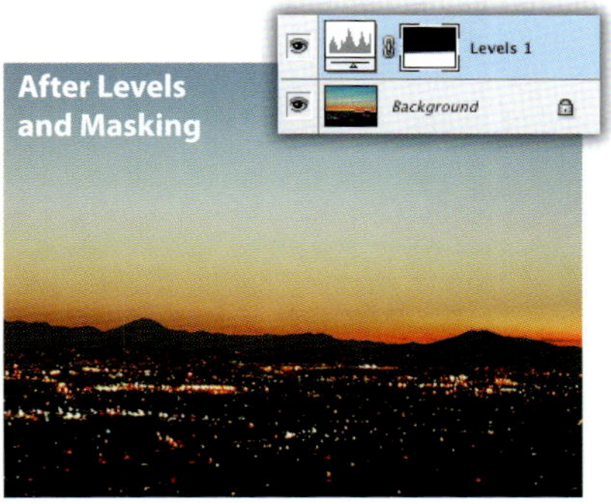

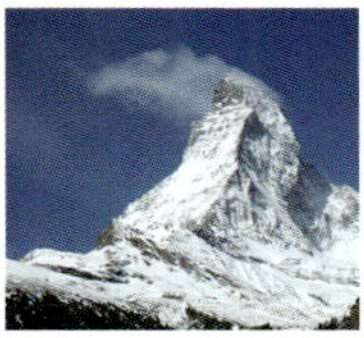

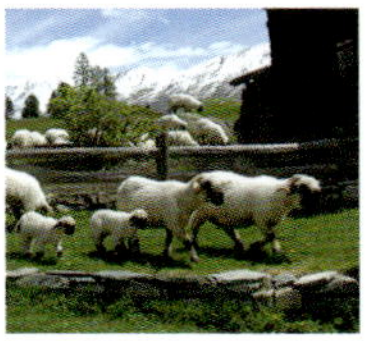

Gradients can also be used in conjunction with layer masks to do quick and dirty compositing. Let's say that we wanted to blend these two images together into one image. We could do an extraction and feather and then a copy and paste. But look at the effect we can quickly get with the Gradient tool and layer masks. We duplicate the 1st image (Layers panel menu), pasting it as a new layer in the 2nd image). With that copied layer selected, we add a layer mask and select it. Next we choose the Gradient tool, set on Black,White and linear, and drag across where we would like a blending boundary between the two images to occur. Voilà. Instant blending!

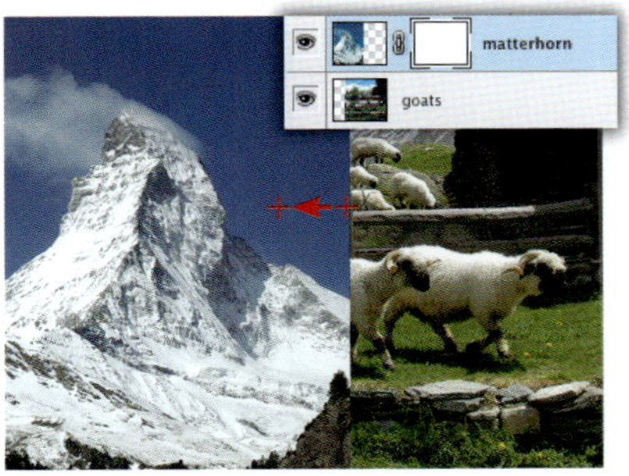

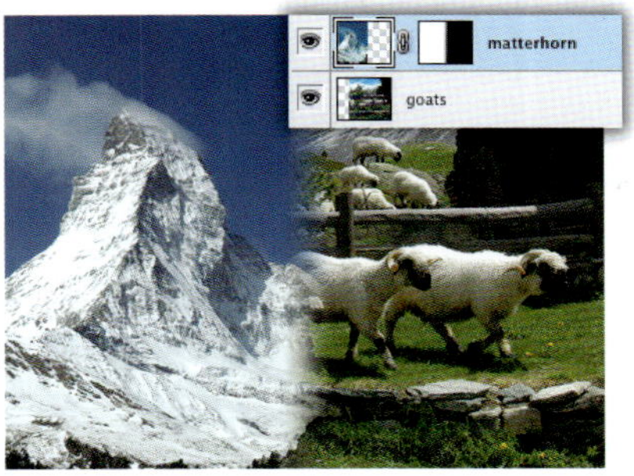

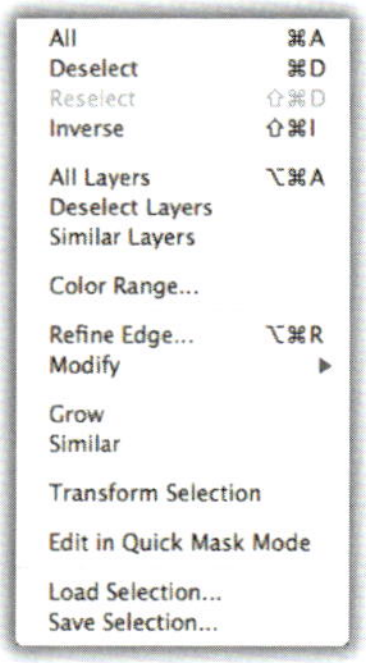

Time to visit selections again. Like layers, they are central to everything we do in Photoshop. In Chapters 6 and 12, we learned valuable tools and techniques for making selections. In this chapter, we will have a look at some of the commands available under Select in the menu bar that can save us lots of time and frustration. We already know a few of these commands We have used "Deselect" and "Inverse" already. "All" simply selects the entire canvas, independent of its contents. And we have also used "Transform Selection" to make refinements to Marquee selections. Now let's check out a few of the others.

Let's say we spent tons of time making a perfect selection of a tree (leaf by leaf by leaf). Perhaps we will use the selection to do an extraction or a hue/saturation change. Of course we already know that we'll want to convert the selection into a layer mask so that it is later editable. But since we spent so much time on this selection, wouldn't it be nice to save it? Just in case...

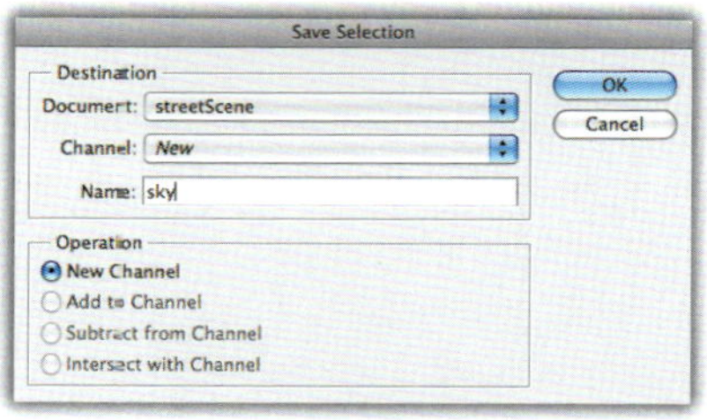

This is what **Save Selection** does for us. With a selection active, we just choose Select>Save Selection. A dialog box pops up with some options to consider, but for now, all we really need to do is to type a meaningful name (I used "sky") and click OK. By default, Photoshop then saves this selection as what it calls a new channel and permanently attaches it to the file.

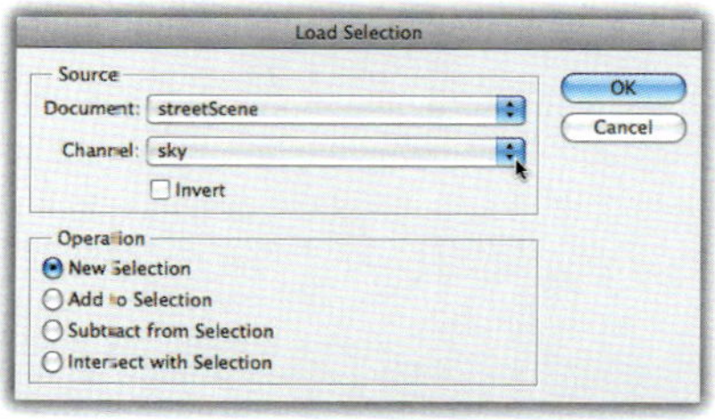

So what if sometime later, we realize we could really use that selection again? It's simple. We choose Select>**Load Selection**, open the Channel menu in the dialog box and choose our saved selection. We click OK and the selection reappears.

The Save Selection and Load Selection dialog boxes also give us the ability to add and subtract from selections. If, for example, we wanted to create and save a selection of two beach balls, we could select one ball and save the selection as, say, "Beach Balls." Then we could select the second ball, choose Select>Save Selection, and under Channel, choose Beach Balls instead of New. The last step is to click the Add to Channel radio button. Now Beach Balls will have both selections saved as one. For additional details on adding to and subtracting from selections, check out Help.

If we didn't save a selection and later wished we had, there may be ways to recover it. If we had jumped a selection of pixels to a new layer, for example, we'd be in luck. Cmd(Ctrl)-Click on a layer's thumbnail and a selection of all non-transparent pixels is loaded. Here, I Cmd(Ctrl)-Clicked on the ET thumbnail and its former selection returned. (Of course we would save it this time, right?)

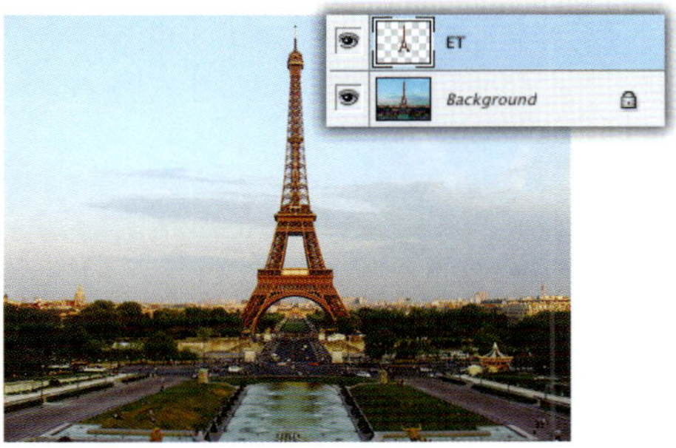

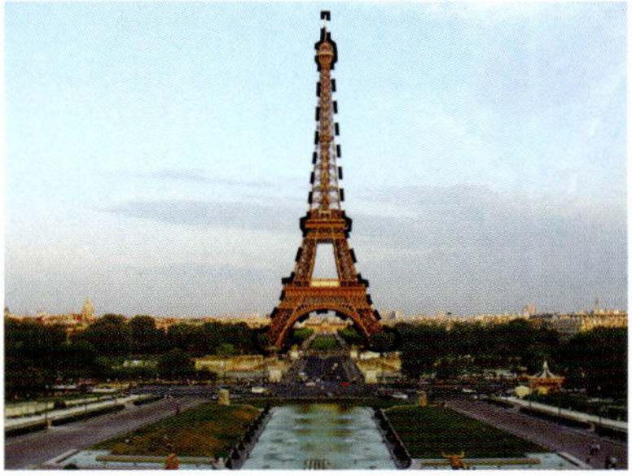

If, instead of jumping pixels to a new layer, we had followed a more prudent approach of creating a layer mask, we can still get back to the selection. We can Opt(Alt)-Click on the layer mask thumbnail to display it in the document window. And then we can use the Magic Wand tool to select all of the black pixels. (I will explain why not white in a moment.) Select>Inverse brings us back to our original selection. Opt(Alt)-Click on the layer mask thumbnail again to return to the normal display.

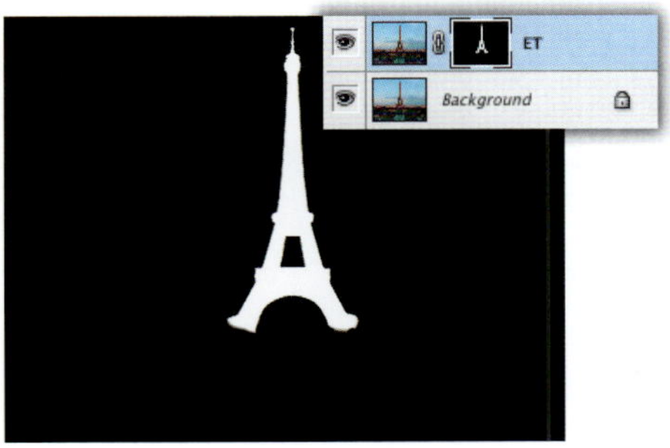

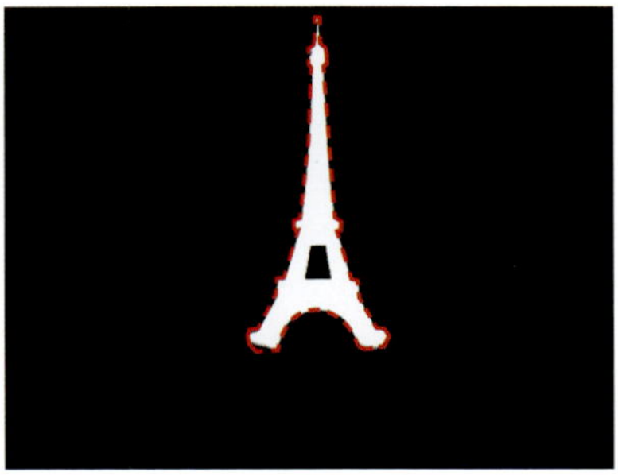

This last technique will run into problems if our layer mask has gray on it (in other words it is not just black and white). Gray would show up if we had feathered the original selection, blurred the layer mask, or used any other technique to create gray, partially transmissive regions. Unfortunately in this case, we really cannot get back to the original selection. So we just do the best we can. This is why I suggested using the Magic Wand tool to select black and then do a Select>Inverse as opposed to just selecting white. This method includes gray mask areas in the selection whereas selecting on white would have excluded them.

Choosing **Select>Modify** opens a dialog box with a few more commands for us. Right now, we will look at only **Expand** and Contract. Expand simply expands or grows our selection by the number of pixels that we specify in its dialog box. **Contract**, as you might have guessed, contracts our selection by a specified number of pixels.

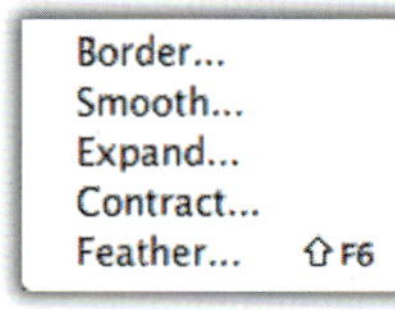

How might we use this in the real world? Let’s say we wanted to remove this white sky and replace it with a pleasing blue sky, maybe with clouds. First we duplicate the Background and then select the copied layer. Next I'd use my Magic Wand tool to select the sky, invert the selection, and create a layer mask. Then I would grab another sky from a different picture, copy that sky over to my document and drag its layer under the Street Scene layer. We did this already in Chapter 20. Here's the result.

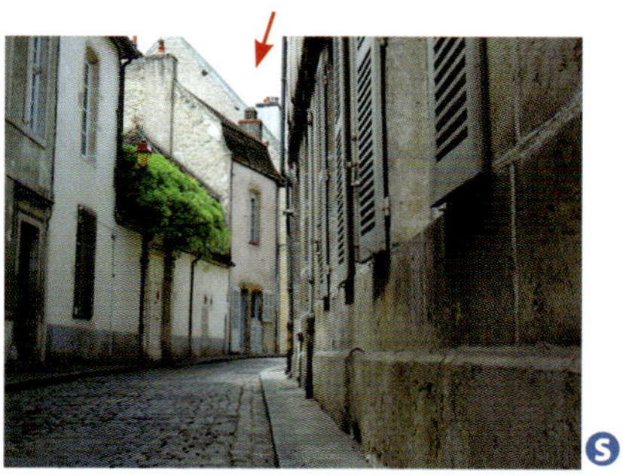

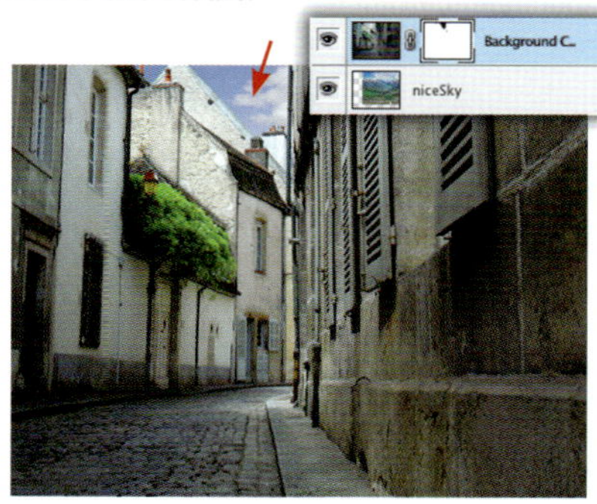

It's okay. But if we look closely, we notice that there is an ugly halo of greenish white around the rooftop. These are edge pixels at the border the roof and the sky that were not selected because they are a slightly different color than the sky. This halo is maybe 3 pixels wide.

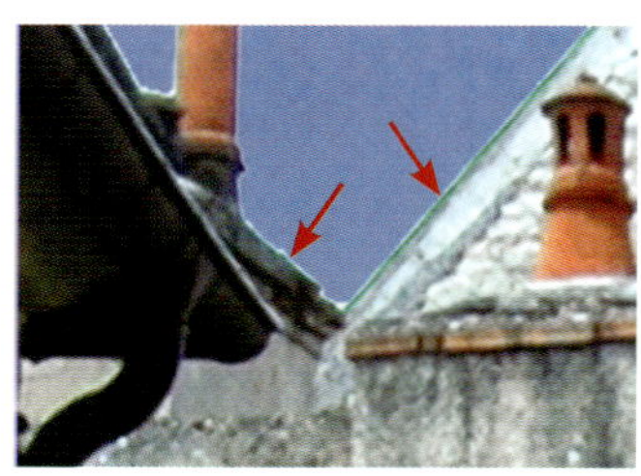

Halo...

We could have avoided this problem by expanding the original Magic Wand selection of the sky by 3 pixels. Then those edge pixels would have been included in the selection so when we inverted the selection and created our layer mask, those pixels would have been masked off along with the rest of the sky. So then when we insert in our new sky, the halo is gone.

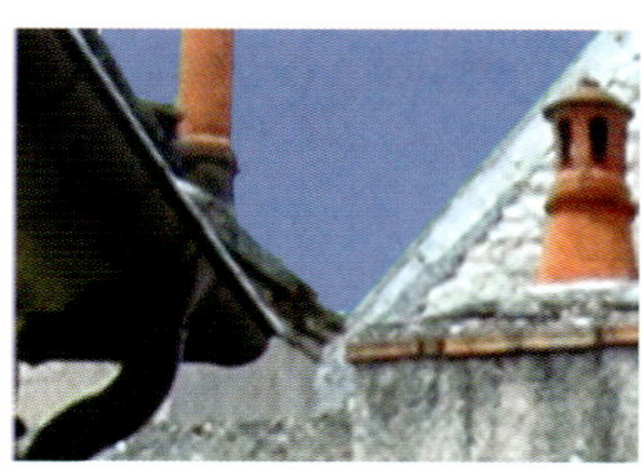

No Halo

The halo is gone but we have a new issue. The edge of our original selection is nice and sharp, sharper in fact than the rest of the image. Compare the sharp edge of the chimney on the left with the soft edge on the right chimney. This type of problem jumps out on an enlargement. Here is where we use Select>Modify>**Feather**.

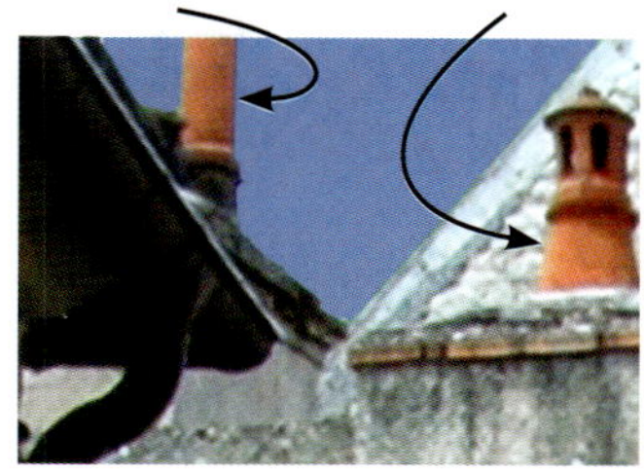

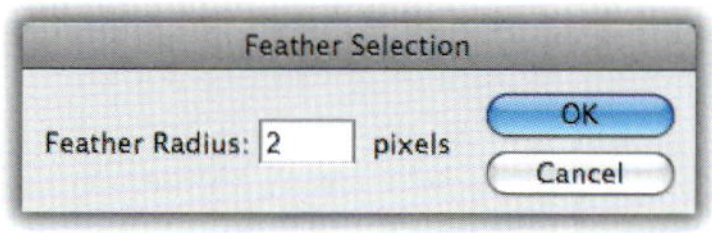

Recall that many of the selection tools we discussed earlier have feathering options. But some do not. In particular the Magic Wand tool does not. But we can still feather our selection by using the Feather command. We first use our Magic Wand to make our selection of the sky. To get rid of the halo, we expand the selection as before (and I will choose 5 pixels this time). And then we choose Select>Modify>Feather and specify 2 pixels. Now when we create our layer mask to mask the sky, the halo is gone and the roof top is softer. (A little hard to see with these small pictures, I know!)

Here the selection was feathered and the image elements match better.

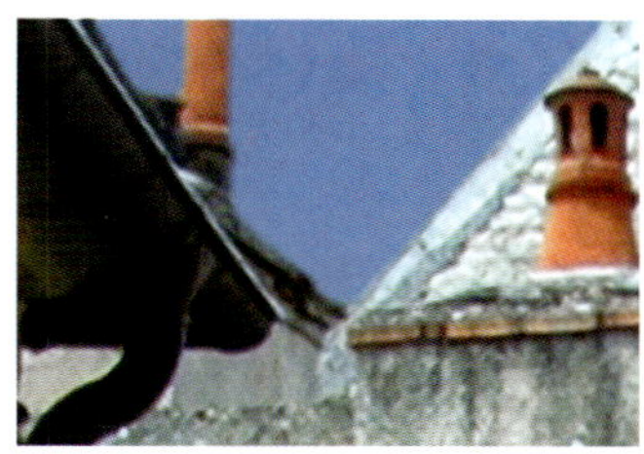

Can you figure out why we chose to expand the sky selection by those couple of extra pixels? We have to envision what is going on with feathering. As we know, when Photoshop feathers, it pegs the selection border to 50% selected. The selection transitions to 100% inside the border and to 0% outside the border at a rate dependent on the amount of the feathering. In our sky example, this would have meant that the halo might still have been visible in the transition region of the selection. It would have been fainter, but it would have been there. We expanded the selection more to prevent this.

Here's a visual that might help. The screen shot here is a blow up of the layer mask border where I feathered the original selection by 2 pixels. The selection border gets pegged at 50% gray with pixels inside transitioning to white and those outside to black. Note that a feather of 2 still gives 8 to 10 pixels of transition. (No, I don't know why.)

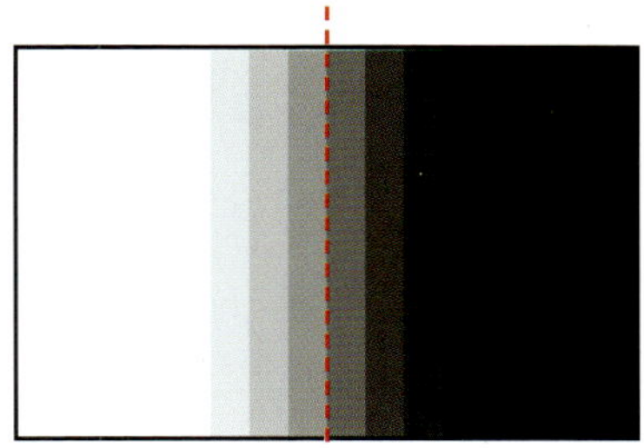

28. THE TRANSFORM COMMAND

For a section on layers, we seem to be spending a lot of time discussing other things, like gradients, selections, and now the **Transform command**. The reason is that these items are best described in the context of layers–their purpose in life just makes more sense. So bear with me... The next two chapters will be back to hardcore layers.

In past chapters, we've extracted part of one image and placed it in a second image. More often than not when we do this, the extracted item will not be exactly the right size in second image. With careful planning and diligent use of Image>Image Size, we could fix this problem up front. But that's a lot work. (And who wants to carefully plan and be diligent?) The easier solution is to use the Transform command to resize the extracted object once we've placed it in its new image.

Here's our street scene (Beaune, France by the way) from the last chapter. It's a nice image but could it use something more? How about, oh, a gorilla?

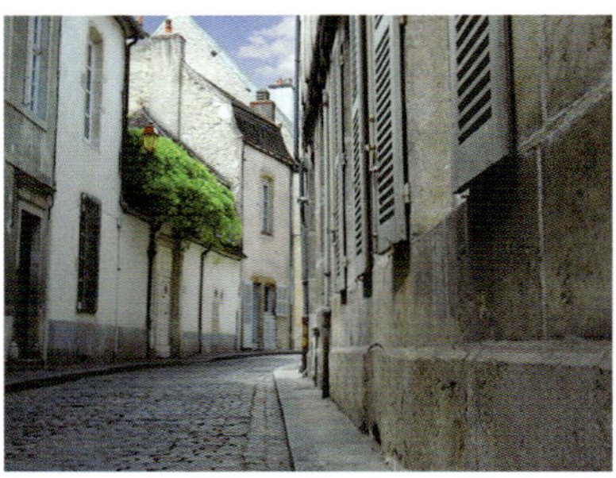

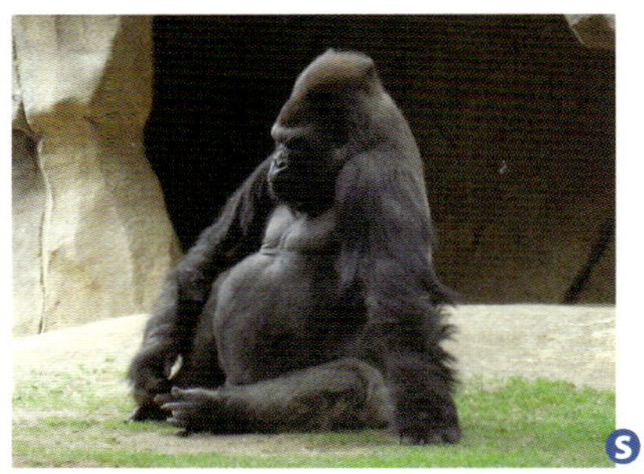

We follow the steps described in Chapter 20 and extract the gorilla's pixels onto a new layer within its document and then duplicate that layer into the destination image, the street scene. (We really should have done this with a layer mask but it is a little easier to see what is going on with Transform if we use this method. As a general rule, though, use the layer mask technique.) The copied gorilla is sized according to its original size in pixels in relation to the destination image's size in pixels.

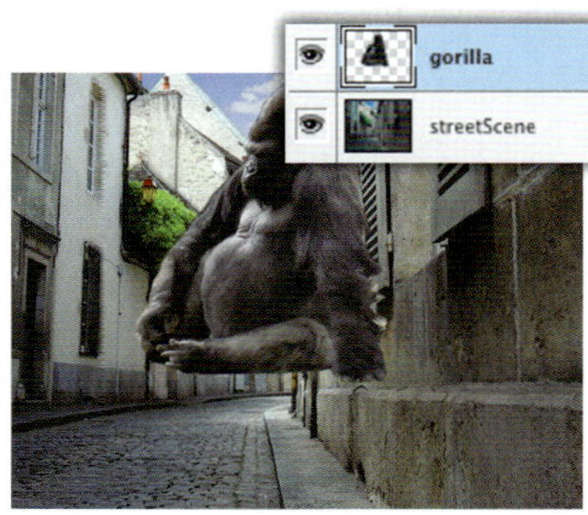

Of course the gorilla is not located correctly in its new home and let's say it should be smaller. (Not that there is a really correct size for a gorilla in this scene!) We are able to correct both of these issues with the Transform command. Let's see how.

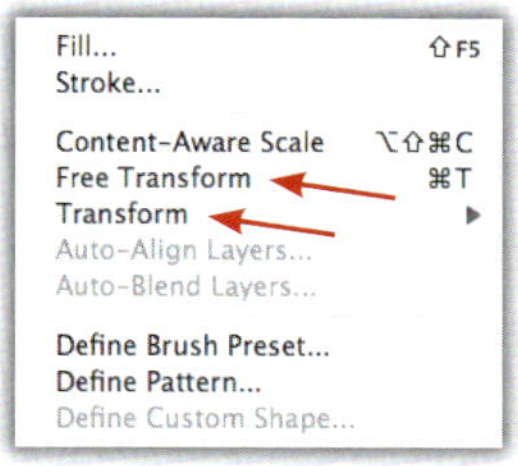

The Transform command is found under Edit in the menu bar and comes in two different flavors, Free Transform and Transform. Both of these commands have very similar capabilities. For the most part, though, I use the Free Transform version, opting for Transform only for specialized needs. But we will review them both and you can pick your favorite. Let's start with Free Transform.

When we choose Edit>**Free Transform**, we get a rectangle, called a bounding box, around all of the non-transparent pixels on the layer we have selected. If the layer is an image that fills the canvas, then the bounding box goes around the full canvas. If the layer is our extraction, which has lots of transparency, then the bounding box is sized to just include the non-transparent pixels, like the gorilla. (If we have a layer mask in place, then the bounding box will include the full layer mask as well.)

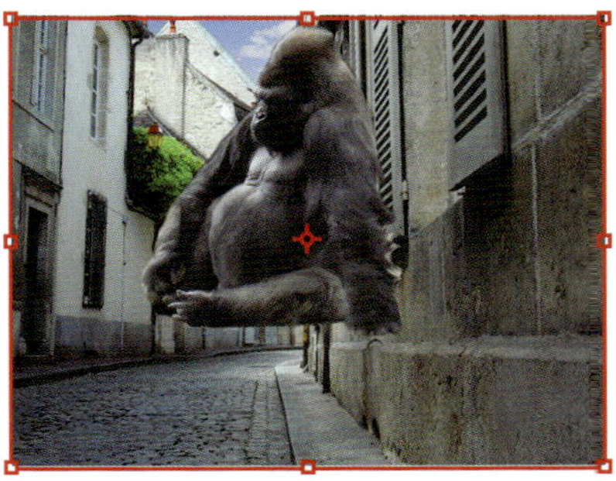

Free transform, street scene layer selected

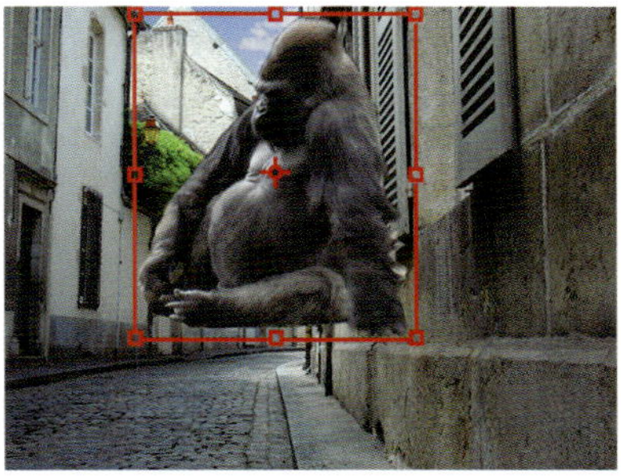

Free transform, gorilla layer selected

Around the Transform rectangle, we see resizing handles. These should be getting familiar by now. They work exactly like those we reviewed for transforming selections in Chapter 6 and for cropping in Chapter 16.

As before, our cursor changes depending on where we are hovering to indicate the type of transform that will occur on a click and drag. Clicking and dragging within the bounding box moves the box.

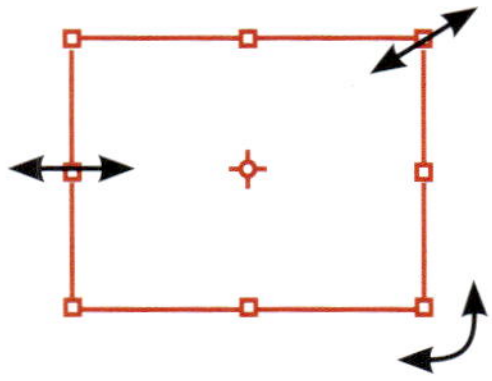

But there is a very important distinction between the Transform Selection and Crop resizing handles and Free Transform resizing handles. Transform Selection and Crop handles transform boundaries. The Free Transform handles transform both the boundary as well as all of the content within that boundary on the chosen layer. This is how we are going to resize our gorilla.

Let's go back to our example. So far, we have gotten our gorilla into the street scene. But it's too big and in the wrong place. To fix that, we select the gorilla layer in the Layers panel and choose Edit>Free Transform. Holding down the shift key to maintain aspect ratio, we push in on one of the corners to shrink the gorilla to a more appropriate size. Then, with the cursor inside the bounding box, we click and drag the gorilla to a better location. When we're satisfied, we either hit Return(Enter) or click the Commit check mark in the options bar just as with Transform Selection and Crop.

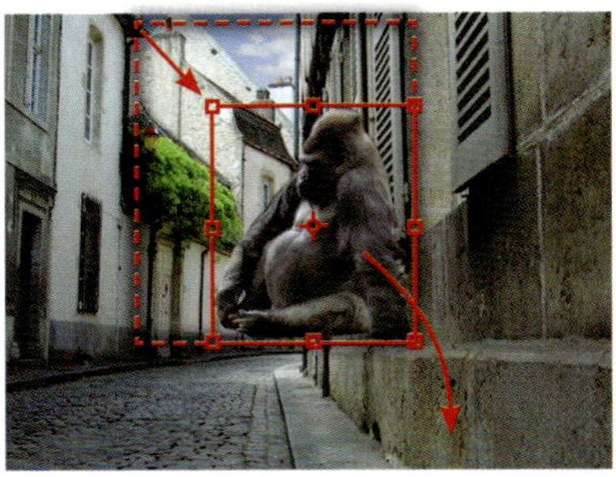

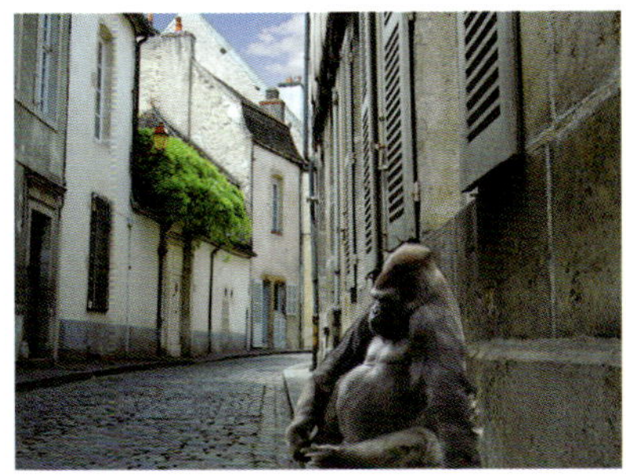

Yes, the Free Transform command has its own options bar. If we want specific, by the numbers transformations, we can make entries here as opposed to using the click and drag technique. From left to right, we have the X and Y location, width and height (click the chain link to lock in aspect ratio), rotation (always starts at 0 degrees), horizontal and vertical skew and warp (I will come back to this one). We simply enter numbers in the boxes to get our desired effect. Generally, however, I am using my eyes as a guide so I am clicking and dragging as opposed to entering numbers.

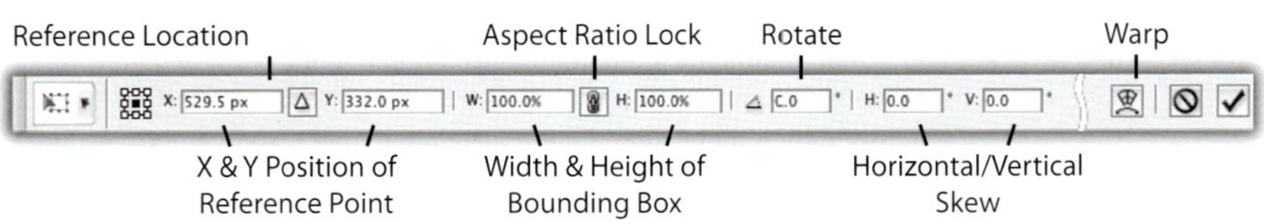

This is probably a good time to issue a big warning. Our gorilla was too big so we scaled it down. And how did this happen? When we transformed it, Photoshop actually downsampled the gorilla, just as if we had done it with Image>Image Size.

That's fine. But what if we had needed to make it bigger? Well, Photoshop will do our bidding. But in this case, it will do it by upsampling and, unfortunately, degrading the quality of the gorilla. Refer back to Chapter 5 if you need a refresher on this. In some ways, this situation is even worse than upsampling a whole image because the reduced quality of the gorilla might stand out against a higher quality background. So proceed carefully with Free Transform. The pixels are permanently altered.

Now on to the **Transform** command. If we chose Edit>Transform, we get a new menu with even more commands. Most are actually in the Free Transform options bar and work in the same way. The preset Rotates (180° etc.) and the Flips are new and can save you some keystrokes when you need to apply those specific transforms. Perspective creates, well, perspective but it is much easier to accomplish the same thing with Distort.

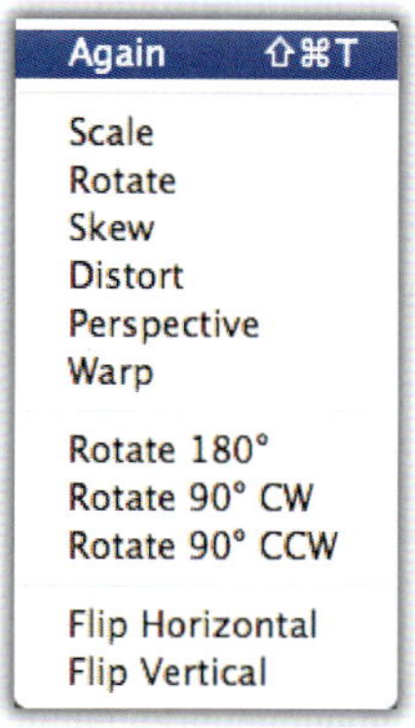

Distort allows us to freely distort the transform bounding box by dragging on its corner handles independently. Here's an example–let's put our gorilla in a picture frame. With an imported gorilla layer on top of the frame layer, we choose Distort and line up the corner handles of the gorilla with the underlying print. I've lowered the gorilla's opacity to make it easier to line things up. Then I hit Commit, reset opacity, and I'm done.

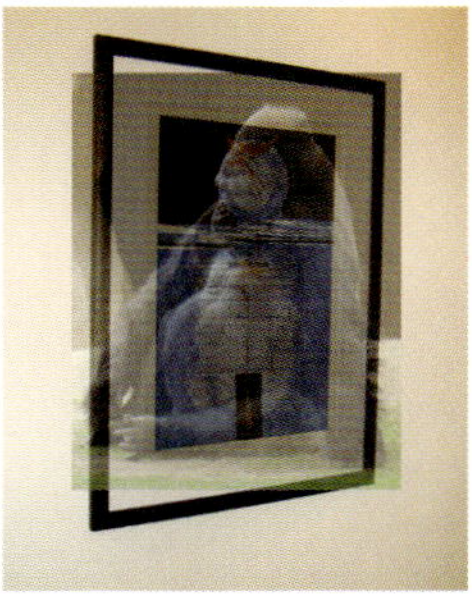

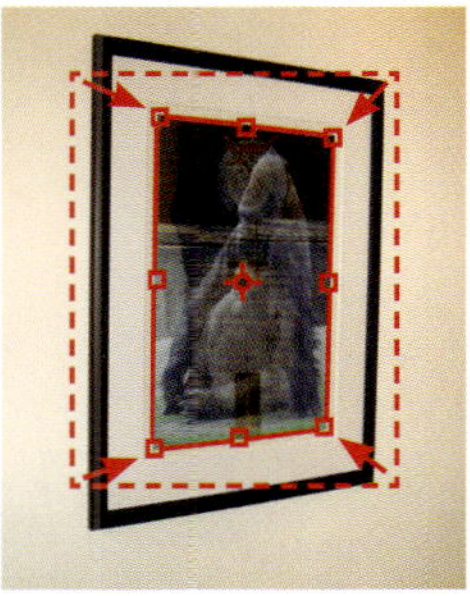

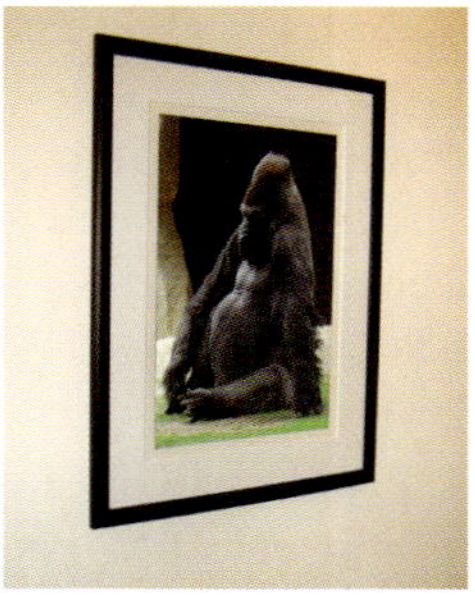

And last, there is **Warp**. With it, we can correct horizon curvatures that often occur with point and shoot cameras. Here we correct the upper left of the image by dragging on the intersections of the warping grid that appears when we select the function.

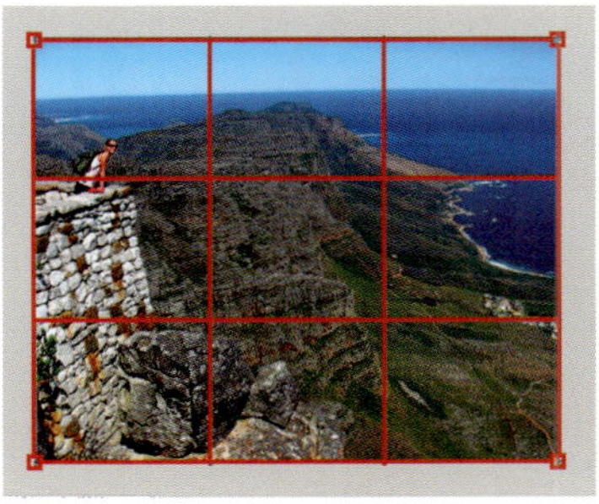

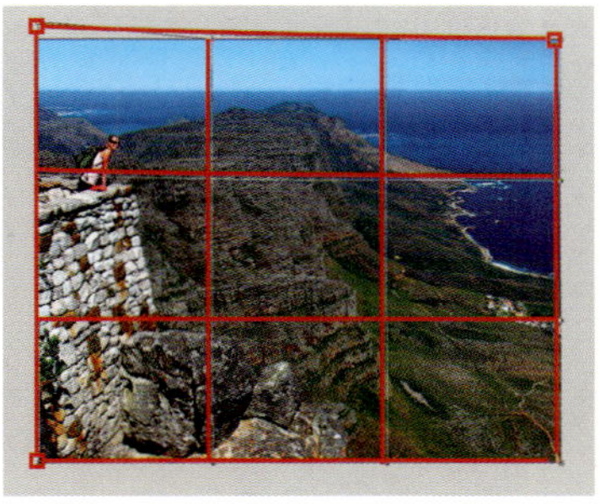

29. WANAKA SUNRISE EXAMPLE

In this chapter we will pull many of the techniques we've learned together to do a simple composite. This is a real life example of mine and you'll see that the basic flow will be applicable to many of your projects. Below left is a sunrise picture of Lake Wanaka in New Zealand. Not a bad starting point. But I remembered another shot I had taken the previous day of a bird on a rock (below right). If only that bird could have been standing on one of the protruding posts at the sunrise. Well, let's put it there!

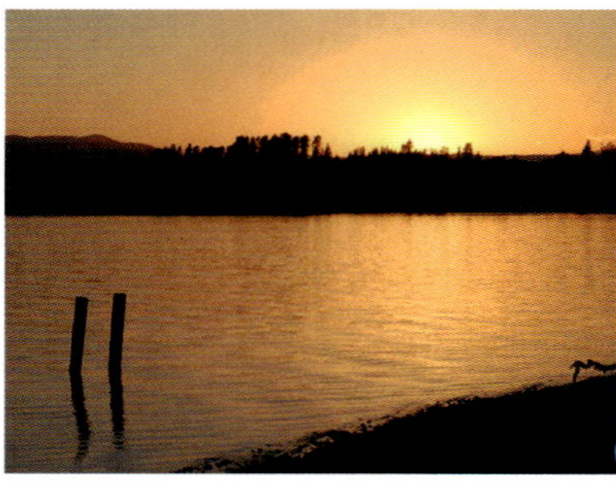

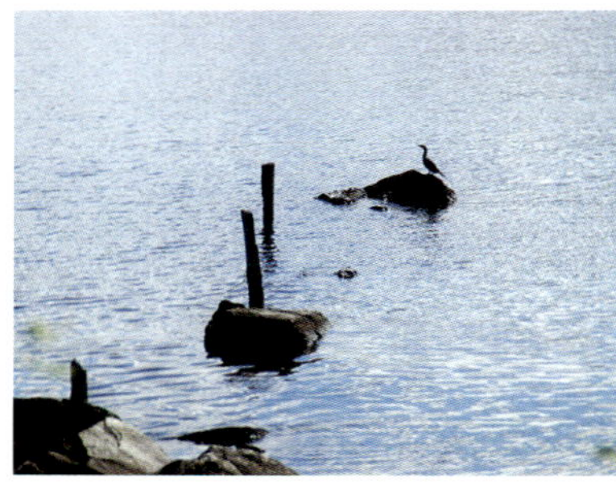

We will do this step by step. There is nothing new here; we have discussed it all. We are just putting it all together.

We open the "bird" image and make a copy of Background by dragging that layer onto the New Layer icon in the Layers panel. We rename the layer "Bird." (Chapter 19) We will do our bird extraction with a Layer Mask but to simplify life down the line (I will point out when), we crop the picture closer to the size of the bird. (Chapter 16)

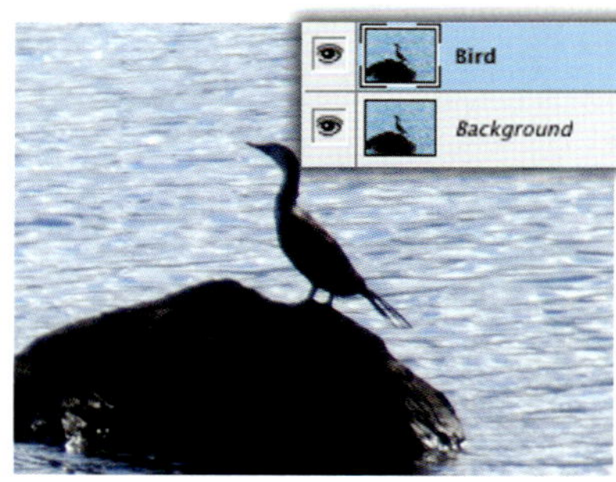

Now we select the bird using the tool of our choice. I used the Magnetic Lasso with a feather of 1 pixel. (Chapter 12) We will see why we needed the feathering in a few steps.

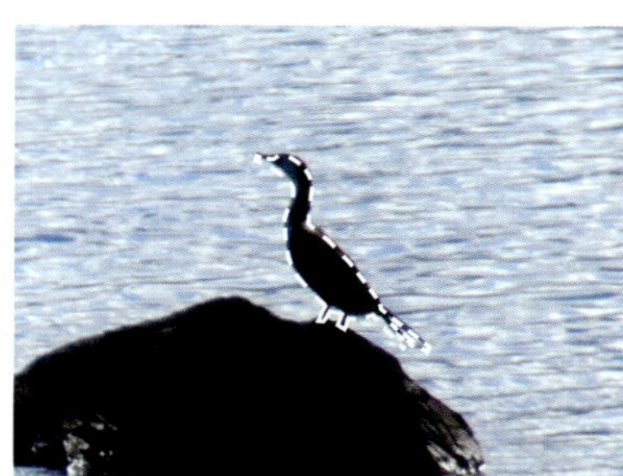

With the selection still active and the "Bird" layer chosen, we click the Add Layer Mask icon in the Layers panel. Now the background is masked off with only the bird showing. And if later we see that our selection needs work, we can just edit the layer mask. (Chapter 25).

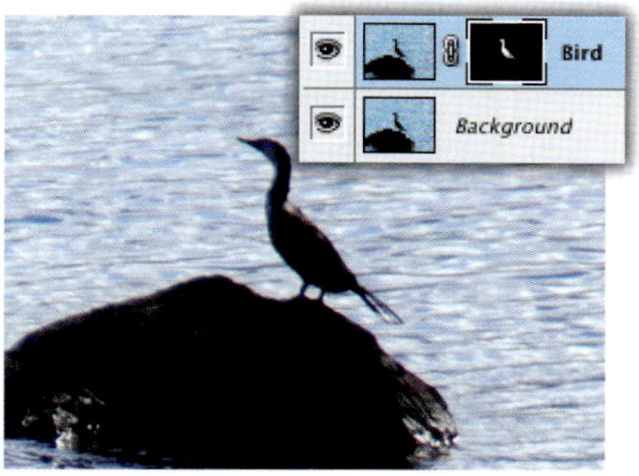

Now we open up our sunrise image to bring in the bird. To do this, we make our bird image active again by selecting it under Window in the menu bar. We select the Bird layer and, using the Layers panel menu, duplicate it with the sunrise image as the destination. Now the bird is in the sunrise image as a new layer. (Chapter 20) We use the Move tool to reposition it.

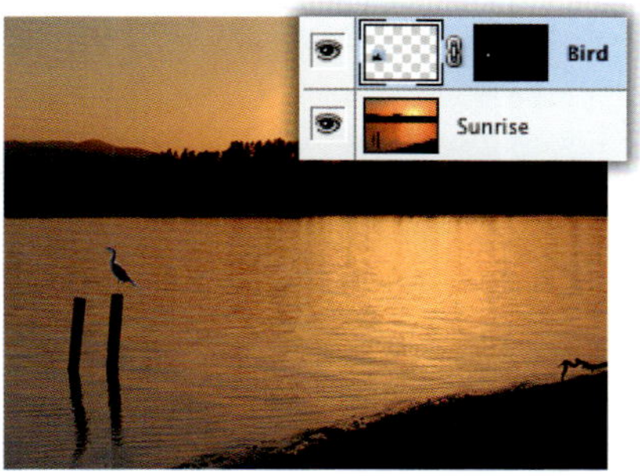

I think the bird should be looking towards the sunrise so, with the Bird layer selected, we do an Edit>Transform>Flip Horizontal. (Chapter 28)

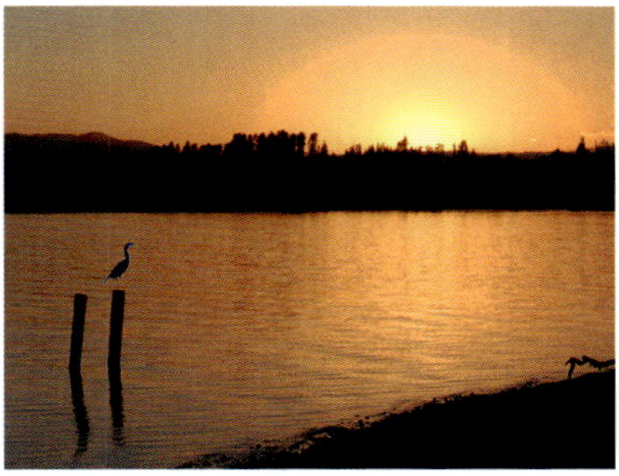

The bird is a bit big as well. We choose Edit>Free Transform and, holding the shift key down, push a corner handle in to shrink the bird proportionally. Then placing the cursor within the transform box, we drag the bird to one of the posts. Its legs look too short though. We can fix that in a moment. (Chapter 28)

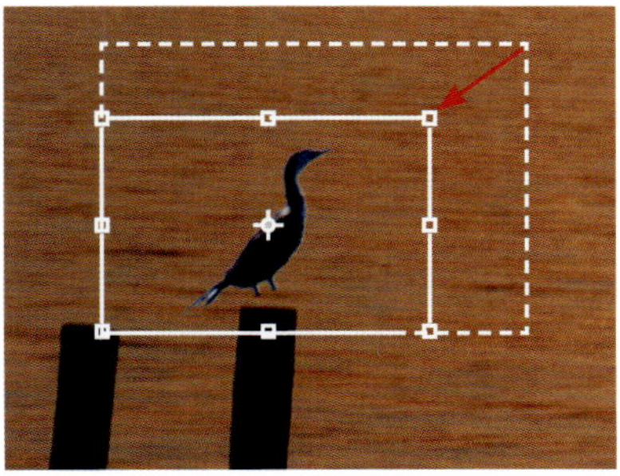

If we hadn't cropped the bird image, our transform box in the previous step would have conformed to the original full-sized image. This would have made it a bit more unwieldy to deal with. It would still work, of course. It's just more convenient to be able to zoom in and still have the transform handles visible and available.

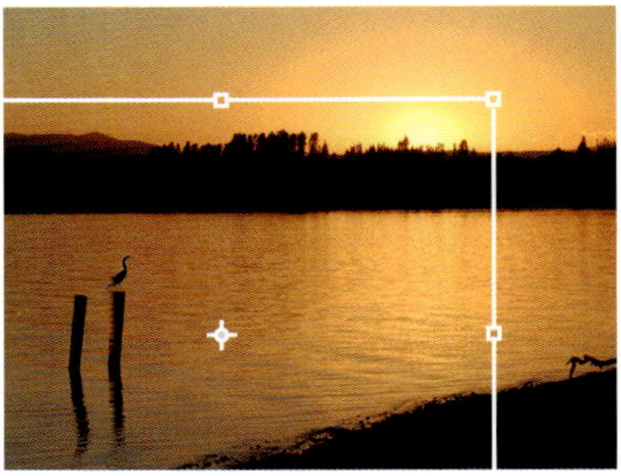

We can see that the bird is much lighter than it should be. We would like it to be a total silhouette, much like the posts. Let's use the actual post color since it is not exactly black. We select the Eyedropper tool in the toolbox and click on the post. This sets the foreground color to the post color (almost black but not quite). (Chapter 8)

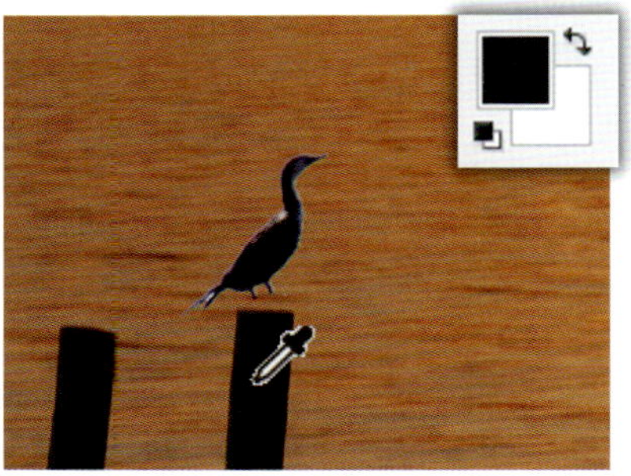

Since we are just looking for a silhouette of the bird, we can fill the layer with the foreground color and count on the layer mask to maintain our shape for us. With the layer thumbnail selected, we choose Edit>Fill and choose Foreground Color.

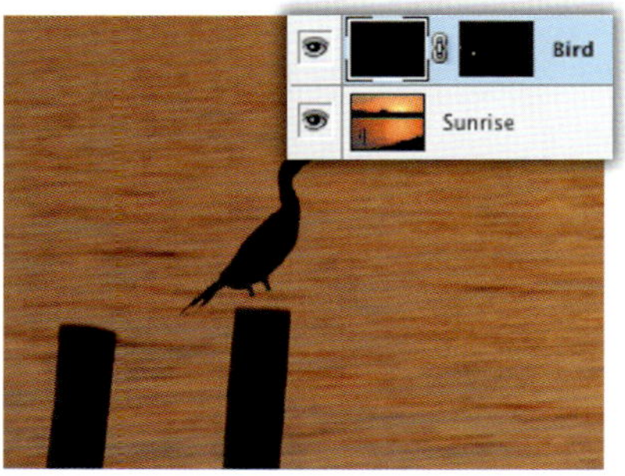

When we did our initial bird selection, I had us use a feather of 1 pixel. Had we not done so, the outline of the bird would have looked unrealistically hard compared to the posts. If further blurring is required, we could select the layer mask and choose Filter>Blur>Gaussian Blur and adjust it (or check out this section's CS4 tips). But it actually looks pretty good. (Chapter 25)

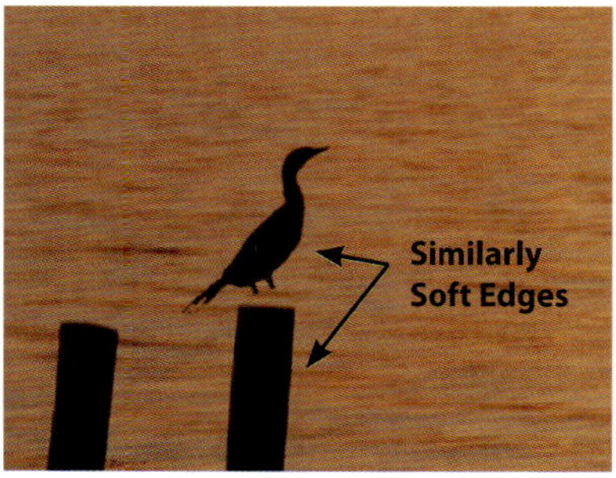

Time to fix those legs. We click on the New Layer icon in the Layers panel and rename it Legs. We choose the Brush tool, noting that the foreground color still corresponds to the bird/post color. We pick a diameter near the bird's leg size, set Hardness to around 50%, and, after zooming in, draw in the missing legs. (Chapter 11)

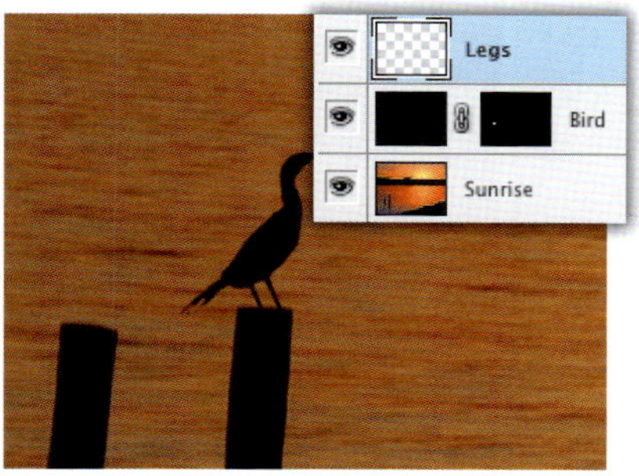

Now the compositing is complete and we can do our normal enhancing. With the Legs layer selected, we click the Create New Adjustment Layer icon in the Layers panel and choose Levels. The black and white points look pretty good but perhaps the picture could be darkened a bit. We choose the Midtone slider and move it slightly to the right. (Chapters 14 and 21)

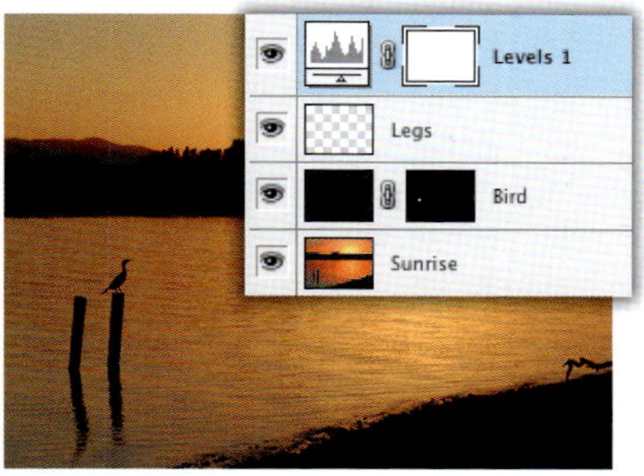

On to Hue/Saturation. We click the Create New Adjustment Layer icon in the Layers Panel and choose Hue/Saturation. By moving the hue slider a bit to the right, we dampen the reddish tones. (These changes are subtle but can make our images much more pleasing.) We won't bump the saturation as the sun is already pretty bright. (Chapters 15 and 21)

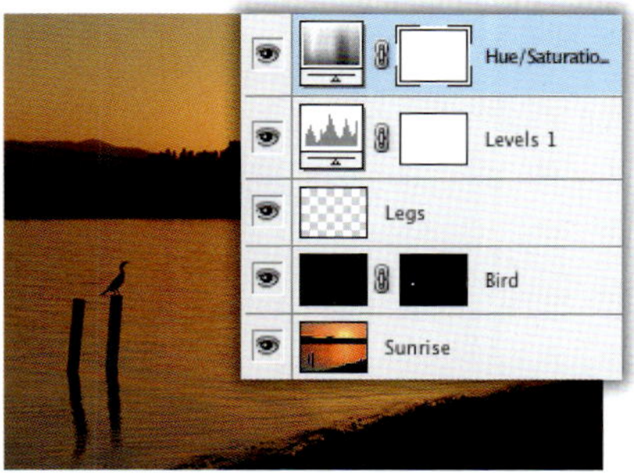

And there you have it, a finished composite. Selections, layers, layer masks, transformations, recoloring, brushes, and adjustment layers all in one exercise. The flow is pretty easy and quick; everything is editable; and the result looks pretty good.

There is the slight matter of the bird's reflection being missing. We'll tackle that in Chapter 45.)

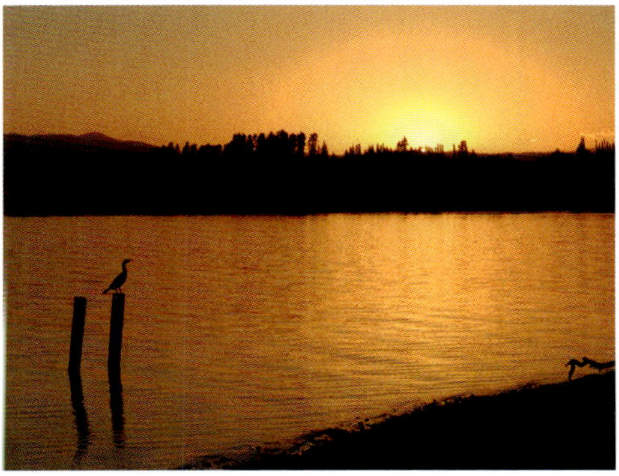

30. OPACITY AND FILL

We know a little about Opacity from Chapter 19 but now it's time to dig into it a bit more. We will find that simple though it is, opacity is actually quite powerful and has a number of useful applications. And we will finally learn about Fill.

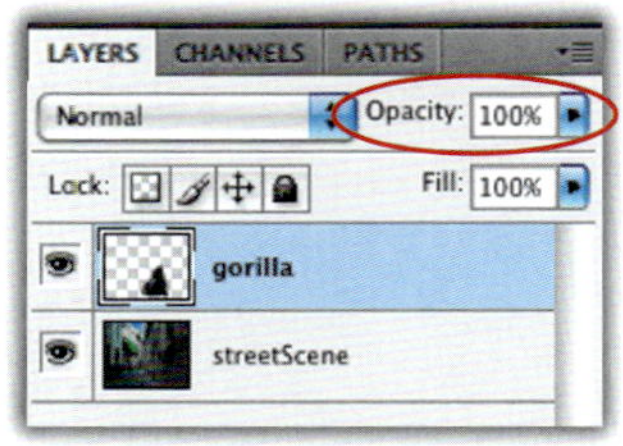

The **Opacity Control** is found in the Layers panel, in the upper right, and is by default set at 100%. Each layer has its own opacity setting; the number in the box is the opacity for the selected layer, our favorite gorilla in this example. At 100% opacity, a layer's content is opaque, blocking anything below it from view. At 0% opacity, the content becomes totally transparent. Anything below is totally visible. At opacities between 0% and 100%, the content becomes partially transparent (in proportion to the setting) and we see a blend of the layer and the underlying layers. (Transparent or empty pixels are always transparent, independent of their layer's opacity setting.)

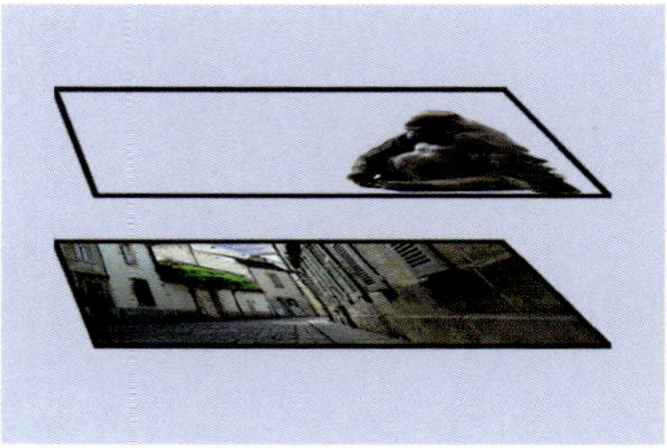

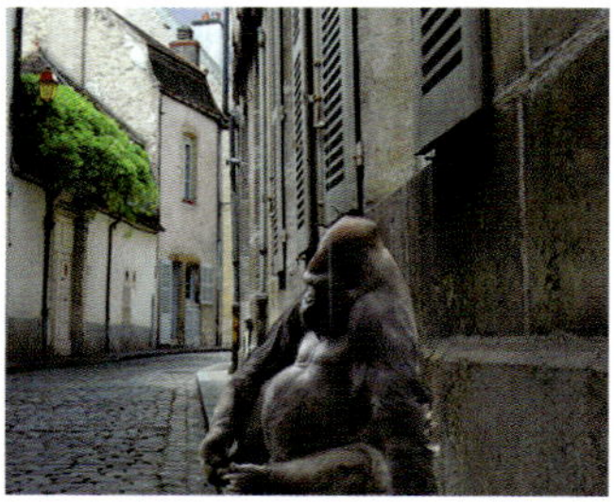

Opacity = 100%

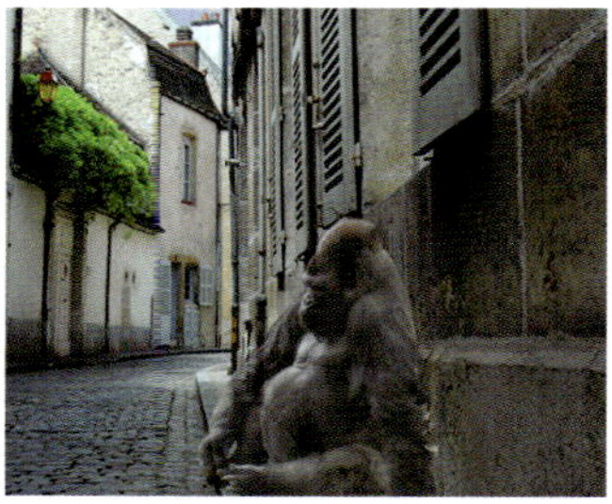

Opacity = 75%

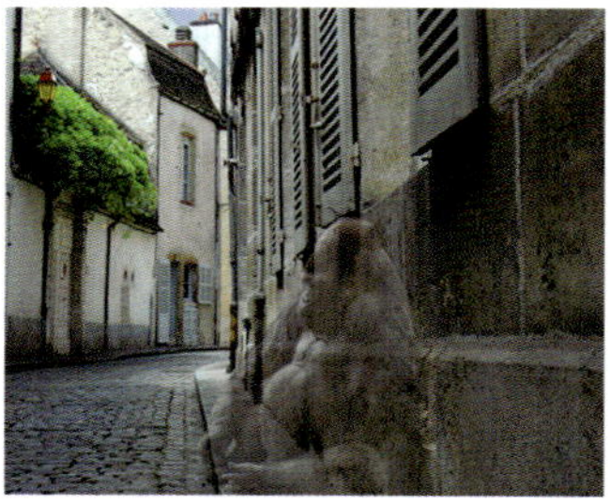

Opacity = 50%

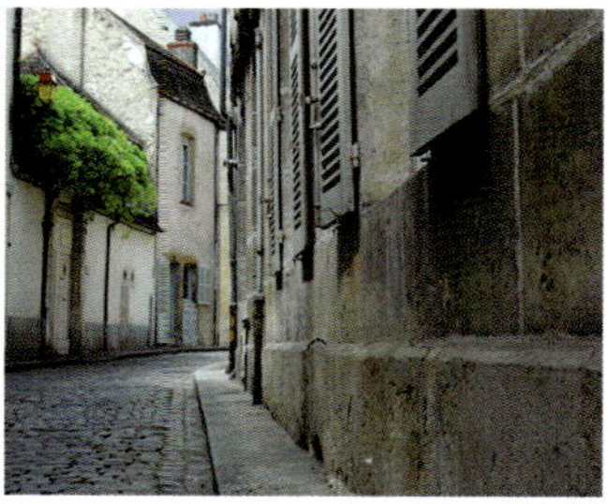

Opacity = 0%

This blending attribute of opacity can be put to easy and effective use. In this example, I opened an image (from our previous chapter) and added a text layer, typing the words Wanaka Sunrise. I used the eyedropper to pull one of the sunrise colors out for the text but perhaps it's a bit bold, grabbing too much attention.

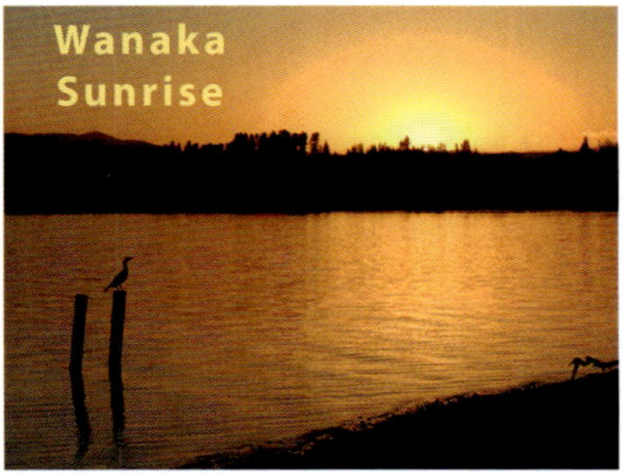

One easy fix is to blend the text with the underlying image using opacity. Here I have chosen 50% opacity for the text layer and the text becomes understated and integrates more naturally with the image.

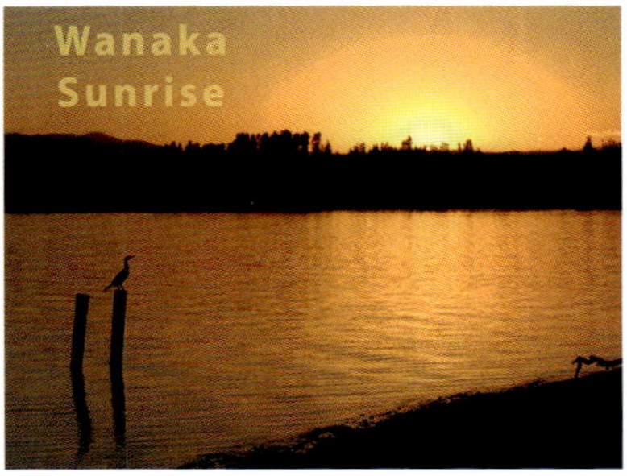

This is a very straightforward, one setting change and it yields an pretty appealing result.

Here is another example that demonstrates opacity blending in a slightly different way. This image was also taken on New Zealand's South Island and I have added a layer on top, "map outline," with a graphic outline of New Zealand. (Notice also that the map outline layer has an Outer Glow layer style attached to it.) By reducing the opacity of the map outline layer, in this example to 60%, the graphic blends into the underlying image in a more pleasing way. (Note that the layer style opacity is affected as well.)

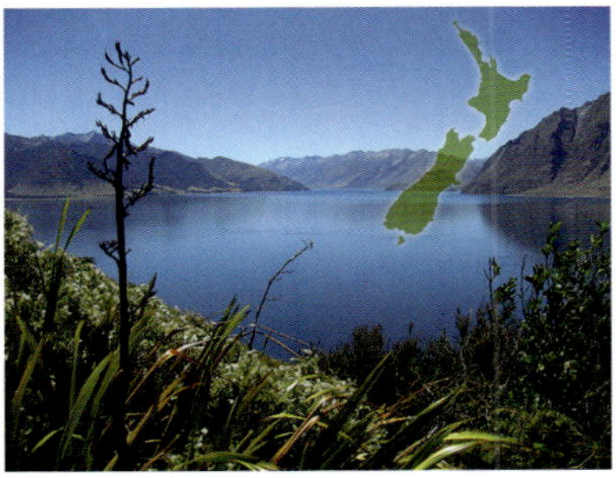

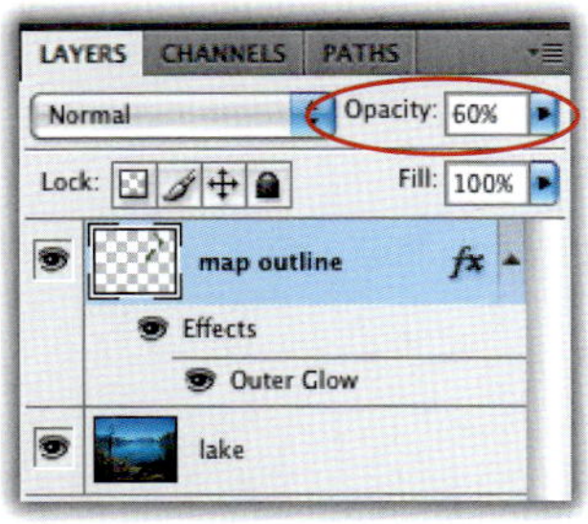

The detail in the underlying image partially shows through the graphic of New Zealand. This is the blending process at work. There are many more powerful methods for creating composites but just using opacity affords us a really quick and easy method for many of our projects.

This is a good time to mention a close cousin of the opacity setting, the **Fill** setting. Fill can be found directly under the opacity setting in the upper right hand corner of the Layers panel and is controlled in exactly the same way. The difference is that whereas opacity sets opacity of everything on a layer, fill sets opacity for everything except layer styles and blending modes. We will talk about blending modes in the next chapter but we are already familiar with layer styles from Chapter 24.

Let me explain further with an example. And by the way, this happens to be the only effect that I regularly use the fill setting for. We will use our Wanaka Sunrise image and apply a Bevel and Emboss layer style to the Wanaka Sunrise text layer. If we drag the fill setting of this layer down to 0%, the color of the text becomes transparent but the bevel and emboss effect stays. Neat!

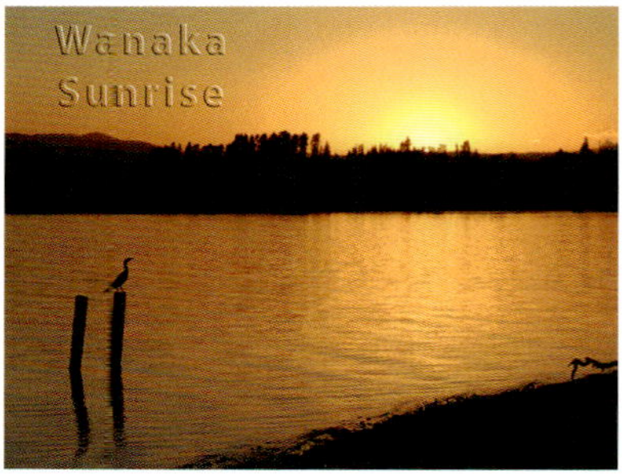

Here's a blown up comparison of the Wanaka Sunrise text with 100% fill and 0% fill. I have moved the text over the top of the mountain so that the transparency effect is more obvious. This is a common and unobtrusive way to create watermarks.

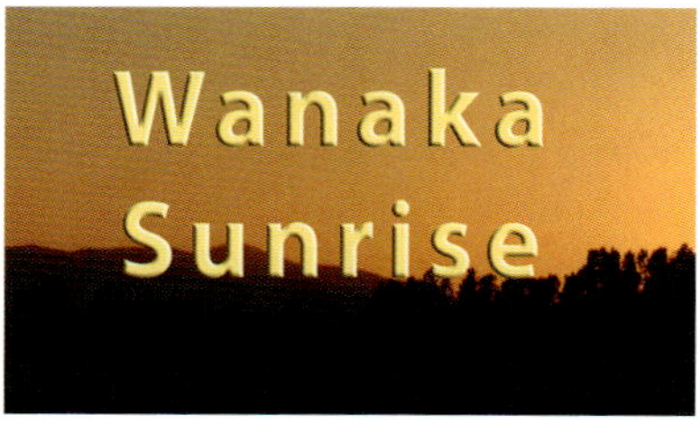

Fill = 100%

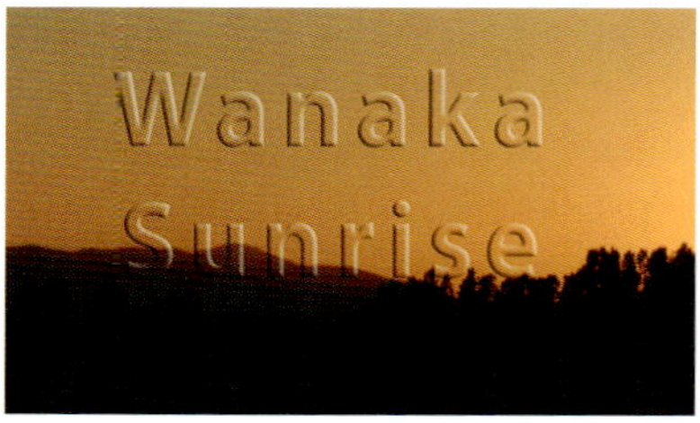

Fill = 0%

Let's go back to our example with the graphic of New Zealand over the lake image. We had spiced up the graphic with an outer glow layer style, right? So were we to reduce the fill setting of that layer to 0%, the map should disappear but the outer glow should stay. And as you can see, that is exactly what happens. I'm not sure the result looks all that special but it illustrates the concept.

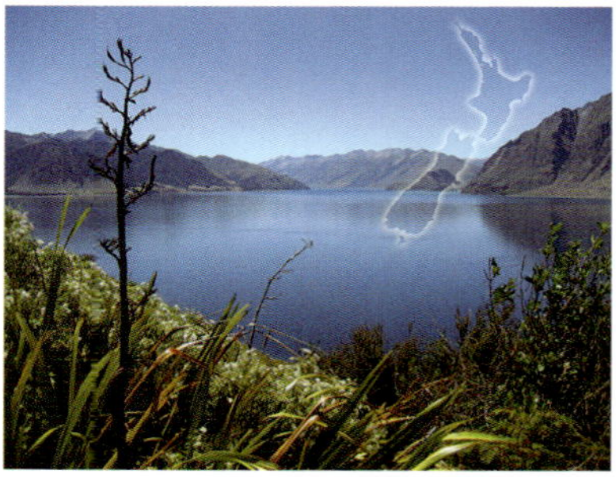

In Chapter 21, we used the opacity setting on an adjustment layer to modulate or decrease the amount of the adjustment. I'd like to use that concept again here to create a demonstration of just how opacity is actually doing blending of layers.

We will start by grabbing our Wanaka Sunrise image from earlier in the chapter. We'll add an Invert adjustment layer by clicking on the New Adjustment Layer icon at the bottom of the Layers panel and then selecting Invert from the pop up menu. Here is the resulting Layers panel.

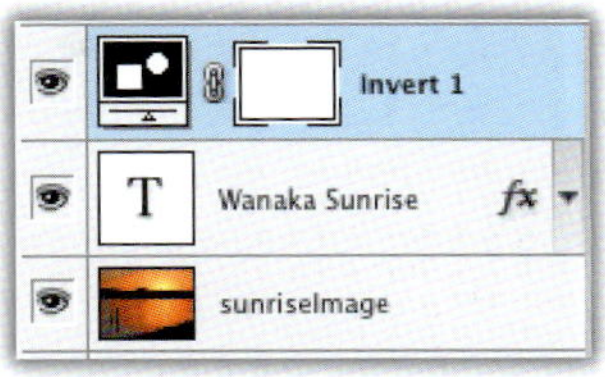

We remember Invert from Chapter 12 on Image Adjustments. It makes color negatives of our images. Back then we didn't implement it as an adjustment layer; we just used Image>Adjustment>Invert. But the better way to do it is with an adjustment layer, right? Yes! Because then it is non destructive and editable.

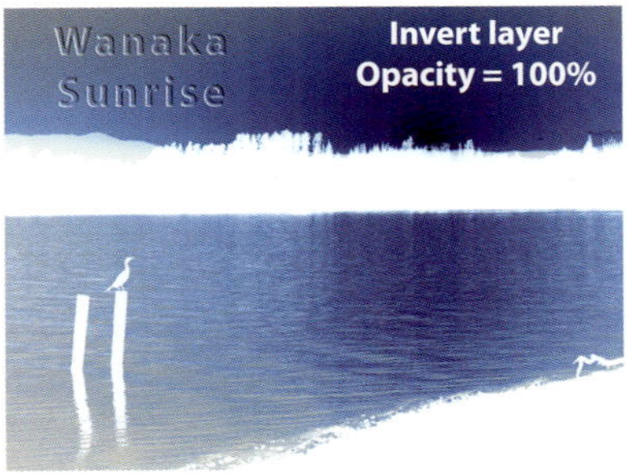

Now if we take the opacity setting of the Invert adjustment layer down to 0%, our initial image returns. The Invert effect, which is to mathematically replace light with dark, dark with light and colors with their compliments, is dialed down to nothing.

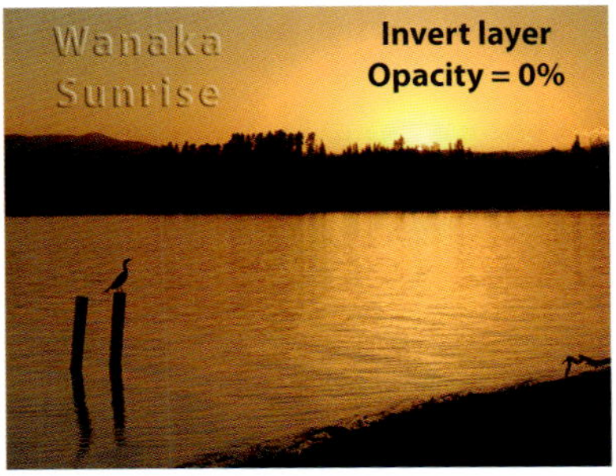

Look what happens when we set opacity to 50%. Everything turns gray! We are blending each pixel with its color-inverted pixel in equal parts. Black blended with white makes gray. Dark blue blended with light yellow makes gray. Everything turns into exactly neutral gray. This type of interaction between layers is what blending, and our next chapter, is all about.

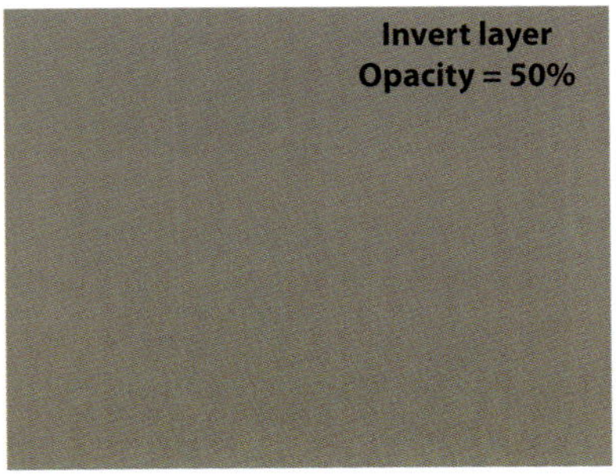

31. BLENDING MODES

In the last chapter, we discussed the Opacity setting and how it could be used to blend a layer with its underlying layers. This method turns out to be only one of many different ways to blend layers. Now I must say I had reservations about adding this chapter because **Blending Modes** can be rather confusing and are really outside the scope of "Just the Skinny." These modes show up in so many options bars and menus, however, that I just can't shake the feeling that we should at least discuss what they are all about, even if we don't use them at this point. Blending modes are fun to play with and can generate some very interesting effects–so we will go over just enough in this chapter that you get the general idea and can play around with them if you choose.

Blending modes are found in many places, most notably in options bars, in the layer style menus, and in the Layers panel. Let's focus on the Layers panel where the concept is a little easier to understand. In the upper left hand corner of that panel, we see a box with "Normal" written in it. This is where blending modes can be specified. Normal is a blending mode and is the standard default for all layers. We can click the disclosure triangles to see the others and, as we see, there are many choices.

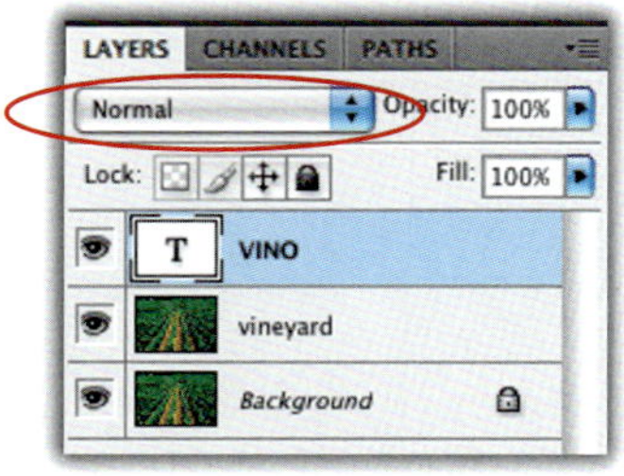

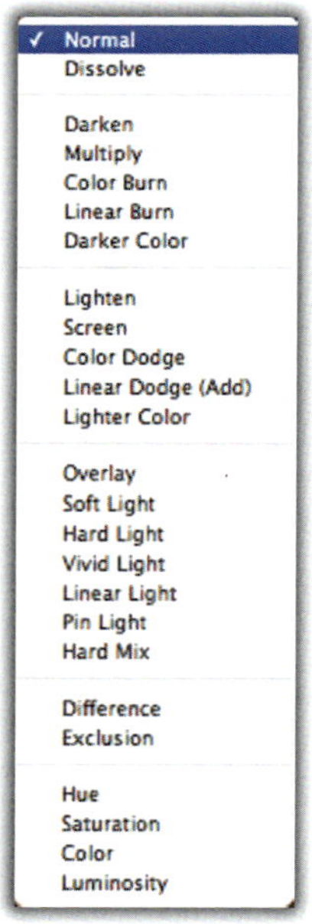

Each layer has its own blending mode and as I said, defaults to Normal. A layer's blending mode specifies a blend, or interaction, between that layer and all of the layers below it. In the Layers panel shown, VINO's blending mode specifies how the layer VINO interacts with the layer vineyard and Background. The resulting blend is displayed, not the layer itself. This will get clearer with examples.

The Normal blending mode is pretty straightforward. Non-transparent pixels on layer VINO cover those on the layers below; transparent pixels on layer VINO allow the underlying layers to show through. So the normal blending mode is really more like no blending at all.

I promised some examples so here we go. One of the blending modes is called **Color**. It is actually the one I seem to use the most. This blending mode displays a blend of the hue and saturation of the selected layer with the luminance, or grayscale, information of the underlying layers. With it, we can make quick and easy duotones (an image with only two colors) or do simple recoloring operations.

Let's say that we wanted to turn this image into a blue/black **Duotone.** It is currently full color, but we want to blend the grayscale version of it with a blue color of our choosing. Fortunately, this is exactly what the blending mode Color does for us.

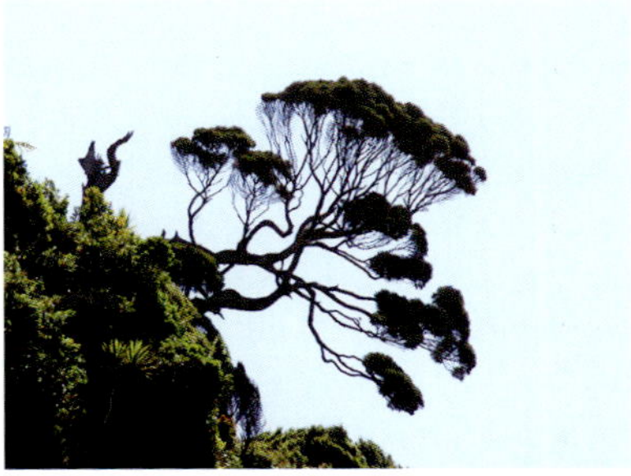

We add a new adjustment layer (use the icon in the Layers panel) and pick Solid Color. This gives us just that, a solid color layer. (I could have just made a new layer and filled it with a color but what fun is that?) When we choose this adjustment layer, our color picker automatically opens and we choose our color. (Again, I'm picking a blue.) Then we set that layer's blending mode to Color and we are done.

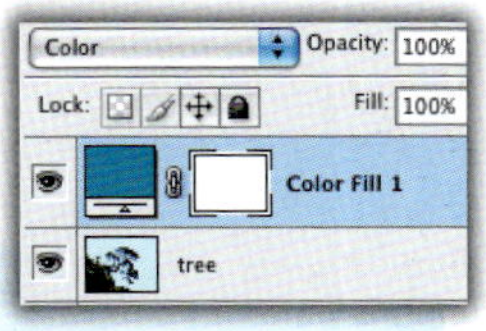

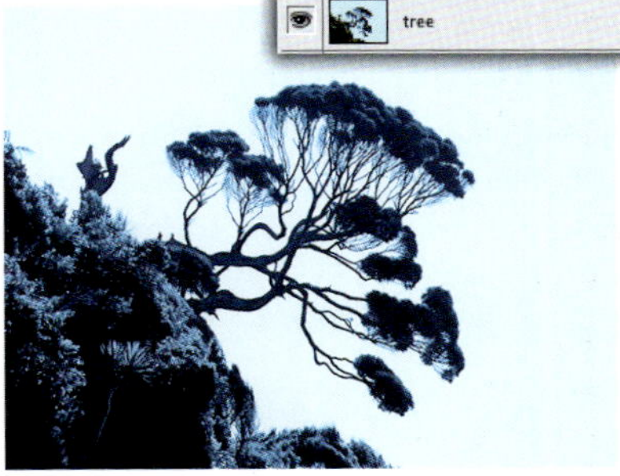

Our blue has been blended with the luminance of the image to create the duotone. If we want to change the blue, we can simply double click on the color thumbnail in the adjustment layer and use the Color Picker to make changes.

Now you might be saying to yourself that we've done this before. And you would be right. Back in Chapter 15, we used the colorize feature of the Hue/Saturation command to create exactly this same effect. Much of what we can do with blending modes, we can do with other techniques as well. So you shouldn't feel too badly if you avoid blending modes for the time being. But don't forget them either because you can do a host of things with them that you can't do any other way.

Let's do another example with Color to make sure we really have the hang of it.

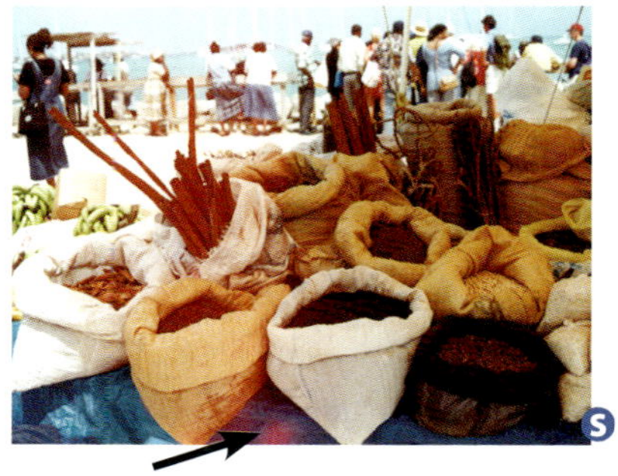

This picture was taken in St. Martin and suffers from a serious lens flare problem. That's what has led to the magenta-looking splotches on the otherwise blue tarp. With the Color blending mode, however, we can make a pretty good fix.

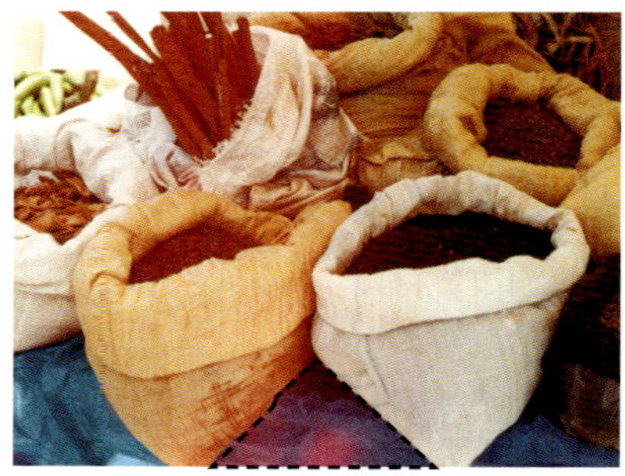

The trick is to Color blend the correct tarp color over the lens flare. To start, we make a feathered selection around the magenta area using our tool of choice. In the Layers panel, we click on the New Adjustment Layer icon and pick Solid Color.

This creates a solid color layer (using our foreground color) with a built-in layer mask based on our selection. So only the selected area gets affected.

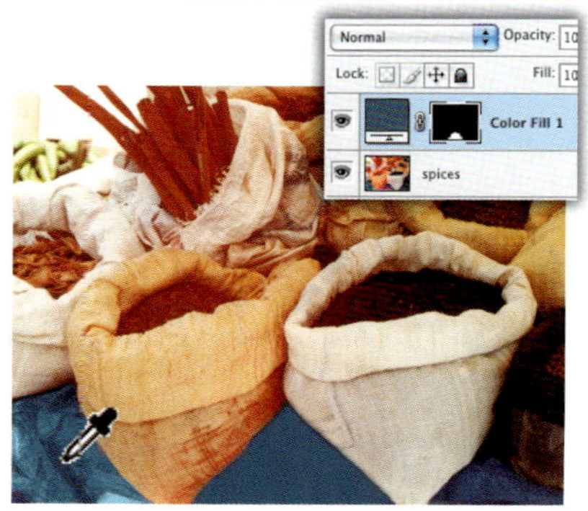

The Color Picker automatically opens and we click with the eyedropper on the tarp in a region adjacent to the flare where the color looks good. We click OK and that color is transferred to the adjustment layer.

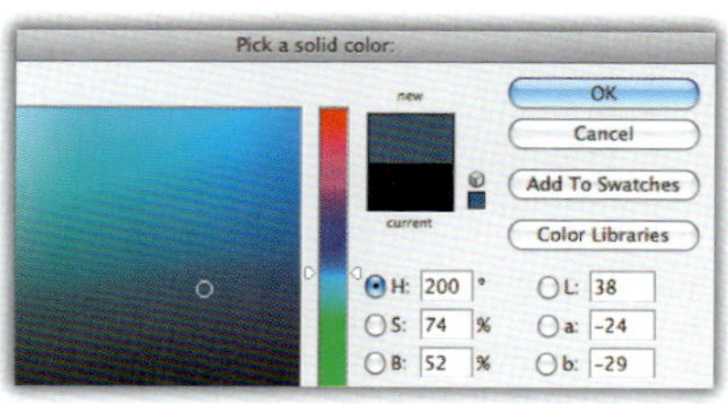

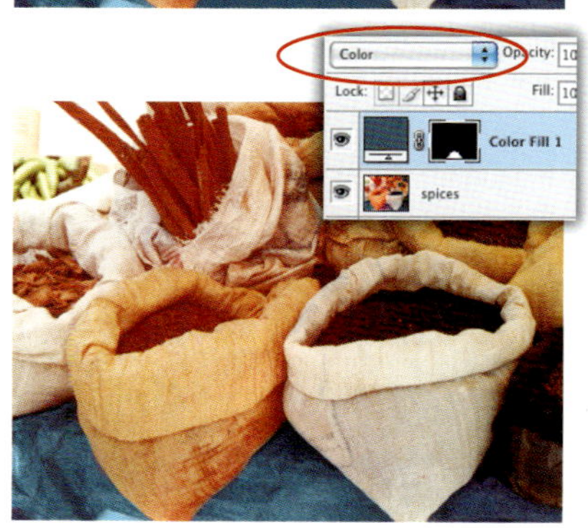

Now our last step is to change the blending mode of the adjustment layer to Color. Now the original tarp topology shows through..

This would have been difficult to do with Hue/Saturation. (I know from experience.) But with Color blending, we can chose exactly the right color and blend it in.

If there is one adjective that describes most blending modes for me, it is "unpredictable." Color is one of the three or four modes that seem to make sense. In fact, if we go to Photoshop Help and search on Blending Mode Examples, we are presented with visual examples of each of the modes. Even with those examples, it is hard for me to predict how they will behave in all but the simplest of situations.

While in Help, search on List of Blending Modes and find definitions for each. I'm guessing that those won't make a lot of sense either. But this doesn't mean that we can't have fun with blending modes. Try them out and see what you get!

Here are a few examples. (The associated Layers panel is the first figure in this chapter.) The VINO layer is on top of the vineyard layer and we can compare results with the VINO layer blend mode set to Normal, Color Burn, Lighten, and Linear Light.

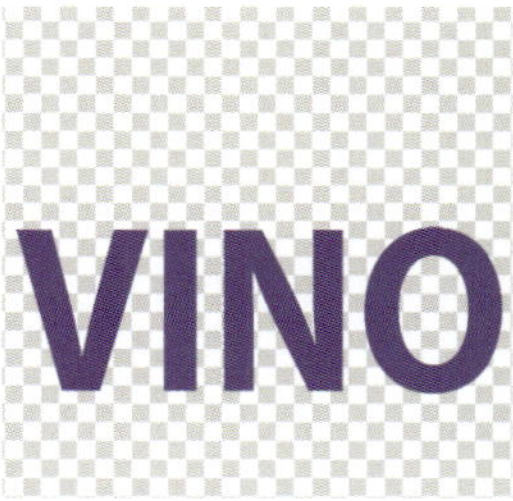

VINO Layer

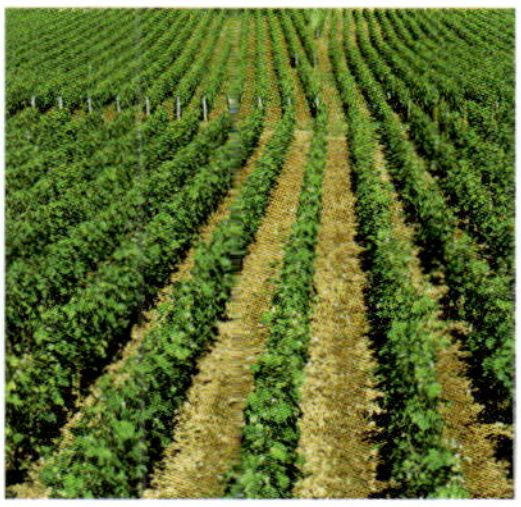

Vineyard Layer

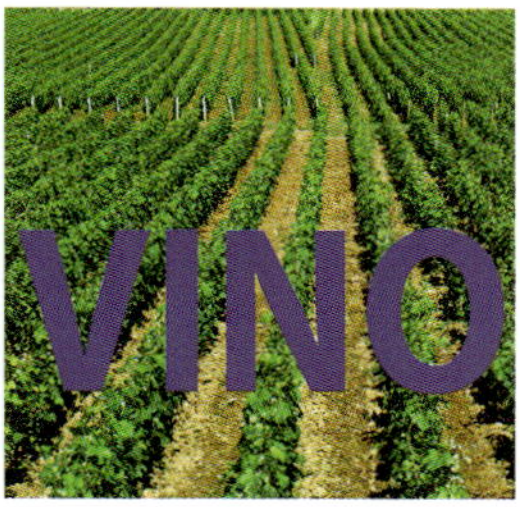

VINO Blending Mode = Normal

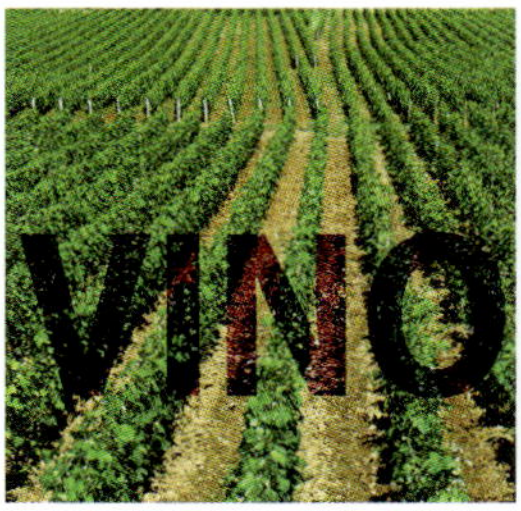

VINO Blending Mode = Color Burn

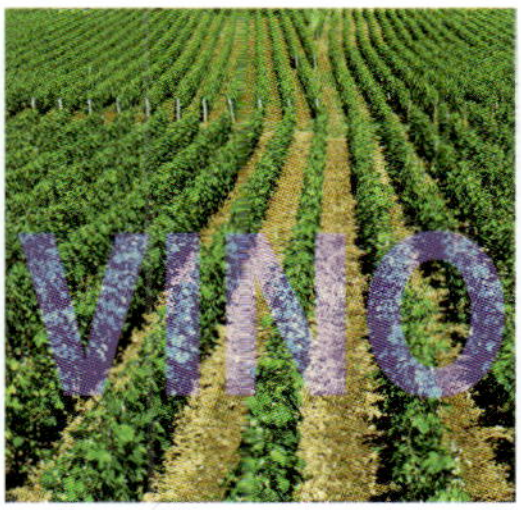

VINO Blending Mode = Lighten

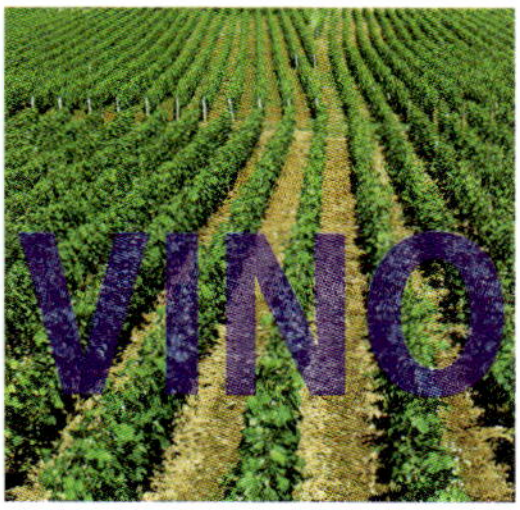

VINO Blending Mode = Linear Light

Let's finish our chapter on blending modes by discussing where else they show up. We've talked about the Layers panel and how we can set the blending mode for a given layer. Another very common place to see blending modes is in the options bar of any of the tools that are brush-like. This includes the Brush tool, the Spot Healing Brush tool, the Healing Brush tool, and the yet-to-be-discussed Clone tool. A blending mode on a brush tool causes blending of the specific brush effect with the underlying layers. As if layer blending wasn't difficult enough to visualize...

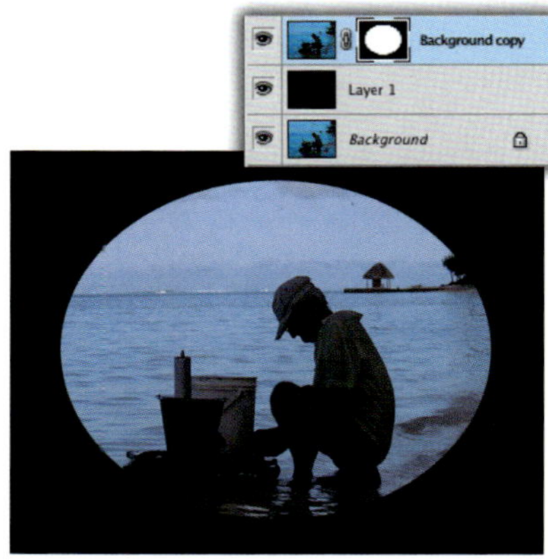

Vignetting with the CS4 Mask Panel: In our Section III CS4 Tips we mentioned the new Masks panel. This CS4 feature is very powerful and can simplify a lot of what we do. We will review it by way of an example, using the vignetting technique we discussed in Chapter 25.

The final vignetting flow we had discussed was creating an image layer with a hard elliptical layer mask, stacked over a layer filled with solid black. This intermediate step is shown here. Then we used the Gaussian Blur filter to soften the edges of the mask. This was great because we could dial in the amount of blur we wanted. The downside is that the filter step is not reversible.

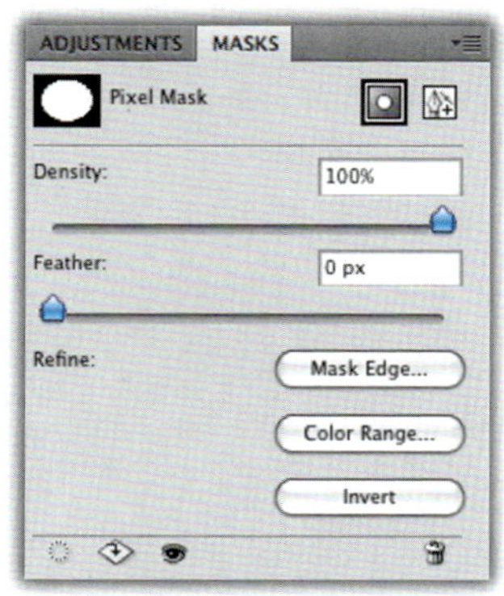

So check this out. Instead of the filter step, we click on the Masks panel. (Our masked layer must be selected.) See the Feather slider? If we move that to the right, it feathers the mask edge in the same way. But with this control, it is reversible. We can go back and change it. If we want the edges to show through a bit, all we need to do is dial back Density to our liking. Very powerful.

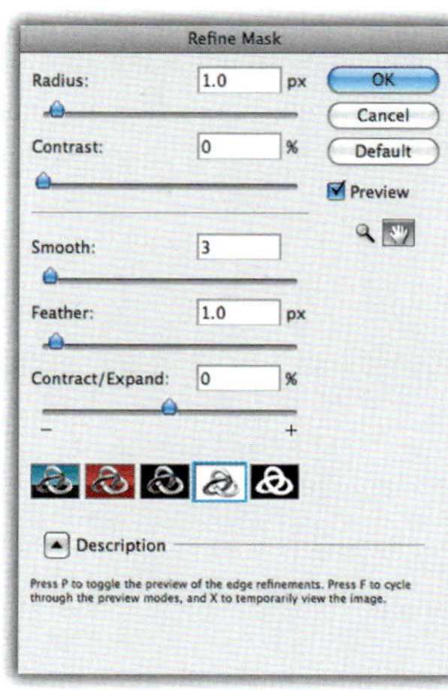

And while we are talking powerful, click on the Mask Edge button. Here we can make further adjustments to our mask, like expanding and contracting. Much easier than what we went through trying to remove the halo effect in Chapter 27. The row of icons at the bottom switches views for us. Hover over anything and you'll get a complete description at the bottom of the dialog box.

Where's the Solid Color Adjustment in CS4? Not all of the adjustments are represented by icons in the new Adjustments panel. But you can still get to them by clicking on the New Adjustment Layer icon at the bottom of the Layers panel.

SECTION

V

MORE IMAGE ENHANCING

In a sense, we are coming full circle now. Way back in Section II, we spent quite a bit of time going through different ways to enhance our images. After that, we jumped into a discussion of layers and explored some of the many ways they can be utilized to alter our images. Now we are back to image enhancement again.

In a sense, we really never left the subject. After all, image enhancement is really what Photoshop is all about. But in these chapters, we will return to the subject more directly.

Aside from improving contrast and color and refining composition via cropping, the next biggest improvement we can generally make is by slightly altering content. (Major alterations would be more consistent with a new image altogether, not an enhancement.) We already touched on this back in Chapter 18, Fixing Defects. Now we will learn some heavier duty techniques.

In this section, we will start with the Clone tool, my personal favorite tool in Photoshop. Ever take an outdoor picture of someone only to see later that a tree branch appears to be growing out of his or her head? (Why can't we see these things at the time?) The Clone tool will fix this. In this section we will talk about filters, a general category of Photoshop effects that will help your dormant inner artist to come to life. And then we'll talk about two filters in particular that should become part of your everyday arsenal, the sharpen filter and the blur filter. We are cruising in fourth gear now!

32. THE CLONE TOOL

We start this new section on image enhancing with the **Clone Stamp** tool (aka the Clone tool). For the novice user, this tool is probably the biggest-bang-for-the-buck tool in Photoshop. To clone is to make an identical copy and that is exactly what the Clone tool allows us to do. I find, though, that more often than not, I use the Clone tool to get rid of something, not to duplicate it. I'll explain shortly.

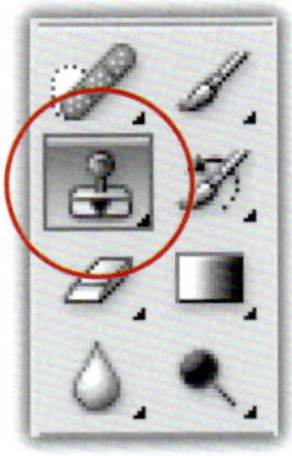

The Clone tool can be found in our toolbox; its icon looks like a rubber stamp. When we select the Clone tool, its unique options bar appears. The Clone tool is another of the tools that is brush-like at its core with diameter and softness/hardness that are variable. It also has Mode, which, from our last chapter, we know refers to blending modes.

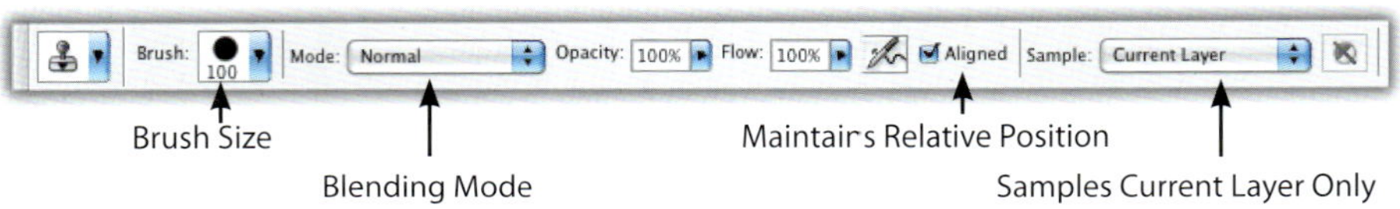

NOTE: Before we start, please select Window>Clone Source and uncheck Show Overlay in that panel. Then close the panel. I'll explain in the CS4 Tips after this section.

The Clone tool works by sampling pixels from one location (the source) and painting them at another location (the destination), duplicating, or cloning, the pixels. We establish the source point by holding down the Opt(Alt) key and clicking on the desired source location. (When we hold down Opt(Alt), the cursor turns into a little target as a clue that when we click, the source point will be chosen.)

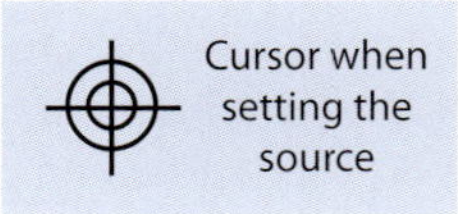

Next, we move the cursor to the destination point where we would like to paint the source pixels. When we click the cursor at this new location, the Clone tool copies the pixels from source point and paints them at the destination point, using the diameter and hardness of the brush specified in the options bar. (Conceptually, this is very similar to the Spot Healing Brush.)

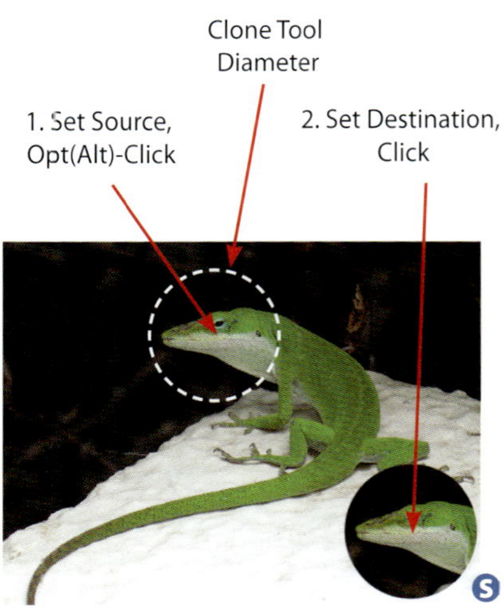

If, instead of clicking at the destination point, we were to click and drag, the Clone tool will sample and paint continuously, maintaining the relative position of the source and destination points. (As long as Align is checked in the options bar, if we release the mouse and then click and drag again, the Clone tool will remember the relative positions of source and destination. It will continue to do so until we establish a new source point by holding down Opt(Alt) and clicking on a new location.)

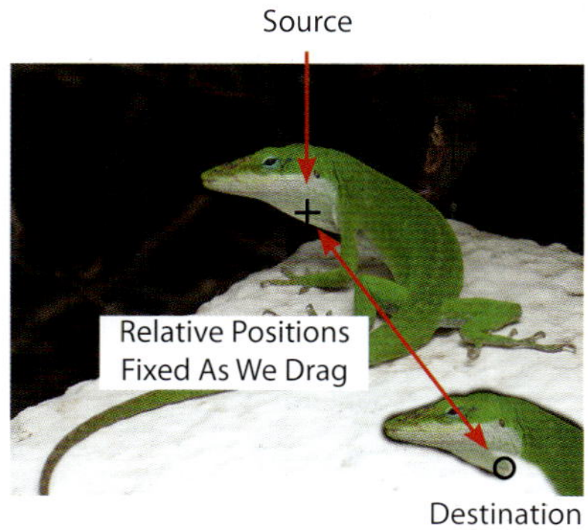

One more little tip before we dive into a couple of examples. Pay close attention, because this is huge. We just discussed how the Clone tool samples from the source to paint at the destination. What we didn't mention, but should be clear, is that the Clone tool paints over the existing pixels at the destination. That is "paints over" as in replaces. The old pixels are gone. This isn't good, even if we want the old pixels replaced. What if we made a mistake, for example, and cloned more than we had intended? Or what if we later want our old pixels back? We'd be out of luck.

The solution is to make use of the fact that the Clone tool not only works from a source to a destination on the same layer, but can also clone from a source on one layer to a destination on another layer. In this example, we have created a new layer, CloneDest, just above the CloneSource layer. We select the CloneSource layer and choose our source point. Then we select the CloneDest layer and click and drag at our destination point. The cloned pixels end up on the CloneDest layer. The result looks just as before. But since the cloned pixels are on a new layer, the originals were not destroyed. So if we want to make edits of some kind, we still have everything at our disposal.

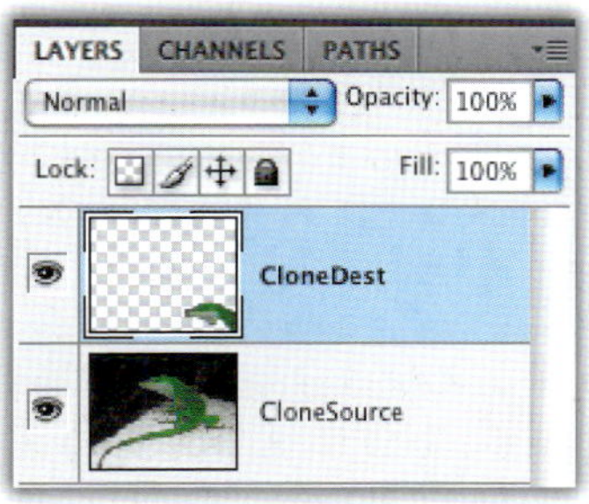

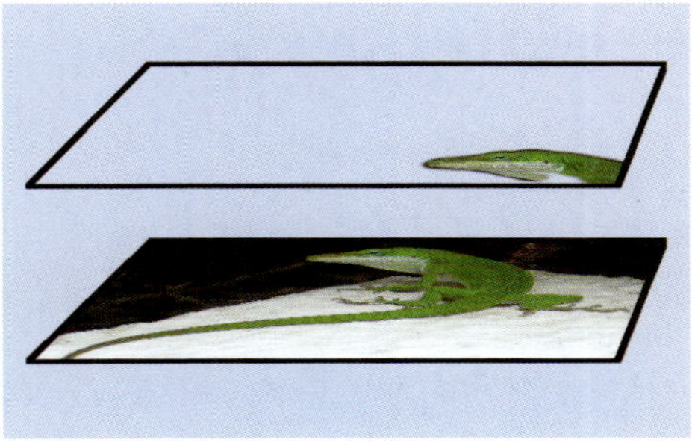

Let's say this image from Chapter 29 was an original (i.e. a flat JPEG) and we wanted to move the bird to the other post. With our image open and the Clone tool selected, we adjust our diameter to an appropriate size prior to setting the source. That diameter can be modified as we go, so we can start larger and then shrink it to do the smaller details. Choose a 50% hardness.

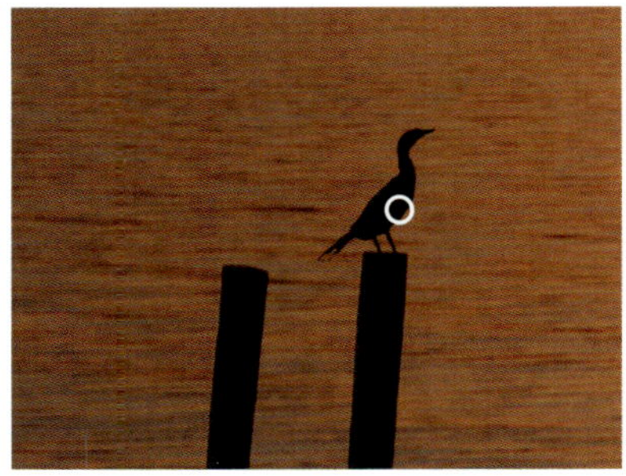

We make a new blank layer for the cloned bird, select the original layer and set the source point (Opt(Alt)-Click) on our bird. Next we select the clone data layer, pick our destination (on the second post), and begin cloning. As we clone, we can see our brush size at the destination and we can see the target tracking at the source. At any time we can release the mouse, reset the diameter, and start the click and drag again. With Align in the options bar selected, the spatial relationship between source and destination stays constant.

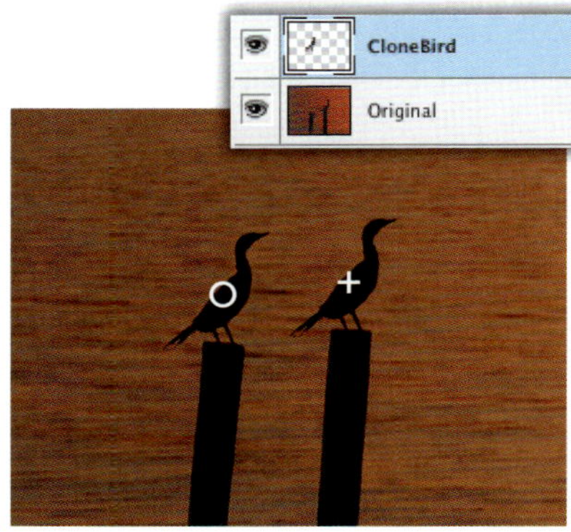

Our cloning is on its own layer, so we can easily do touch ups. We simply turn off the visibility on the source layer (using the eyeball in the Layers panel), select the destination layer and, with the Eraser tool set to an appropriate diameter and hardness, erase any cloning (lake in this case). We don't need perfection because the background blends in nicely.

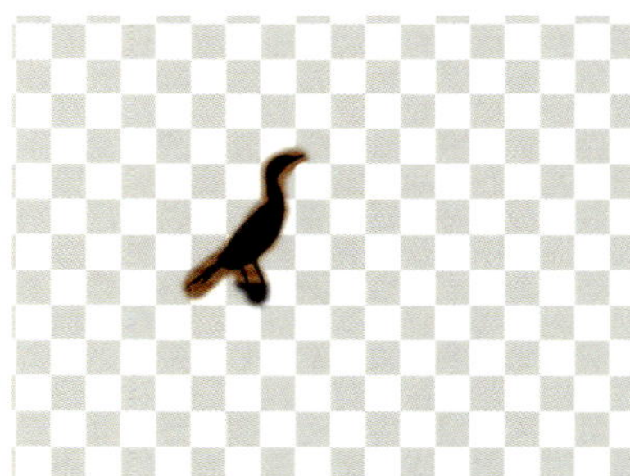

Here is the finished result. Since the cloned bird is on its own layer, we can move it or transform it to our heart's content. I made it a bit bigger with the Free Transform command just as an example. (Yes, I know this is upsampling!)

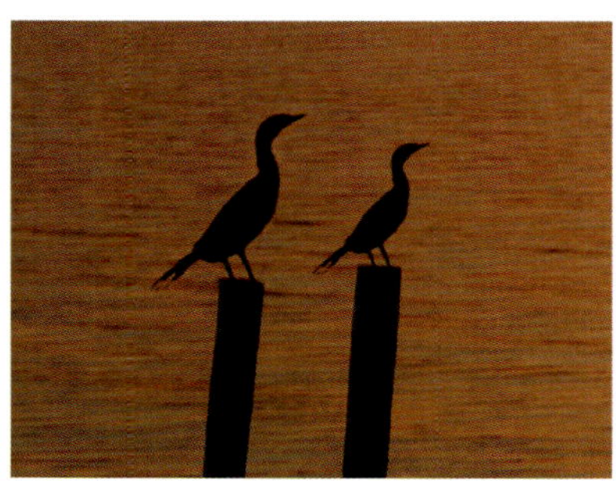

Now having two nearly identical birds in the last example doesn't look all that realistic, does it? So let's go ahead and remove one. But to keep it interesting, let's remove the original one. As I said earlier, I tend to use the Clone tool more often than not for removing things, not duplicating them. Now I can show you just what I meant when I said that.

Our plan will be to clone some lake to cover the original bird. We start by adding a new layer, CloneLake, just above our original layer. We select our Clone tool and give it an appropriately sized brush with a very soft edge. With the Original layer selected, we choose a source point on the lake where the water seems to have similar lighting to the water around the bird we are going to remove. (In this example, I chose a point to the right of the bird.)

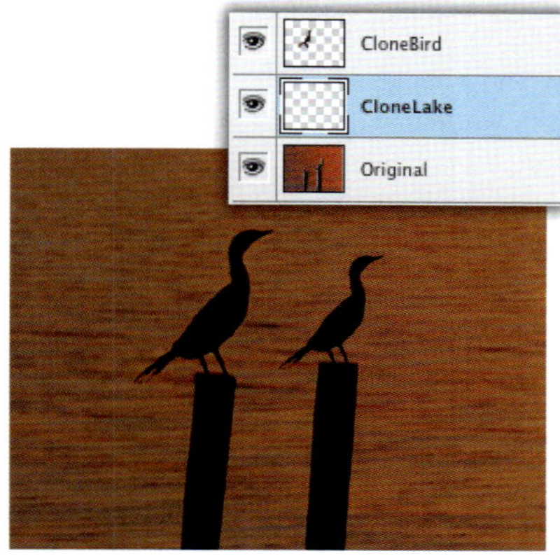

Now we select the CloneLake layer (the new layer) and click and drag, painting over the original bird. Because we picked a soft-edged brush, the cloned lake blends in very nicely with the original lake. When doing this kind of removal, always use a soft brush to better blend the border of the cloned pixels. (The plus sign is showing us our instantaneous source point.)

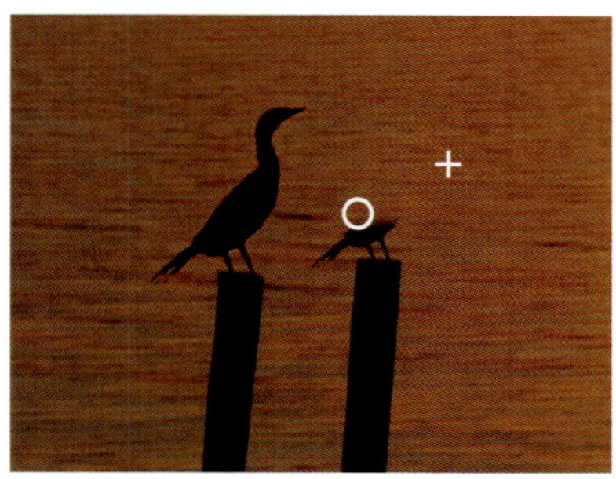

Looks pretty good. We are aided by the fact that the lake surface is pretty random. This makes it harder for our eyes to pick up the new versus the old. But this cloning technique still works well with less random objects; we just have to be more careful with our choice of source and destination points. We'll see how in the next chapter.

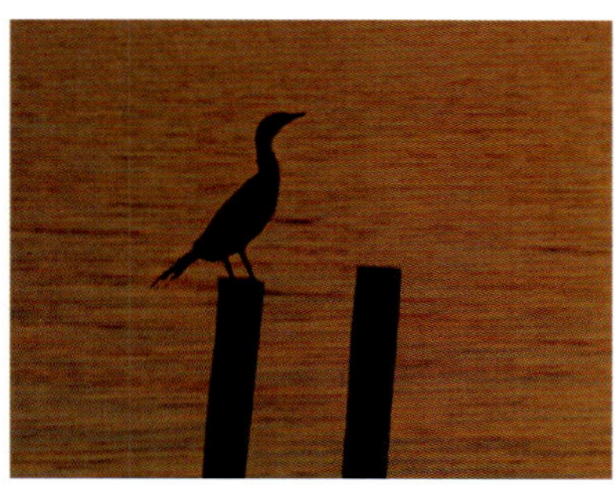

That's the Clone tool in a nutshell. But just knowing how it works doesn't get us too far with respect to knowing where to use it. So let's press on with another chapter on this very handy tool.

33. THE CLONE TOOL–PART 2

In the last example in the previous chapter, we cloned some lake water to cover up one of the two birds in our image. It was a snap to do and the results looked good. As I pointed out, what we had going for us was the randomness in the lake ripple pattern. When that type of randomness is not there, we need to work a little harder to achieve similarly good results.

Actually, really definite patterns are almost as easy to deal with. Here is an image taken of the Sacré Coeur Basilica in Paris. For a grouping I was doing, I wanted to crop it as shown. But I was bothered by the fact that my crop was cutting off a few of the tower openings, creating so-called edge intrusions at the bottom of the photo. Still, I wanted this particular crop. My solution was to use Photoshop to resize the openings.

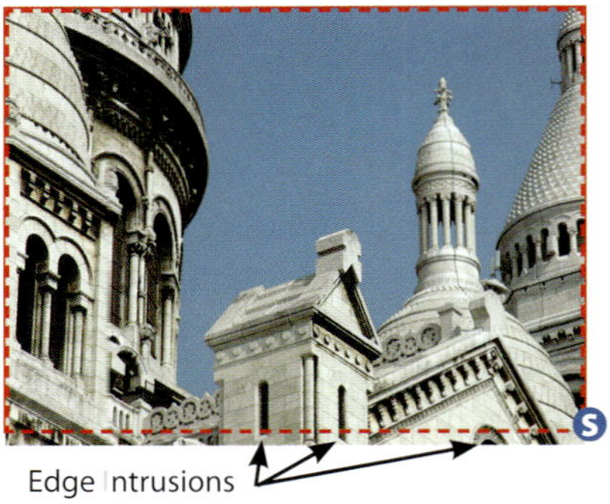

Since the basilica is constructed from rectangular blocks, we have a very regular pattern with which to work. The first thing we do is to create a new blank layer to use for our cloning destination. We can use the name CloneBlock. Our objective is to raise the bottom of the opening so that it is above the crop boundary. We select the Original layer and, with the Clone tool, we set the source at the lower right of the existing opening, as shown. (Opt(Alt)-Click)

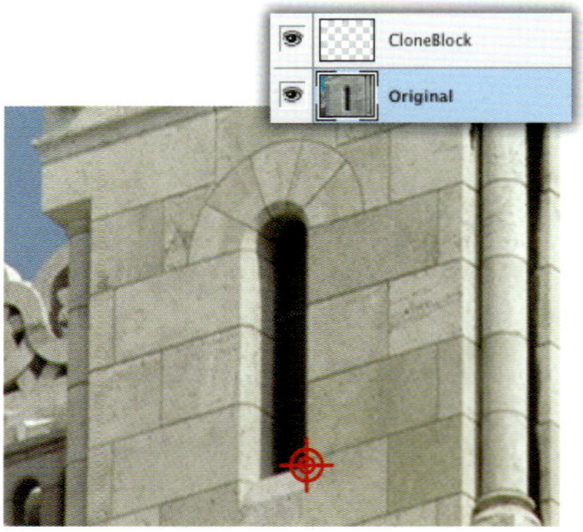

In the Layers panel, we select the CloneBlock layer and click exactly one block up from where we set the source. See the example. If we now click and drag, we are able to copy the bottom of the original opening to a location one block up.

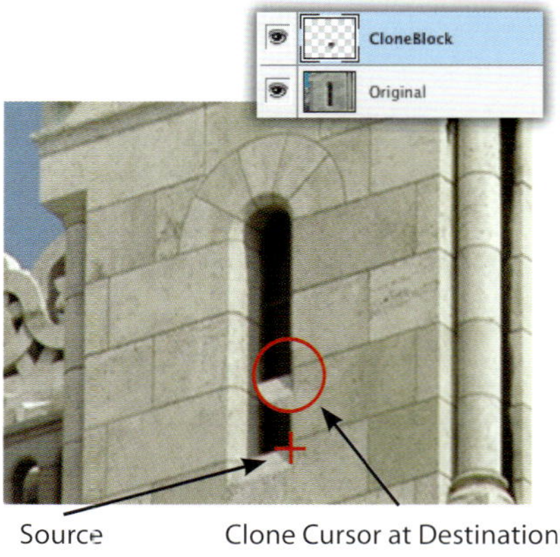

Anytime there is some repeating element in our image, in this case it is the blocks, we can use that element almost like a grid to choose our source and destination points so that the cloned pixels line up correctly.

Setting the diameter and hardness of the Clone Stamp tool is a matter of experience. I rarely work with a hardness of 100% because I want the edges to blend in for a more realistic look. In the last screen shot, you can see the diameter I chose.

Here are before and after blowups of the area we just modified, along with a third blowup where I have turned off the visibility on all but the CloneBlock layer.

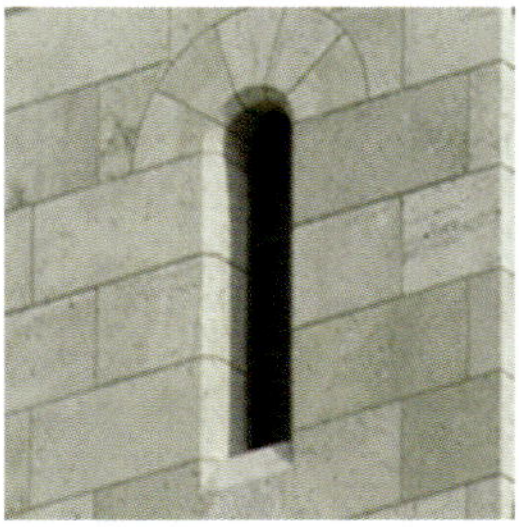

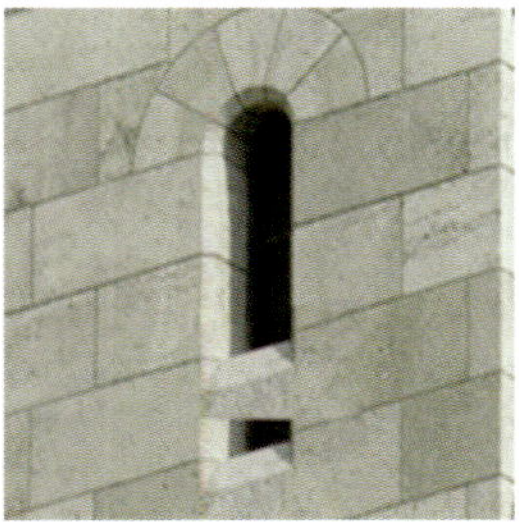

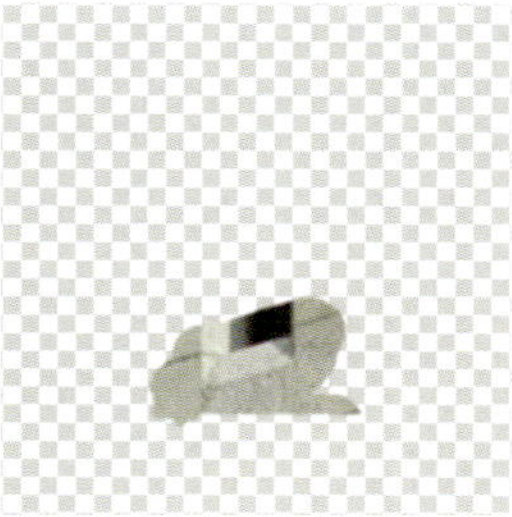

We can handle the middle intrusion in the exact same way, raising its bottom up by one stone. The arched intrusion on the right has to be handled a little differently since we need to cover its top. To do this, we clone stone blocks from above the arch down over the arch, enough to cover it up within the edge of the crop.

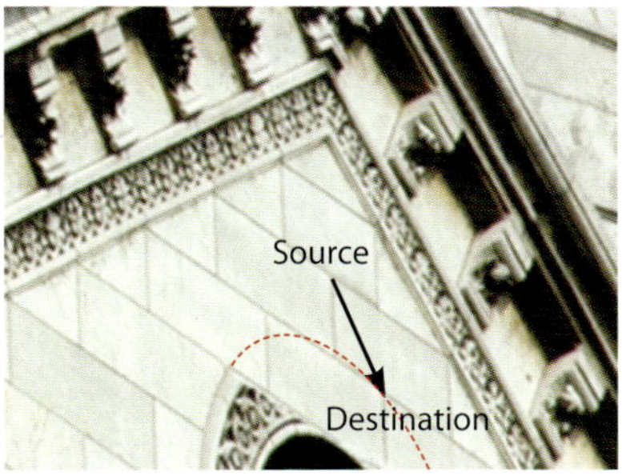

(From now on, when I draw a line with an arrowhead for cloning, the tail of the line will be the initial source point and the arrowhead will be the initial destination.)

Here is our final result after fixing all three openings and cropping the image. It came out looking pretty realistic owing to (1) the repetitive pattern of the blocks and (2) the very even lighting of the wall.

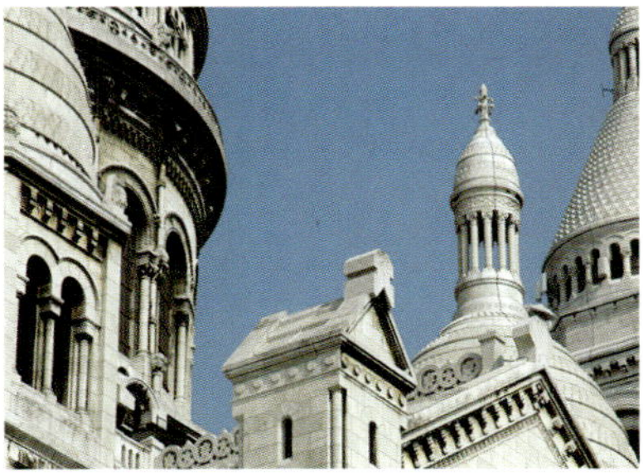

When I do my cloning, I generally work at the highest possible magnification in order to be as precise as possible. But I will routinely switch back to lower magnifications to double check. Sometimes that last little artifact I am trying to fix at high magnification just isn't visible at a normal view. And at other times, a cloning job that looks perfect at high magnification may have some obvious issues at normal magnifications.

Now let's tackle a slightly more complicated situation but one which is more typical of what we will likely encounter. The mechanics of cloning are pretty simple. The challenge is making good choices of what to clone. We'll focus on that in this example.

I am continually amazed by what I don't see when I take a picture. Here, I didn't see the air conditioning condenser peeking out on the left behind the arch. I guess I was too focused on lining up all of the arches. (We are in Beijing's Forbidden City.) Anyway, the image would clearly be better off without it, so let's use the Clone Stamp tool to remove it.

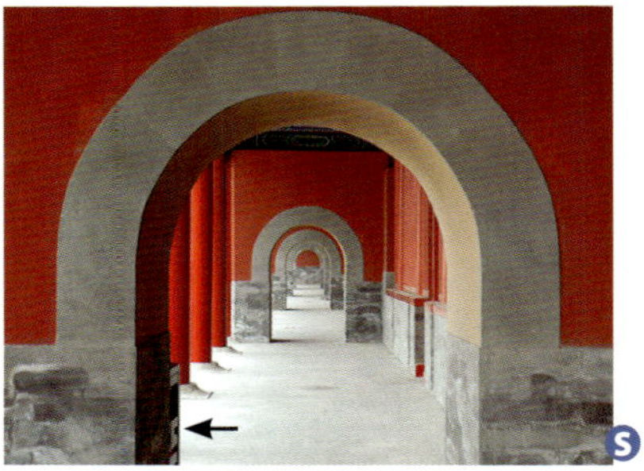

The first thing we notice is that the condenser pixels abut the arch so it would be very easy to inadvertently mess up the arch pixels. A technique to avoid this is to create a selection around the condenser. Recall that when we have an active selection, only those pixels within the selection can be modified. We make the selection (use a 2-3 pixel feather) and leave it active. I've left the selection very loose on the right side.

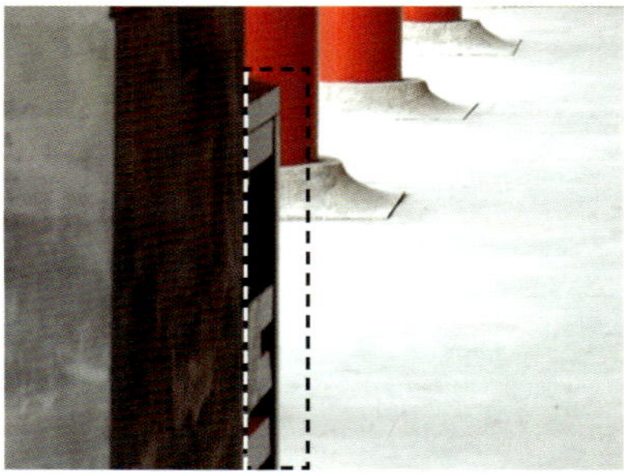

To set things up, we duplicate the Background layer (call it Arches) and create a new blank layer on top of it (CloneDst). We will clone from Arches to CloneDst.

The first thing we work on is the top of the base of the pillar behind the condenser. Notice that the next base back looks similar so we can line up source and destination as shown and clone. The image on the right shows the result.

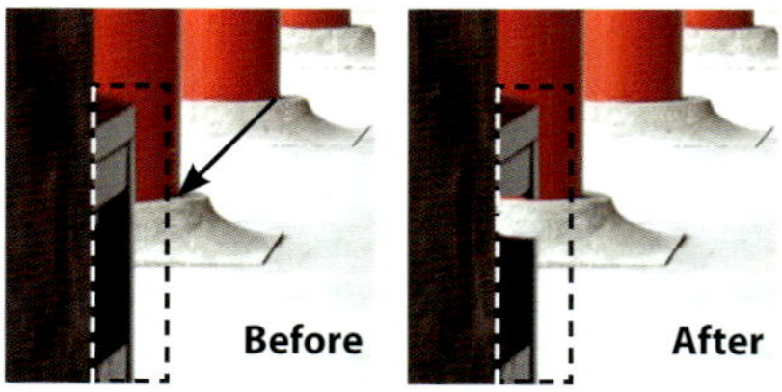

We can clone the right-hand side of the base bottom to create the left-hand side. (The back pillar base is too light.) And we can clone right up to the arch edge without a problem because the selection protects it.

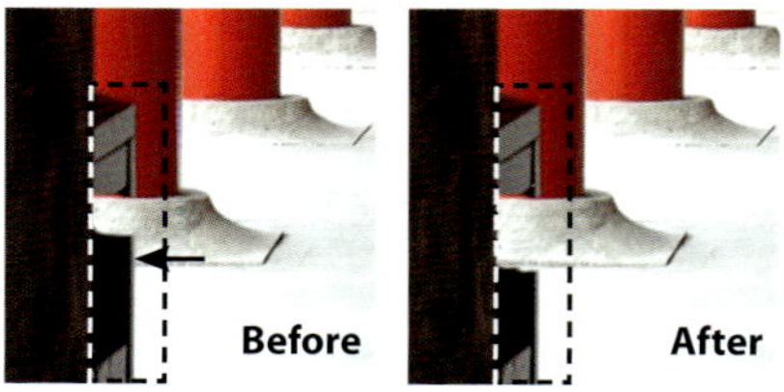

Now we fill in the orange pillar column. For this, we choose a source above the condenser and clone it down, being careful to make the destination exactly under the source. We always look for the most similar area in selecting our clone source.

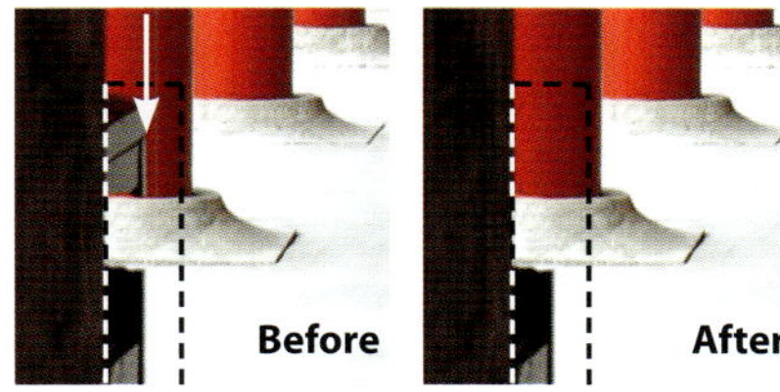

Lastly, we have to fill in the floor. We use a slightly larger diameter and softer brush here and play close attention to the lighting. Near the pillar, the flooring is almost blown out so we have to be careful to match things up.

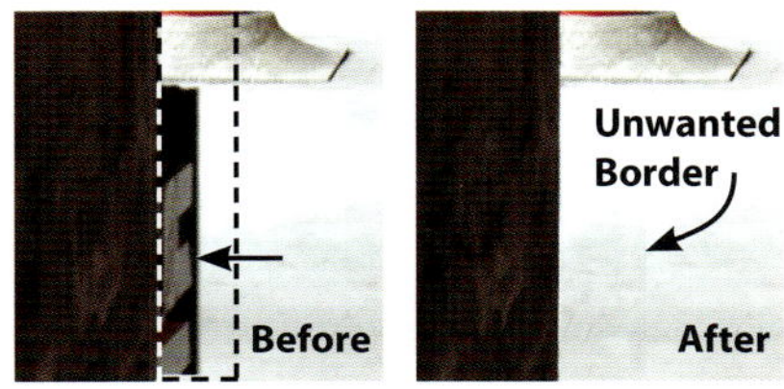

Most of our work looks fine but there is an obvious unwanted border on the flooring left from our last step (the After image). This is because of the selection we had in place to protect the arch. The problem is easily fixed, however. We get rid of the selection (Select>Deselect), choose a nice soft brush for our Clone Stamp tool and re-clone over the edge, mussing up the border.

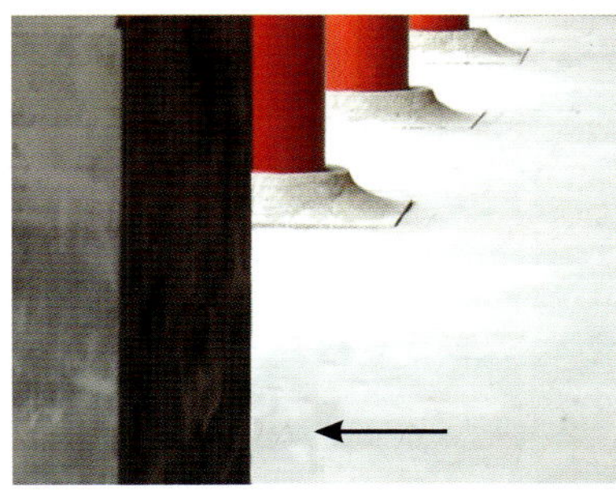

And here is the final result. It might not withstand the scrutiny of a microscopic examination but it certainly would pass a casual examination on a family room wall. (At least it has on mine.) Whether it is the condenser you didn't see or the guy in the lime green shorts walking through your otherwise perfect landscape, the Clone tool is your best choice for "artifact" removal.

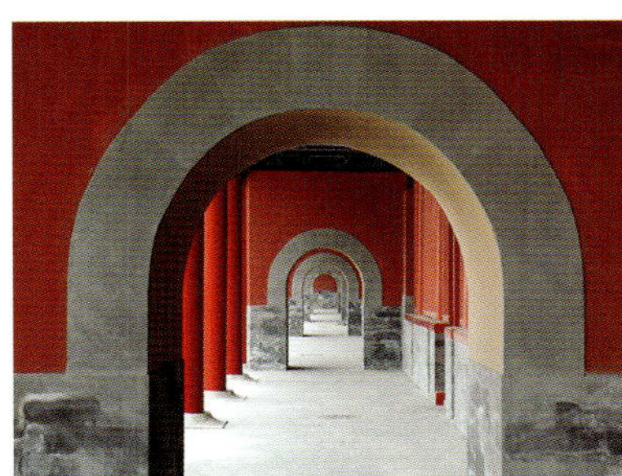

Always pay attention to lighting. If the lighting in the vicinity of the source pixels doesn't match the lighting in the vicinity of the destination, the clone won't look right. Here's another advantage of placing cloned pixels on their own layer; we can use an adjustment layer to fix the lighting if need be. We simply Cmd(Ctrl)-Click our Clone layer thumbnail on the Layers panel to create a selection around the cloned pixels and then create a new Levels adjustment layer. The adjustment layer then comes with a layer mask confining its effects to just the cloned pixels and we adjust their lighting.

34. FILTERS

I know that everything we have done with Photoshop thus far is fun, but filters are where it goes over the top. Filters, in essence, are a set of canned special effects that allow us to stylize images, or portions of images. The results can be pretty dramatic and are often unpredictable. But they are almost always interesting.

Here is a sneak peek at what I'm talking about. The left image below is an image as taken. The right image below is that same image with a Palette Knife filter applied.

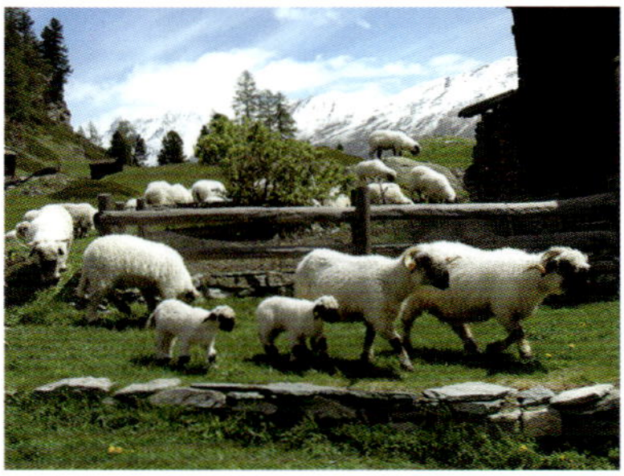

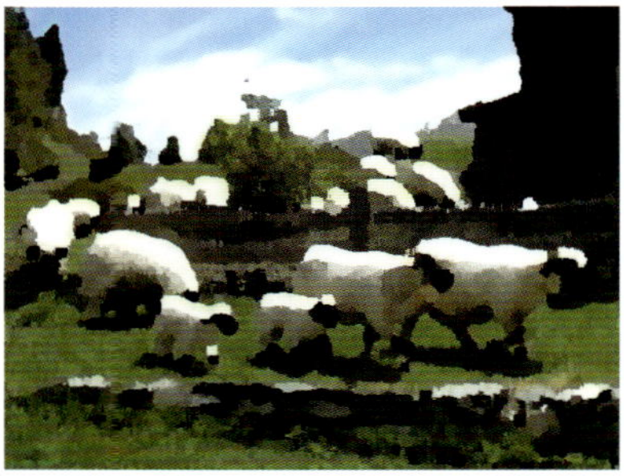

These effects are accessed through the menu bar by clicking on Filter. As we can see, there are more than just a couple to choose from.

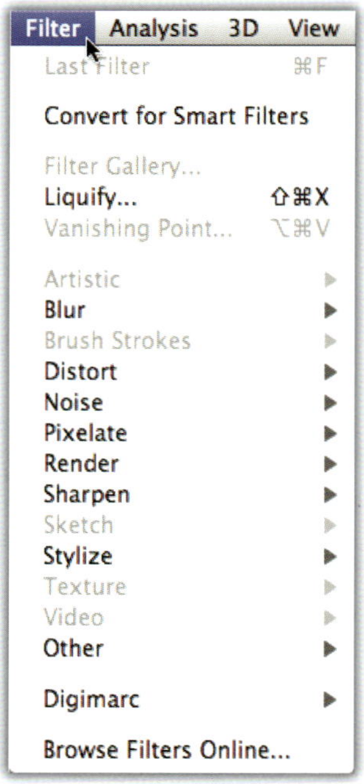

The third grouping, starting with Artistic and ending with Other are the basic filters. Click on any one of them and a submenu pops up with even more choices. All in all, there are over 100 distinct filters and most of those have editable attributes. So the sky is the limit. (Actually, our time is probably the limit.) Palette Knife is found under Artistic.

When we apply a filter, it does its magic on whichever layer is selected. If we have an active selection on that layer, the filtering affects only those selected pixels. The filtering process is a mathematical manipulation and the original pixels are modified, as in changed forever. In a bit we'll discuss how to avoid this with extra layers.

The filter listed at the very top of the Filter menu is the last filter we've used in the current session. In the example on the previous page, Palette Knife was what I had used last. Selecting this repeats the filtering action with all of the settings we had in place the last time around; there is no opportunity to make changes. I rarely do this, opting instead to navigate again to the filter so that I may make changes if necessary.

"Convert for Smart Filters" and the group of filters starting with Extract and ending with Vanishing Point are outside of the scope of this book. The exception to that is the Filter Gallery. The Filter Gallery isn't actually a filter; it is a graphical interface to many (but not all) of the filters in the third grouping. When we select it, we get the following screen:

Preview Panel (displaying Palette Knife) | Filter Gallery | Filter Settings

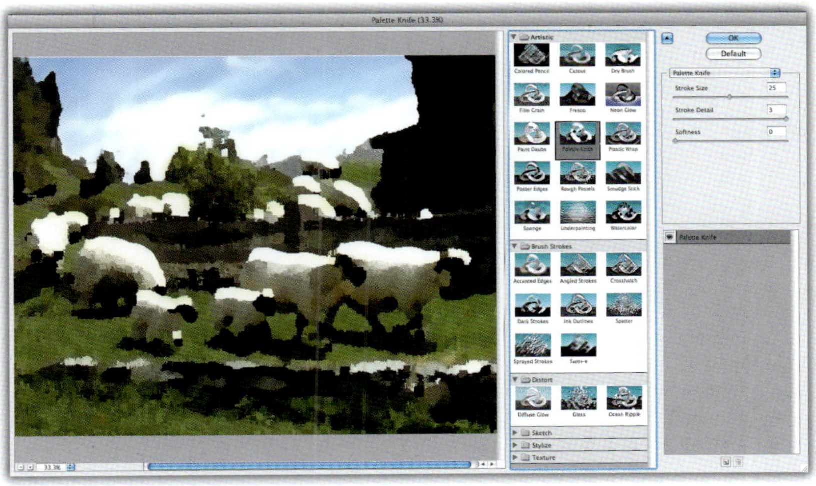

The best way to get a feeling for filters is to play around with them and there is no better vehicle than the Filter Gallery. The middle panel is a gallery that lists filter categories which, when opened, show icons for each of its filters. We choose a filter by selecting its icon. When we do, the left-hand panel displays a preview of the filtering effect on our image. (Note we can adjust the zoom at the lower left.) The right-hand panel allows us to customize the filter effects to our taste. When we click OK, the filter, with our settings, is applied to the selected layer (or the selection on that layer if there is one).

So go experiment. A word of warning though. Filtering is very computationally intensive, meaning that when we select a filter icon, there may be a lag in time while our computer crunches the numbers. The warning is that if anything might drive you to upgrade to a faster computer, a fondness for filtering would be it.

Here are some examples for those of you that didn't stop reading to go off to try out every filter combination.

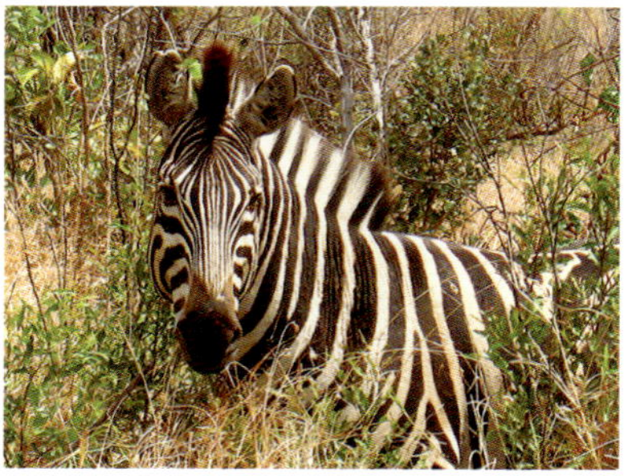

Original Image

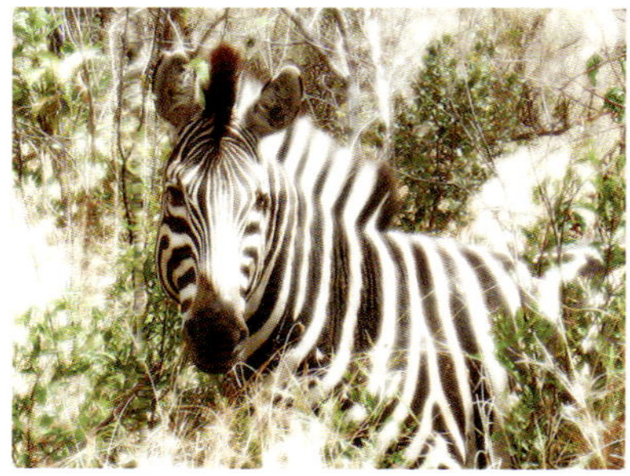

Diffuse Glow (under Distort)

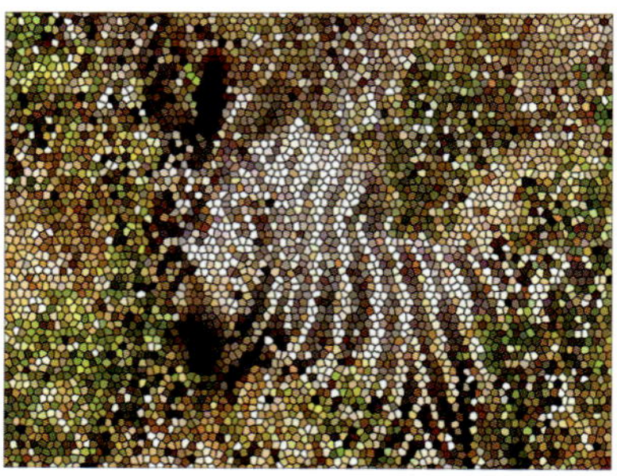

Stain Glass (under Texture)

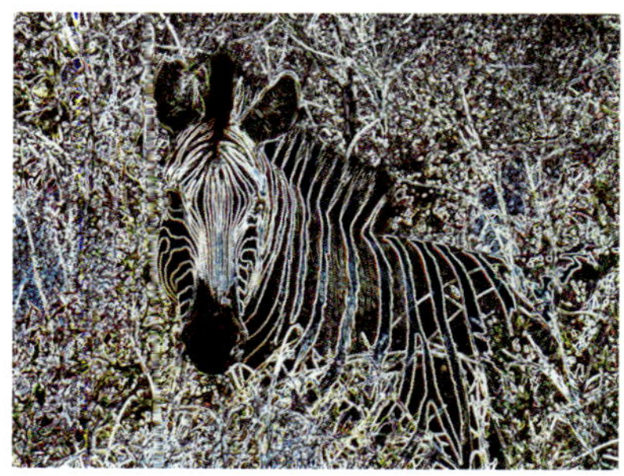

Glowing Edges (under Stylize)

Since filtering affects only one layer, what if we want to filter a document made up of several layers? Well there's an easy way to do this and it's a very neat technique, so listen up. If we select the top layer in our document and hold down Cmd(Ctrl) plus Opt(Alt) plus Shift and click E, a new single layer (automatically named Layer 1 here) that is a composite of all visible layers below it is inserted above the stack. We may then run our filter on that layer. (This composite layer won't update if we later make changes on the underlying layers. In that case, we'd make our changes, delete the composite layer, replace it and refilter.)

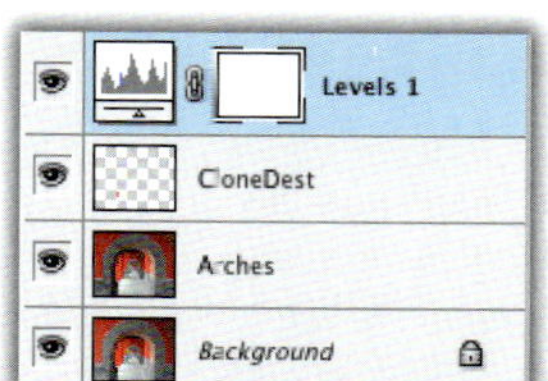

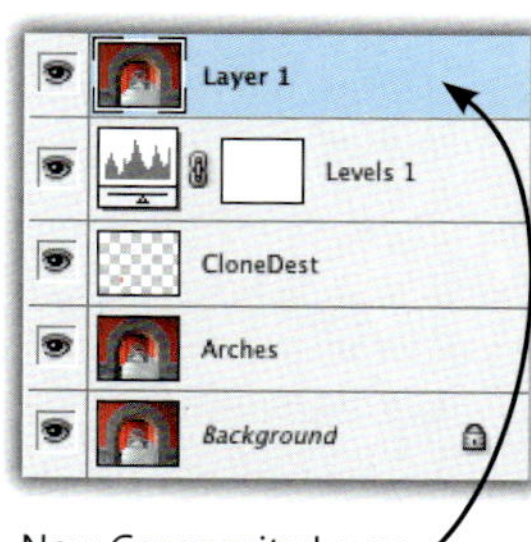

New Composite Layer

The two filters I use most often, Sharpening and Blurring, are covered in the next two chapters. Of the others, I tend to make use of those that help me make interesting lighting or backgrounds. Here are a few examples.

This is an example of the Lighting Effects filter, found under Filter>Render. The particular style shown here is the default, an Omni light (creating a soft spotlight effect). But there are many styles available with multiple settings for each. With them, we can simulate a host of specialized lighting conditions. Remember, the filter affects only the selected layer.

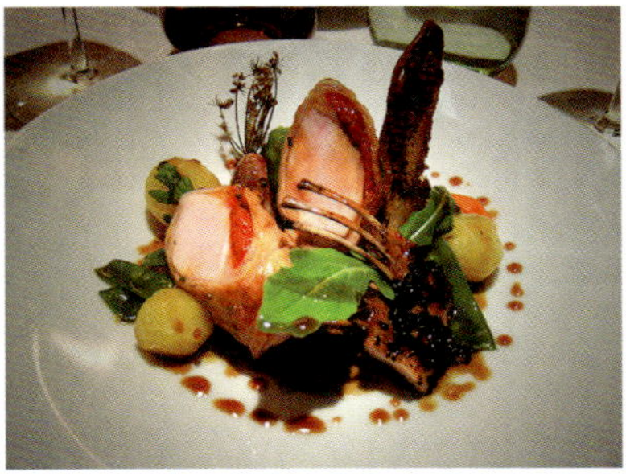

The Fibers filter is another favorite of mine, good for making backgrounds for text and slides. It is also found under Filter>Render and it creates customizable fibers using the existing foreground and background colors. So select your colors first and then run the filter. (Always run Fibers on a blank layer as it completely replaces all of the layer contents.) Looks like oak, doesn't it?

Under Filter>Texture, we find the Texturizer filter. We can use it to create simulated burlap or canvas (shown here), among others. Texturizer uses the color of the selected layer, not the foreground or background color, so set that color before running the filter.

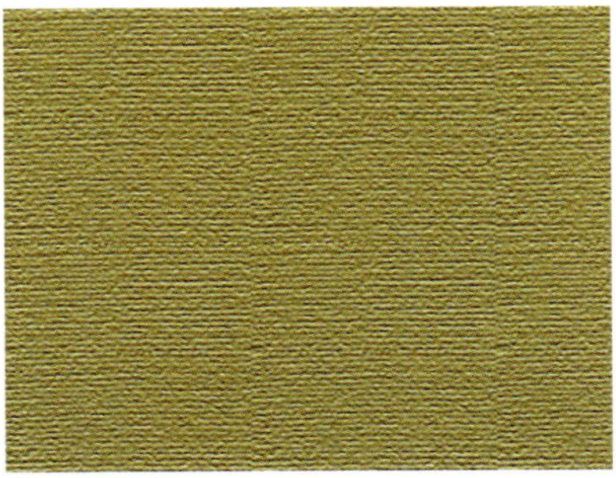

I like to use Texturizer to make simulated matting around pictures to be framed, using the canvas filter along with a Bevel and Emboss layer style. (I do spring for real matting on occasion.) Check out Chapter 46 for the details on how to do this.

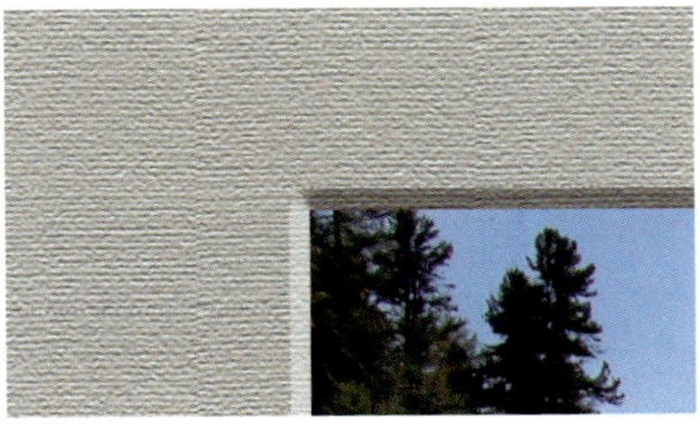

35. THE SHARPEN FILTER

Sharpness is one of a photograph's most critical attributes. Photographers go to great lengths (and expense) to get the sharpest images possible because our eyes are very sensitive to focus. Big huge lenses, tripods, gigapixels (OK, megapixels) are all employed by the pros. But probably not by you and me.

Fortunately, Photoshop has the ability to sharpen images. It won't take a badly-out-of-focus image and correct it, but it will take a reasonably focused image and improve it immensely. Actually, all digital photographs need a measure of sharpening, even those taken with huge lenses, tripods, etc., owing to the digital nature of our sensors.

The Sharpen filters are found under Filter>Sharpen. As we see, there are several choices. Let's pick the least likely choice, the Unsharp Mask. I know... It sounds like the opposite of what we want but the name is a holdover from film processing days; it refers to the method by which film-based sharpening was done. There are other Sharpen filters but I think the Unsharp Mask is the most straightforward.

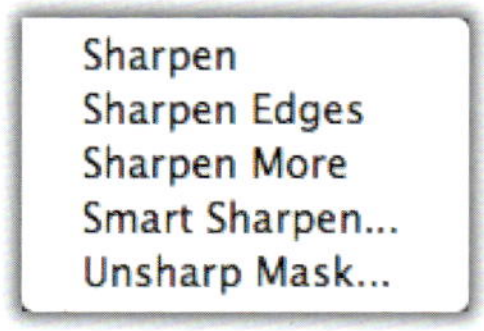

Photoshop can't really retroactively improve the focus of an image. But what it can do is trick our eyes into thinking that the image is sharper than it actually is. Our eyes are sensitive to edges, to sharp variations in contrast. To sharpen, Photoshop scans our image looking for these edges (light to dark or dark to light) and then, in the immediate vicinity of those edges, makes the lights lighter and the darks darker. Our eyes pick up the heightened contrast and say "Wow! Better focus!" It is basically an optical illusion. But illusion or not, the resulting image is more pleasing to our eye. (It's hard to see in these small images, I know. Try comparing the windows in the before and after.)

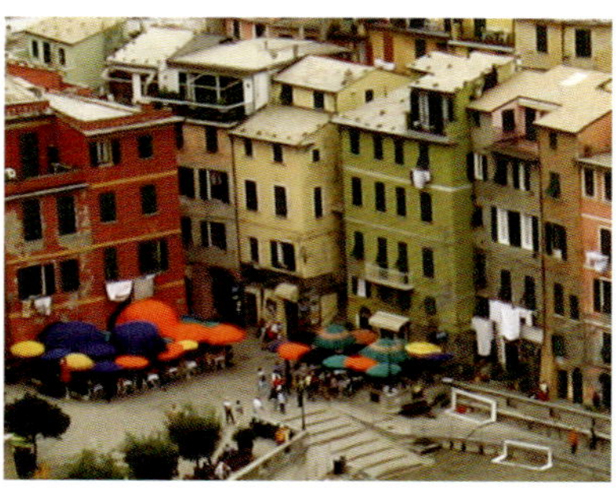

Original

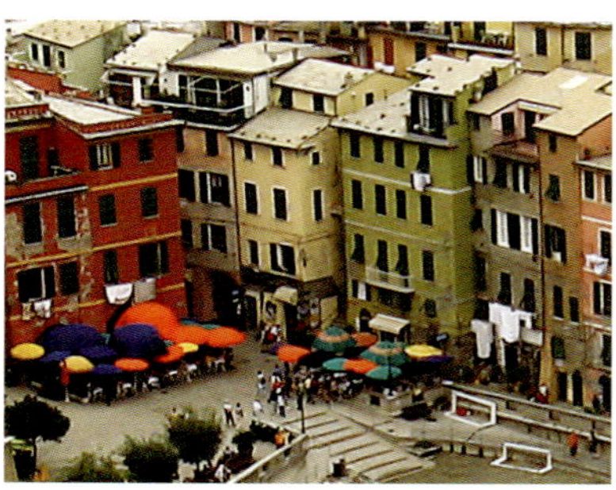

Sharpened

Unfortunately, Photoshop needs help from us to optimize sharpening. Every image is different and we have to play with settings that can be very confusing at first. But if we understand how sharpening is done, they get far less confusing. So let's invest just a moment digging in.

Here is an edge. It is a transition from dark gray to light gray and, because it is a computer-generated edge, it is perfectly sharp. Neither the 100% zoom nor the 3200% zoom (Photoshop's maximum) show any blurriness.

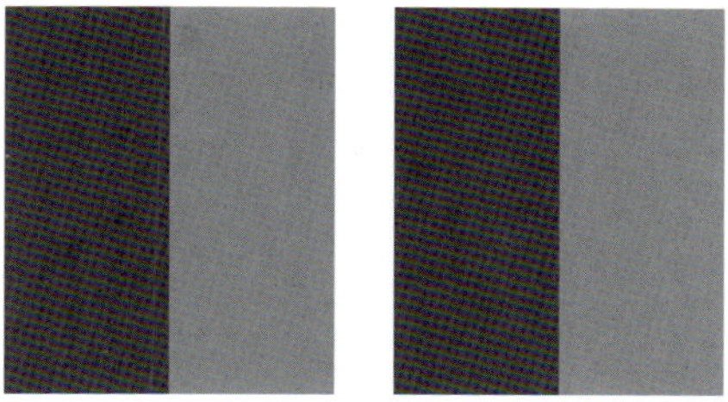

100% 3200%

Here are the same two views of the edge after performing a sharpening. Right at the edge, the dark gray has been made darker and the light gray lighter. The transition now has a slight halo to it because of the enhanced contrast. We can see this effect quite clearly at the 3200% zoom.

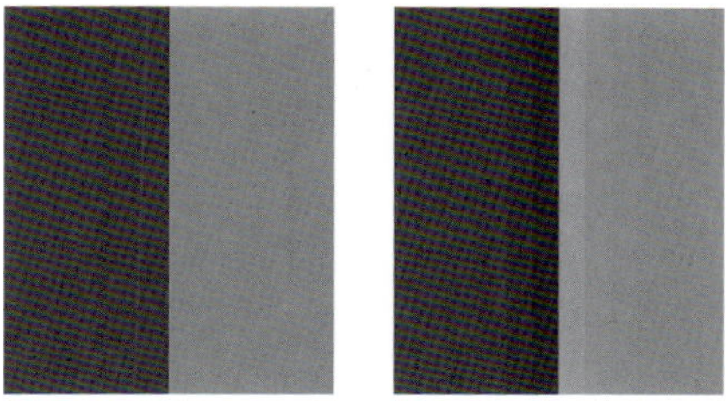

100% 3200%

If we take the original edge and blur it slightly, we get an edge that is more representative of what we might see from our camera. The edge is not sharp. There is a more gentle transition from dark gray to light gray.

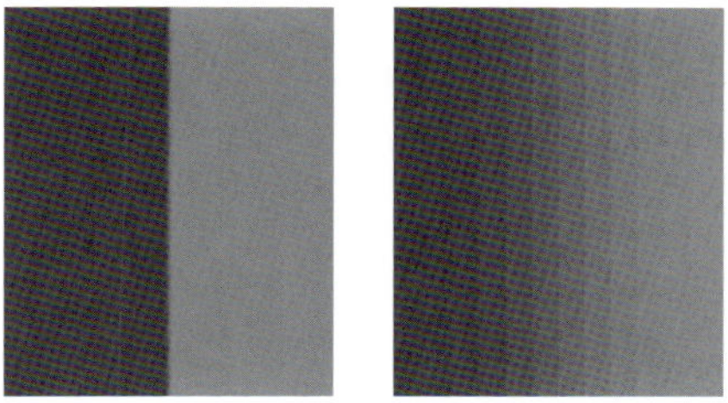

100% 3200%

In this last example, I have sharpened the blurred edge from the previous example, counteracting some of the gentle transition, pushing the transition pixels back towards darker and lighter. Our result is optimum when the strength and width of sharpening line up with the degree of blurring.

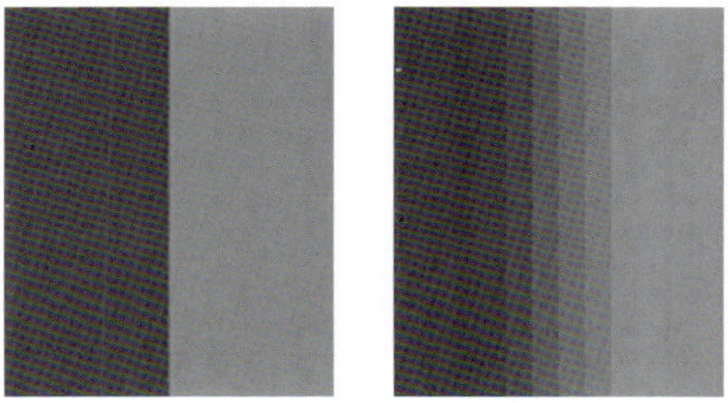

100% 3200%

When we choose Filter>Sharpen>Unsharp Mask, here is the dialog box that opens. We have three sliders to play with: Amount, Radius, and Threshold. Amount is just the strength. A higher Amount pushes the darks darker and the lights lighter at the edges. Radius refers to the width of the sharpening. We use a bigger radius to counteract a softer edge. Threshold tells Photoshop to ignore contrast differences below a certain level (to look for stronger edges).

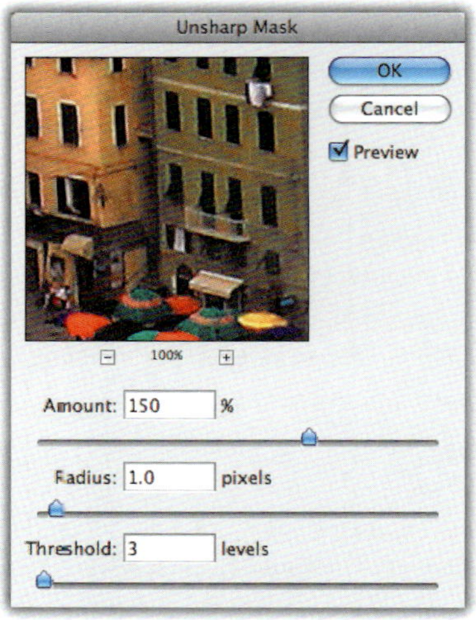

The small preview box shows us what the filter result will look like. If we check Preview (please do), our document window will update as well. Toggling preview on and off helps with doing real-time, original to sharpened comparisons. Otherwise it is sometimes hard to see the change.

"So what settings do I use?" you might ask. And that would be a very good question. And one, unfortunately, for which there is no good answer. Sorry! But there are some general guidelines. First and foremost, we need to trust our eyes. As we play with the sliders, we should toggle Preview on and off and follow our perception as to what looks good and what looks bad. The more we do this, the more comfortable we will become in controlling the sharpening effect.

Check out these three pictures. On the left, we have the original. In the middle, there's a sharpened version. Notice how the detail pops. On the right, we have an over sharpened version. Notice the telltale halos–either Amount or Radius needs to be reduced.

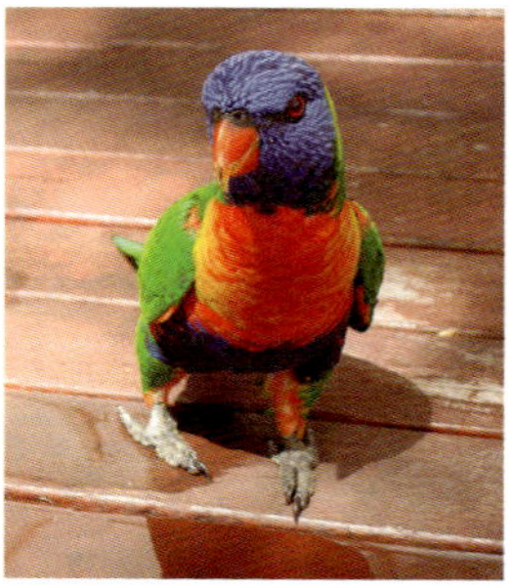
Original

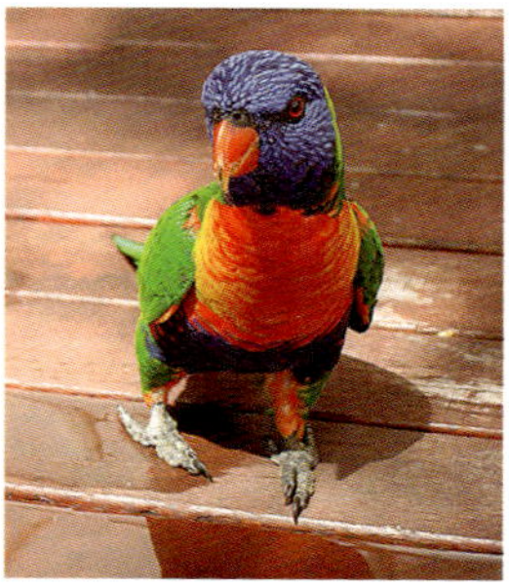
Sharpened

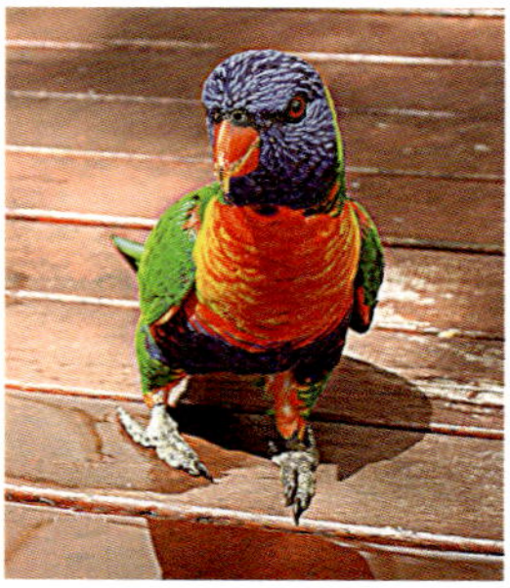
Over Sharpened

Okay, so let's go ahead and sharpen something. The first thing I do, as I mentioned in the last chapter, is to make a composite layer, even if I'm dealing with a single layer image. If we do have a single layer image, we just drag its layer onto the New Layer icon in the Layers panel. If we have multiple layers, we select the top one, hold down Cmd(Ctrl) plus Opt(Alt) plus Shift and hit E. I usually name the new layer "CompSh" for Composite Sharpened.

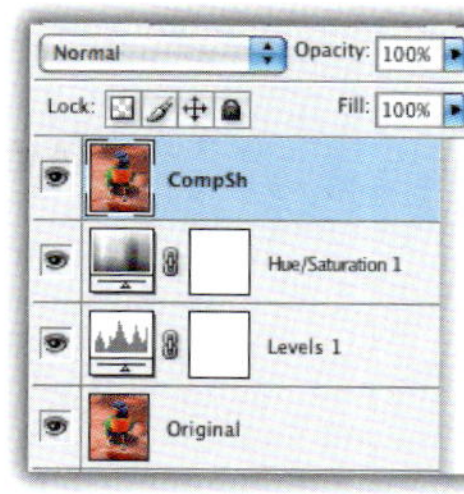

Select the CompSh layer and choose Filter>Sharpen>Unsharp Mask. Suggested starting points are Amount=200%, Radius=2, and Threshold=3. This should be a little over sharpened so back off a bit on both Amount and Radius (toggling Preview on and off to compare progress) until the image is crisp but realistic. Then click OK. And that's it.

STARTING SHARPEN SETTINGS

Amount = 200%
Radius = 2
Threshold = 3

Optimized settings will vary from image to image. Amount will probably be between 50% and 200%, Radius between .5 and 2 pixels, and Threshold between 3 and 6. If the image has smoothly varying tones, like in a sky or a skin close-up, sharpening can have negative consequences. Try increasing Threshold to eliminate these.

I generally err to the side of over sharpening a bit. The reason is that I still have one more trick up my sleeve. Since I sharpened my CompSh layer, essentially a duplicate, I have the ability to tone down the sharpening by simply lowering the opacity on that layer. This works because the sharpened CompSh blends with the unsharpened underlayers. (At 0% opacity, the sharpening is completely gone.)

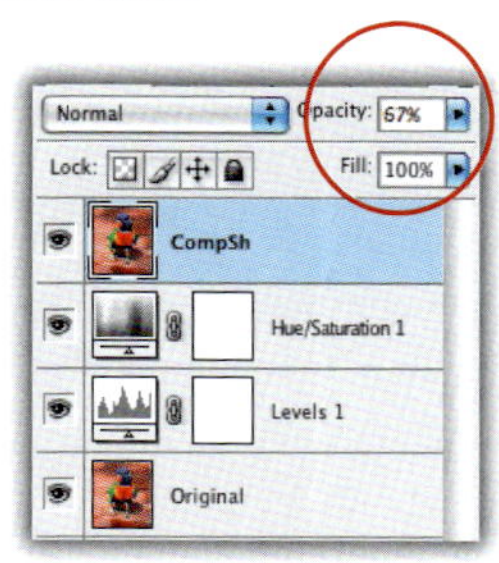

One last reminder regarding sharpening... When we run the filter, we affect only the selected layer or the selected pixels on that layer if there is an active selection. So if we have a portrait and want the eyes to really pop out, we might consider making a soft selection on the eyes and giving them a special sharpening. A better solution, though, is to jump those selected pixels to a new layer and sharpen them there. With this technique, you have the ability to use opacity to independently adjust sharpening for each layer.

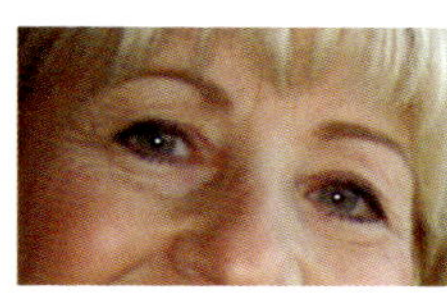

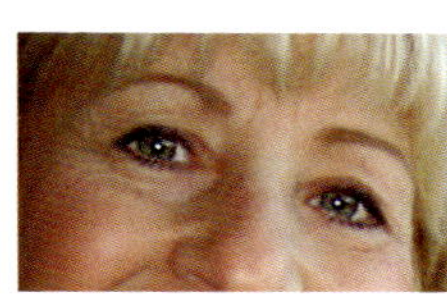

36. THE BLUR FILTER

If you were struggling with the complexity of the Sharpen filter, you'll now be able to breath a sigh of relief. Why? Our new topic, the Blur filter, has only one setting. And it is intuitive on top of that! We discussed it briefly back in Chapter 27.

Blurring, of course, is just the opposite of sharpening. The Blur filters smooth out sharp edges. But since focus (sharpness) is so central to good photography, why in the world would we need to blur? The answer is for special effects!

The Blur filters are found under Filter>Blur. As with Sharpening, there are lots of choices but we will concentrate on just one, Gaussian Blur. The name Gaussian Blur is derived from the German mathematician Karl Friedrich Gauss, inventor of the mathematics used by the filter. (Gauss, by the way, is pronounced like house, not like gauze, as it is commonly mispronounced in most Photoshop seminars I've attended.)

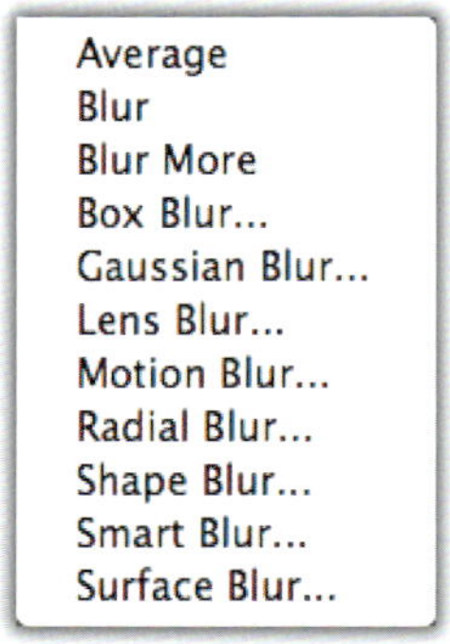

The Gaussian Blur is simple to use and the most general purpose of the blur filters. The two others that may be interesting to you are the Lens blur, which more precisely simulates a defocussed image, and Motion blur, which simulates the blur resulting from a moving subject taken with a long exposure.

Here is our original edge from the last chapter again. Recall it is a transition from dark gray to light gray and, because it is a computer-generated edge, it is perfectly sharp. Neither the 100% zoom nor the 3200% zoom show any blurriness.

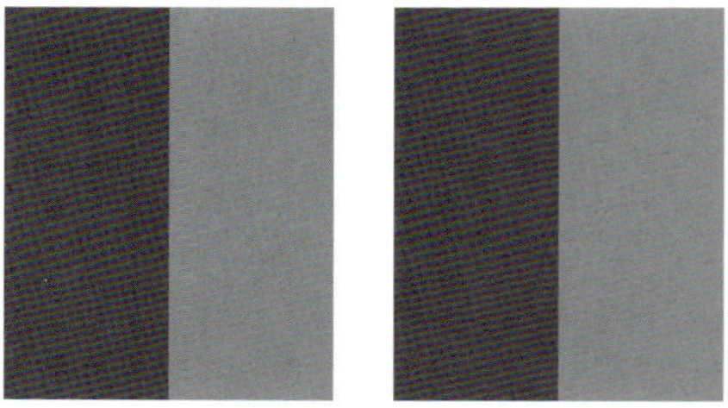

100% 3200%

Here are the same two views of the edge after performing a blur. There is now a smoother transition from dark gray to light gray with several intermediate shades in between. The more we blur, the wider this transition. So far, this is just review.

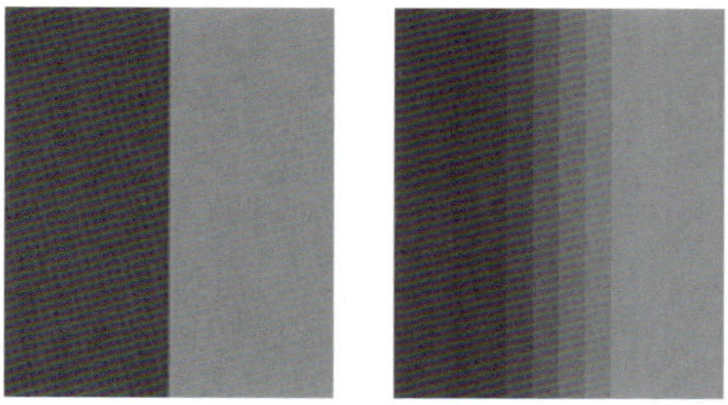

100% 3200%

When we choose Filter>Blur>Gaussian Blur, here is the dialog box that opens. See what I mean about simple? We get the same preview window that we had with Sharpening and the same Preview check box. But now there is a single setting, Radius. Radius is the width of the blur; setting it higher increases the blur. Setting it lower reduces the blur. In this context, it is much easier to understand what Radius for sharpening means. It is the width of the blur that the sharpening tries to counteract!

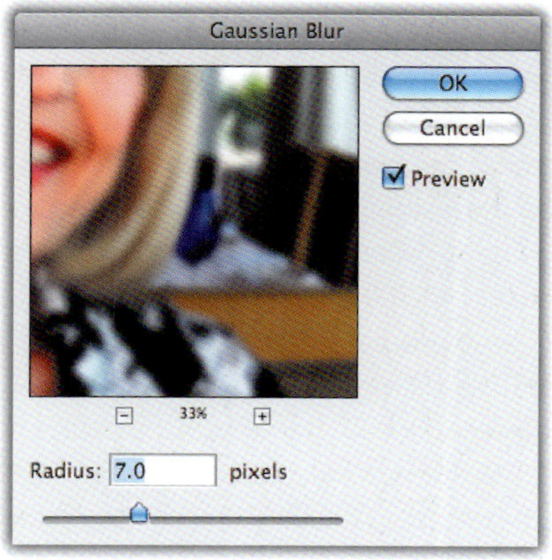

We have a bit more room in this chapter so I'll mention some additional tips on this dialog box that pertain to the Unsharp Mask dialog box as well. If we click and hold in the preview box, the preview reverts to the unfiltered original (sort of like the image does when we toggle the Preview check box on and off). If we click and drag in the preview box, we can reposition the preview. Easier yet, we can click anywhere in original image and the preview box will center on where we clicked in the image.

Okay, we have a simple dialog box and only one very intuitive setting... Now let's use it for something. One application is to simulate a shallow depth of field image, where our subject is in focus while the background is blurred. It is a great way to draw attention to the subject (my wife in this case) and away from an unimportant setting. (This same effect can be achieved with our camera by shooting with a wide aperture.)

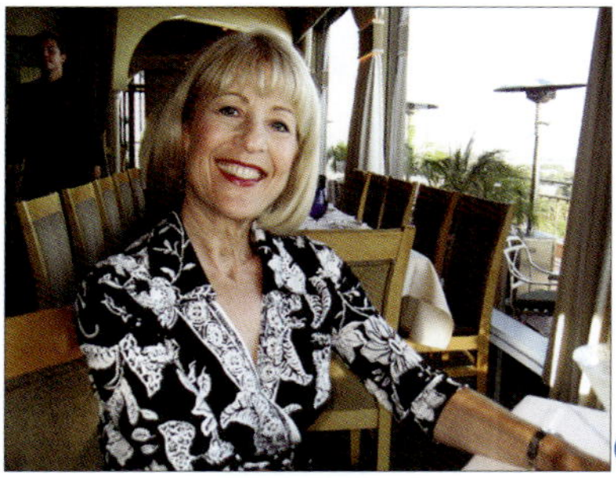

Original

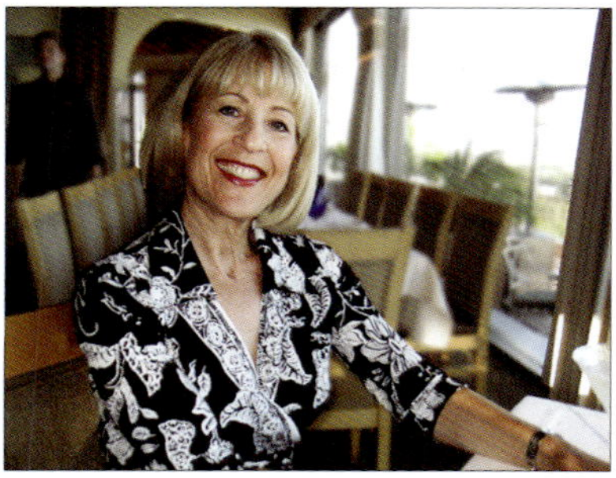

Background Gaussian Blurred

The image on the left is as taken. The camera was set for a relatively large depth of field so the background feels in focus (and is a bit distracting). In the image on the right, the Gaussian Blur filter has been used to slightly blur the background (we will go through an example of how to do this next), simulating a shallower depth of field.

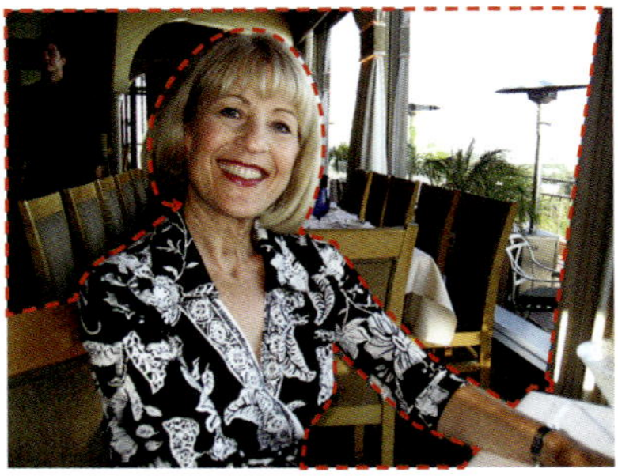

Here is how we go about doing this, using the example from the previous page. We use our selection tools to create a selection around the area we wish to blur. Now let's save this selection (Select>Save Selection), calling it BlurArea. With the selection still active, we choose Layer>New>Layer Via Copy (or use the shortcut Cmd(Ctrl)-J to jump the background pixels to a new layer and name it BlurBackground. (I will get to why we didn't use a layer mask.)

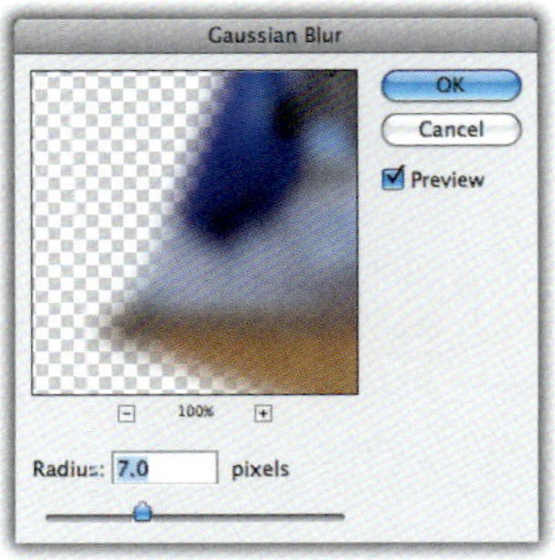

With the BlurBackground layer selected, we choose Filter>Blur>Gaussian Blur and adjust the setting per our taste. Before we hit OK, look at what is happening in the preview box! The border of BlurBackground has blurred as well. This is an unintended consequence of the blurring. I will get back to this as well.

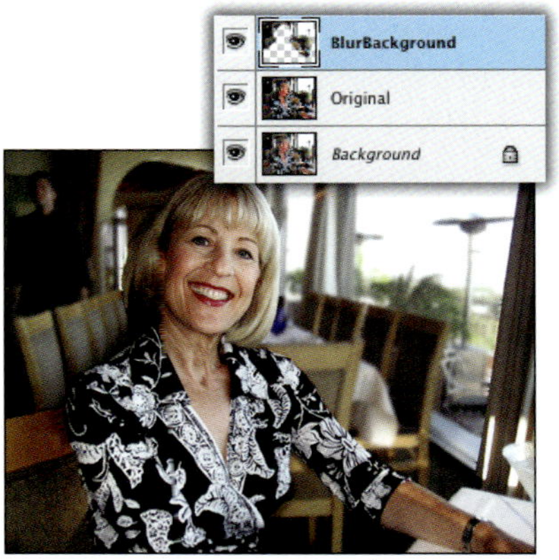

When we hit OK, BlurBackground blurs and our image is complete. The foreground remains in focus and the background has been slightly blurred. So our attention is directed to the foreground.

If we had done a heavier blur, the BlurBackground edge might have blurred so much that it encroached on the foreground edge, making it look blurred. The fix for this, if you run into it, is to select the BlurBackground layer, load the BlurArea selection (Select>Load Selection) and then click the Add Layer Mask icon. The mask hides the blurred edge and fixes everything. (By the way, this is why we didn't use a layer mask to begin with. The mask would have blurred as well when we applied our filter and then we wouldn't have this "Add Layer Mask" trick at our disposal.

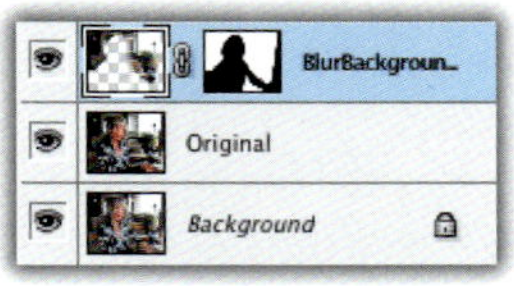

Layer Mask Added

Although we didn't want to do it in the previous example, running the Gaussian Blur filter on a layer with a layer mask can have useful applications. In fact I would say that this is how I most commonly use this filter.

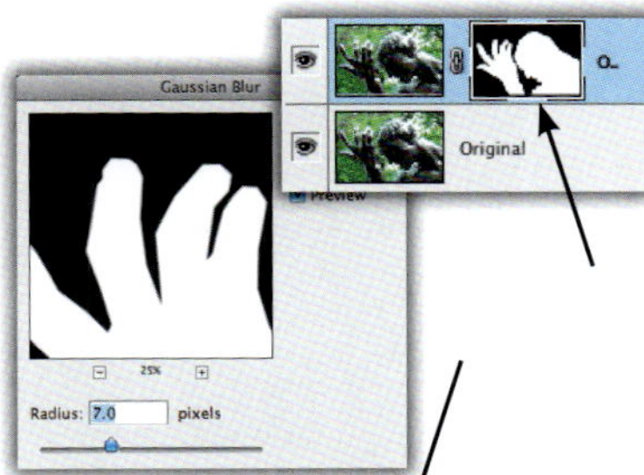

When we run a blur filter on a layer that has a layer mask, we have to pay extra attention to which thumbnail is selected. If the layer mask thumbnail is selected, then only the layer mask blurs. (And only the layer mask will show up in the preview.)

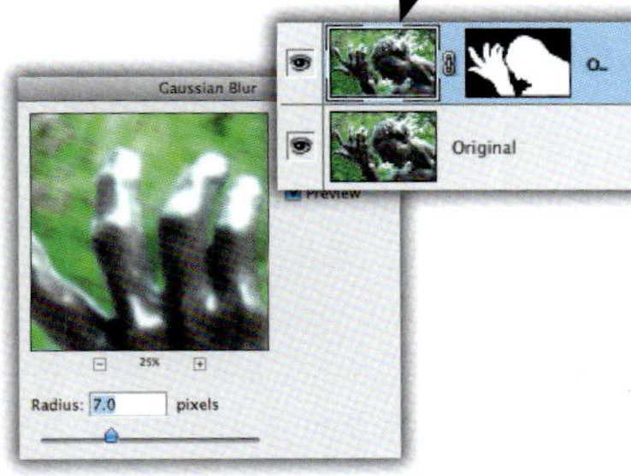

But if the image thumbnail is selected, then the image and the layer mask are both blurred, not just the image. I imagine there must be a good reason for this but I don't know what it is. This is why we waited until the end of the process in our last example to apply the layer mask.

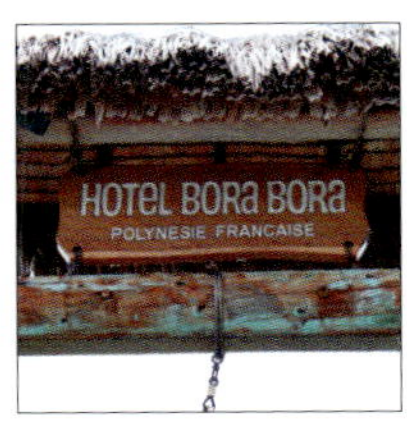

Remember the vignette effect using layer masks that we demonstrated in Chapter 25? We can look back now and see that what we did was to blur the layer mask to create the feathered border around the vignette. Let's use this exact same technique to do a quick composite.

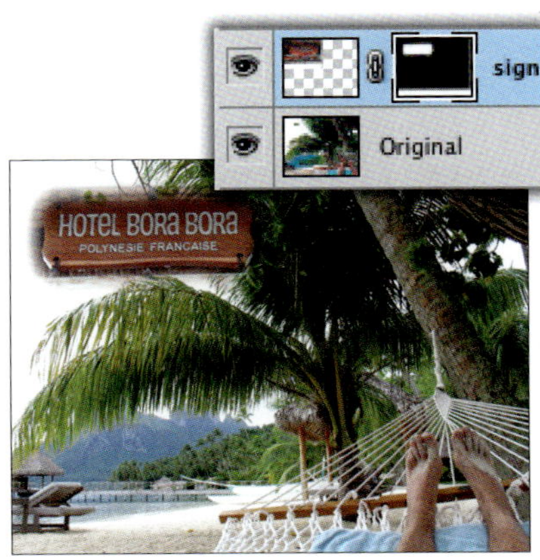

We'll add a Hotel Bora Bora sign to a second image, one I took from a hammock at that hotel. We duplicate the sign as a new layer in hammock scene and then transform size and location as desired.

With the sign layer active, we make a rectangular marquee selection around the sign and create a new layer mask. The selection is reflected in the mask. Then with the layer mask thumbnail selected, we choose Filter>Blur>Gaussian Blur and blur appropriately. We hit OK and we are done.

CS4 Clone Tool Preview: Although not totally new to CS4, a feature called Clone Preview has gone from clunky (in CS3) to polished in CS4. With Clone Preview turned on, we get to see a preview of what we are about to do. Let me explain...

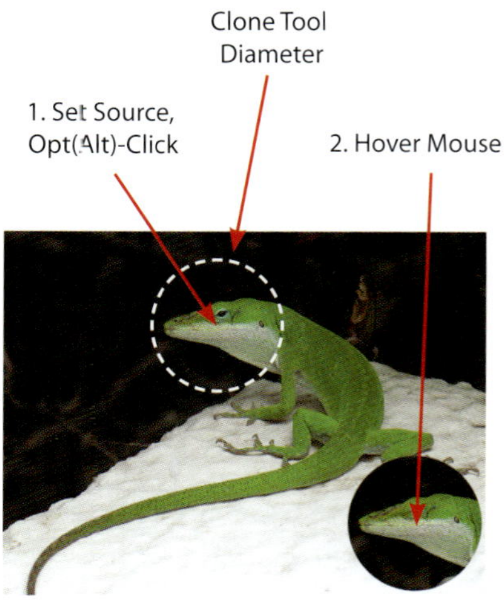

Here is the example we were playing with in Chapter 32. I set my source point by Opt(Alt)-Clicking. But now, with Clone Preview turned on, when I move my mouse towards my destination, I see a live preview of what I am about to clone. Now I can locate my clone exactly where I want it prior to committing (by clicking).

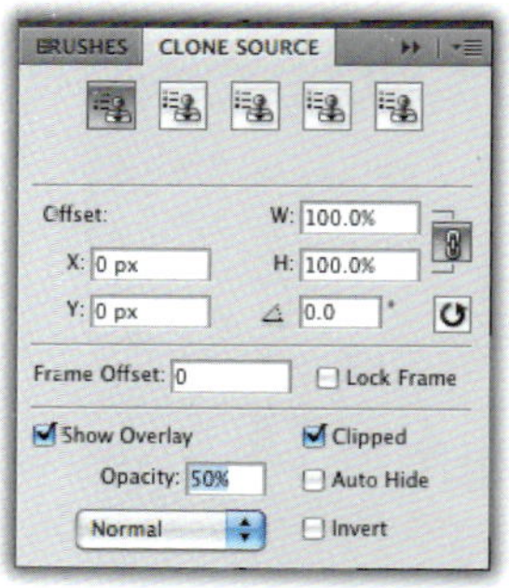

To see the live preview go to Window>Clone Source and you will be presented with this panel. (Alternatively, there is a link to this panel on the right side of the Clone tool options bar.) Check both Show Overlay and Clipped. Show Overlay tells Photoshop to show the preview and Clipped tells it to bound the preview by the Clone tool diameter. (CS3 didn't have this Clipped control so the entire image appeared in the overlay. Yecch! This is why we turned it off in Chapter 32.)

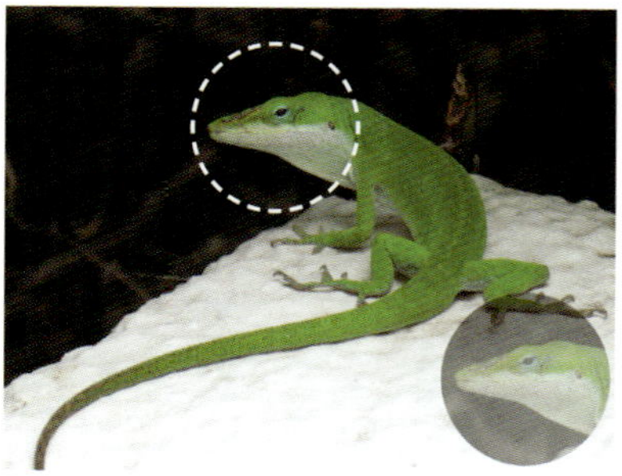

I find Clone Preview to be even more useful if the overlay is reduced in opacity. In this example (and in the dialog box above it), I have reduced the opacity to 50%. Now I can see through the preview to the underlying image. This makes it even easier to locate the clone exactly where I want it to be.

Healing Brush Tool Preview: In CS4, the Healing Brush that we reviewed in Chapter 18 also has a live preview associated with it. Our same Clone Source panel controls it as well (and its options bar has a quick link to that panel).

SECTION

VI DRAWING & PAINTING

Time to shift gears altogether.

Although Photoshop is primarily an image editing application, it does have the capability to create graphics. There are other applications more directly suited to this, such as Illustrator, but for simple jobs, especially those you might want to integrate with an image in Photoshop, you really don't need to go elsewhere.

Way back in Chapter 11, we introduced the Brush tool. But we really only talked about it in the context of those characteristics that were common to a number of other Photoshop tools–diameter, softness and hardness, etc. I imagine that it will not surprise you to learn that the Brush tool can also be used to actually paint, to create art. In this section, we will learn how.

We will also delve into a completely parallel universe, vector graphics. This is the world of geometric objects and scalability. Remember my admonitions never to upsample images (at least not by much) because of the resulting quality loss? Vector graphics don't suffer from this constraint. They'll scale up to our heart's content. We'll see how.

And then there is the Pen tool, about which entire books are written and which people have spent their entire lives attempting to master. We'll spend a part of a chapter...

Okay, seriously! Vector graphics is a huge subject and we will not even start to do it justice. But what we can do is introduce it, show how it fits into Photoshop, and take some of the mystery out of it for when you do want to throw more energy at it.

37. BRUSH ENCORE & PENCIL TOOL

Back in Chapter 10, we discussed the basics of the **Brush tool** and learned that its core functionality is replicated in many of Photoshop's other tools. In this chapter, we will focus more on the Brush tool's drawing and painting capabilities. Along the way, we will also learn about the Pencil tool, a close cousin of the Brush.

As we know, the Brush tool is accessed in the toolbox and brings up an options bar with which we are already familiar. In Chapter 10, we left Mode on Normal because we had not yet discussed blending modes. If we pull down that menu now, we see that we can set our brush to blend with underlying pixels with all of those blending modes. That said, I still suggest you leave it set to Normal until you've developed good skills with blending.

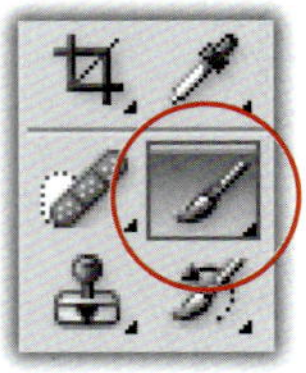

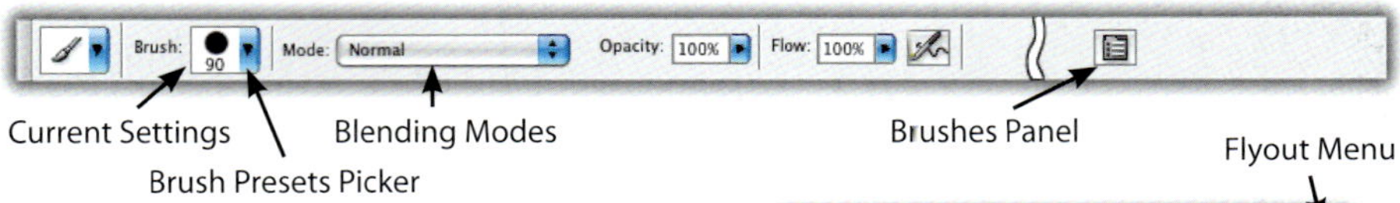

Recall that in the **Brush Presets Picker** menu, we have our diameter and hardness settings. (Although I didn't mention it the first time around, you probably also noticed the menu's array of preset brush sizes. We will come back to this group in a moment.) Dragging out the lower right hand corner, as I have done, will expand the menu size, so that more options can be seen at once.

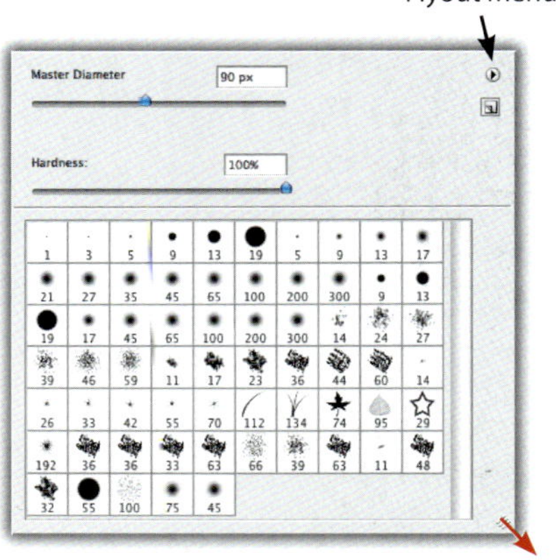

To paint with our brush, we set the diameter and hardness, set the foreground color (this will be our brush color), and click and drag on our canvas. Our brush starts painting where we click, follows our mouse movement as we drag, and stops painting when we release the mouse. To draw a straight line, by the way, just click and release on the starting point and then shift click and release on the ending point. The Brush tool will connect the two points with a straight line.

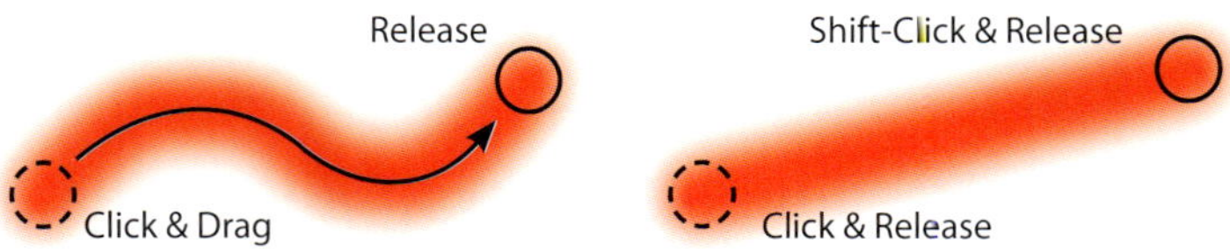

Let's go back to that Brush Presets Picker menu we just discussed. Looking at it, we see the first group of presets has a hardness setting of 100% with diameters ranging from 1 to 19 pixels. Then comes a group with hardness settings of 0% and various diameters. All in all, this isn't very interesting–I would really rather pick my diameter and hardness visually using the brush cursor size and keyboard shortcuts. But if we continue down the list, we see a whole bunch of wild and crazy brushes (spatter, chalk, etc.) and a whole bunch of others that aren't even conventional brushes (leaves, grass, etc.).

We can hover our mouse over any thumbnail for a tool tip that tells us what it is. Alternatively, we can click the flyout menu in the upper right hand corner of the Brush Presets Picker menu and choose "Large List" to see the names with the brush shape.

The special brushes are lots of fun. To appreciate them, just open a blank canvas and start experimenting. And I advise you to do just that. You will see that many of them, like the leaves and grass brushes, scatter shapes along the path we describe with our mouse. Some even take their own liberties with color (varying the hue), using the foreground color as a basis. Here is some doodling of mine as an example.

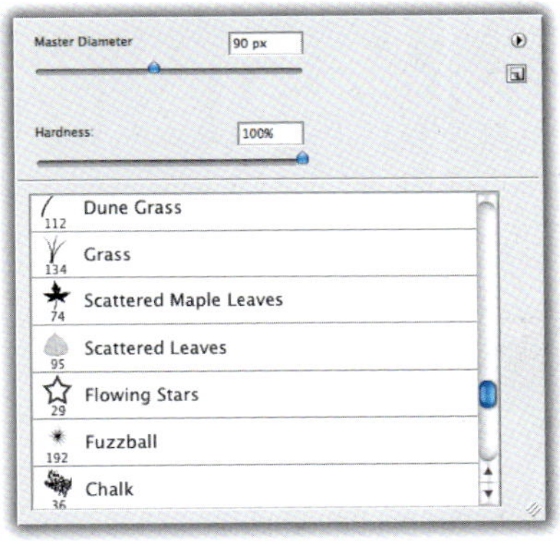

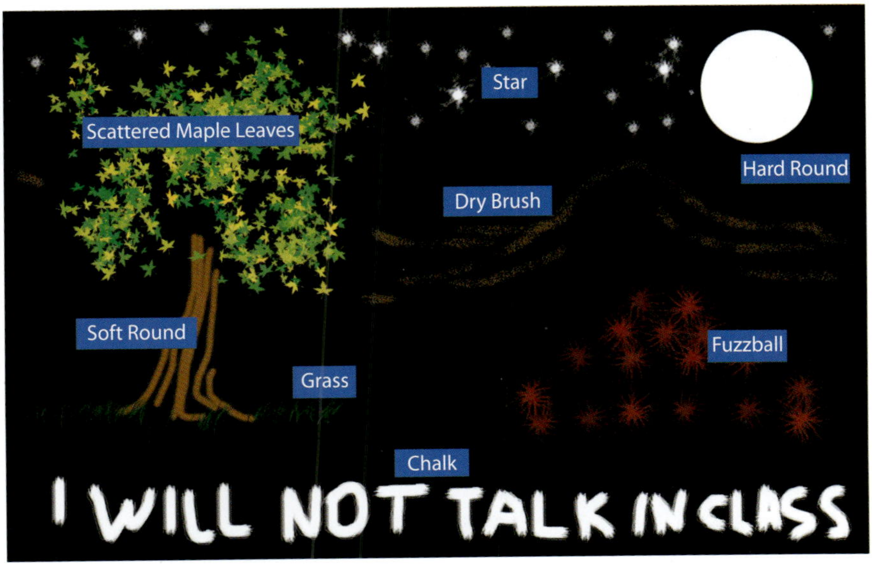

There is an entire world to explore within Photoshop regarding the Brush tool, including the capability for us to modify existing presets or to create and store our own custom styles. As we will see, there are also several additional libraries of presets that come with Photoshop that we can access if we know where to look.

Panel Menu

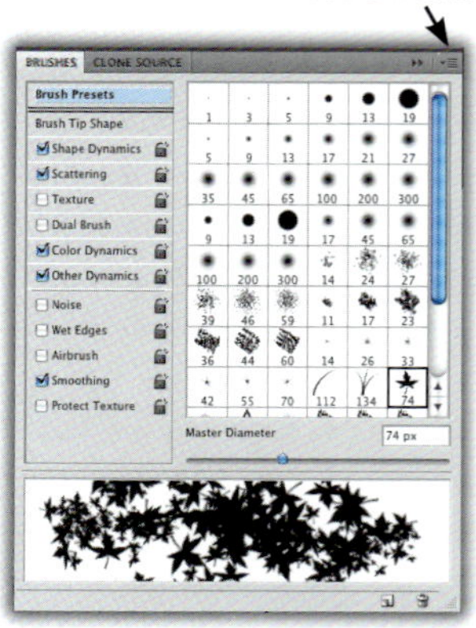

We won't spend a lot of time on all of the available options but the best place to start is with the **Brushes panel**. With the Brush tool selected, choose Window>Brushes to bring it up. (Now its icon is available in the collapsed panel dock. It looks like three brushes in a brush holder.) If your panel does not look like this, click on the panel menu and choose "Expanded View."

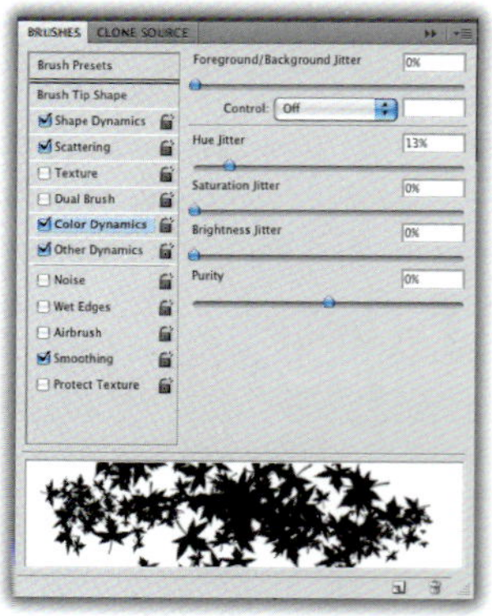

Click on a brush thumbnail to select that brush. (Note it shows as selected in the options bar at the same time.) Click a checked brush attribute (under Brush Tip Shape) to edit it. Only the checked attributes apply to a given brush. For example, choosing Scattered Maple Leaves and clicking on Color Dynamics gives us this. "Hue jitter" controls how much color variation there is among the leaves. And so on. Click "Brush Presets" to reset to the brush thumbnails.

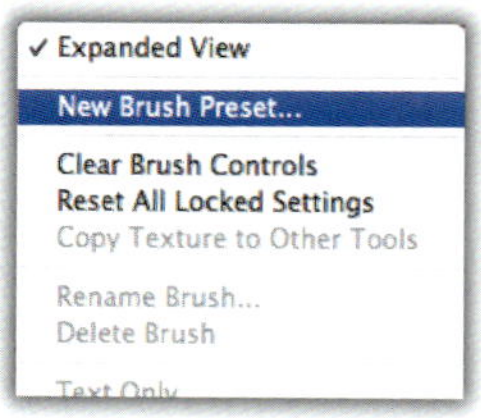

Did you create a variation on one of the presets you would like to save for future use? Not a problem. Once the settings are to your liking, open the panel menu and choose "New Brush Preset." A pop up will prompt you to name it and, from then on, that preset will reside in your Brush Preset Picker as well.

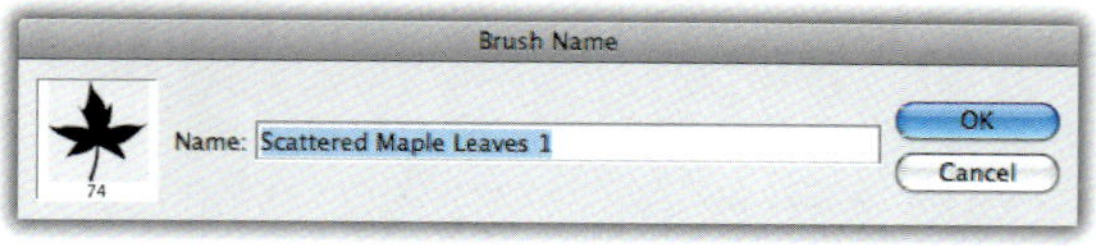

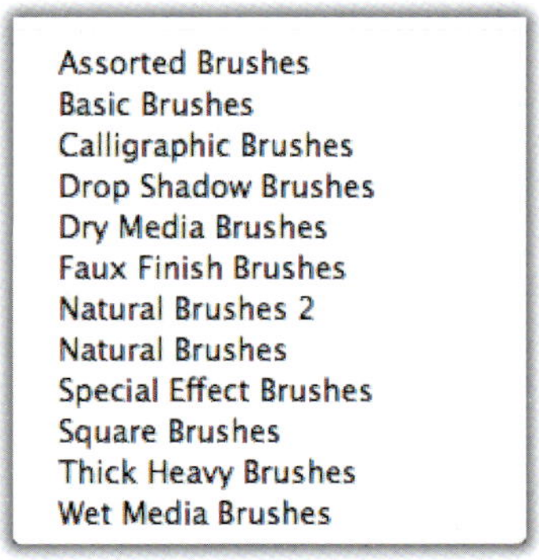

Not feeling that enterprising but interested in more brush choices? Open the Brush panel menu and look at the bottom section. There are a number of additional libraries of brushes we can load. We just select it and then either Append (add them) to the current set of brushes, or Replace, which replaces the existing presets with the new group. The same flyout menu has a Reset Brushes command to get back to where we started.

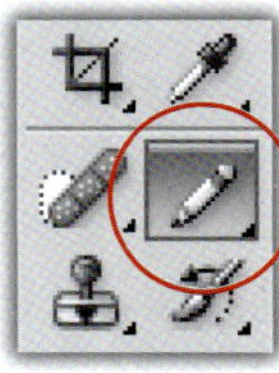

Once we have mastered the Brush tool, we pretty much know all there is to know about the **Pencil tool** as well. Hidden underneath the Brush tool in the toolbox (click and hold on the Brush tool to access it), the Pencil tool has the same brush styles menu and works with all of the same blending modes. The same Brush panel applies as well.

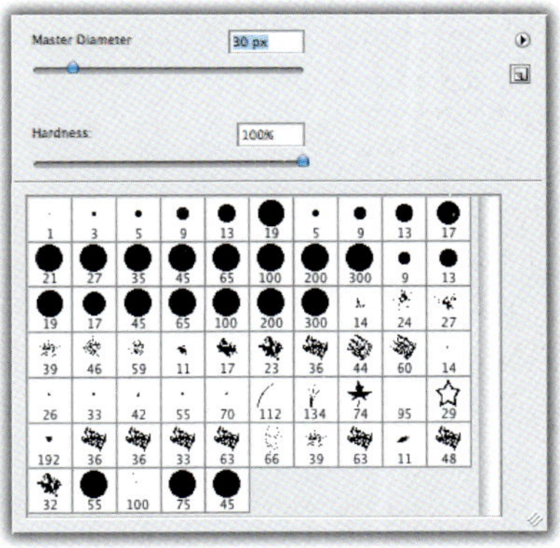

So what is the difference? The bottom line is that the Pencil tool always draws with a hard edge. That's pretty much it. (There are some other slight differences visible in the options bar that you can check out in Help if you want to.) We can pull down the Pencil menu and pick a brush tip that is soft, but notice that when we do, the little thumbnail indicating our selection shows a hard edge. We can even play with the softness/hardness slider but it won't change the softness/hardness. The Pencil is hard.

To tell you the truth, I never use the Pencil. The Brush gives me more flexibility and can duplicate almost everything that the pencil can do. But if you are an artist (and as you have seen above, I am not), perhaps you will find it useful in its own right.

We have talked about the Brush tool and we've talked about the Pencil tool. It only seems logical to talk about the Pen tool next, right? Well… No! While the Brush and Pencil tools are closely related to each other, the Pen tool is a completely different animal. The Brush and Pencil tools paint pixels while the Pen tool creates vector paths. But since we have not discussed vectors at this point, let's go there first.

So what is a **Vector**?

The short answer is that it's a mathematical formula. Instead of saving information pixel by pixel (often called a bitmap), vector graphics saves it as mathematical formulas. These formulas (for lines, circles, rectangles, and much, much more) are built into the program and can represent anything we can think up. Photoshop takes care of all this.

To display these vectors, Photoshop constructs how the pixels should look based on the formulas. What might seem like extra effort can be well worth it.

Check this out, for example. Picture a straight line, 1 pixel wide by 300 pixels long. When we save it pixel by pixel, the following information, or something like it, will be saved:

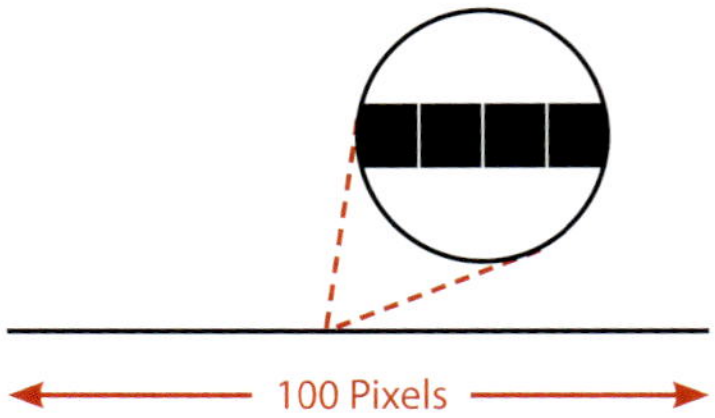


```
Pixel 1     (x-coordinate=0, y-coordinate=0, color=black, opacity=100)
Pixel 2     (x-coordinate=1, y-coordinate=0, color=black, opacity=100)
Pixel 3     (x-coordinate=2, y-coordinate=0, color=black, opacity=100)
  .
  .
  .
Pixel 298   (x-coordinate=297, y-coordinate=0, color=black, opacity=100)
Pixel 299   (x-coordinate=298, y-coordinate=0, color=black, opacity=100)
Pixel 300   (x-coordinate=299, y-coordinate=0, color=black, opacity=100)
```

Each pixel has its own line of code. There are 300 lines of code in all, one for each pixel.

But as an alternative, imagine representing the straight line as follows:

```
Line 1      (starting x-coordinate=0, starting y-coordinate=0, direction=right, length=300,
            color=black, opacity=100)
```

The program knows what a line is, it's a group of pixels starting at a point and extending in one direction for a given length, so it can construct it with these parameters. We get the same result but with a lot less code. A lot less! This translates to smaller file sizes.

If we wanted to double the straight-line length, we would need to double the code in the bitmap case, adding new lines of code for pixels 301 to 600. In the vector case, we simply change the length to 600 and we are done. This is the essence of scalability.

This sounds so great, why bother with pixel by pixel? The answer is that not all content lends itself to being represented as formulas. Geometrical objects do, like circles and rectangles. Bold graphics do, like solid colors and smooth curves. But our image of a landscape with wisps of clouds in the sky and pompous grass in the foreground would not be a good candidate. Nor would any image with continuously varying tones and lots of detail like we get from our digital camera. That's why there are pixel-by-pixel (or bitmap) programs, like Photoshop.

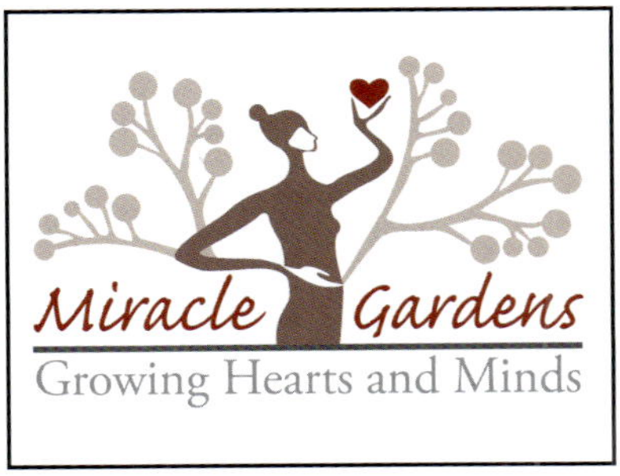

This image lends itself to vector graphics.

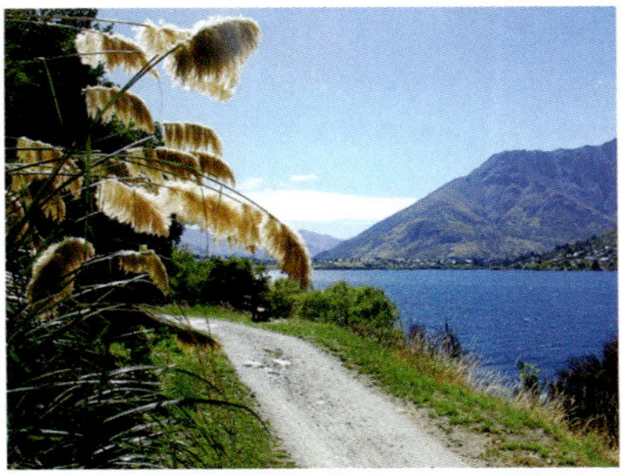

This image lends itself to bitmap graphics.

I mentioned above that when Photoshop displays a vector, it constructs a pixel-by-pixel representation of the vector and displays that. It does this by internally constructing the results of the formula–this is called a **Path**–and then using pixels to draw out the path. So the pixels drawn are drawn along the path and the path represents the formula. The punch line is that we can directly access this path, modifying it as needed, and the drawn pixels will follow along. We'll do some examples in the upcoming chapters.

Here I have constructed a solid blue circle using Photoshop's vector tools. In the blow-up, there is a barely visible smooth line at the boundary–this is the path. We can also see how Photoshop has chosen to shade the pixels at the edge of circle to best replicate the circular shape. This shading technique is called anti-aliasing.

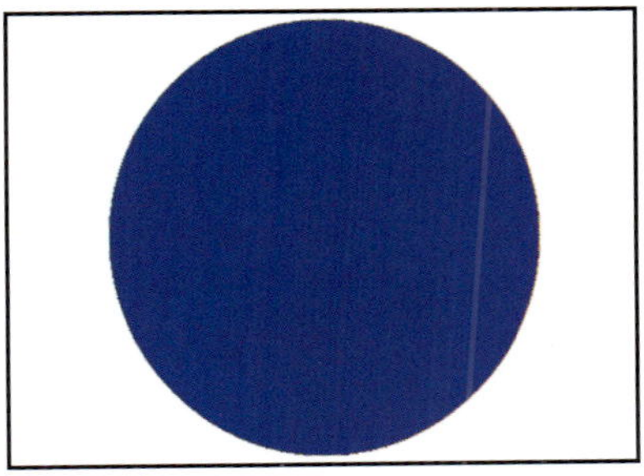

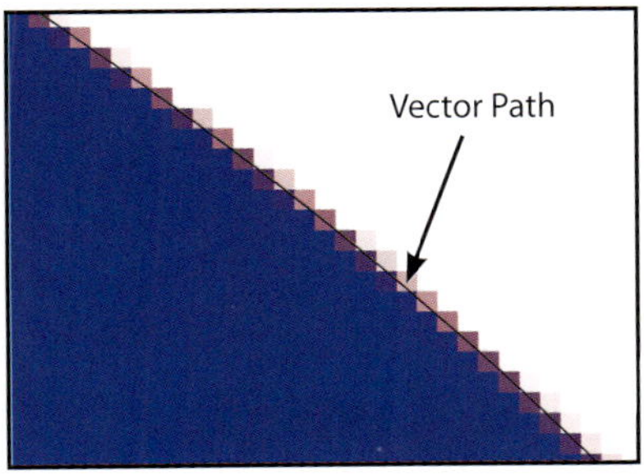

We have been talking pretty theoretically about vector graphics without actually making any. You might be wondering when we are going to get around to that. Actually, we already have. Back in Chapter 23, we went through an introduction to Photoshop's text capability. Text, as it happens, is all done with vectors.

Recall that when we type text, it goes on to its own layer. At any later time, we can go back, select that text and edit it. We can change spelling, font, color, etc. We can also choose a larger font to make the text bigger, with no loss in quality.

We are certainly used to this behavior from our word processors, but it is not the norm for Photoshop, is it? For everything bitmap, if we try and blow it up, we get pixelization, a loss of quality. But this T blows up from 12 points to 72 points with no problem. The reason is that text is made from vectors. And vectors can be scaled.

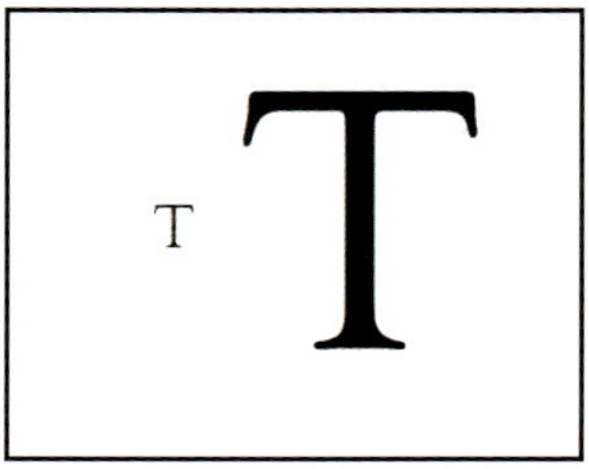

As another illustration of this, let's convert our 12 point T into bitmap and then blow it up to a 72 point version. At 12 points, the difference between vector and bitmap is not noticeable. But the difference becomes quite obvious at 72 points.

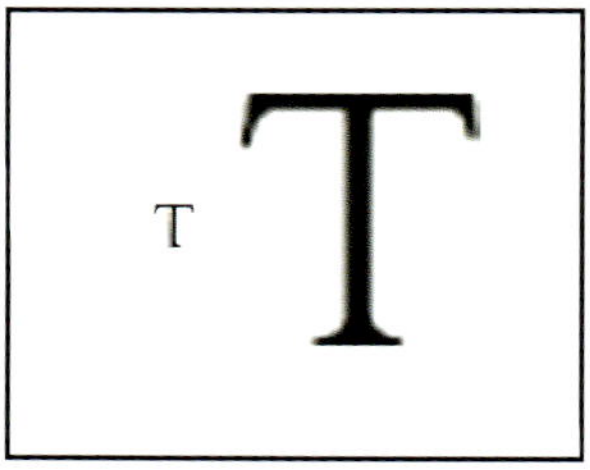

We discussed how a vector path is a visual representation of the vector formula. Path is a term we will run across often in Photoshop. But now we will know it is just this vector graphics thing. Here is the actual path for the letter T, blown up so we can see it. Just smooth thin gray lines with little boxes. Those boxes are known as anchor points and are the key to the path's editability. More later on this.

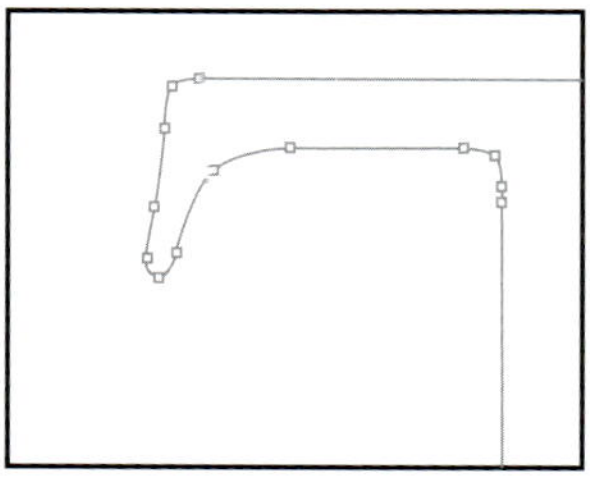

Text gives us a very good example of the benefits of vector graphics. It is editable. It is scalable. And as mentioned earlier, it is also very efficient with respect to memory usage.

There are some things to watch out for with vector graphics, though. Here's one you are guaranteed to run into. (I know that it scared me the first time I ran into it.) In our last section, we reviewed Photoshop's filtering capability. We should be able to create some very interesting text effects with those filters, right? Well, yes and no.

Let's create some text and run the Stained Glass filter (found under Filter>Texture). We start by opening a new document and select the Text tool. We choose a font, color, and a size of our liking and type something clever.

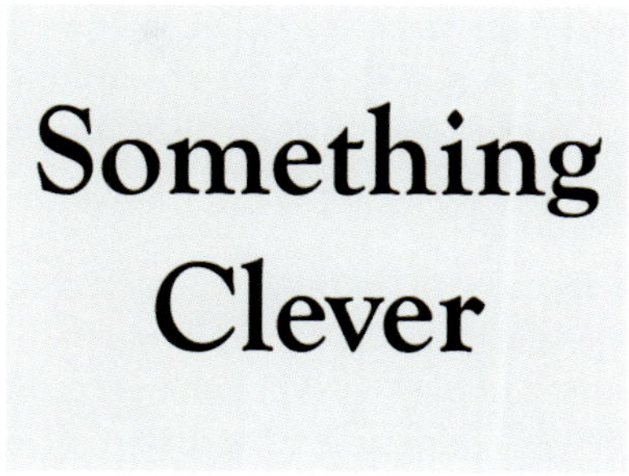

With our type layer selected, we choose Filter>Texture>Stained Glass and sit back to view our really neat effect. What we get, however, is this ominous message. Our text must be rasterized… It will no longer be editable… Yikes!

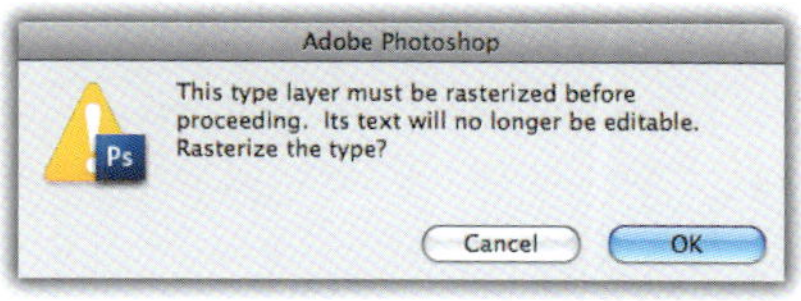

Photoshop, as we've discussed, is basically a pixel-by-pixel program that dabbles with vector graphics. Many of its tools, filters in particular, only work on pixel data. What this message is telling us is that to run the filter, the text has to be converted to pixels (this is what rasterizing does) and that once converted, our normal text editing tools won't work anymore. The text is a picture at this point, not vector.

If we are satisfied our text won't need further editing, we can safely click OK and apply the filter. Here is a tip, though. Before filtering, duplicate the text layer and turn off the visibility on the original. Then run the filter on (and rasterize) the copy. If you later find that your text does need editing, delete the filtered layer, edit the original text, duplicate the layer and then filter (and rasterize) again. Note that we can tell that the filtered layer is no longer an editable text layer because the "T" thumbnail has been replaced with a little image.

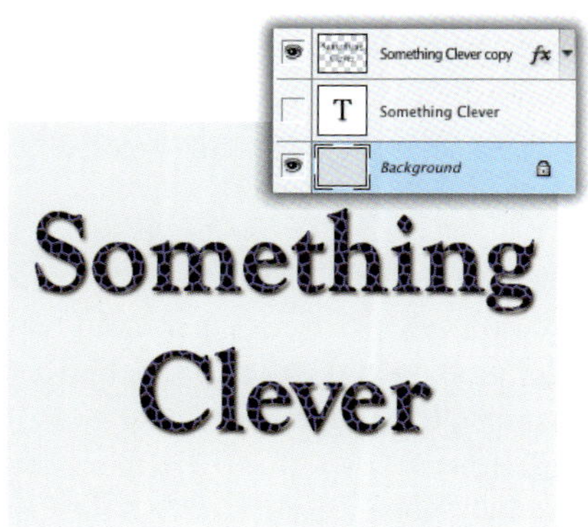

39. THE SHAPE TOOL

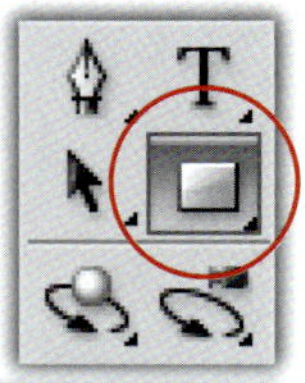

Perhaps the easiest way to start working with vector paths is with the **Shape tool**. This tool, which allows us to create some standard and some not-so-standard geometric shapes, can be found, as you might expect, in the toolbox.

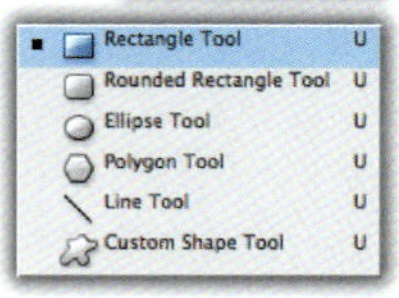

The default shape is a rectangle. If we click and hold on the tool, we see that nested underneath are a variety of different shape tools, including a Custom Shape tool whose icon reminds me a little of a bloated starfish.

There's actually an easier way to access these other shape tools, however. We just choose the rectangle tool and notice that in the options bar, all of those hidden tools (and some additional ones) are immediately available for the clicking. The little triangle to the right of this little mini toolbox gives us a tool options menu that varies depending on which tool we have selected.

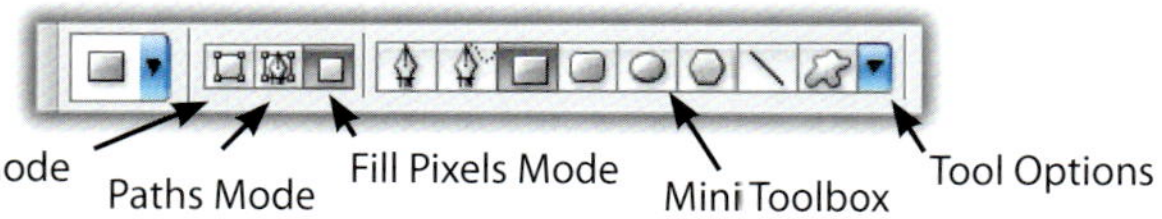

The options bar also has three shape tool modes. Let's start with the "Fill Pixels" mode.

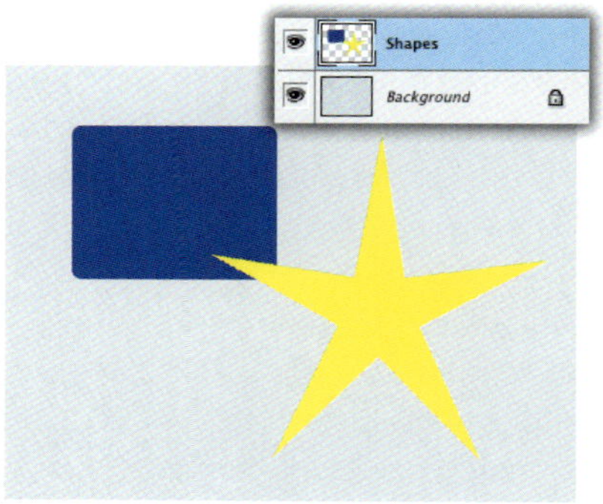

When we are in the **Fill Pixels** mode, we click and drag to create a shape and that resulting shape is filled with the foreground color. (This is pretty much like creating a selection with a Marquee tool and then choosing Edit>Fill.) This is pure bitmap pixels; no vectors involved. Here is a rounded rectangle and a star. (We make stars by choosing the Polygon tool and selecting Star in its options menu.)

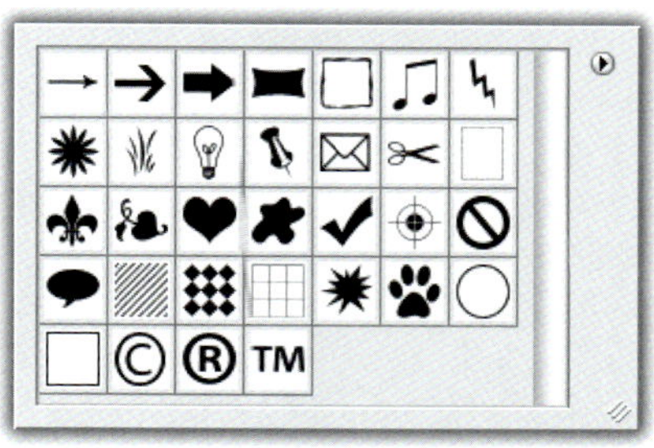

The Custom Shape tool is actually a menu of custom shapes. Select that tool in the mini toolbox in the options bar and a Shape pulldown menu becomes available where there are another 32 shapes at our disposal. Not enough? Click on the Custom Shapes flyout menu (triangle) and pick from a number of other shape suites.

Here are a few indispensable tips to help us get the exact results we want.

- Hold down SHIFT while clicking and dragging to make squares, circles, etc.
- Hold down Opt(Alt) while clicking and dragging to grow the shape out from its center (where you first clicked) as opposed to its edge.
- Hold down the spacebar during dragging to suspend sizing the object and to move it around. Release the space bar to resume sizing. Get used to fine tuning shape size and location by pressing and releasing the spacebar without ever releasing the mouse.

Okay, I need to say it again. In the Fill Pixels mode, the shape tools create pixels, bit-mapped pixels. Now if we select as our shape mode the left most box, the **Shape Layers** mode, we get something entirely different; we get vectors!

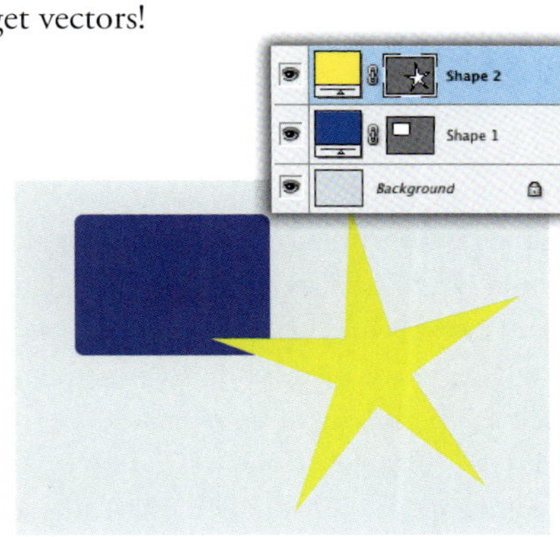

Here, I have chosen the Rounded Rectangle and then the Star, clicking and dragging as before. The shapes look exactly the same as we got with Fill Pixels. But if we look at our Layers panel, we see that we got there in a completely different way. Two new layers have been added (called shape layers) and the shapes were actually created by a layer mask (a special layer mask called a vector mask).

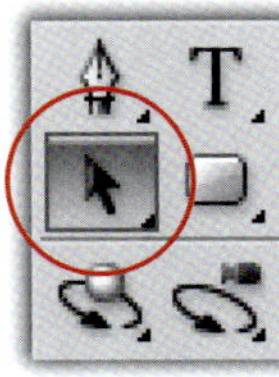

The outward appearance is the same but the difference is immense. The vector mask that creates the shape is in fact tied to a vector path. As we mentioned in the previous chapter, this means that it is editable. To do so, we choose the Path Selection tool, found in the toolbox. Clicking this tool within a shape will select the path that bounds the shape.

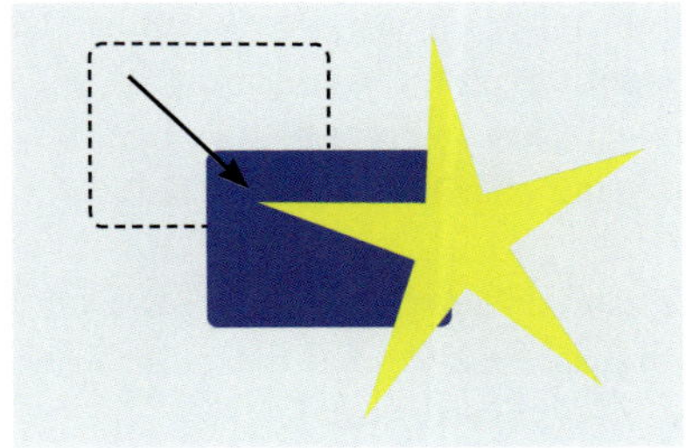

We can then click and drag the shape and, voilà, we are able to move it around the canvas. The vector mask thumbnail updates as we go. We are actually selecting the vector path that is used in the mask and moving that around. So far this is nothing that can't be done as easily with layers. But there is more, so read on.

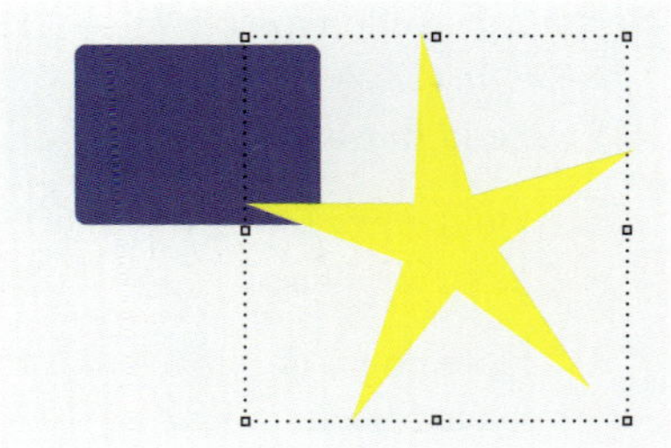

How about scaling? We said vector paths were scalable. With the Path Selection tool selected, look in the options bar and check Show Bounding Box. Up pops a transformation box around our path and we can transform to our hearts content. (As usual, we need to hit return or click Commit to apply the transformation.)

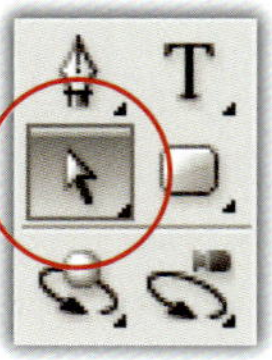

If you are still not impressed, hopefully this will put you over the top. Hidden under the Path Selection tool in the toolbox, we find the Direct Selection tool. It looks like the Path Selection tool but is hollowed out. With it, we can really modify the shape's vector path.

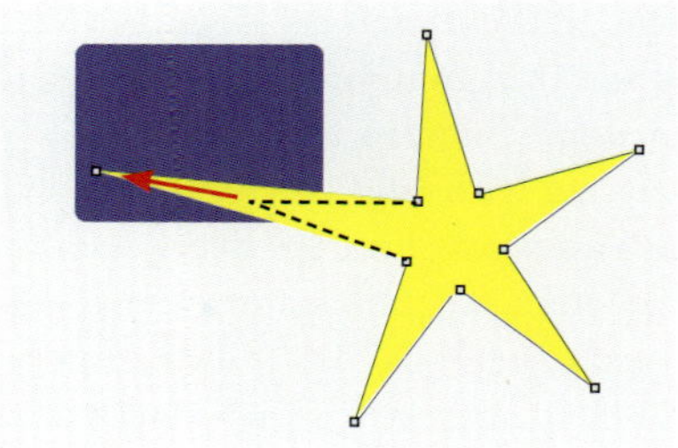

With our Direct Selection tool (and the shape layer selected), we click a spot on the path (the shape boundary) that we would like to modify, making the anchor points visible. Then we can click and drag that spot to make a transformation. We get different behavior depending on whether we choose a handle or a segment.

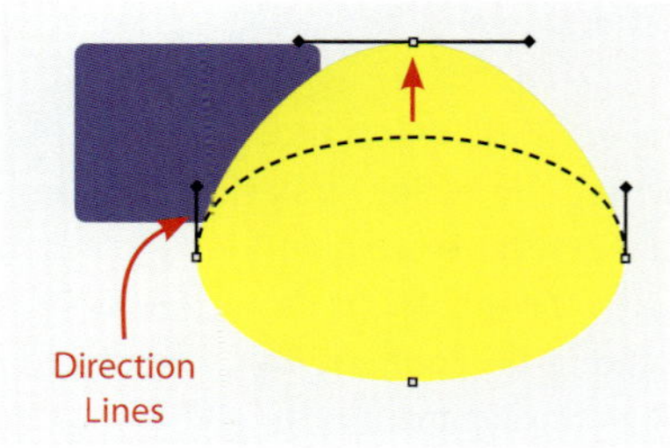

If our shape is curved, such as an ellipse, we can still do exactly the same thing. Again, choosing handles or segments gives different results. Now in this case, we also see direction lines. More on them in the next chapter.

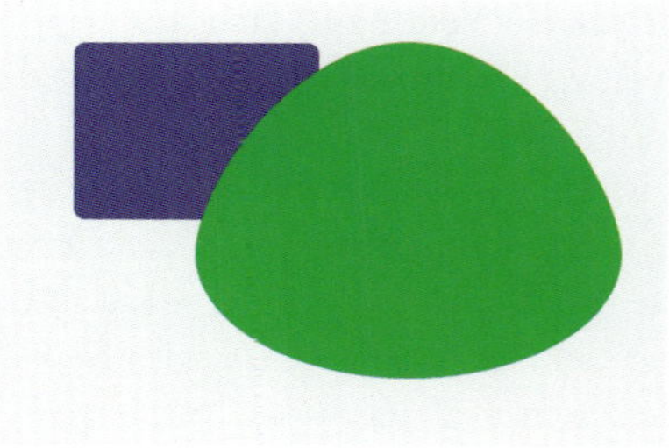

Would you like to change the color? Go to the Layers panel and select the shape layer. Double click on the layer thumbnail (the colored box, not the vector mask), and the Color Picker will pop up. Change your color and click OK. Just that simple!

We can't do these kinds of transformations with just layers. And at this point, we have only scratched the surface.

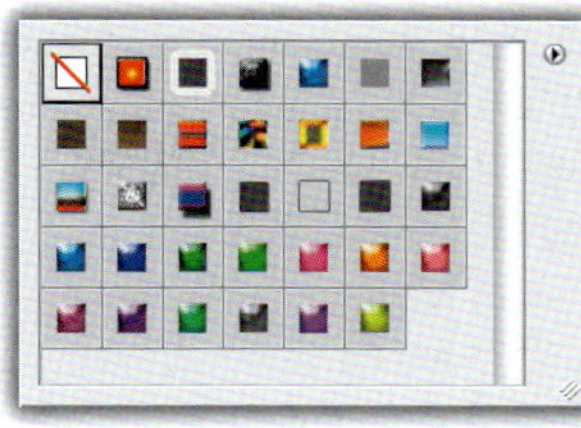

Of course Photoshop isn't going to leave us dangling with just plain old color choices. When we're in the Shape Layer mode, we also have styles available to us. A pull down Style menu on the right side of the options bar gives us a variety of fill alternatives. And if we want more, we can click the flyout menu and have at it.

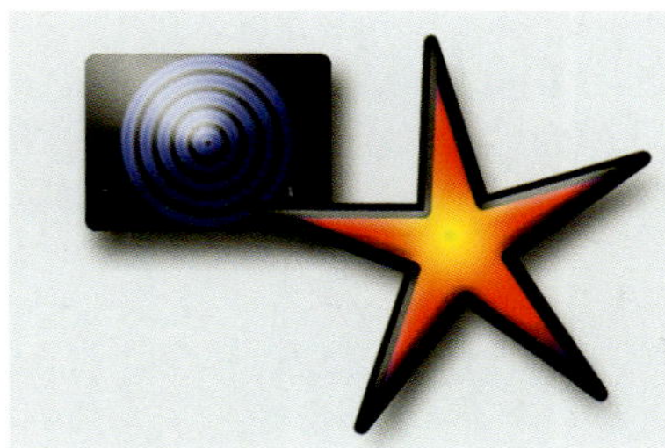

In most cases, these styles supersede any color we may have already chosen. Also note that these styles may also automatically add layer styles, as they did in this case with drop shadows. If they do so, the layer style icon will show up in its usual place.

There's a last grouping of icons in the options bar that I'll mention but won't go over how they work. The grouping of little box icons are for merging paths together in different ways. The same set of functions exists with selection marquee tools. Search Help for "Work Path" and read "To create a new work path" for explanations.

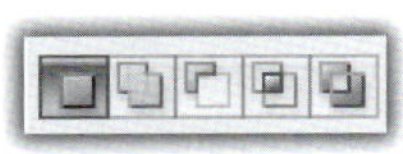

The Merge Path Icons

This is our second exposure to vector paths (our first being with text). So what do you think is going to happen if we decided to run a filter on our shape layer, maybe to add a little texture to it? Remember the ominous message that showed up with text? We get the same thing here. The Shape Layer is a vector graphic, not bitmap, and our filters won't work with it.

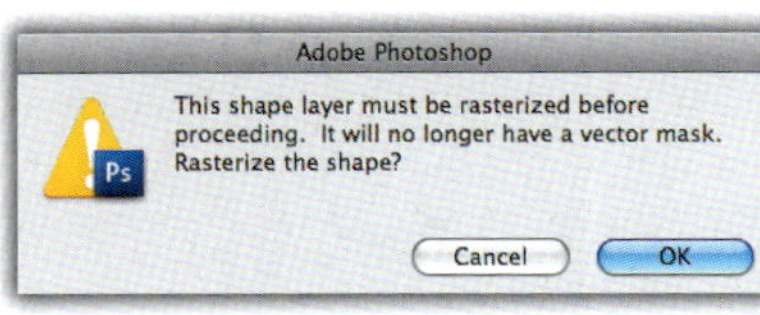

So as with text, Photoshop alerts us that it has to rasterize the layer and that the vector mask will be gone. If we are done with our edits, we are good to go. (As before, though, we make a copy of our shape layer first and hide it in case we need it later.)

We have talked about two of the shape modes in the options bar, the Fill Pixels mode and the Shape Layer mode. What about the third one, the one called Paths? As its name suggests, this one uses the Shape tool we have chosen to directly make a vector path. No vector mask is created and no pixels are affected. We simply get a vector path. So what good is that? Find the answer to this and more in the next chapter.

40. PATHS & THE PEN TOOL

If you are focused on using Photoshop for image enhancement, as opposed to drawing, you might have snoozed a bit during the last couple of chapters. Well, time to wake up, sleepy head. In this chapter, we will see how drawing and paths might just be indispensable for everyone.

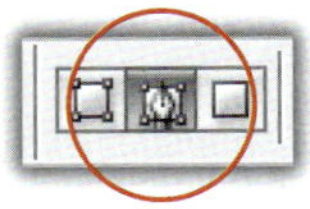

Let's start by creating a path, just a path. We start by opening a new blank document with Photoshop's default. We click the Rectangle tool and, in the options bar, select the middle shape mode, **Paths**. And, just for variety, let's choose the polygon tool. (Make sure under options that Star is not chosen.) If we set Sides to 8, we get an octagon when we click and drag.

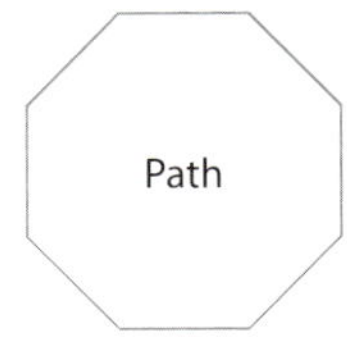

In the Paths mode, when we click and drag, we draw just the vector path. None of the pixels are affected yet; we just have a path. (Were we to print right now, by the way, we would get a blank white image because paths do not print.) If we click our new path with the Path Selection tool, we see the telltale anchor points displayed, just as with a shape layer.

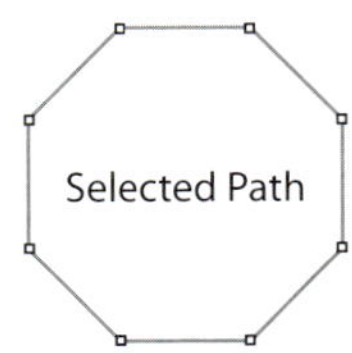

With our Path Selection tool, we can select the path and perform basic transformations. And with our Direct Selection tool, we can modify the path by moving anchor points and path segments around. This is all as it was with the Shape Layer mode. But now, only the path is being edited; no pixels are involved.

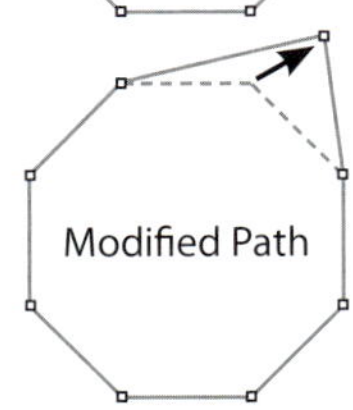

The new wrinkle here is that we can use paths for more than just drawing neat shapes that are editable later. The fact is that paths can be used to make incredibly accurate selections. (And we all know how important selections are!)

With our octagon path still in place, we open the Paths panel (behind the Layers panel) and see a thumbnail for our octagon path with the name Work Path (a default).

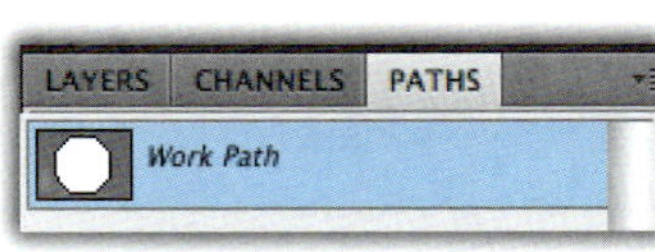

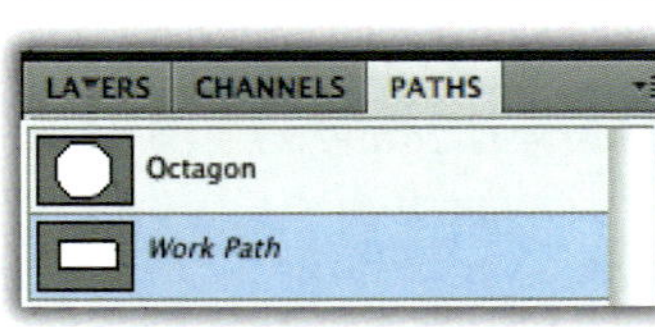

Paths, like selections, are temporary. If, sometime later we were to make a new path, say a rectangle, that rectangle would replace the octagon. But also like selections, we can save a path, giving it a unique name, like Octagon. Then if we were to later make a new rectangle path, it would become the Work Path, but the Octagon path would still be available for us.

To save a path, we access the Paths panel menu, choose **Save Path** and, when prompted, give it a name. In the example I just used, I named it Octagon.

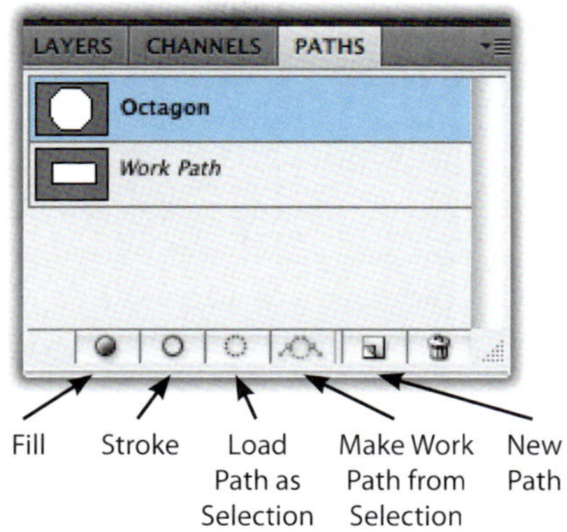

At the bottom of the Paths panel, we see icons for filling or stroking a path. A path is like a selection. If we choose Fill, the pixels within the path on the active layer are filled with the foreground color. This is just like Edit>Fill with a selection. Stroking creates a visible border on the path.

It's no coincidence that selections keep coming up. Paths and selections have many properties in common. In fact, look at the Paths panel menu above; there is a command called Load Path as Selection. If we have an active path (one selected on the Paths panel) and choose Load Path as Selection, Photoshop creates a selection from the path. (The path is still saved.) And if we have an active selection, we can save it as a path, if we wished, by going to the Paths panel and choosing Make Work Path from Selection and then saving that path.

So we can make paths from selections and selections from paths. What's the big deal? Well first of all, because paths are vectors, we have much more flexibility to modify them. This in turn means that we have much more flexibility to modify selections. The point here is that to make really, really accurate selections, our best bet is to make a path instead, refine the heck out of it using the Path Selection and Direct Selection tools, and then convert it into a selection.

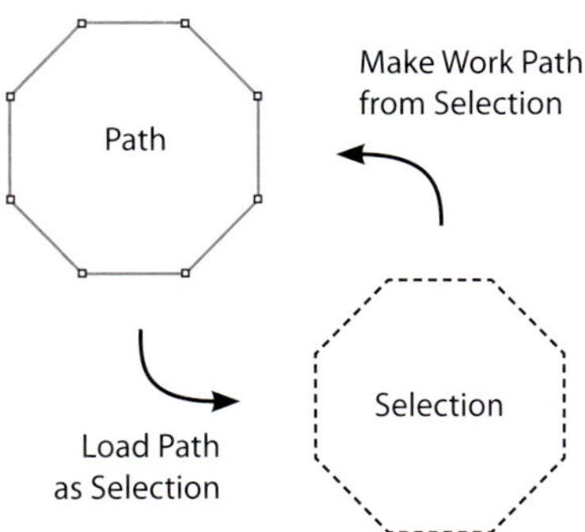

Enter the **Pen tool**. There are some that love it and some that are frustrated by it but everyone probably agrees that it is extremely powerful. It is located in the toolbox and also in the mini toolbox in the options bar of the Shape tool. Don't try and understand it. Learn by drawing, and drawing, and drawing some more. Think of it like learning to ride a bike. You can read all you want but you only learn by doing. The good news with the Pen tool is that any bruises along the way will be to your ego, not your derrière.

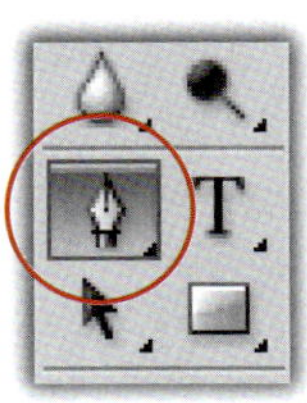

What follows is a quick overview of the Pen tool and certainly doesn't do it justice. But it should be enough to get you on your way and to allow you to get more out of various tutorials you might find. Consider Photoshop Help as well, searching on Pen Tool.

It starts simply enough. With a new blank document open, we select the Pen tool (not the Freeform Pen tool under it) and, in the options bar, we choose the Paths mode we just used above. We click once to define where we will begin the path, creating an anchor point. We click again to create a second anchor point and a straight-line path segment between it and the first anchor point. We repeat the process to make a third anchor point with a second path segment. And so on...

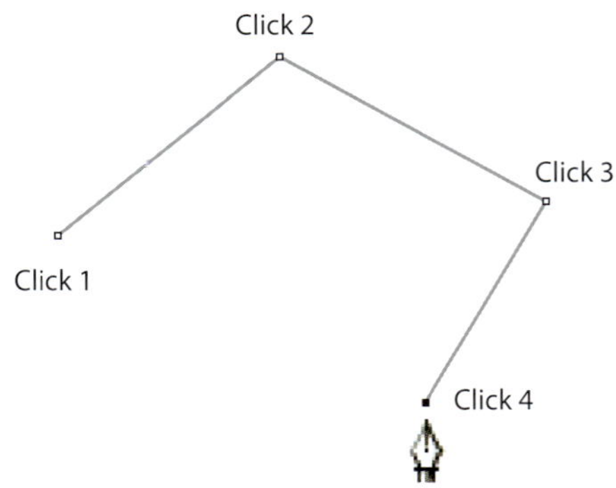

To close the path, we hover over the initial anchor point until we see a small circle by the cursor (which indicates we are positioned to close) and click. These instructions should seem familiar. Used in this way, the Pen tool works exactly like the Polygonal Lasso tool.

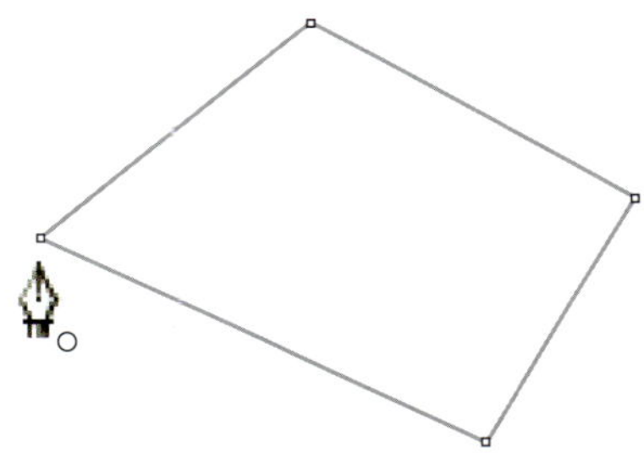

The real fun begins when we create an anchor point by clicking and dragging, not just clicking. Instead of creating a straight-line path segment, the tool creates a smoothly curving path segment that passes through the anchor point in the direction that we drag. And the further we drag, the flatter the curve going through the anchor point becomes.

Okay, time to get on the bike. With a clean canvas (select and erase any existing paths), we click and release to set the first anchor point. Then we click, drag, and release at a second point, getting a curved path that starts at the first point, moves through the second in the direction of our drag, and has a shape determined by how far we had dragged at the second point. (The direction line shows us how far we dragged.)

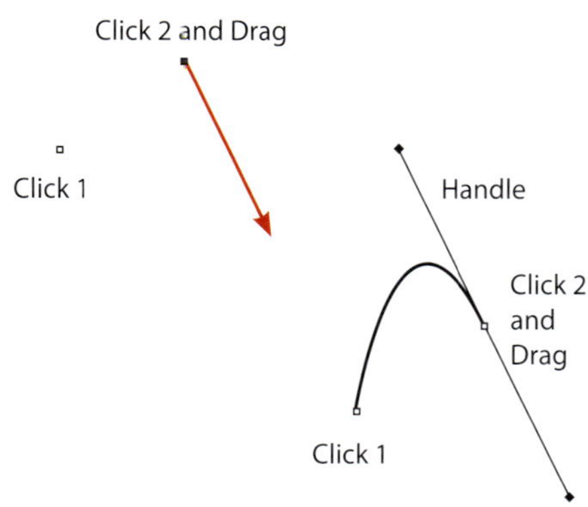

Close the path as before by hovering over the first point until the little circle shows up and then clicking. Remember, trial and error. This takes time. More than likely, you will get out of control quite quickly. When this happens, Cmd(Ctrl)-Click anywhere to terminate the path. Then select and delete the path, take a breath, and try again.

Here's an example of an irregular shape created with the Pen tool. The clicks and the approximate drag lengths (direction lines) are shown so you should be able to reproduce it. Just keep riding and you will be up and balancing in no time.

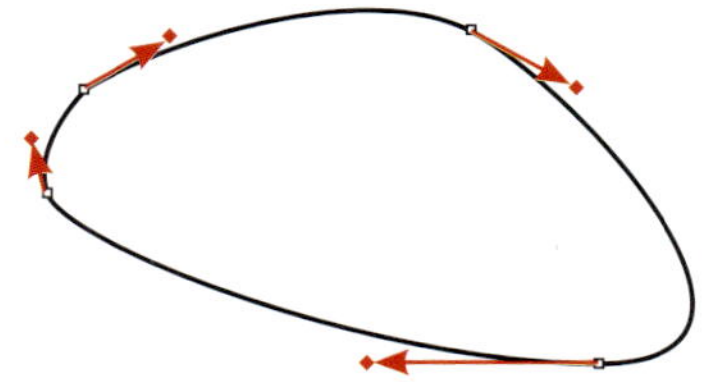

Here are two tips that might confuse you now but which you'll want to know later. To have an inbound curved path with an outbound straight path, click and drag to set the inbound direction and then Opt(Alt)-Click again on the anchor. This will make your outbound path a straight-line segment to the next anchor. To have an inbound straight path with an outbound curved path, click to set the inbound straight path and then click and drag again on the anchor to set an outbound direction.

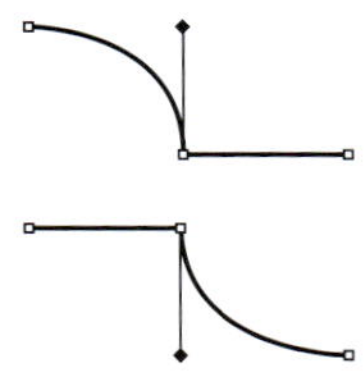

Now on to why we're putting ourselves through this misery. With our Direct Selection tool, we can select either corner or curve anchor points or path segments and modify them. When we select a curve anchor point, we see the anchor and the direction lines corresponding to the direction and the smoothness of the curve. We can extend the direction lines, making a smoother curve or change their direction.

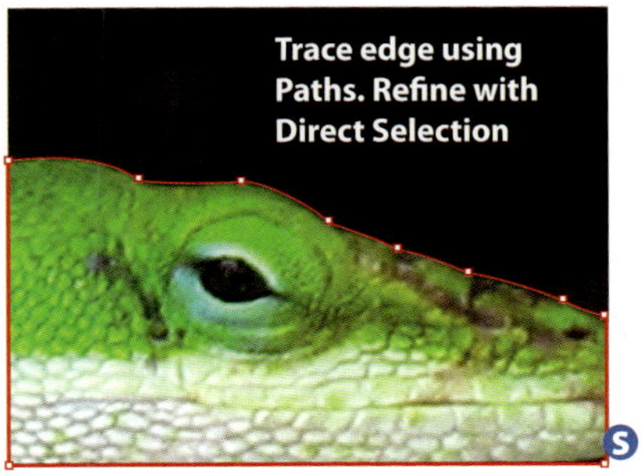

So do you now see how we can make incredibly accurate selections? We use our Pen tool to make a very accurate path around our subject. We refine the path with the Direct Selection tool to make it even more accurate. We save this path with a unique name. And then we convert the path into a selection using the Paths panel. Keep pedaling–you'll get it.

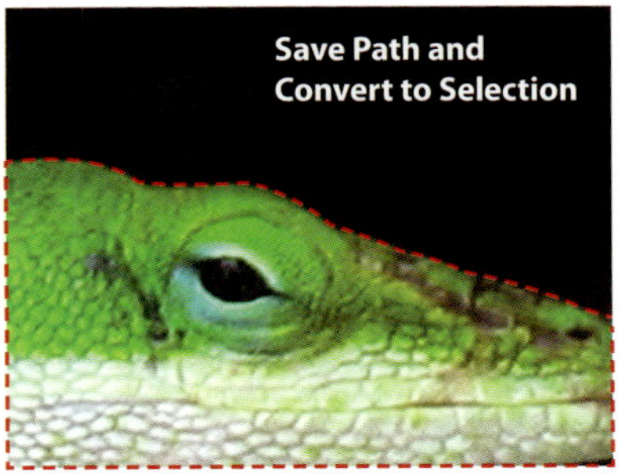

Here we are at the end of Section VI and there really aren't any special CS4-only features that jump out as worthy of review. With regard to drawing and painting, CS4 is pretty much just like CS3 and CS2. So we could twiddle our thumbs and make ready for Section VII. Or, we could switch gears entirely and discuss something new.

At the end of Section IV, in the CS4 Tips, we had a look at the new Masks panel and reviewed how it could really simplify our work flow with respect to layer masking. In particular, we looked at a Refine Mask dialog box (accessed from the Mask Edge button in the Masks panel) and saw how it allowed us to alter our mask in terms of contrast, size, feathering, smoothness, etc. Wouldn't it be nice if we had the same sort of power over selections? Well of course it would.

Refine Edge: Under the Select menu, there is a command called Refine Edge. Choose it and its dialog box pops open. Now if this dialog box looks a little familiar, it's because it is exactly identical to the Refine Mask dialog box. All of the sliders are the same as are the viewing option icons at the bottom. (By the way, the Refine Edge command is grayed out unless there is a selection. It makes sense; without a selection there is nothing to refine.)

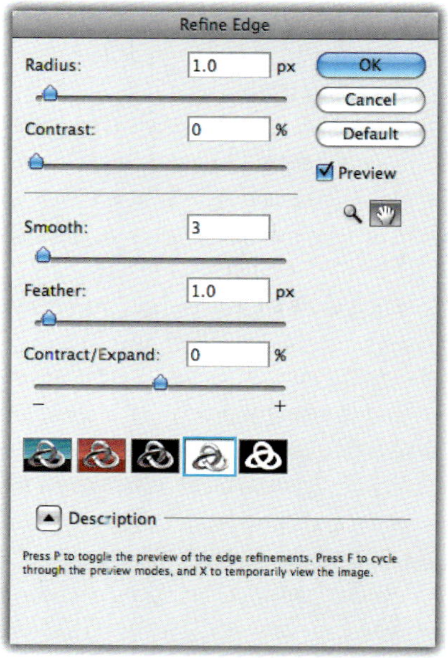

As before, the Description at the bottom of the box updates to describe each slider as we hover over it. Since Feather is here, we never have to worry about setting the feather right before doing a selection (or even which tools allow us to). We can just do our selection, adjust our feathering, and view the result before committing.

Now here's a little secret that might tie a few things together for you. The Refine Edge and the Refine Mask dialog boxes work the same because down inside the Photoshop code, selections and masks are really the same thing. And you know what? So are paths. All the same. That's why they have so many characteristics in common. They look and feel different but deep down, under the hood... the same!

Anyway, don't forget about using Refine Edge to optimize your selections. It's as useful for selections as Refine Mask is for layer masks.

SECTION

VII FINISHING UP

We have spent a lot of time learning how to enhance, reshape, modify, alter, and merge our images. So what's the last thing we're going to want to do after investing all this work (I mean fun time) on an image? We're going to want to save our work and then maybe print it, send it to someone, or post it on the web. So that is what we are going to talk about in this section.

Saving may seem like a pretty simple topic but as usual, there are little details to worry about. Are we saving as a Photoshop document or do we need to save in a different format? Is file size an issue as it would be if we wanted to email the image or post it on the web? Do we need to worry about all of the options that Photoshop presents to us or can we just count on the defaults? Like I said, a few details.

Printing is not something we want to glide right through either. I personally really enjoy creating my own prints and getting them just right. But this process of getting them just right can be a little complicated. You will find rather rapidly that all of the color fine-tuning you did in front of your monitor probably won't be reflected accurately in your printed copy. What you see is not what you get!

But not to worry! Everything is possible with Photoshop. In our chapter on printing, we will learn how to make everything synchronize so that our prints will match what we created on our monitor as closely as possible. The good news is that once we get our system set up once, we will be able to pretty much count on it every time.

41. SAVING YOUR WORK

File>Save! Right? Well, yes. And no.

File>Save does work like File>Save in most applications. If we are working on a previously saved file, File>Save will overwrite that file, updating it with our edits. We get no prompts of any kind; the saved file just updates. A caveat to this is if we've made edits to the file that are incompatible with the original file type (like adding layers to a JPEG image), we will be automatically prompted with a Save As dialog box.

If we are working on a file that has not been previously saved, then we will always be prompted with a Save As dialog box. So the Save As dialog box is where all the action is. Access it with File>Save As.

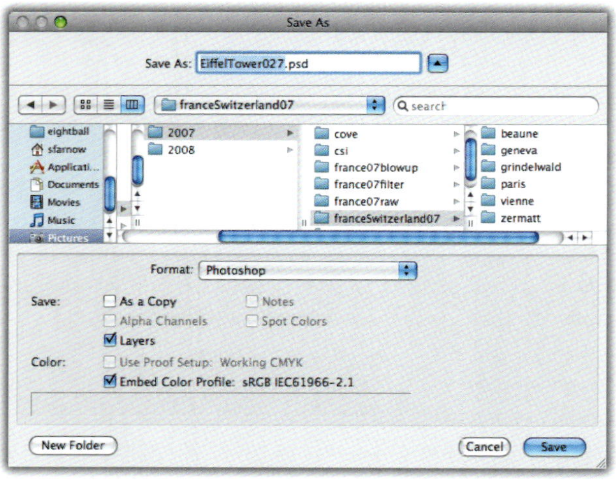

If we want to rename our file (or need to name it for the first time), this is where we do it. This is also where we browse for a location to save the file.

Here is where we also select the file format. If we are working on a brand new document, Photoshop (PSD) will be the default format. If we have opened a JPEG and have made only JPEG compatible edits (like no layers), JPEG will be the default. If we have opened a JPEG but have made incompatible edits (like adding layers), then PSD will be the default. But we can always choose to override the default by popping open the format menu. The other formats we discussed in Chapter 10 are available (along with many others).

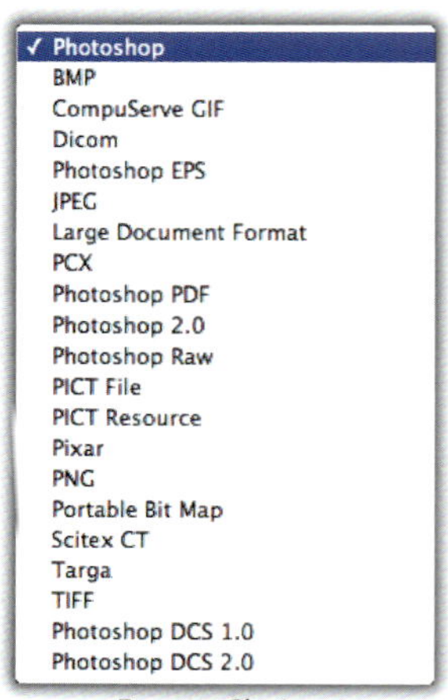

Format Choices

Keep in mind that the best way to insure we have continued access to all of our layers, edits and so on (i.e. all of our hard work) is to save our file in Photoshop format. This uses up more disk space but external drives just keep getting cheaper. If we want to email an image, we can save a copy as a JPEG, keeping the original PSD.

Since JPEGs do not support layers, if we save a copy of a layered Photoshop file as a JPEG, the layers are flattened, that is merged into a single layer, and then compressed. (For some applications, we might actually want a flattened image but without JPEG compression. To do this, we open the Layers panel menu and choose Flatten Image. Note this is not reversible. Remember we mentioned that there were two document sizes shown at the bottom of the document window? Well now I can tell you that the second number is actual file size and the first is the size we'd get if we flattened. So for single layer files, they are the same.)

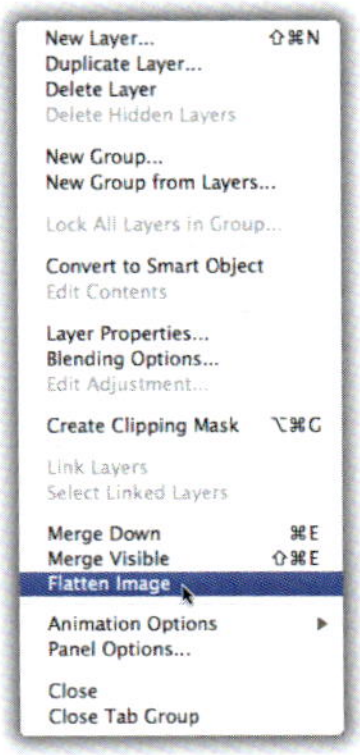

Now is also a good time to bring up the Maximize Compatibility dialog warning that I first mentioned in Chapter 10. When Maximize Compatibility is turned on, Photoshop saves a flattened version of our image within the file. This allows those applications that don't deal well with layers to accept PSD files (i.e. maximizing compatibility). The sacrifice? File size of course. On my Mac with the Leopard OS, I can preview Photoshop documents saved with Max Compatibility but not those without it. Sorry Windows users, this doesn't work on either XP or Vista.

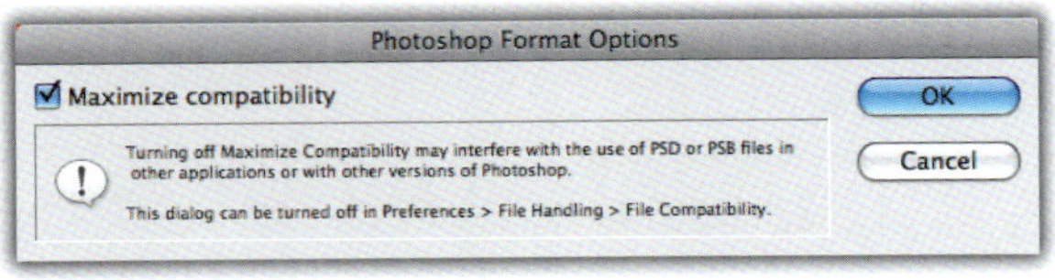

See Chapter 10 for instructions on turning Maximize Compatibility on or off or leaving it in an "always ask" mode (my preference).

So PSDs have layers and JPEGs don't. And recall that TIFFs do and GIFs don't. This is a lot to remember but fortunately the Photoshop Save As dialog box helps us out. Under the Save Options, there is a check box for Layers. If a file type, such as JPEG, does not support layers, this box will be grayed out and a compatibility-warning icon will be displayed.

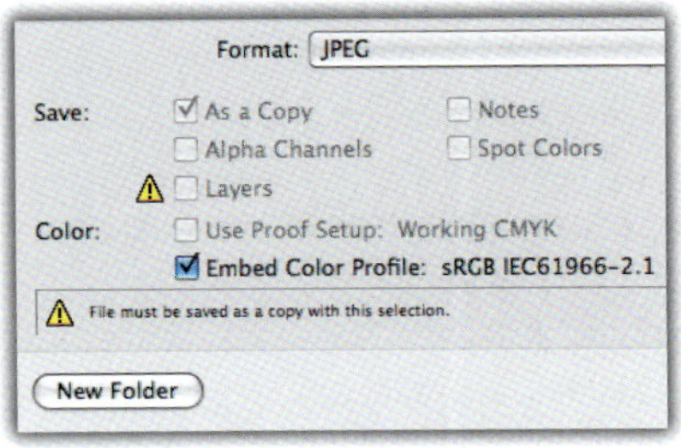

Let's have a look at the other options listed in the Save As dialog box. "As a Copy" can be a real time saver if we want to save interim copies of our work as we go. When we choose File>Save As and check As a Copy, Photoshop automatically appends our file name with "copy" and saves the file where we choose. The active document remains the non-copy version. If a while later we do a Save As with As a Copy again, Photoshop will overwrite the original copy (after asking permission). This is like backing up.

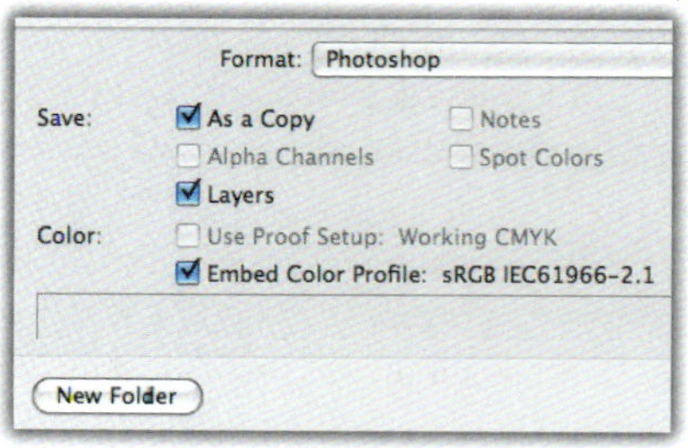

I seem to create flattened copies fairly often, perhaps for another's review or for importing into another application where my layers aren't needed and I'd rather have a smaller file size. An easy way to get this done with what we just learned is to choose File>Save As, check As a Copy and uncheck Layers. Then click Save and Photoshop renames our file (appending "copy"), flattens it and saves it.

We have not talked about Alpha Channels but you can safely ignore that check box. Leave it either checked or unchecked, whatever state it's in.

The Notes check box refers to little sticky notes we can paste on our image. Imagine we have just opened an image and see a number of improvements we would like to make. We could write our ideas down or, using Photoshop, we can choose the Note tool (located under the Eyedropper), click in the vicinity of a potential change, and describe it in the panel dialog box that opens. When we close the dialog box, a little sticky note icon remains on the image.

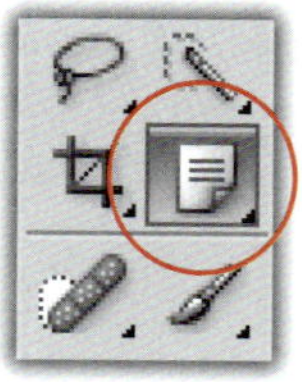

We can right click on the icon to open it or delete it. Or choose View>Show> Notes to toggle the icons on and off.

And, oh yes, checking Notes in the Save As dialog box retains these notes with our saved file.

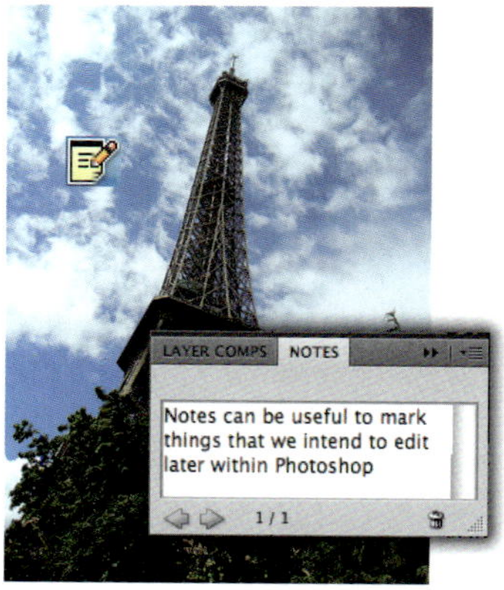

The Spot Color check box and the Use Proof Setup Color check box both relate to working in CMYK. Since we've worked exclusively in RGB, we will ignore those. (They should be grayed out anyway.) The Embed Color Profile check box should always be checked. (We discussed color profiles in Chapter 3.)

Let's circle back now and talk about saving in JPEG. We've already discussed that we will lose our layers and that the image will be compressed. If we want to attach the image to an email or post it on the web, this is probably exactly what we want to do.

When we choose JPEG for our file format in the Save As dialog box and hit Save, Photoshop opens a JPEG Options dialog box that allows us to dial in exactly what kind of compression we want. Under Quality, ignore both the box with the number in it and the pull down menu and just play with the slider. Move the slider to the right for better quality/larger file sizes and to the left for lesser quality/smaller file sizes.

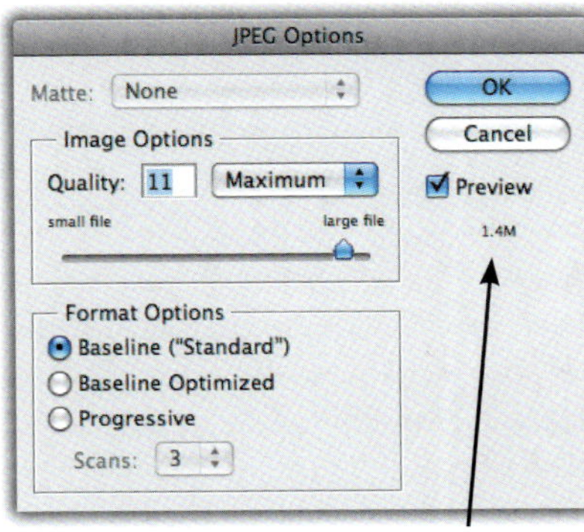

Projected File Size

With Preview checked, Photoshop will display a projected file size and the image will reflect the chosen quality setting. If we are sensitive to file size, however, perhaps for emailing or for the Web, we are better off using Save for Web & Devices, as discussed in the next chapter.

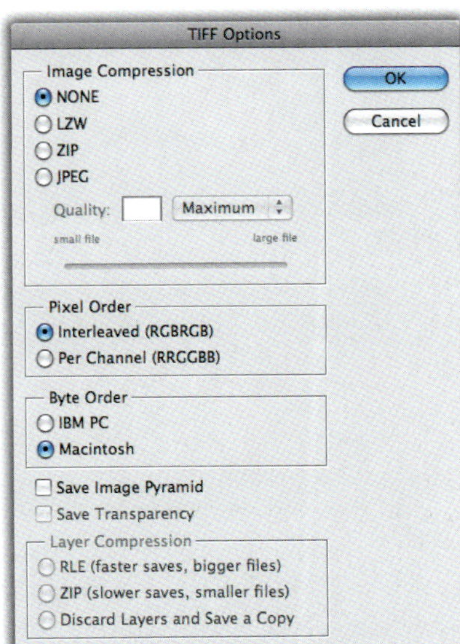

When we choose File>Save As and select TIFF for our file format, we notice that the Save As dialog allows us the option of keeping our layers. I generally don't, keeping my layered files as PSDs. When we hit Save, we get the TIFF's own unique dialog box and lots and lots of options. But we can safely accept the default settings and click OK. One option to note, though, is compression. Unlike JPEGs, TIFFs can be compressed without loss. Choose LZW if you need to use the TIFF format but wish to have smaller file sizes.

42. SAVE FOR WEB & DEVICES

Photoshop has an alternative to the Save As method discussed in the last chapter. It is called Save for Web & Devices (or just Save for Web prior to CS3). Now you might not be planning to be a web graphics specialist but I suggest that you read on anyway because this method has general application.

When we save for the web, the quality/file size compromise becomes paramount. We want our images to look good, but we also want them to download quickly (i.e. have a small file size). Recall from the last chapter, when we save a Photoshop file as a JPEG, we get a JPEG Options dialog box where we can adjust the quality/file size trade off. And we were able to preview the image with our choice of settings.

But choices are easier to make with side-by-side comparisons than they are by looking at them one at a time. This is exactly what Save for Web allows us to do. It does much more than this, actually, allowing for really detailed fine-tuning of the quality/file size trade off. Most of this detail is outside our scope, but we can still use this tool as a Save As on steroids without too much intellectual investment.

With an active Photoshop document up, if we choose File>Save for Web, we get a screen similar to that shown below. If you are following along, choose the 4-up tab above the image(s) and adjust magnification (lower left) to a 100%.

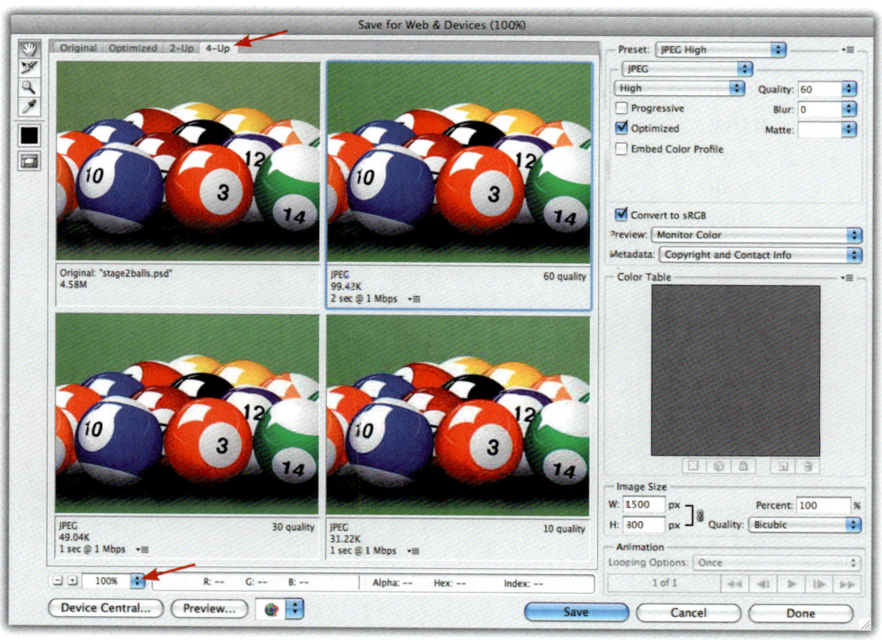

Save for Web & Devices allows us to do side-by-side comparisons of the image quality of various file formats, quality settings, and file sizes. In the 4-up mode, we see our original in one pane along with three alternatives, usually ranging from high to low quality. If we select an alternative by clicking on it (the blue outline denotes the selected alternative), Photoshop considers it our current choice for the optimized image. So if we click on the Optimized tab at the top, that alternative is what is shown in a larger view. And if we click on the 2-up tab, Photoshop compares the original to that optimized image side-by-side. The Original tab, of course, just displays the original.

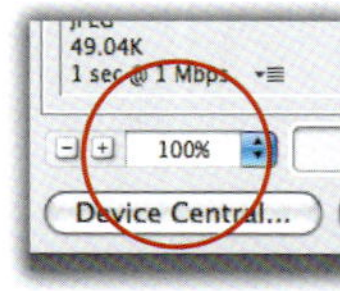

A couple of navigation tips... Save for Web always comes up in 100% magnification. For our multi-megapixel images, this might be too large to begin with. Reset the magnification in the lower left hand corner to something better. Type in a number or pick from the menu. All four image views adjust at the same time. Keep in mind that high magnifications are useful too; they allow us to focus in on specific areas in our image in order to really compare compression artifacts.

At higher magnifications, when we can only see part of the image, we can adjust what's visible within the panes by selecting a pane, hovering our mouse within it, and noticing that our cursor changes into a hand. We can then click and drag to move the image around within the pane. Note also that all of the panes update in unison.

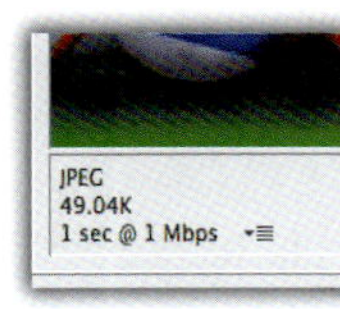

In the lower left hand corner of each image pane, the vital statistics regarding that alternative are displayed. We see the file format (we can compare GIFs to JPEGs here), the file size (warning to follow) and the download time for a given modem speed. My warning regarding file sizes is that these numbers are good indicators but are not completely accurate. We should always double check the final file size by saving the file and then using our operating system to double check the real number.

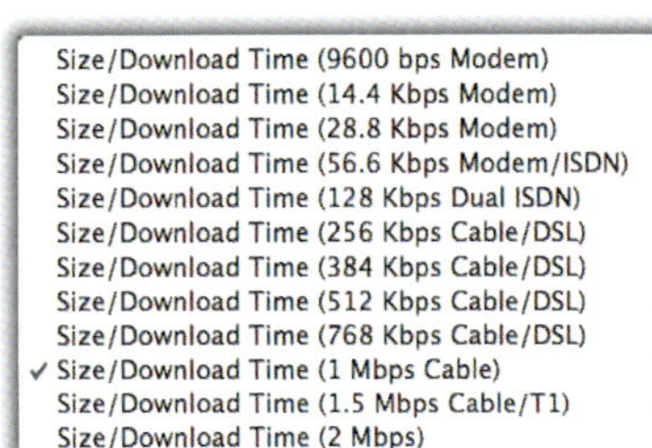

If you would like to adjust the download speed used in the download time calculation (the 28.8K default is just a bit archaic), click on the flyout menu just to the right of the download speed. There are lots of choices. (In CS3 and earlier, this flyout menu can be found in the upper right hand corner of the 4-Up images.)

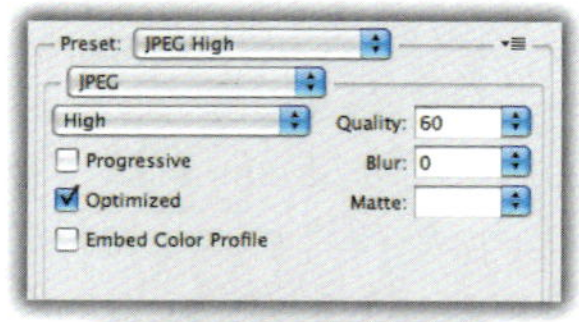

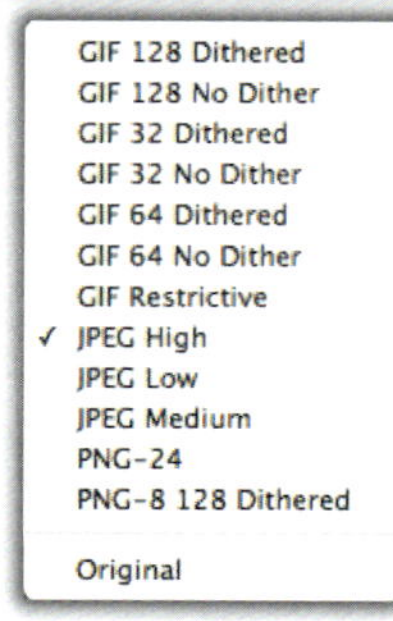

On the right side of the Save for Web dialog box, we are presented with a number of options and controls. These are what we use to create the settings for the three alternatives. (Photoshop will made choices right out of the chute but probably not what we want.) Starting out, ignore all the options and just stick with the Presets. Within the preset menu are pre-existing choices for JPEG, GIF, and PNG (another file format) quality settings. When we select an image pane by clicking on it and then select a preset from the Preset menu, that preset gets applied to that image pane.

To keep this as simple as possible, use the following guidelines. If you want to save as a JPEG, select the upper right hand pane and choose the JPEG High (standing for High Quality) preset. Likewise, assign JPEG Medium to the lower left pane and JPEG Low to the lower right hand pane. Magnify your images and move them around (click and drag) to help with comparison. Then choose the best one, considering both quality and file size. And finally, with your choice selected, use the Quality box back on the right side to fine tune quality and size (if need be).

This is the absolute best vehicle to play with to get a good feel for image degradation resulting from compression. Take a close look at what happens to both sharp edges and smooth color variations. The images below show quite a difference but there is almost a 3X difference in file size too. So this is where we get to decide what to compromise.

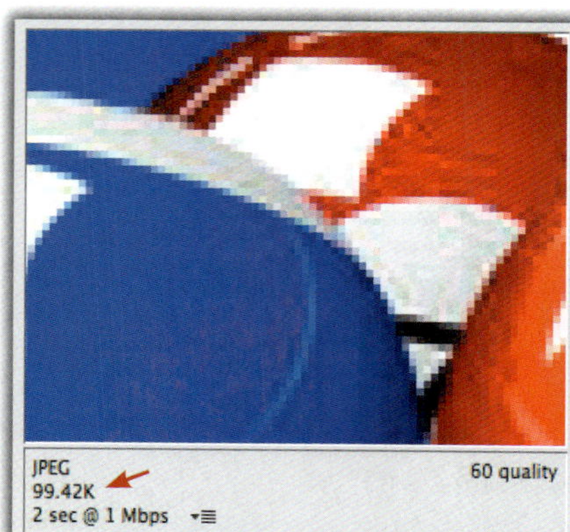

JPEG High Quality at 300%

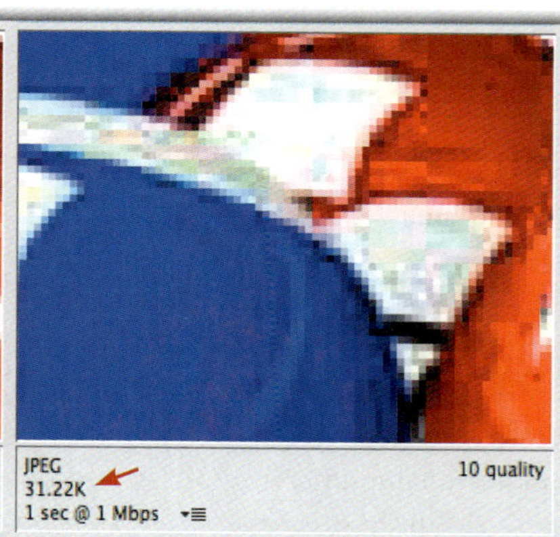

JPEG Low Quality at 300%

The same sort of methodology applies to saving files as GIFs. Recall that GIFs are particularly well suited to line art or logos. This is because GIFs compress by constraining the number of colors in the image; line art and logos don't usually have all that many colors. In the presets, we see there are choices for GIFs ranging from GIF 128 down to GIF 32. (I will get to the "Dithered" option in a moment.) The numbers here refer to the number of available colors in the preset (the colors are uniquely generated as a best fit to the image). So GIF 128 has four times as many colors as does GIF 32.

Photoshop even shows us the colors it has chosen for the GIF. They are shown under the Color Table tab, in the lower right.

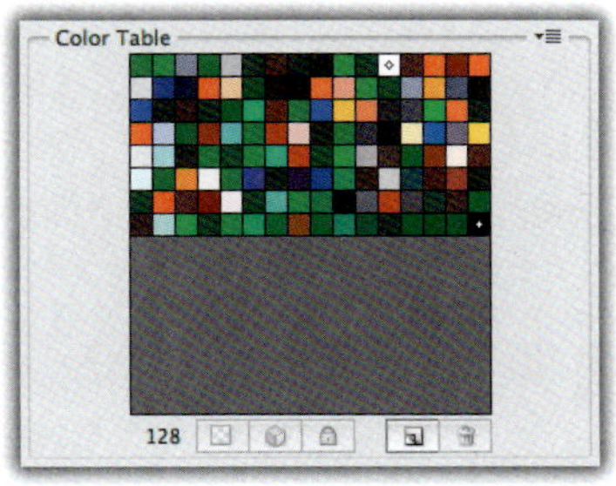

So to do our comparison, we use GIF128 for our high quality, GIF 64 for medium and GIF 32 for low. We'll leave all of the other choices on their defaults.

And what's with dithering? Well, when we constrict the number of colors in an image, we can get sort of a posterization effect, especially where colors are gradually changing. Dithering tries to compensate for this by interspersing pixels of one color with pixels of another color to trick your eye into seeing a blend of the two colors. For any GIFs that have picture-like qualities, choose the Dithered option.

What if we have selected our minimum acceptable quality and the file size is still a bit too large? Now what? There is one more trick up Save for Web's sleeve and that is to change the image size. Under the Image Size tab, right next to the Color Table, there are a group of settings that look awfully similar to what we get under Image>Image Size. And they work in exactly the same way.

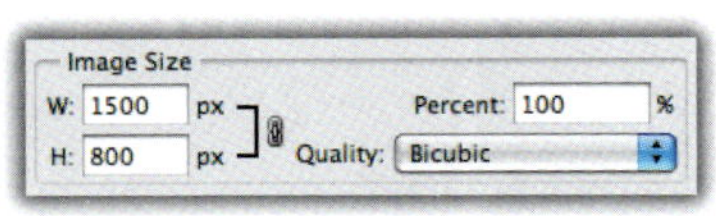

Shrinking the image size (by altering the pixel counts or by adjusting percentage) may solve our problem. But we need to keep in mind that we are changing pixel count so we really are changing the size of the image. Probably not a winner.

To save our final results, we select the alternative of our choice (if it is not already selected) and hit Save. Photoshop will go to a Save Optimized As dialog box to allow us to rename the file and choose where to store it.

43. PRINTING

Printing can be as simple as File>Print or as complex as we want it to be. We can print at home on our inkjet printer, take files to a camera store, or go to an offset printer. We'll discuss the first two of these printing methods. The offset printer option is outside our scope.

If you are headed for a camera store (or an online vendor), there's not too much to discuss either. They will typically want you to provide your images in a JPEG format (be sure to use the best quality you can). And don't get confused with the "CMYK is for printing" stuff you hear. CMYK is for professional offset printers–not your camera store and not your home printer. Stick with RGB... trust me!

If I have a bunch of 4x6" snapshots to print, I might consider using a camera store or an online vendor. But I prefer to do my own enlargements. Good quality photo printers are not all that expensive and we get all sorts of control by printing directly from Photoshop (not to mention instant gratification).

There are a number of excellent photo printer manufacturers out there–I use an Epson R1800 (now it's the R1900) with great results. One of the first things you may notice when looking at these printers is that they specify dots per inch significantly above the 250 dpi we talked about earlier. This is because, in order to create a large gamut of colors with just a few inks, inkjet printers print dots within dots, mixing the colors of the smaller dots so that we perceive the desired color on the larger dot. These smaller dot resolutions are what are advertised. The larger dots are what correspond to our pixels.

Once we have our printer, we need to choose our paper. The choice of matte, semigloss, or glossy is a matter of personal preference. For me, glossy creates the most pleasing result. When we do print, though, it is vitally important that we identify and choose our specific paper in the printer dialog box (which is unique to our printer). Each type of paper accepts ink a little differently and the printer will do a much better job if it knows exactly what paper it is printing to. Along these same lines, I would suggest you match your printer and paper brands. If you have an Epson printer, print on Epson paper. If you have a HP printer, print on HP paper. The manufacturers work hard to optimize results on their own paper and their printer dialog boxes may even reference their specific papers by name.

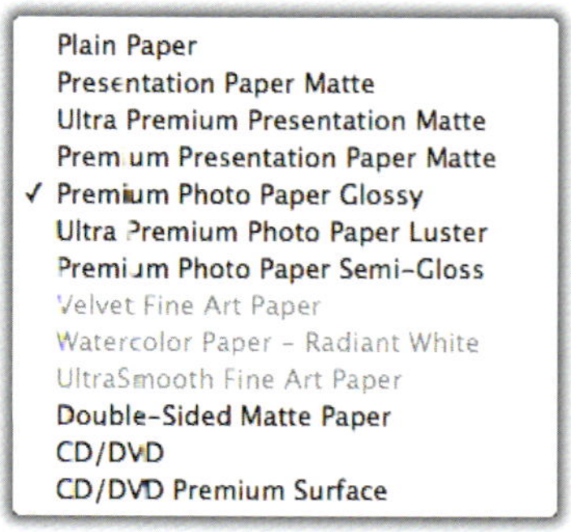

Our color mode (I will say it again) needs to stay RGB. If you have individual ink cartridges, they may be cyan, magenta, yellow, black, and perhaps some others. Don't let this confuse you. The printer is expecting RGB from your computer and will handle all of the conversions.

On the topic of color, wouldn't it be nice if what we see on our screen were to match what we print on paper. I hate to break it to you, but it won't. We see images on our screen with transmitted light while the printed page is seen with reflected light. Some colors on your screen, a vibrant purple for example, won't look nearly as vibrant on paper. But the fact that we can't get perfection doesn't mean we shouldn't strive for the best possible compromise.

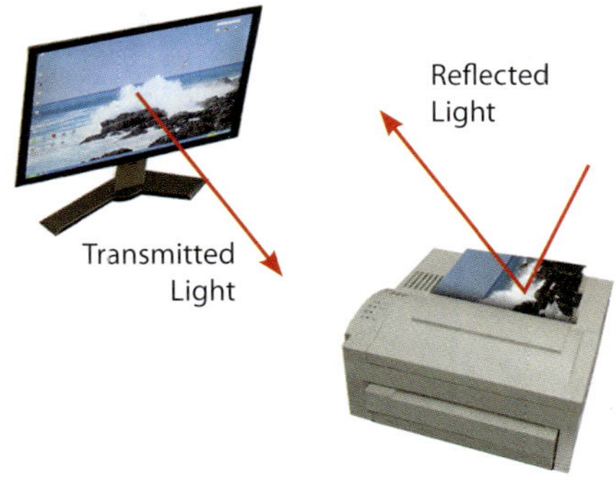

To get our colors to match up as closely as possible, we have to manage them. Step 1 is to calibrate our display so that we are seeing the exact colors Photoshop thinks it is displaying. Our OS can do a free but marginally effective process. (For Mac's, go to System Preferences>Display>Color>Calibrate and follow the instructions. For PC's, you need to use Adobe Gamma; search on Adobe.com for more information.) The better solution is to buy a hardware calibrator. These solutions come with a sensor you place on your display and software that performs an automatic calibration using that sensor. Expect to pay between $100 and $300 from manufacturers like Pantone and Colorvision.

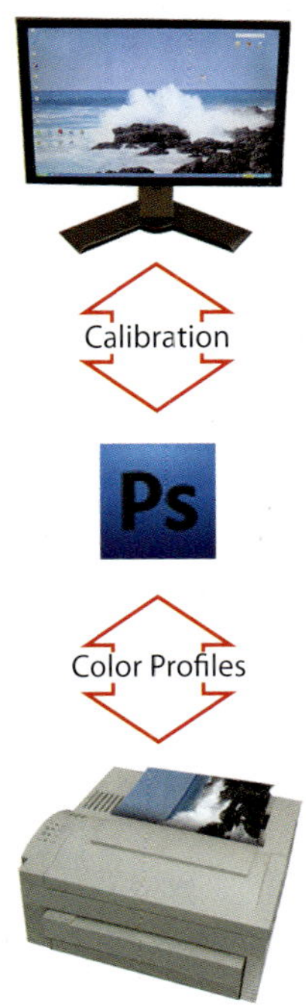

Step 2 is to calibrate Photoshop for our printer so it prints the exact colors (or as close to them as possible) that Photoshop has in mind. For this, we need a printer profile (called an ICC printer profile) for our printer/paper combination that installs right into Photoshop. For Epson printers, this is an easy process. On their web site, access Drivers and Downloads for your printer, find the profiles, hit download and follow the instructions. If your manufacturer's web site doesn't have this, consult with them or Google for third party providers (using your manufacturer's name and "ICC profile"). We will access these profiles during the printing process and they will help guarantee the colors that print are the colors that we were expecting.

Okay, we've chatted long enough; let's actually print something. To do so (with our file of choice open), we select File>Print. (For CS2 and earlier, the best option to choose is Print with Preview.) Up pops the following Print dialog box:

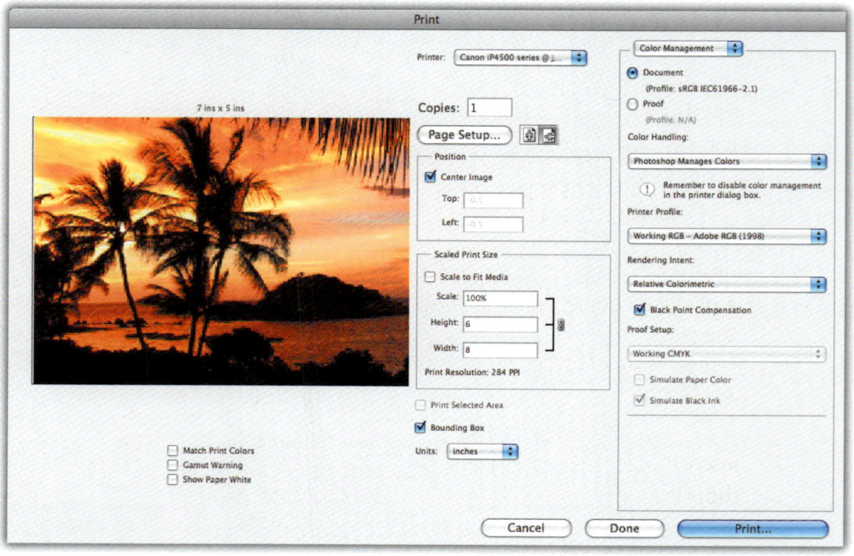

The preview in the upper left immediately tells us if we have some major paper size or image orientation error. Use the Page Setup button in the middle column to correct any of these issues. With the Position options we can either center our image or, by unchecking Center Image, move it around in the window with our cursor.

The Scale Print Size options allow us to grow or shrink our image for a better fit. Keep in mind that quality suffers with magnification. Any scaling we do here affects the print only–the image file itself is not altered in any way.

Now if we don't want to fool with all of the fancy printer profile stuff, we are one click from printing. Under Color Management/ Color Handling, select Printer Manages Colors (or similar). With this option, Photoshop makes no attempt at color matching, leaving it up to our printer to do its best possible job. (Please note the warning on the next page.) All that's left to do is to click Print.

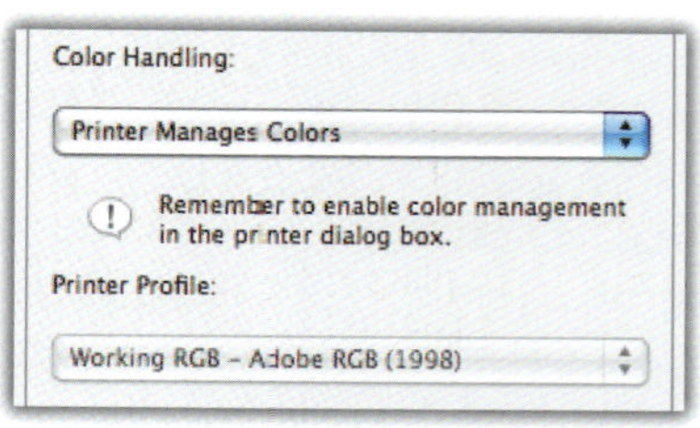

Using printer profiles isn't actually much more involved. Under Color Management/ Color Handling, select Photoshop Manages Colors (or similar). Notice the Printer Profile is no longer grayed out and we can select the profile we installed earlier. Here my R1800 with glossy paper is selected. Leave Rendering Intent on Relative Colorimetric and leave Black Point Compensation checked. Next, click Print.

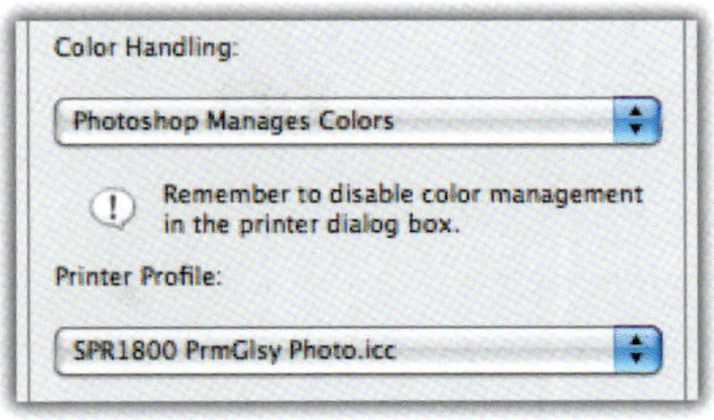

When we click Print, we are sent to our printer's dialog box. So far, we have only been talking to Photoshop; now we are talking to our printer. Every printer is different, but there will be a place to choose paper, quality (choose the highest), and color management (or maybe color correction). This last one we turn off. This tells the printer not to color manage. If we don't do this, Photoshop and the printer will both try to manage the colors and, well, there will be too many cooks in the kitchen.

If we have chosen Printer Manages Colors in the Photoshop Print dialog box, our printer must be set to manage color in its dialog boxes. But again, if we have chosen Photoshop Manages Colors in the Photoshop Print dialog box, we must tell the printer not to manage color. Here I've turned off color management for my R1800. This is important!

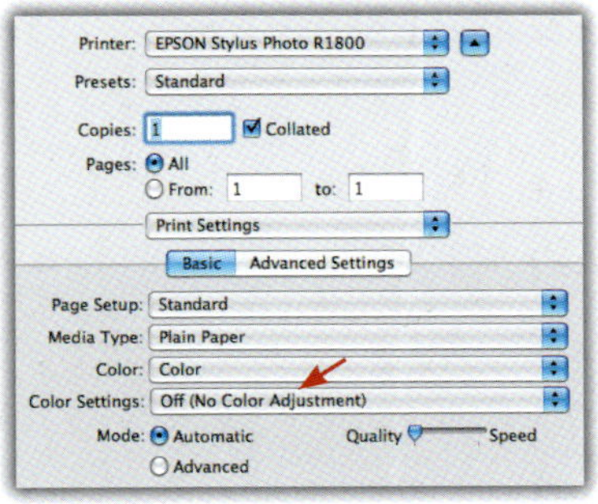

Having heeded the warnings and correctly set things up, we hit Print in the printer's print dialog box and await our results.

There are a couple of interesting options under Output (hidden under Color Management at the top right of the Photoshop Print dialog box). Background allows us to select a color to print around our image if the image is smaller than the paper. By default, we get a white (no ink) background. If we select Background, the Color Picker pops up and we are free to choose a different color. A similar option, Border, allows us to specify a border to be placed around our image. While we cannot control the color (would you like black or black?), we can specify the width.

Printing and color management are meaty subjects with entire books devoted to them. But with these simple steps, we can achieve pretty impressive results at home.

Saving and printing in CS4 is pretty much identical to how it is done in CS3 and earlier. All of the changes are really cosmetic in nature; the functionality remains the same. One thing that struck me as I was writing this section, though, is that some time spent on managing collapsible panel icons might be time well spent.

Managing Collapsible Panels: Way back in Chapter 4, we reviewed how there were panels visible by default and others that could be accessed by selecting them under the menu bar's Window dropdown. Recall, for example, that the Navigator panel in CS4 is not active by default so we select Window>Navigator to bring it up (along with its panel group).

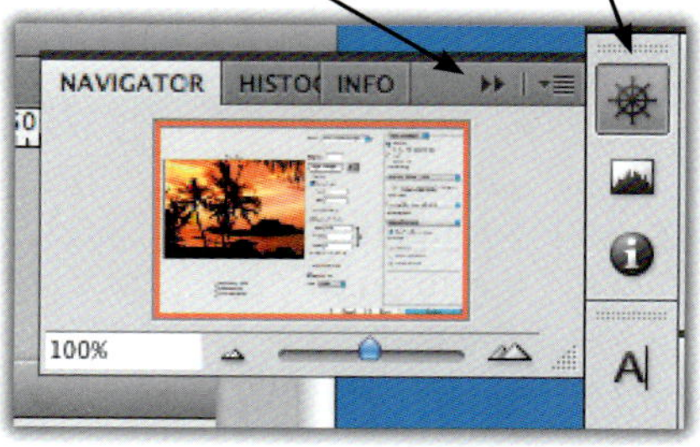

And you will probably also remember that when we are done with one of these, we can collapse it back into an icon which would thereafter give one-click access to the panel. This is a really nice feature, presuming that we want continued access to this panel group. But over time, as we use more and more of the panels, they're going to begin to stack up.

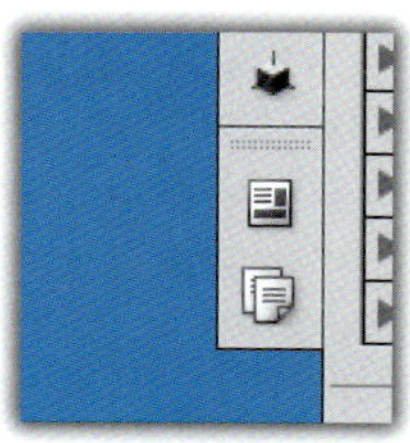

To tell you the truth, this struck me when I was writing the little section on the Notes tool. While I'm sure it is useful for some, I don't use that tool all that often. But as soon as I inserted a note, there was the panel icon, available in perpetuity.

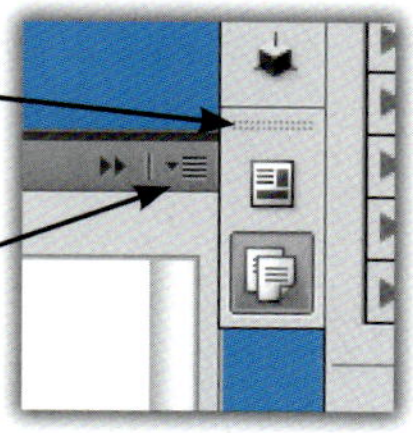

Okay, maybe not in perpetuity. In fact it is quite simple to delete. To do so, open the panel group with any of the icons. Now click on the panel menu and choose Close Tab Group.

We are not stuck with keeping these icons docked here, either. Simply click and drag on the double-dotted lines and move the panel group anywhere you please.

SECTION

VIII SOME EXAMPLES

We've now reached the end of instruction. This last section contains six examples that incorporate many of the techniques we've reviewed. Each example deals with a specific issue, either an image with some problems or a desired effect to achieve. All of the images are real life vacation pictures. And they all needed some degree of help.

These are not tutorials in the sense that I don't give you every click and keystroke to get from start to finish. Rather the idea is to show how our techniques can be used in a workflow to correct many of the problems we encounter in everyday photography. Each chapter will present starting and ending points and discuss the actions taken, one by one. But again, without a lot of the click by click description.

If you would like to follow along, you can download a zip file which includes most of these images. Just go to www.justtheskinny.com/support.

44. THE ZEBRA

Let's start out with this picture of a zebra, taken at the Kruger National Park in South Africa. There are a number of issues to work on. We will start by cropping the photo to try and get in a little closer on the animal. Then we will address a few of the distractions in the image before finishing it off with corrections to the contrast and the hue/saturation.

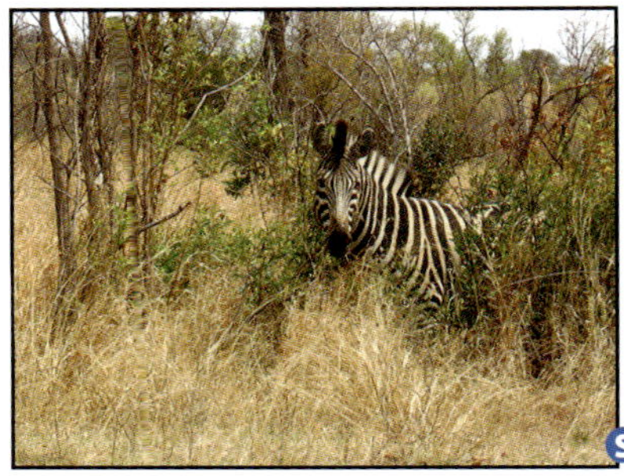

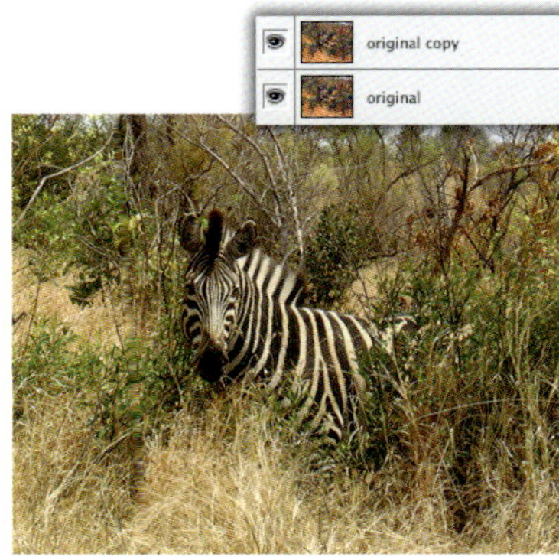

I want to crop to an 10x8 aspect ratio while getting in a little closer. How close is a matter of personal preference, resolution permitting. Here is the crop that I chose, closer in but still maintaining a lot of the background. Notice that I have made a copy of the original layer just to be sure that I always have an untouched original layer.

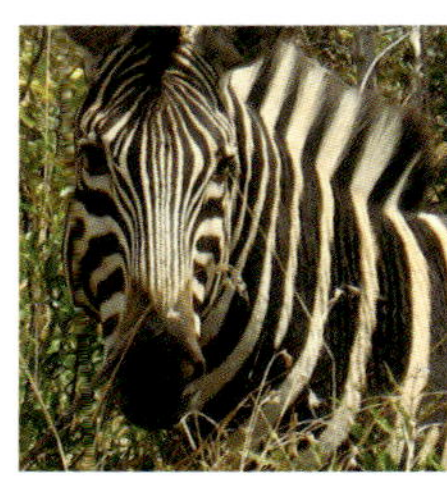

There are two major distractions to address. First, there are the blades of grass positioned in front of the zebra's face. And second, there are a bunch of dead leaves on the tree in the upper right of the original that detract from the image.

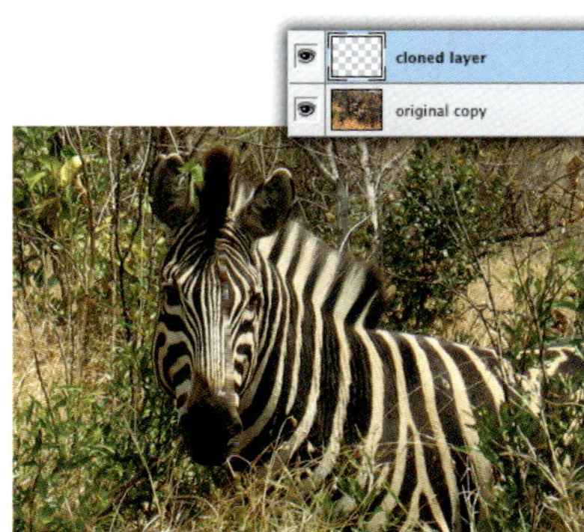

To remove the distracting blades of grass, I used the clone tool at high magnification to locally clone adjacent fur over each blade. Notice also, as we discussed in Chapter 32, I have cloned the grass-covering fur onto its own layer (the cloned pixels are too small to show on the thumbnail). (The original layer is still there–the bottom of the layer stack is just not shown to save space.)

The dead leaves are fixed with a Solid Color adjustment layer. We create that layer and chose a green, using the Eyedropper tool to sample an existing, live leaf. We create the adjustment layer, fill its layer mask with black (Edit/Fill) and set the blending mode for that layer to Color. With a small, soft brush set to white and the adjustment layer still selected, we paint the dead leaves. Before our eyes, they turn green.

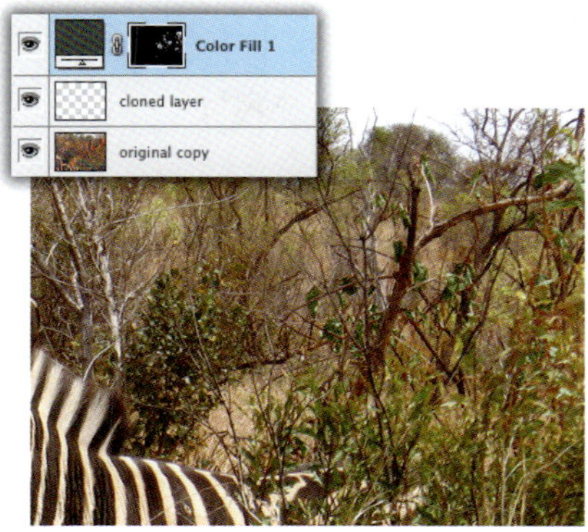

With the distractions fixed, I optimize Levels and Hue/Saturation with adjustment layers. I also subtly vignette the image with another Levels adjustment layer, darkening it with the midtone slider, but masking the effect everywhere but in the corners. (Fill the mask with black and use a big soft brush with white to paint the corners.) The image looks a little warm (yellow/red), so I'll add a cooling Photo Filter adjustment layer and then sharpen a composite layer to get the final image.

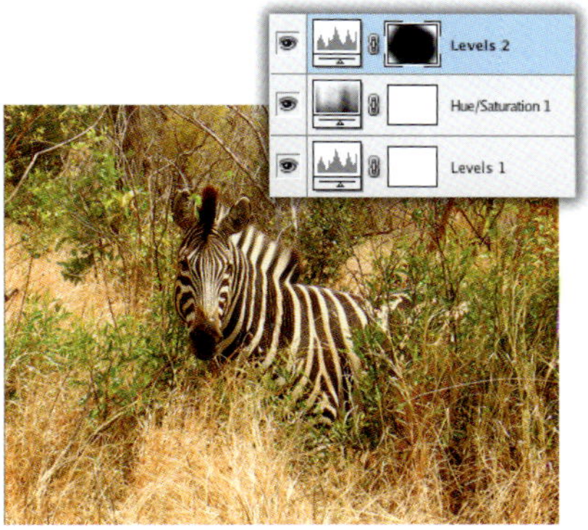

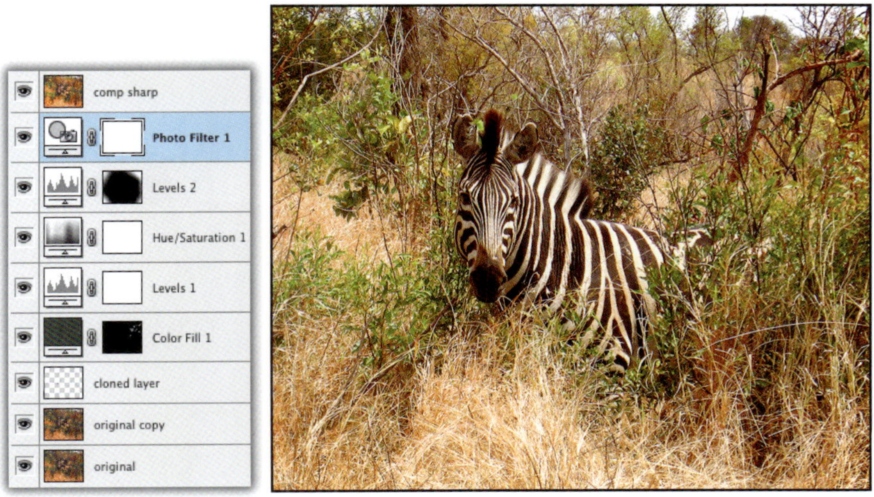

45. WANAKA SUNRISE

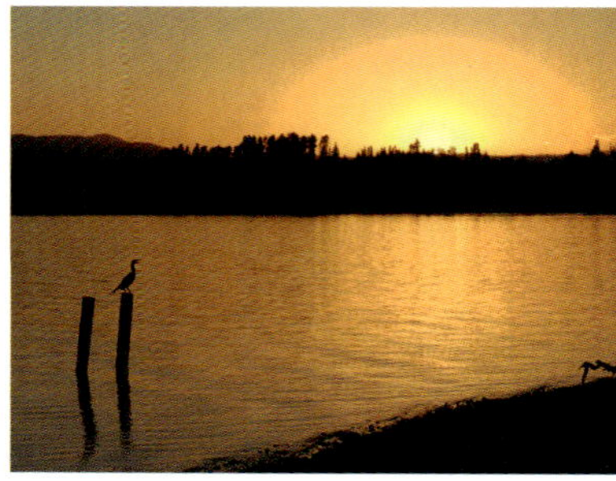

Back in Chapter 29, we worked on this image of Lake Wanaka in New Zealand. Recall that the original image was lacking the bird and we cloned it in from another image. At the time, I pointed out that the bird's reflection was missing from the top of the post's reflection. And we want it to look real, right? So we'll fix that in this example.

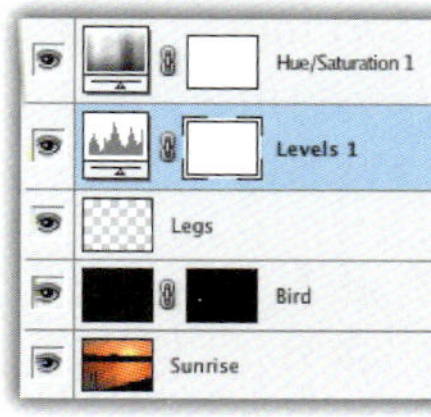

Here is the layers stack from that original example. Recall we brought in the bird and created a layer mask with its outline. The color of the layer itself (Bird) is the same as the post. And then, because the legs weren't long enough, we just used our Brush tool to create "leg extensions" (Legs). The pixels in the thumbnails of the Legs and Bird layers are too small to be visible.

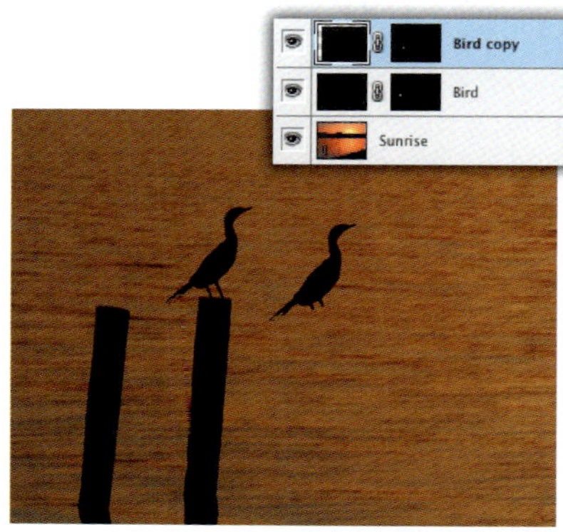

Since the reflection is broken up by the ripples in the water, we can safely ignore the little leg extensions. The first thing we do is duplicate the bird layer, complete with layer mask. Here, I have offset it a bit so that we can see it. Notice that this offsetting is reflected in the layer thumbnail as the solid layer and mask have been moved. (The extra transparency, the checkerboard at the top, doesn't affect us.)

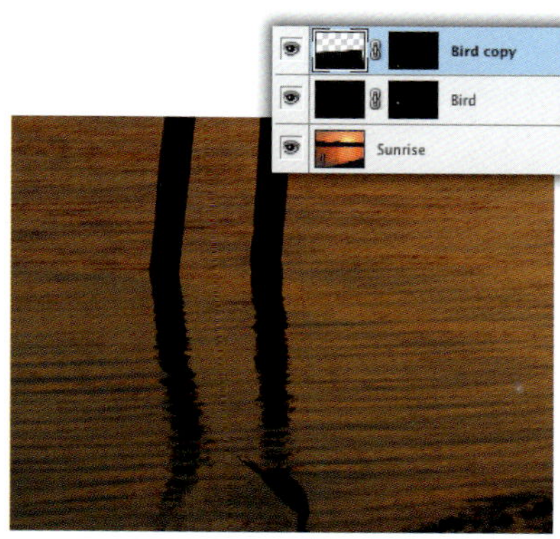

Next we do a series of transformations on the whole Bird copy layer. First we flip it vertically to get it in the right orientation. Then we translate it down to where the reflection should have been. (The correct location cuts some of the head off.) And then we rotate it slightly to correspond to the angle of the rotation of the post. (More transparency now shows in the Bird Copy layer. But again, the layer mask blocks it.)

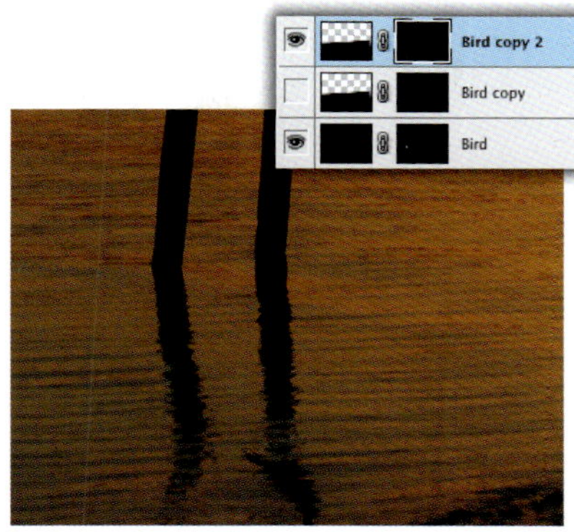

The ripples in the lake are distorting the post reflections so how can we mimic this in the bird's reflection? Let's use the Smudge tool (Chapter 17). We make a copy of the "Bird copy" layer and turn off visibility for the first copy. (If we mess up, we have a saved copy.) Now with the layer mask on this new layer selected, we use the Smudge tool, working left and right, to distort the edges of our reflection. Again, we have a hidden copy if we need another go at it.

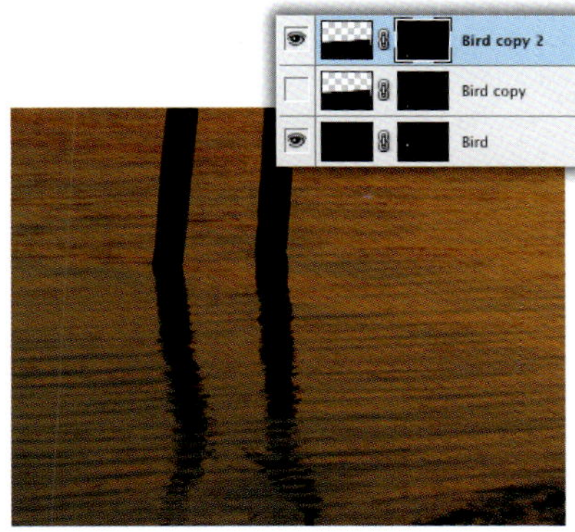

So far, so good, but the reflection is still too bold; it is not blending in with the ripples. One solution is to switch to a small, soft brush set to black and, with the layer mask still selected, draw some left to right lines mimicking the ripples we see on the post reflection. As a final touch, we can lower the opacity of the reflection layer (I chose 65%) just to soften the effect even more.

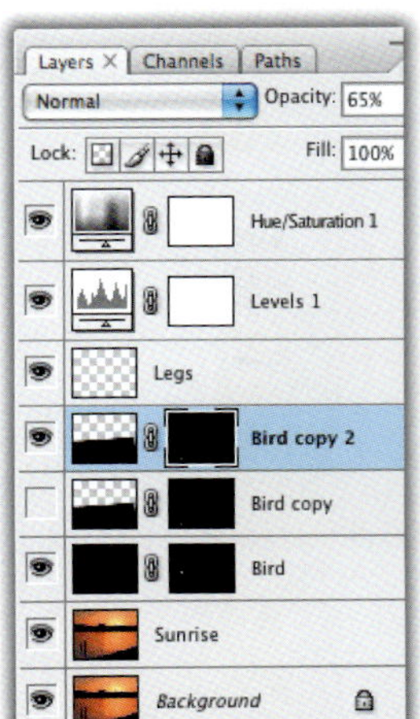

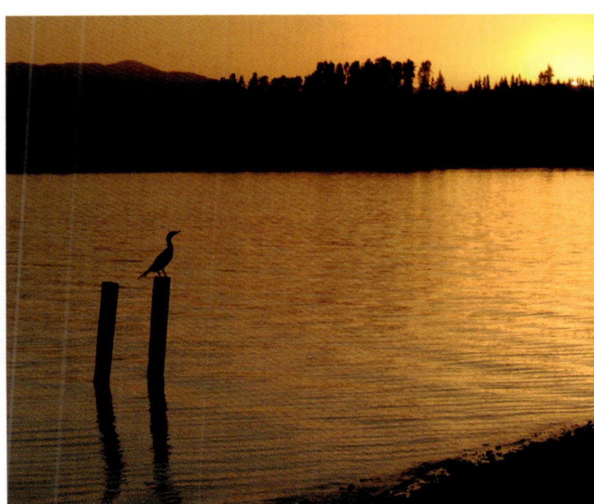

46. FAUX MATTING

Back in Chapter 34, I mentioned making simulated picture matting. Here is how to do it. We start by sizing our image appropriately. Let's say we want a total size of 8"x10" (so that we can buy a stock frame) with a 1" matt. This means our image needs to be 6"x8". With the Crop tool and the Image>Image Size dialog, we make those changes. (Refer to Ch. 5 and Ch. 16.)

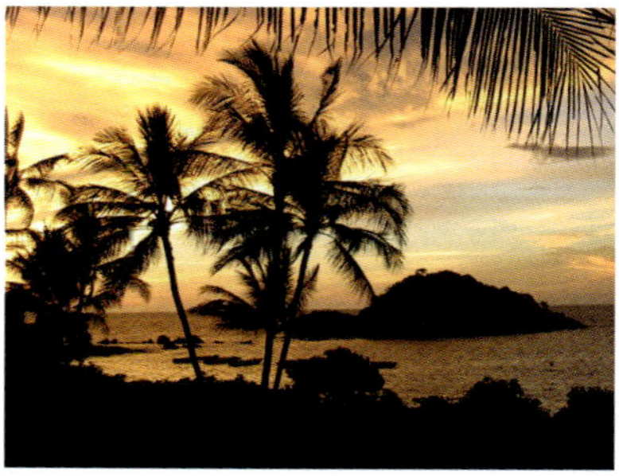

Now I'll introduce a new menu item. Under Image in the menu bar, we select Canvas Size. With Canvas Size, we can resize our canvas without affecting the image pixels. Here I have set the new height to 8" and the new width to 10". Set the Canvas extension color to Background and make sure Relative is unchecked.

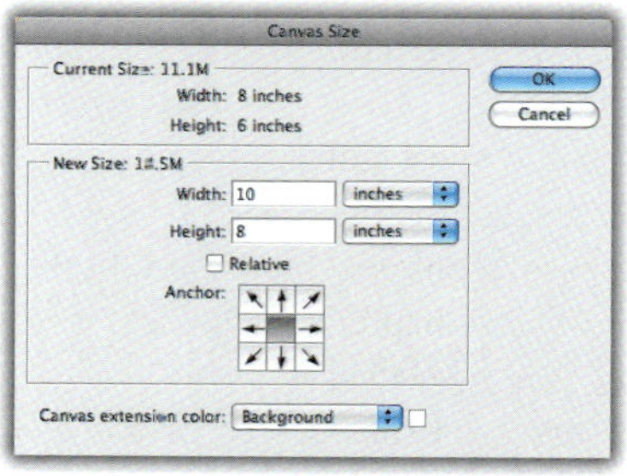

And here is what we get. The canvas has now grown by an inch all around, leaving our image centered within. The new border is the Background color, in this case white. By setting the anchor in the dialog box on a corner or a side, we can make the canvas grow preferentially in any direction. Our anchor was in the middle so the canvas grew in all directions uniformly. Growing the canvas turns out to have a lot of applications.

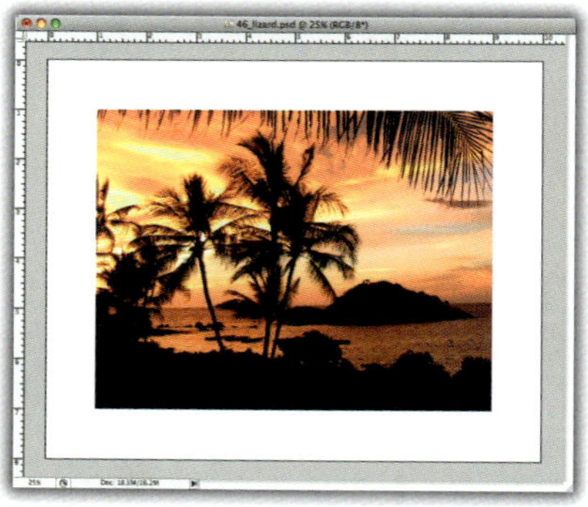

Our next step is to make a selection around our original image using the Rectangular Marquee. As this selection will end up defining the matting, we want to make sure it just overlaps the image. So zooming in, we use Select>Transform Selection to nudge our selection over the edge of the image. The last step is to use Select>Inverse to invert the selection. Now our matting area is selected. Here is a magnified corner.

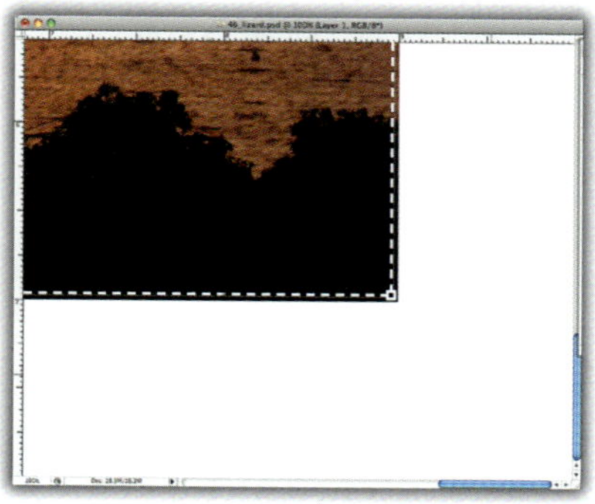

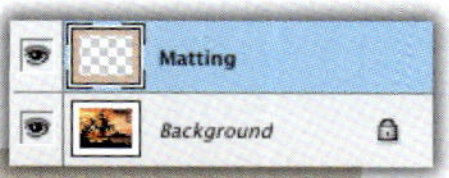

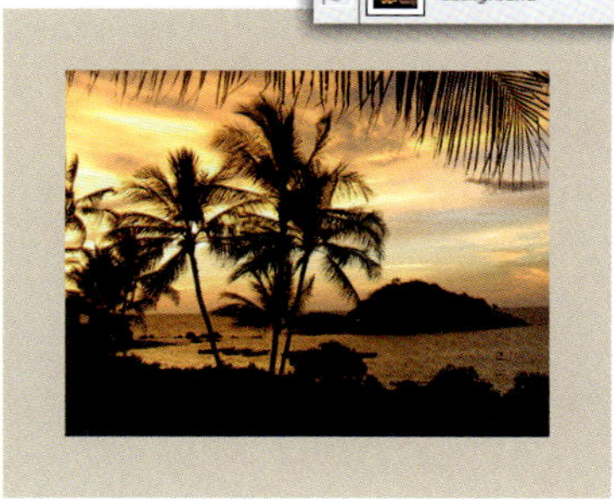

With our selection still in place, we add a new layer (we can call it Matting). By double clicking on the foreground color in the toolbox, we can use the Color Picker to choose a matting color. I grabbed a color from the image with the Eyedropper tool. We choose Edit>Fill with the foreground color and the matting changes color. We deselect the selection and move on.

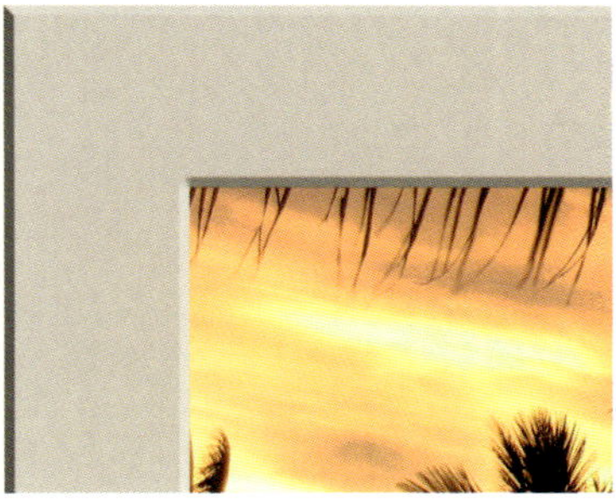

We only have a couple more things to do. To simulate the matte cuts, we apply a Bevel and Emboss layer style to the Matting layer (Chapter 24). Note that the outer edge gets beveled as well. But it will be hidden under the edge of the frame so this is okay. I like to use the Chisel Hard option under Technique in the settings. We adjust Depth and Size to get a pleasing result.

The last step is to apply the filter to the Matting layer. Let's duplicate the Matting layer and filter the duplicate just in case we later want to change. To filter, we choose Filter>Texture>Texturizer and choose Canvas as our texture.

Zoom in to get a better feel for the texture.

(By the way, this image was taken on Lizard Island, out in Australia's Great Barrier Reef.)

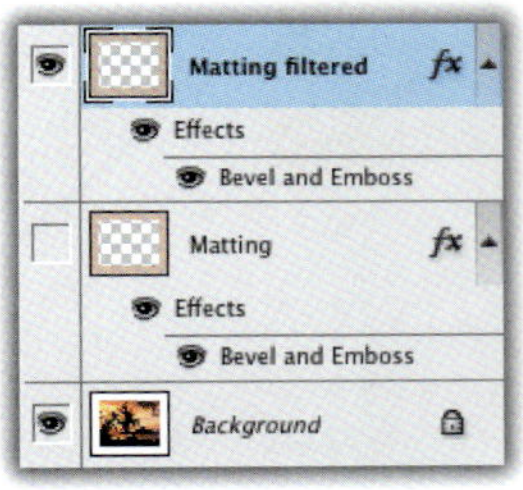

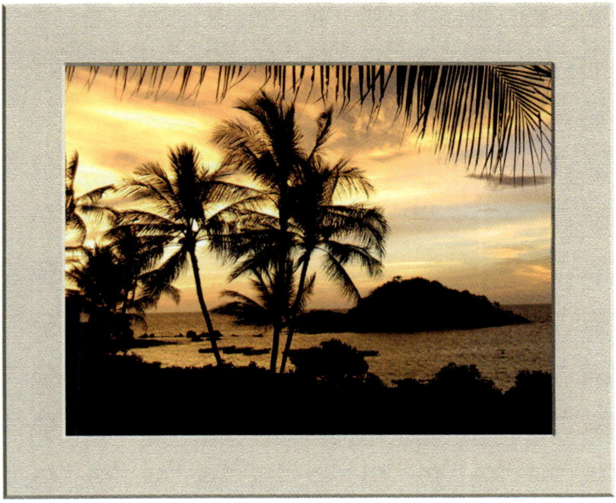

47. CINQUE TERRA

Now we travel to Cinque Terra, Italy. I have already cropped the image so that it has an 8x10 aspect ratio. This image, however, was taken on a hazy day and suffers from contrast issues, a curved horizon (lens distortion), and an ocean that lacks any color. So let's go fix those things and see what we get.

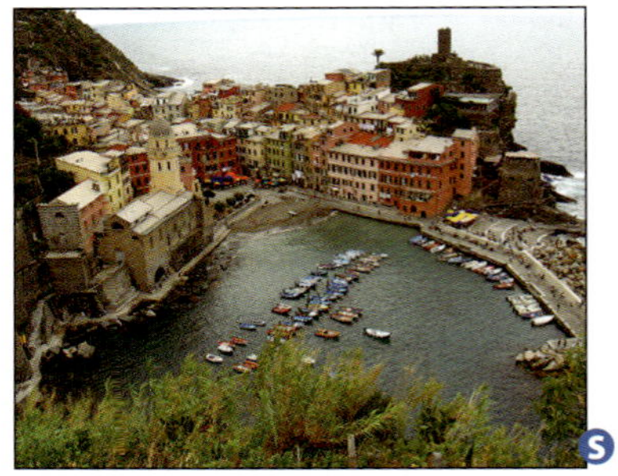

We start by making the obligatory copy of our original layer. And then, using Edit>Transform>Warp (Chapter 28), we lift up the horizon in the upper left by pulling up on the grid intersection. It is important to realize that the whole document is not being warped–the original layer is unchanged. We are warping pixels on the original copy layer only. Once done, we hit Return(Enter) to accept the change.

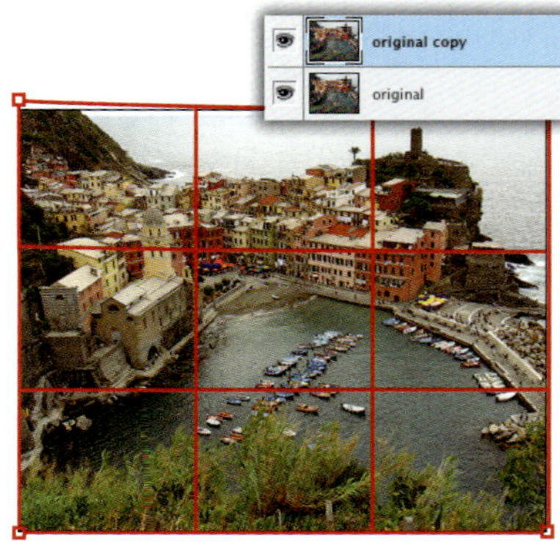

We need to improve the contrast of the overall image but the ocean is so hazy that we'll tackle it separately. Let's start by making a selection of the ocean. We can use the Magic Wand, adjust threshold until we get a reasonable selection, and then refine in Quick Mask mode. Because we will need it later, we'll also save this selection.

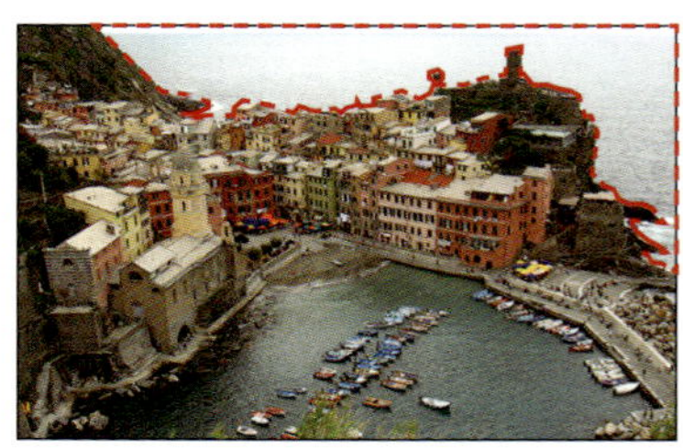

Before proceeding with the ocean, let's fix everything else first. We invert our selection (Select>Inverse) and then make a new Levels adjustment layer. The new adjustment layer shows up with a layer mask in place (created from the selection) that blocks the adjustment from the ocean in the background. Exactly what we want. We make our levels correction and improve the contrast of the buildings and the harbor.

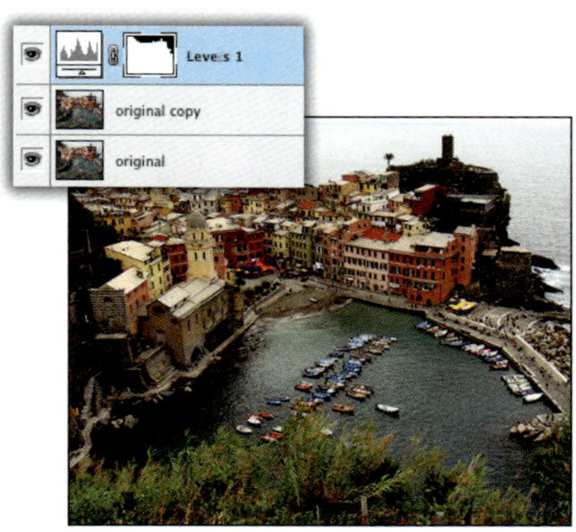

Now let's tackle the ocean. Since we saved our ocean selection, we can reload it (Select>Load Selection) and then create a new Levels adjustment layer. Again, the layer mask is automatically created from our selection. This time everything but the ocean is blocked. We use the Levels dialog box to darken up the ocean, to give it more contrast. We are starting to look pretty good but the background ocean has a slightly different hue. Let's tackle that.

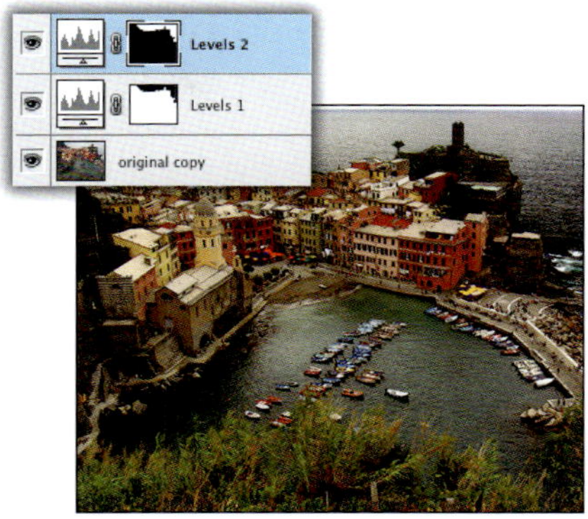

We'll start by reloading our ocean selection. Then we'll make yet another adjustment layer, this time a Solid Color adjustment layer. Again, it shows up with a layer mask based on the selection. With the Color Picker dialog box that automatically pops up, we use our Eyedropper to pick a dark greenish color from the water in the harbor. We click OK and then, the last step, set the blending mode for the adjustment layer to Color.

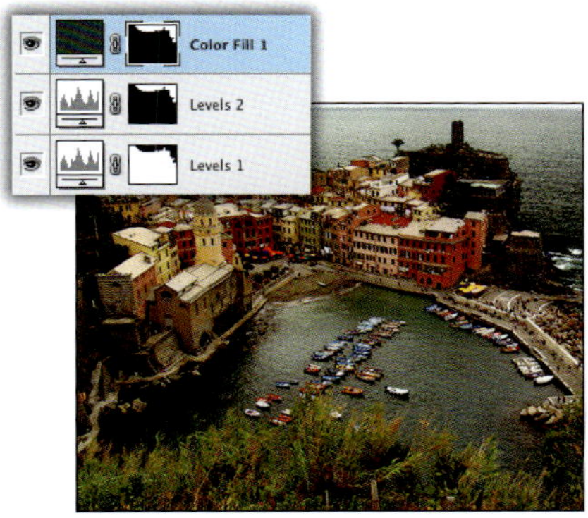

Saturation looks good, so we create a composite layer, sharpen it, and we are done.

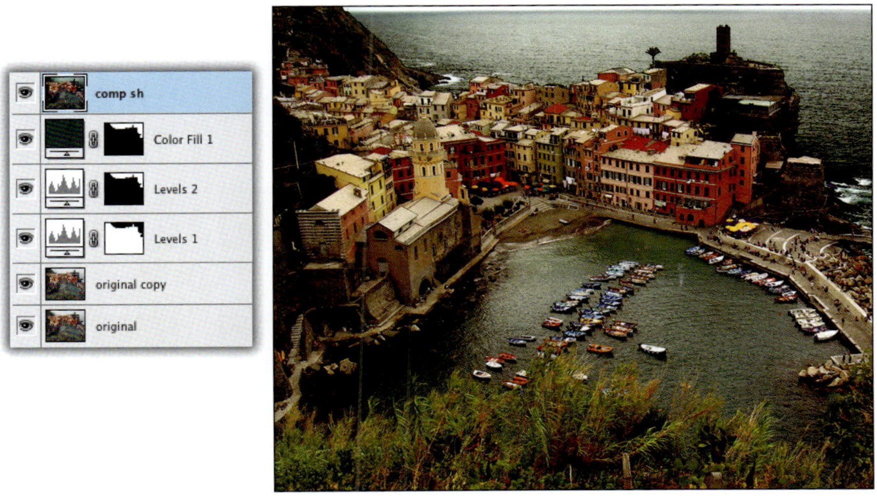

48. AN IMAGE GROUPING

The object of this chapter is to make a grouping of images within a larger master image. We need to start by deciding how large the little images will be and how large the master image will be. I have chosen 1.5" x 2" for my little images and I'll place them on an 8" x 8" master image. To start out, we prepare and separately save our little images, using Crop (Ch. 16) and Image>Image Size (Ch. 5)to get just what we want. We also perform any image enhancements or sharpening required.

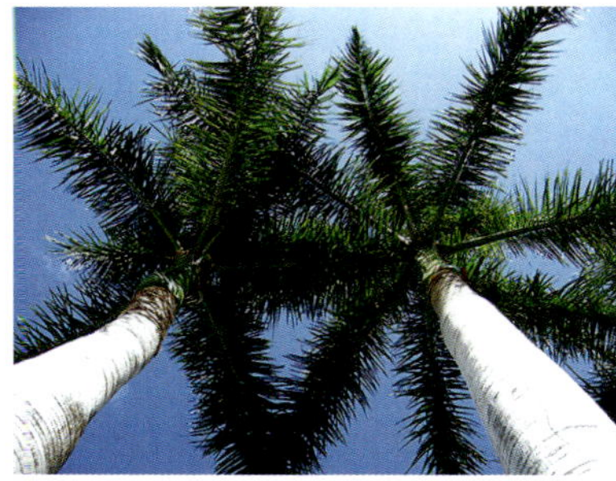

We open up a new document, setting the dimensions to 8" x 8" with a resolution matching that of the little images–in my case this is 250 pixels/inch. In the menu bar, under View, we select Show>Grid and a non-printing grid appears. Under View, make sure that Snap To>Grid is checked. The default grid has major grids every inch and minor grids every quarter inch. (You can change this under Photoshop Preferences>Guides, Grids, etc.)

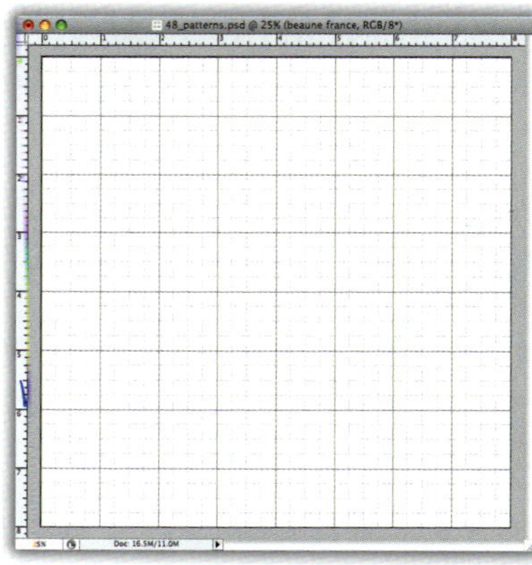

Now we open our individual images and duplicate them into the master image, each on its own layer (Chapter 20). (If an image has multiple layers, we can create a composite layer and duplicate that layer over.) As to where to place the images, we are on our own; Photoshop won't do our planning for us. But with the grid, it's pretty easy to line everything up in a pleasing fashion. I chose a 1½" left and right border with 1¼" on top and 2¼" on the bottom. The interior horizontal spacing is 1" and the vertical spacing is 1½". Again the grid helps us locate everything (using the Move tool). Having the Snap to Grid function enabled helps insure everything is lined up.

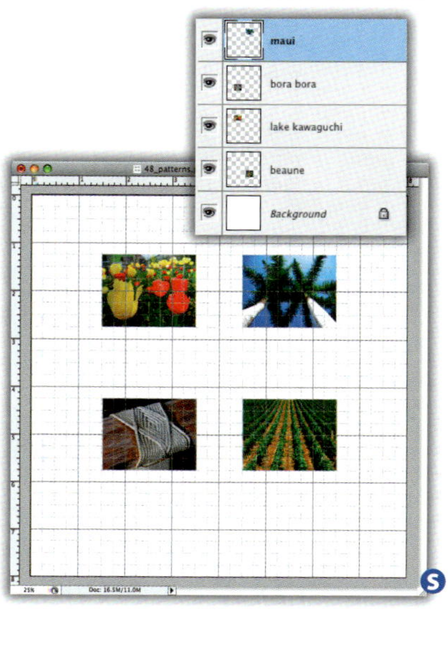

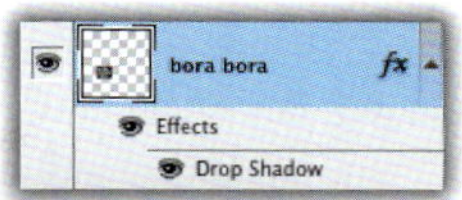

Granted the result so far lacks punch. Let's add a little excitement with a layer style. Here, I have added a drop shadow to the rope image, taken at Bora Bora, making it appear to be suspended above the page. We can add the same layer style to each of the other layers; the drop shadow settings are sticky so they will all be the same.

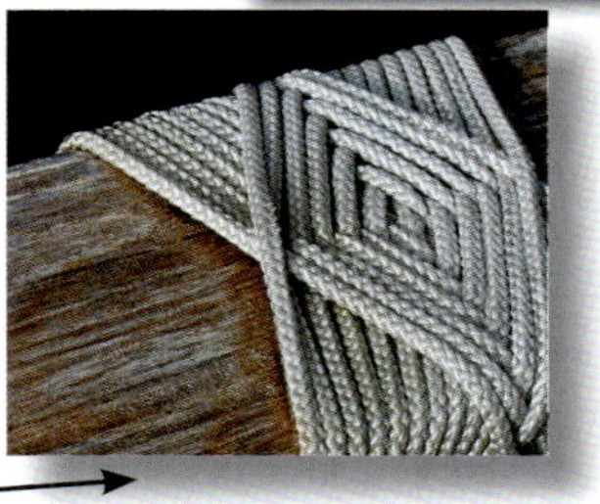

Or alternatively, recall we learned a shortcut for this. We can duplicate a layer style from one layer to another by Opt(Alt) dragging the "fx" icon from the styled layer to the new layer. Bingo, it's copied.

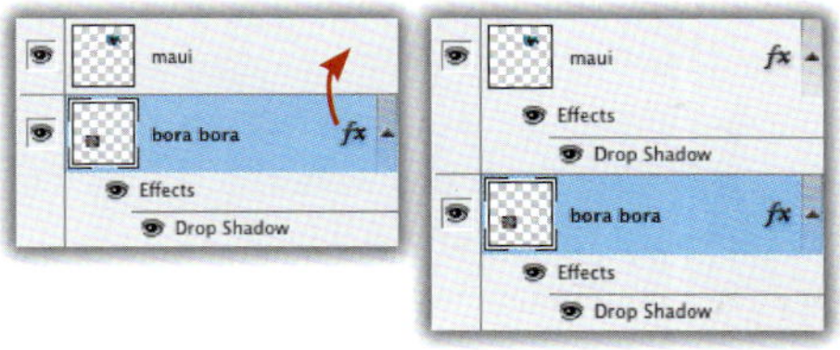

Finally, we can dress things up more by adding text under each of the images indicating its origin. (In the final Layers panel, I collapsed the layer style, using the disclosure triangle, for all but the Maui layer, to hide the extra details. But they are all still there.)

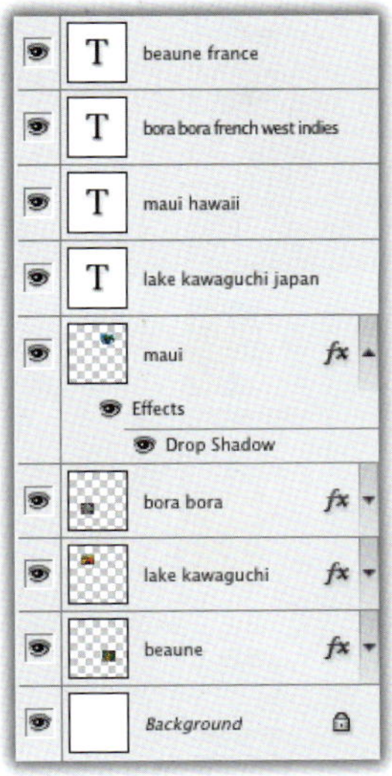

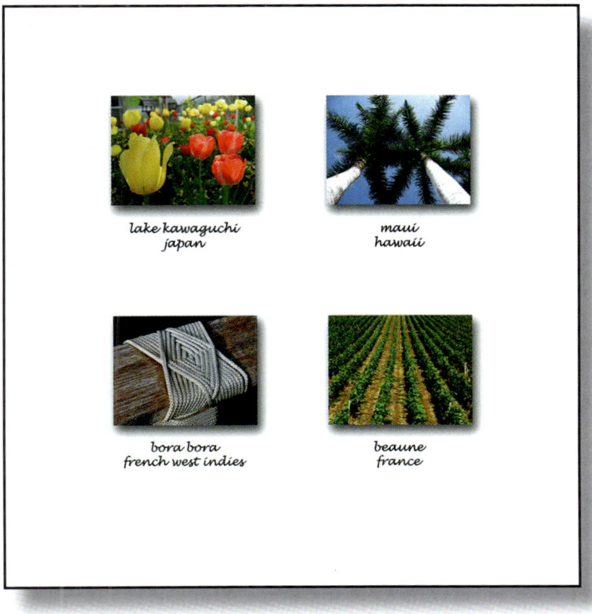

49. THE TAJ MAHAL

This building probably doesn't need any introduction; it is the famous Taj Mahal in India. The day this was taken, there was unfortunately some scaffolding in place (on the left most column), and some inconsiderate visitors were walking in front of the building! So let's go about removing the scaffolding and those visitors. Then we'll brighten up the image a bit.

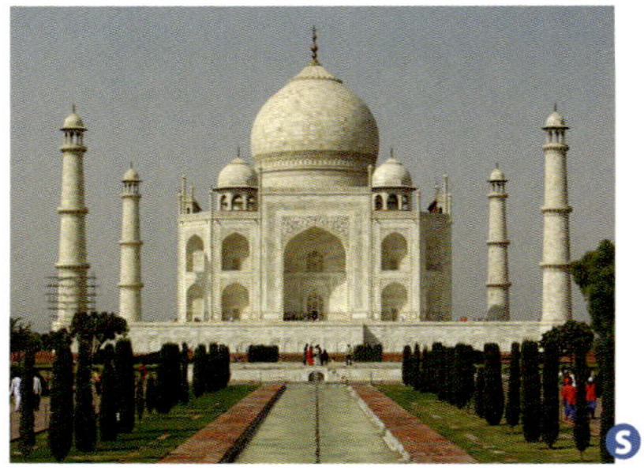

Let's start by addressing that scaffolding on the column (actually it's called a minaret) on the left. We start by creating a new layer (I called it Clone layer) and using the Clone tool to remove the scaffolding that is protruding from the column. We use the nearby sky on the original copy layer as the source and clone it to the Clone layer, over the scaffolding, hiding it. In this image, I have completed the left side and have yet to do the right side.

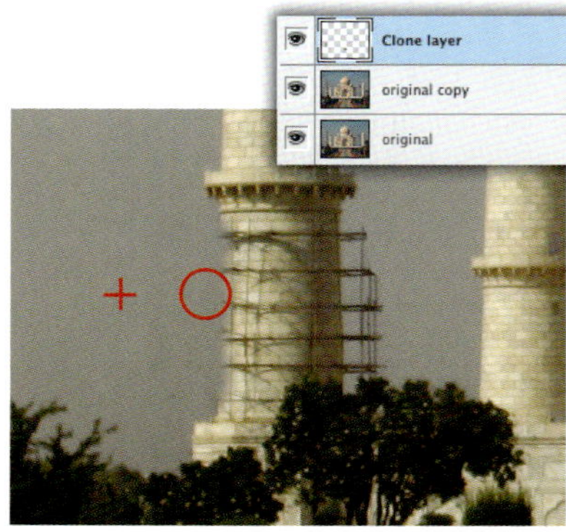

Next we remove the visitors in a similar fashion. The repetitive pattern on the building makes the job easy. We set the source on an unobstructed section just to the right of the left-side bushes on the original copy layer. We then pick a destination one section over and carefully clone left to right to the Clone layer. We will have to reset the source several times before we are done. (Again, I am about half done.)

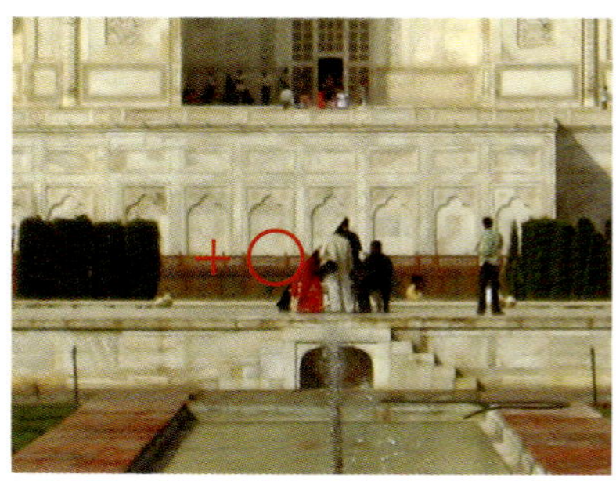

Now to get rid of the scaffolding still left in front of the left column, we make use of the right column; it fortunately doesn't have any scaffolding. Using a selection tool of choice (I used the Pen tool) we make a selection around the lower section of the column on the right. We keep this selection in place for the next step.

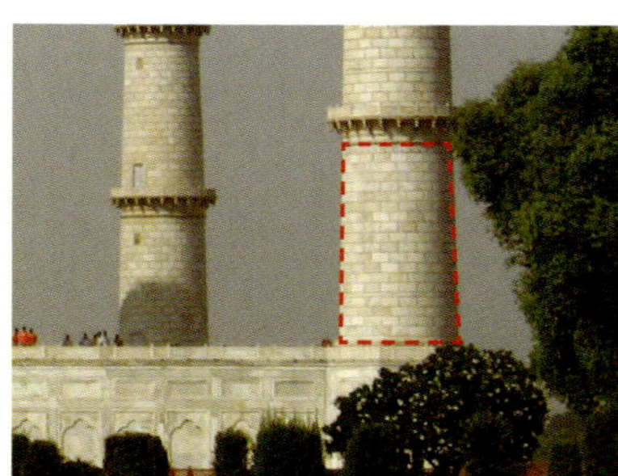

Now we do the following: We make a duplicate of the original copy layer and drag it to the top, above the Clone layer. I called it columnCopy. With our selection still in place, and with the new columnCopy layer selected, we choose New Layer Mask from the bottom of the Layers panel. Nothing on the image has visibly changed but we now have a new lower section of the right column on its own layer (and with an editable layer mask).

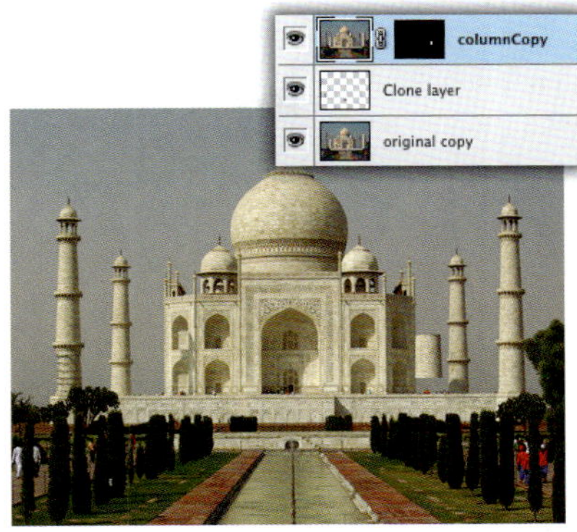

With the columnCopy layer still selected, we use the Move tool to move the duplicate column section over the top of the column on the left, covering up the scaffolding. Two problems are immediately evident. The new section is covering up part of the tree and also appears just a little too light. But of course these really aren't problems, not for us.

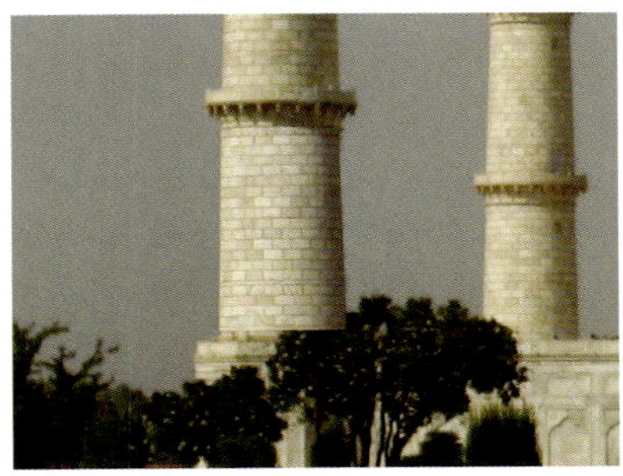

Because we defined our column section with a layer mask, the tree issue is a snap to solve. We lower the opacity on the columnCopy layer to where the underlying tree is easy to see. Now before we fix the tree, notice in the columnCopy layer that the layer thumbnail is mostly transparency. This is because we moved the whole layer, including the mask from the right to the left. It is not a problem, just worth noting.

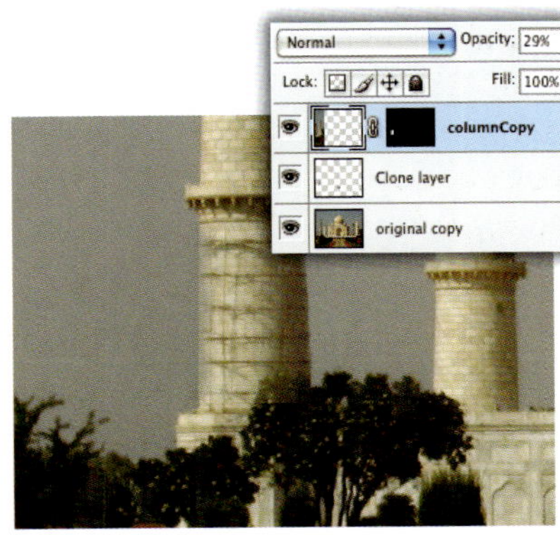

With the layer mask on the columnCopy layer selected, we chose a small soft brush with black as our foreground color and paint over the tree. Where we paint the mask, the column pixels get blocked, allowing the tree to show through as it should. We don't even need to be all that precise.

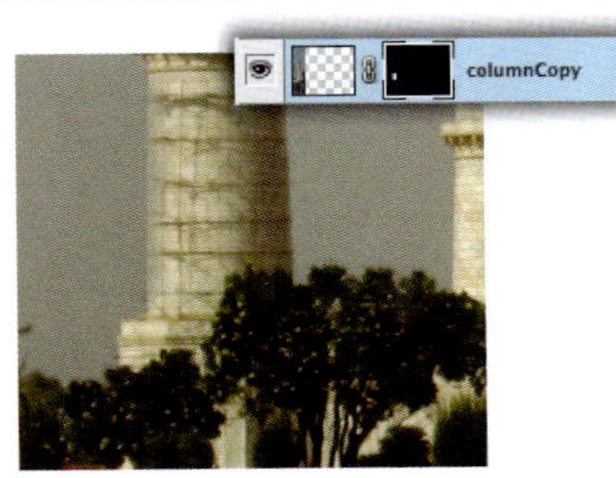

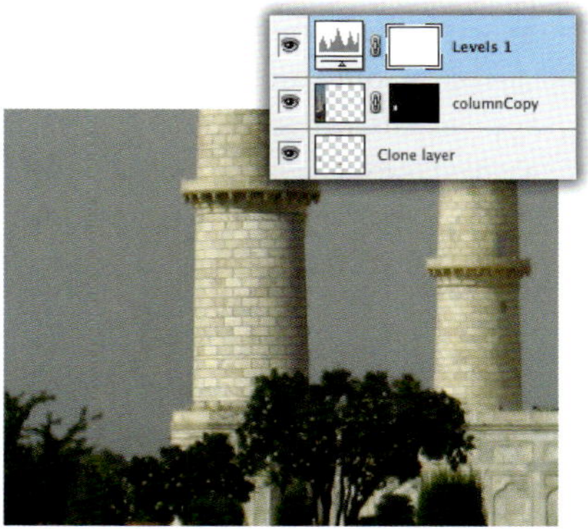

Bringing the opacity of the columnCopy layer back up to 100%, we can see that we are in pretty good shape. The section we replaced is still a little lighter than the section above it, however. The right side of the image must have been just a bit brighter than the left side. We can easily fix this with levels–in fact let's go ahead and add a Levels adjustment layer. But that Levels adjust affects the entire image. Not what we want! Not to worry–we'll fix that next.

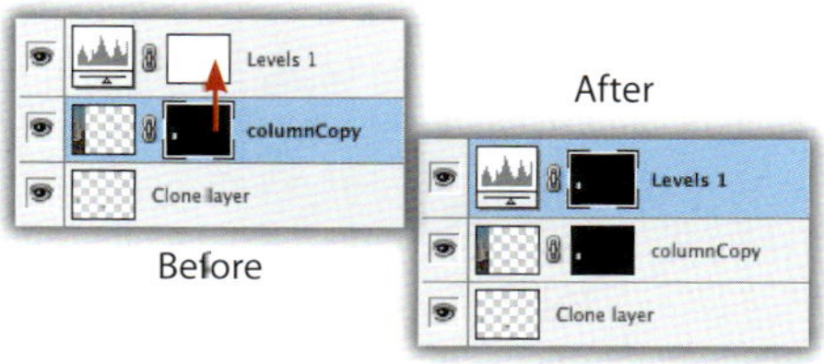

What if we had the same layer mask on the Levels 1 adjustment layer as we have on the columnCopy layer. Well that would fix things, wouldn't it? Then we could adjust the new section without affecting the remainder of the image. To do this, we select the columnCopy layer mask and then, holding down our Opt(Alt) key, we drag it onto the Levels 1 layer. We answer "yes" when asked if we wish to replace the existing layer mask. Neat!

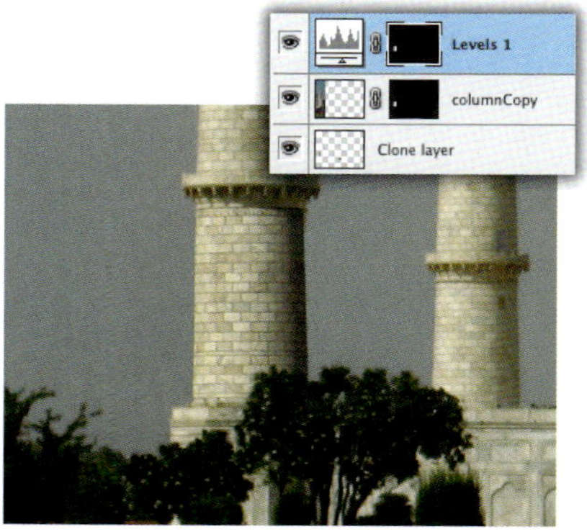

Now we open the Levels dialog box by double clicking on the layer thumbnail. Moving the neutral slider to the right darkens up the column section to match. (We could also consider a slight blur to the columnCopy layer but since it is so small, it's not really needed.)

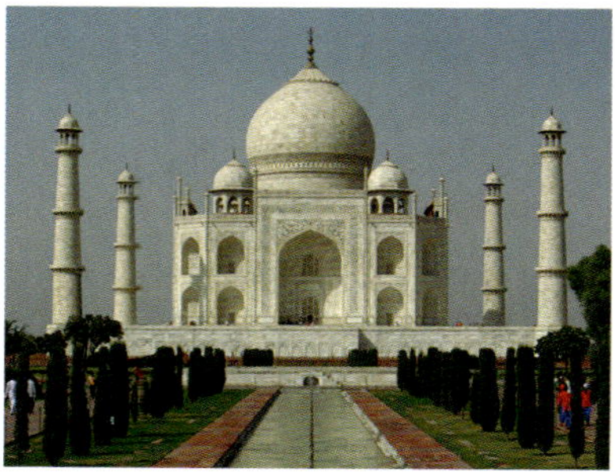

Here is the same image, pulling back to full frame. The column on the left looks pretty good. And of course the inconsiderate visitors are now gone from the front of the building. More than anything, both fixes are unobtrusive.

Now that we have our alterations done, we can perform some overall image enhancement. We start with a new Levels adjustment layer. Notice that Photoshop automatically serializes adjustment layers. These names are editable, however, if you would like to create something more meaningful.

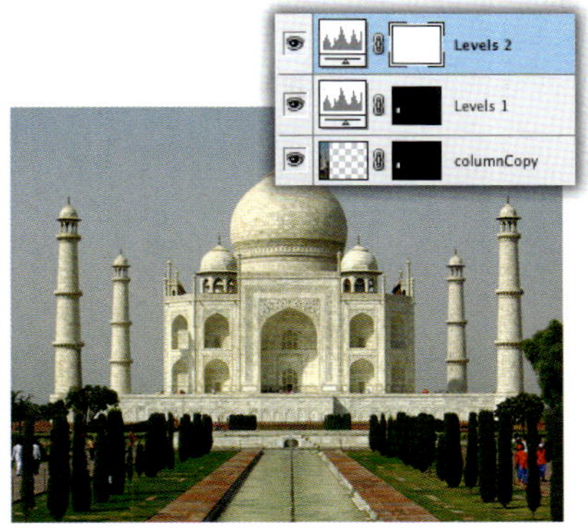

After adjusting Levels, we can boost the saturation a bit to liven up the colors. I also put in a very slight hue shift that made the sky a more pleasing blue. Make it a point to play with your sliders to see what pleases you. Most likely you won't need anything too dramatic for most of your images.

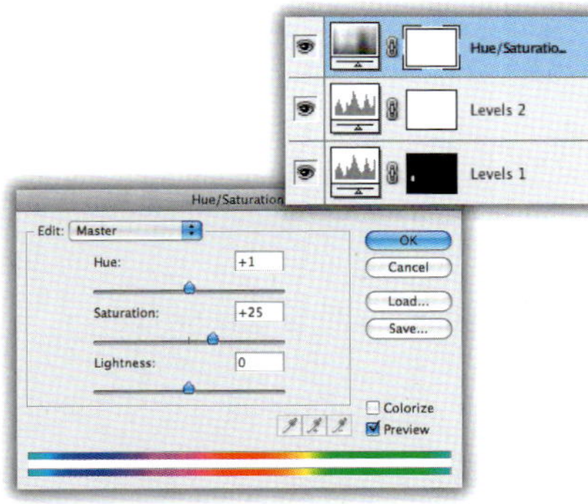

As a last step, we create a composite layer by selecting the top layer and hitting Opt-Cmd-Shift-E (Alt-Ctrl-Shift-E). As I have been doing in earlier examples, I have named it "comp sh." We can then use this layer for sharpening.

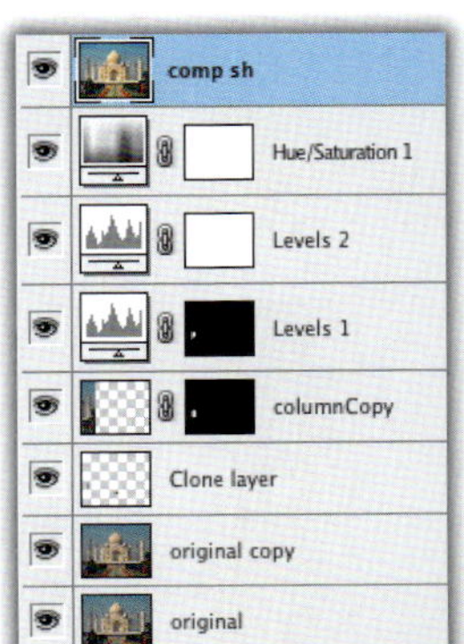

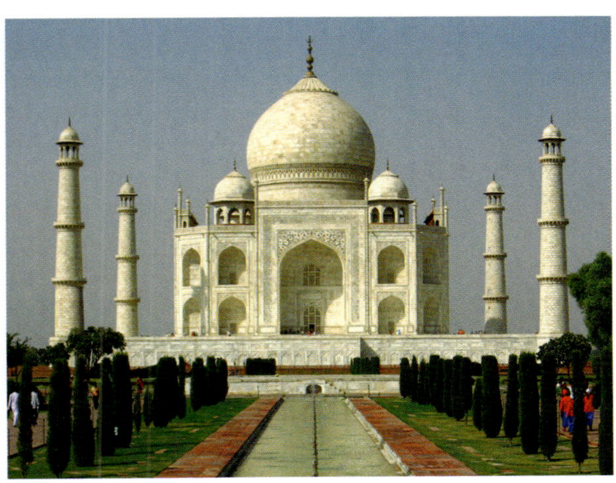

50. FINAL THOUGHTS

So that's Photoshop–at least a quick introduction to it. And that, after all, was one of my main goals. Quick and easy, just the skinny.

We talked about enhancing, altering, and combining our images. We talked about adding text and graphic elements. We spent a little time under the hood, talking about color models, histograms, bitmaps and vectors. And hopefully, in a relatively short amount of time, we've got you to the point where you can perform most of the basic Photoshop tasks.

I've always said that Photoshop is hard to learn unless you already know how to use it. But if you start by learning basic skills (which you've done) and then play with the program for a while to let those skills sink in, you'll find that mastering Photoshop's more sophisticated techniques is much easier. So start playing...

And finally, I hope you've enjoyed this book as much as I have enjoyed writing it. I actually have a new saying now–the best way to learn Photoshop is to write a book about it.

INDEX

A
Adjustment layers, 86-88
  solid color, 130, 189
  layer masks, 90-93
  levels, 86
  photo filter, 89, 189
Adjustments
  image, 52-55, 76
  panel, 102, 50
Adobe RGB, 10
Annotations, 176
Anti-aliasing, 161

B
Background color, 32
Background layer, 12, 81
Bevel and Emboss, 100, 193
Bitmap graphics, 161
Black and White image adjustment, 53
Blending modes, 128-131
  color, 129
  color burn, 131
  lighten, 131
  linear light, 131
  normal, 128
Blur filters, 150-153
  Gaussian blur, 150
Blur tool, 70
Bridge, 10
Brush presets
  presets picker, 156
  saving, 158
Brush tool, 16, 42-45, 156-159
  hardness, 42
  opacity, 43
Burn tool, 69

C
Calibration, 183
Canvas, 6
Canvas size, 192
Character panel, 96
Clone tool, 134-141, 188, 198, 154
  clone preview, 154
CMYK, 33
Color, 30-33
  background, 32
  foreground, 30, 32
Color blend, 130, 189
Color mode, 33
  CMYK, 33
  indexed, 33
  LAB, 33
  RGB, 2, 30
Color panel, 15
Color picker, 31
  eyedropper, 31-32
Color profiles, 183
Colorize, 61
Compression
  JPEG, 3, 38
  lossless, 40,177
  lossy, 3, 38
  TIFF, 40,177
Contrast, 36
Copy
  adjustment layers, 88
  layer styles, 101
Crop tool, 64-67
  perspective, 67
  width/height, 66
CS4, 50, 76, 102, 132, 154, 172, 186
Custom swatches, 32

D
Direct Selection tool, 166
Distort, 119
Dithering, 181
Document window, 7
Dodge tool, 68
Dots per inch, 18
Downsampling, 21
DPI, 18
Drop shadow, 100, 197
Duplicate layer, 84
    adjustment layers, 88

E
Elliptical Marquee tool, 24
Embedded Profile Mismatch Warning, 10-11
Eraser tool, 44-45
Eyedropper tool, 31-32, 50, 186
    hue/saturation adjustment, 62
    levels adjustment, 59

F
Feathering, 46-47
    selection, 115, 172
File formats, 38-41
    GIF, 41
    JPEG, 38-39
    PSD, 40
    TIFF, 40
Fill, 126
Filter gallery, 143
Filters, 142-145
    blur, 150-153
    diffuse glow, 144
    fibers, 145
    Gaussian blur, 106
    glowing edges, 144
    lighting effects, 145
    sharpen, 146-149
    stain glass, 144
    texturizer, 145
Flattening, 175
Font, 94
Foreground color, 30, 32
Free transform, 117

G
Gaussian blur, 106, 150-153
    vignette, 106
GIF, 41
Gradient tool, 108-111
    compositing, 111
    with layer masking, 110
Gradient picker, 108
Grid, 196

H
Hand tool, 26-29
    keyboard shortcut, 29
Healing Brush tool, 73, 154
Histogram, 34-37, 50
History panel, 16, 50
Horizontal Type tool, 94
HSB, 30
Hue/Saturation image adjustment, 60-63
    colorize, 61
    eyedropper tool, 62

I
ICC printer profiles, 183
Image adjustments, 52-55
    auto, 52
    black and white, 53
    hue/saturation, 60-63
    invert, 53
    levels, 56-59
    posterize, 53
    variations, 54
    vibrance, 76
Image size, 18-21
Indexed color, 33
Invert image adjustment, 53

J-L
JPEG, 2, 13, 38-39
LAB, 33
Lasso tool, 25
Layer masks, 104-107
    adjustment layers, 90-93
    gradient tool, 110
    linking/unlinking, 107
    disabling/enabling, 107
    vignette, 106

Layer styles, 98-101
  bevel and emboss, 100
  copying, 101
  drop shadow, 100
  outer glow, 100
Layers, 78-85
  adjustment, 86-89
  background, 81
  blending modes, 128
  duplicating, 84
  layer styles, 98-101
  layer via copy, 85
  naming, 80
  text, 95
Layers panel, 12, 17, 79-80
Levels
  adjustment layers, 86
  image adjustment, 56-59
  eyedropper tool, 59
Load selection, 112

M
Magic Wand tool, 48
Magnetic Lasso tool, 47
Mask panel, 50, 102, 132
Maximize compatibility, 41, 175
Menu bar, 7
Move tool, 23, 83

N
Navigator panel, 15, 50
Non-destructive editing, 103
Note tool, 50, 176, 186

O
Opacity, 43, 80, 124-125, 191
  adjustment layers, 89
Opening a document, 10-13, 102
Options bar, 7
Outer glow, 100

P
Panels dock, 7
Panels, 14-17, 50
  character, 96
  color, 15
  history, 16, 50
  layers, 17, 79-80
  navigator, 15, 50
  swatches, 15
Patch tool, 74
Path selection tool, 165
Paths, 161, 168-171
  converting to selection, 169
  saving, 169
Paths panel, 169
Pen tool, 169-171
  making selections with, 171
Pencil tool, 159
Photo filter 89, 189
Photoshop file format, 40
Pixelization, 5
Pixels, 2-5
Pixels per inch, 18
Polygonal Lasso tool, 25
Posterize image adjustment, 53
PPI, 18
Preferences, resetting, 13
Printing, 182-185, 186
PSD extension, 13, 40

Q-R
Quick mask, 49
Rasterizing
  shape layer, 167
  type layer, 163
Rectangular Marquee tool, 22
Red Eye tool, 75
Refine Edge, 172
Refine Mask, 132
Resampling, 19
  downsampling/upsampling, 21
Resolution, 18-21
Revert, 23
RGB, 2, 30

S
Save As, 174, 186
  as a Copy, 176
Save for Web & Devices, 178-181, 186
Save selection, 112
Saving files, 12, 174-177
  JPEG options, 177
  TIFF options, 177

Selections, 22-25, 46-49, 112-115, 172
converting to paths, 169
feathering, 46-47, 115
load selection, 112
modifying, 114
refine edge, 172
save selection, 112
transform, 24
Shape tool, 164-167
fill pixels mode, 164
paths mode, 168
shape layers mode, 165
Sharpen filters, 146-149
unsharp Mask, 146
Sharpen tool, 71
Smudge tool, 71, 191
Solid Color adjustment layer, 130, 132,189
Sponge tool, 70
Spot Healing Brush tool, 72
sRGB IC61966-2.1, 10
Status bar, 7
Swatches, custom, 32
Swatches panel, 15

T

Text, 94-97
character panel, 96
font, 94
text box, 95
warping, 97
TIFF, 40
Toolbox, 7-8, 50
Transform, 116-119
distort, 119
free transform, 117
warp, 119
selection, 24
Type tool, 94

U-V

Unsharp mask, 146
Upsampling, 21
Variations image adjustment, 54
Vector graphics, 160-163
Vector mask, 165
Vector path, 161
Vibrance image adjustment, 76
Vignetting 106, 132, 189
Gaussian blur, 106

W-Z

Warp, 119, 194
Warp text, 97
Work path, 168
Workspace, 6-9
Zoom tool, 26-29
keyboard shortcut, 29